# MISSION IN ACTS

American Society of Missiology Series, No. 34

# MISSION IN ACTS

## Ancient Narratives
## in Contemporary Context

**Robert L. Gallagher**
**Paul Hertig**
editors

ORBIS BOOKS

Maryknoll, New York 10545

**Library of Congress Cataloging-in-Publication Data**

Mission in Acts : ancient narratives in contemporary context / [edited by] Robert L. Gallagher, Paul Hertig.
    p. cm. — (The American Society of Missiology series ; no. 34)
Includes bibliographical references.
  ISBN 1–57075–493–4 (pbk.)
  1. Bible. N.T. Acts—Criticism, interpretation, etc. I. Gallagher, Robert L. II. Hertig, Paul, 1955– III. Series.
  BS2625.52.M57 2004
  226.6'06—dc21
                  2003013704

# Contents

# *Preface to the ASM Series*

The purpose of the ASM (American Society of Missiology) Series is to publish—without regard for disciplinary, national, or denominational boundaries—scholarly works of high quality and wide interest on missiological themes from the entire spectrum of scholarly pursuits relevant to Christian mission, which is always the focus of books in the Series.

By *mission* is meant the effort to effect passage over the boundary between faith in Jesus Christ and its absence. In this understanding of mission, the basic functions of Christian proclamation, dialogue, witness, service, worship, liberation, and nurture are of special concern. And in that context questions arise, including, How does the transition from one cultural context to another influence the shape and interaction between these dynamic functions, especially in regard to the cultural and religious plurality that comprises the global context of Christian life and mission?

The promotion of scholarly dialogue among missiologists, and among missiologists and scholars in other fields of inquiry, may involve the publication of views that some missiologists cannot accept, and with which members of the Editorial Committee themselves do not agree. Manuscripts published in the Series, accordingly, reflect the opinions of their authors and are not understood to represent the position of the American Society of Missiology or of the Editorial Committee. Selection is guided by such criteria as intrinsic worth, readability, coherence, and accessibility to a range of interested persons and not merely to experts or specialists.

The ASM Series, in collaboration with Orbis Books, seeks to publish scholarly works of high merit and wide interest on numerous aspects of missiology—the study of mission. Able presentations on new and creative approaches to the practice and understanding of mission will receive close attention.

**The ASM Series Editorial Committee**
Jonathan J. Bonk
Angelyn Dries, OSF
Scott W. Sunquist

# *Acknowledgments*

We thank Bryan Hudkins, Shawn Redford, William R. Burrows, and Keith Reeves for the assistance they provided with final formatting. We are also grateful to our respective schools and those in our departments of Missions and Intercultural Studies at the Wheaton College Graduate School and Global Studies and Sociology at Azusa Pacific University. Most of all, we'd like to thank our wives, Young Lee Hertig and the late Dolores Gallagher, whose gracious love and encouragement provided the momentum to see this project reach its completion.

All scripture quoted is from the New Revised Standard Version (NRSV), unless otherwise specified. In the case of Chapter 19, Paul's Speech on the Areopagus, the translation from the Bible generally follows the NRSV, but when it does not it is the author's own.

# Contributors

*Grace Preedy Barnes*, born in China of missionary parents and grandparents, is professor/program director, Leadership Programs/Operation Impact, Department of College Student Affairs and Leadership Studies, School of Education and Behavioral Studies, Azusa Pacific University, Azusa, California. She coordinates the travel of more than forty faculty members who offer classes to more than three hundred students, both expatriates and nationals, toward the development of transcultural leaders worldwide.

*Evvy Hay Campbell* served two terms at Kamakwie Wesleyan Hospital in Sierra Leone, West Africa, and for nine years in health education and training with the Christian relief and development agency MAP International. For the last seven years she has served as associate professor of Missions and Intercultural Studies at Wheaton College in Wheaton, Illinois, teaching in the areas of public health, community development, and intercultural communication.

*Robert Gallagher* was formerly a Pentecostal executive pastor in Australia and a theological educator in Papua New Guinea and the South Pacific. He currently teaches theology, history, and leadership studies at Wheaton College Graduate School in Illinois and was a co-editor of *Footprints of God: A Narrative Theology of Mission* (MARC, 1999).

*Eddie Gibbs*, the Donald A. McGavran Professor of Church Growth, School of Intercultural Studies, Fuller Theological Seminary, is an ordained Anglican who served as a missionary in Chile 1965 to 1970 with the South American Missionary Society. His most recent book is *ChurchNext* (InterVarsity Press, 2000).

*Dean S. Gilliland* is the senior professor of contextual theology and African studies, School of Intercultural Studies, Fuller Theological Seminary. He was a missionary to Nigeria with the United Methodist Church for twenty-two years and served as principal of the Theological College of Northern Nigeria. He is the author of *Pauline Theology and Mission Practice* (Wipf & Stock, 1998).

*Gene L. Green* is professor of New Testament at Wheaton College in Illinois and previously taught New Testament in the Dominican Republic and Costa Rica for over a decade. He also served as the academic dean and sometime rector of the Seminario ESEPA in San José, Costa Rica. He is author of two commentaries in Spanish (*1 Pedro y 2 Pedro*, Editorial Caribe, and *1 y 2 Tesalonicenses,* Editorial Portavoz) as well as *The Letters to the Thessalonians* (Eerdmans, 2002).

**Roger S. Greenway**, professor emeritus of world missiology at Calvin Theological Seminary in Grand Rapids, Michigan, the founding editor of the journal *Urban Mission,* served in Sri Lanka, Mexico, and other parts of Latin America. He has authored more than a dozen books, including *Apostles to the City* (1973), *Go and Make Disciples* (P&R Publishing, 1999), and *Discipling the City* (2001).

**Paul Hertig**, professor of global studies and sociology at Azusa Pacific University, directs its L.A. term program, a semester-long urban-immersion program in central Los Angeles. He served on the mission field for three years in East Asia and pastored and taught in immigrant churches and seminaries in Los Angeles for twelve years. He is author of *Matthew's Narrative Use of Galilee in the Multicultural and Missiological Journeys of Jesus* (Mellen Biblical Press, 1998).

**Young Lee Hertig** integrates theology, anthropology, and psychology in her teaching in various academic institutions. An ordained Presbyterian, she has served Korean immigrant churches for the last twenty years. She is author of *Cultural Tug of War: The Korean Immigrant Family and Church in Transition* (Abingdon, 2001).

**Mary E. Hinkle**, associate professor of New Testament at Luther Seminary in St. Paul, Minnesota, was the associate editor of *Word & World* and remains a frequent contributor. Her writings are on the intersection of biblical studies and homiletics. She recently published a nine-session Bible study for *Lutheran Woman Today*, "Grace upon Grace: A Study of John's Gospel."

**Robert C. Linthicum** is president of Partners in Urban Transformation (PUT), a ministry that equips churches, mission agencies, and community organizations to work successfully for social and spiritual change in their cities. Over the past quarter century, he has worked through World Vision and PUT with hundreds of churches in Africa, Asia, and Latin and North America in the fields of community organizing, economic and housing development, and evangelism. He is visiting professor of urban ministry and community organizing at Eastern University in Philadelphia. His most recent book is *Transforming Power: Biblical Strategies for Making a Difference in Your Community* (InterVarsity Press, 2003).

**Lynn Allan Losie** is associate professor of New Testament in the Haggard Graduate School of Theology of Azusa Pacific University. His responsibilities include teaching in cross-cultural programs for the development of Korean and Latino pastors and teachers.

*Paul Martinson,* born in China, served with the Lutheran church in Hong Kong in the 1960s and taught at Luther Seminary from 1972 to 2001, where he became the Fredrik A. Schiotz Professor of Missions and Religions. He currently serves as vice president of the China Service Ventures, fostering relationships between Christian communities in North America and communities, including Christian communities, in China. His most recent publication is *Families of Faith: An Introduction to World Religions for Christians* (Fortress Press, 1999).

*A. Scott Moreau* served for fourteen years in Africa, teaching general science in a Swazi public high school and later at the Nairobi International School of Theology. He also served as a deputy administrator for the Accrediting Council for Theological Education in Africa. Since 1991 he has taught in the Missions and Intercultural Studies Department at the graduate school of Wheaton College, where he is now professor and department chair. He was the general editor of the award-winning *Evangelical Dictionary of World Missions* (Baker, 2000) and is the editor of *Evangelical Missions Quarterly.*

*Stephen J. Pettis,* associate professor of missiology and cross-cultural studies at Reformed Bible College in Grand Rapids, Michigan, has participated in church planting, curriculum development, teaching, and small-group leadership in Bermuda, Portugal, the Azores, Romania, and Mexico.

*Shawn Redford,* an adjunct faculty member and Ph.D. candidate in the School of Intercultural Studies at Fuller Theological Seminary, worked as a mechanical engineer before entering into cross-cultural mission work among the Maasai tribe in Kenya, East Africa. He is an editor for *Announcing the Kingdom: The Story of God's Mission in the Bible* (Baker, 2003).

*Keith Howard Reeves,* professor of New Testament and early Christian literature, Department of Religion and Philosophy, Azusa Pacific University, is the founding editor of the *Journal for Christian Theological Research* and has done summer teaching and mission work in Zambia, Honduras, Mexico, and England.

*David Strong* is the professor of missiology and chair of the Theology and Ministry Division, Simpson College, Redding, California. He served for fifteen years with the Christian and Missionary Alliance in Korea and the Philippines. His publications include "The Smokey Horizon: Moving Beyond the American Experience in Filipino Mission," *Journal of Asian Mission* (September 2000).

*Nancy Thomas,* along with her husband, Hal, co-directs a postgraduate program in missiology for the Bolivian Evangelical University in Santa Cruz, Bolivia. She teaches Christian writers in the majority world and co-edited the book *Footprints of God: A Narrative Theology of Mission* (MARC, 1999).

***Norman E. Thomas*** is the Vera B. Blinn Professor Emeritus of World Christianity at United Theological Seminary in Dayton, Ohio. He served for fifteen years as a Methodist missionary in Zimbabwe and Zambia. A biographer, he edited *Classic Texts in Mission and World Christianity* (Orbis Books, 1995) and the *International Mission Bibliography: 1996-2000* (Scarecrow, 2003).

***Charles E. Van Engen*** is the Arthur F. Glasser Professor of Biblical Theology of Mission, School of Intercultural Studies, Fuller Theological Seminary. He served as a missionary, supported by the Reformed Church in America, working with the National Presbyterian Church of Mexico in the state of Chiapas, Mexico, from 1973 to 1985. In partnership with a Mexican director, he developed and served as academic dean for the Theological Education by Extension Seminary for the Chiapas Presbytery. He is the founder and president of Latin American Christian Ministries, Inc., a nonprofit corporation dedicated to creating a Ph.D.-level leadership development program in Latin America. He is author of *God's Missionary People: Rethinking the Purpose of the Local Church* (Baker, 1991).

***Clark A. Walz***, an archaeologist specializing in ritual studies, is currently working on a larger study of magic in the early Christian experience. He is pastor of Cascade and Henderson United Methodist Churches in Erie, Pennsylvania, and adjunct instructor of church history at United Theological Seminary in Dayton, Ohio.

***Santos Yao*** is pastor of Life Christian Fellowship, a church-planting ministry among the Filipino immigrants in the San Gabriel Valley, California, under the auspices of the American Baptist Church, Pacific Southwest region.

# 1

# *Introduction: Background to Acts*

## Paul Hertig and Robert L. Gallagher

The purpose of this book is to introduce students, scholars, biblical interpreters, and mission practitioners to the Book of Acts through the interpretation of key passages and to demonstrate their relevance for contemporary mission practice. The contributors have made genuine connections between the narratives of Acts, their personal narratives, and the narratives of our postmodern context—all with implications for mission.

The editors of this volume have taught the Book of Acts in undergraduate and graduate settings for many years and have found it no easy task to find textbooks that give Acts the full missiological investigation that it deserves. This book has evolved from that challenge. Acts is the most explicitly missional book in the Bible, and it deserves scholarly, missional attention balanced with practical implications.

Each chapter in *Mission in Acts* draws out the missionary nature of Acts through the interpretation of key texts within their original contexts. This interpretive dimension is interconnected with a transformative one through illustrations of the relevance of Acts for contemporary Christian life and missional practice. While it is a given that the narratives in Acts must be interpreted within their socio-historical contexts, a further, pressing challenge is the "hermeneutical" task of discerning the relevance of these ancient texts for missiological practice in the contemporary world. This book seeks genuine connections between the narratives of Acts, the writers' personal narratives, and the narratives of our postmodern context in missiological perspective. The biblical texts are interpreted in their original contexts, utilizing up-to-date tools for interpretation, then understood within various global contexts. The writers' own contexts are vast and varied, from a church planter among Asian American immigrants, to a New Testament scholar in southern California, to a missionary in Bolivia, to an archeologist who pastors in Pennsylvania, to a community organizer in Los Angeles, to a director of an urban-immersion educational program in a multicultural context, to a mission professor in Minnesota, to a director of leadership programs and international education at a Christian University. The writers range in denominational affiliations that include Anglican, Baptist, United Methodist, Christian Missionary Alliance, Presbyterian, Lutheran, Pentecostal, and Reformed. The writers intertwine their own personal narratives in order to ponder the practice of theology within a myriad of postmodern contexts.

Each chapter interprets a specific text within its context as set out in the narrative of the Book of Acts (some chapters interpret a cluster of texts). The writers weave their ministerial and missiological narratives into the tapestry of interpretation to provide relevant applications for contemporary contexts. They utilize a common format of weaving into their scriptural interpretations their personal and/or missiological narratives for an authentically contextual contribution.

## THE UNIQUE GENRE OF ACTS

The Book of Acts is structured around various acts of the Holy Spirit, reaching across spiritual, cultural, social, and political boundaries. A missionary document through and through, it is not intended to be read as a polished book of doctrines or a systematic theology. In the words of James D. G. Dunn, "It tells of the beginnings of Christianity with a vigour and vividness which often leaves the new reader breathless."[1] It is filled with action-packed missionary adventures, power struggles, religious persecution, power encounters, political bullying, the power *(dunamis)* of the Holy Spirit, resurrections of the dead, signs, wonders, miraculous healings, visions, earthquakes from God, dramatic conversions, imprisonments, dramatic prison escapes, beatings, stonings, martyrdom, murders, mob violence, perilous dangers, and incredible rescues. The Book of Acts is theology in action; faith lived out in the trenches of real life.

Some well-intentioned readers of Acts have read it incorrectly. They have studied it in fragments or consulted it as a reference book on doctrines. But Acts is most of all a history book of the early church, structured around the journeys of individuals whom the Holy Spirit sent out into the world. Luke is most concerned with the historical development of the first believers and less concerned with organizing that development into an elaborate set of dogmas. "The evangelists were engaged in proclamation and not just reporting; their concern was to tell the story of the historical Jesus so that their readers might encounter the living Christ."[2] The story of the historical church and its encounters with the living Christ include mysterious and unpredictable power encounters and astonishing works of the Holy Spirit. The church in Acts is guided by the Holy Spirit and not by human governance. The key players are not restricted by dry doctrines or cold creeds as they participate in a new history that unfolds through the guidance and power of the Spirit. Robert Maddox has observed:

> For Luke the church as an institution is remarkably free and spontaneous in the impulses of its communal life. Neither the Apostles nor James exercise authoritarian direction of the church in Jerusalem, nor do Paul or others elsewhere. The church is led not by institutional authorities but by

the Holy Spirit. By the Spirit the church is consolidated, but also disciplined and purified, and at the same time kept open to the mysterious and always new demands of God's will. And there is no trace of a high sacramentalism.[3]

Even Jesus makes appearances in the Book of Acts. He sends his disciples in the power of the Holy Spirit out into the world as his witnesses, then ascends into glory (1:8-10). Later, Jesus meets Saul on the road to Damascus (9:5). Since the second century, our book of study has been traditionally entitled the Acts of the Apostles, but a careful reading has brought scholars and non-scholars alike to conclude that it would be most appropriately entitled the Acts of the Holy Spirit. The Holy Spirit initiates and directs a series of dramatic outpourings and adventures of the early church. Arthur T. Pierson said that this is one book in the Bible without a proper ending, "because it waits for new chapters to be added so fast and so far as the people of God" will follow the leading of the Holy Spirit.[4] Through the Spirit, you and I are invited to become part of the ongoing saga—the history of the church. The church discovers its identity in history when it enters into the narrative where Acts abruptly concludes—in the midst of bold and unhindered proclamation of "the kingdom of God and teaching about the Lord Jesus Christ" (28:31).

Having described Acts as unique in genre, it is nonetheless important to consider that some scholars have described Luke as a biographer. However, Luke shows an interest in events (Lk 1:1-4) more than in people. The two books of Luke-Acts are interwoven by the threads of God's redeeming work in the world more than by the heroics of an individual person or persons—which would be characteristic of the work of a biographer. Certainly, Acts has important biographical features, but Luke begins with a preface that is personal in approach, utilizing first-person pronouns and a dedication. Doubtless, however, Luke is oriented by Old Testament and Jewish historiography, utilizing historical progression to form a narrative theology. His collection of speeches, travel narratives, letters, and trials corresponds to the design of Greco-Roman historiography. But the mysterious and somewhat mystical inner and outer workings of the Holy Spirit provide a unique twist to Luke's two historiographical accounts.

## INTRODUCTION TO LUKE-ACTS

The two volumes of Luke-Acts comprise nearly one-fourth of the New Testament and have been influential in shaping historical Christianity. Today, the church calendar celebrates the festivals of Pentecost and Ascension as a result of the work and witness of Jesus, Peter, Stephen, and Paul as recorded in Acts. Acts enriches our understanding of the apostles of the early church.

The gospel of Luke and the Acts of the Apostles are a twofold work by the same author. Luke and Acts are the two most extended writings in the New Testament. Each volume would have filled a normal papyrus roll, explaining why Luke-Acts was composed as two volumes rather than one. Both have a similar introduction (Lk 1:1-4; Acts 1:1-5) and are addressed to the same person, Theophilus (Lk 1:3; Acts 1:1). Acts 1:1-5 begins with a summary of what the author wrote in Luke and reintroduces material from the end of Luke. It begins in the same city, Jerusalem. In the conclusion of the gospel of Luke the disciples are waiting for the Holy Spirit to come; early in Acts, the same moment of anticipation occurs (1:4-8).

There is a similar literary structure between Luke and Acts, a common style of language, and a similar theological emphasis. Some differences in vocabulary and theological attention are outweighed by the similarities of theological motifs, broad structure, and continued themes. Hence, most scholars see Acts as a continuation of Luke.

Each volume is important in understanding the motivation for writing the whole, since Luke had in mind both the gospel and Acts from the beginning. F. F. Bruce contends that "the purpose of Acts cannot be considered in isolation from the purpose of Luke's gospel. The two parts, for all their stylistic differences, make up an integral whole, with one coherent purpose."[5]

Acts is not only intricately bound to the gospel of Luke, it is also intertwined with the letters of Paul. While occasional references are made to Paul's letters, it is not the purpose of this study to enter into the complex dialogue between the Pauline letters and Acts. Many in-depth studies with this purpose are readily available. The focus of this particular study is on the missiological treatment of Acts itself. Theologically, this study focuses on Acts as a document in its own right and explicitly explores its emerging missiological themes. Structurally, Acts is examined in relation to volume 1, the gospel of Luke.

## AUTHORSHIP AND DATE

Some scholars argue that Luke was a Greek Christian based on Colossians 4:10-14, which lists Paul's Jewish co-workers, concluding with the important comment, "These are the only ones of the circumcision among my co-workers for the kingdom of God" (Col 4:11b). Paul then follows with a list of additional co-workers, which, by implication, must be those *not* of the circumcision, seemingly Gentile converts (Col 4:12-14). Luke, "the beloved physician," is named in this second group, possibly suggesting that Luke is a Gentile Christian of Greek heritage. This is strengthened by the fact that Colossians 4:11 implies that Luke is not one of the converts from Judaism.

An early witness to Luke's authorship is found in the Muratorian Canon (ca. 170-180 C.E.), which also states that Luke was a physician who had not seen the Lord personally but was a companion of Paul. Early church tradition—Clement of Alexandria, Origen, Eusebius, and Jerome—unanimously affirms that Luke authored the third gospel. Such an overwhelming witness from the early church fathers gives strong support for Lukan authorship, especially since he was not an apostle or one of the followers of Jesus.

Due to the unanimous testimony of tradition and the author's implied companionship to Paul in the "we" sections of Acts (16:10-17; 20:5—21:18; 27:1—28:16), which plunge suddenly into first-person plural, we affirm the likelihood of Luke's authorship of Luke-Acts. It is most probable that the author is the same Luke of Colossians 4:14, the "beloved physician" and travel companion of Paul. While some scholars have argued that the "we" passages are stylistic creations or literary conventions, the sudden manner in which they move from third- to first-person plural are better understood as a signal to the reader of a transition to personal involvement; the abrupt move back again from first to third person indicates a change from personal presence to absence. This does not deny that Luke utilized written and oral traditions passed down by eyewitnesses as laid out in his prologue (Lk 1:1-4), but the narratives suggest that Luke himself played the role of eyewitness in certain sequences of his second volume.[6] The "we" narratives, possibly from a personal diary, supplemented the stories from firsthand witnesses concerning the life of the apostle Paul.

Moving from the internal evidence of Luke, the "beloved physician" as author and possible companion of Paul, we now consider his ethnic, educational, and spiritual circumstances. Many scholars believe that the author of Luke-Acts converted to Christianity from a non-Jewish background—a Gentile Christian well educated in the Hellenistic culture and Judaism as evidenced in his sophisticated Greek style of language.

The prologue to Luke (1:1-4) reflects the cultured language of the writer and the serious literary intent of his work. M. Dibelius felt that Acts was intended not only for Christian communities but also for the "book market."[7] Luke is well acquainted with Hellenistic literary styles and Old Testament literary traditions, particularly from the Septuagint, the Greek translation of the Hebrew scriptures. In fact, 90 percent of Luke's vocabulary is also found in the Septuagint (LXX).[8]

It is not possible to be exact about the date of Acts, but a commonly accepted time period is in the 80s. Acts had to be written in a time period after the first volume, the Gospel of Luke (dated in the early 70s), which was itself dependent on Mark (dated in the late 60s or early 70s). The destruction of Jerusalem and turbulent issues lay some time in the past, but not so far back as to prevent Luke's audience from asking questions about the restoration of the kingdom (1:6). Since the Roman government responds favorably at nearly every turn in Acts, the book is likely to have been written after the persecution under Nero (64 C.E.) yet before the outbreak of persecution under Domitian (in the 90s).

Ben Witherington III, observing a rougher style of Greek in Luke's second volume as well as the abrupt ending, hypothesizes that the author died before completing Acts. Surmising that Luke joined Paul as a travel companion while in his thirties (in the 50s C.E.), he would have been in his sixties during the 80s, explaining the rougher and seemingly unfinished work.[9] Dunn argues against the possibility of Luke having in mind a third volume, based on the notion that the second volume gazes into an unknown future (28:30-31). He argues that Luke and Acts were intended to be a matching pair, making up a complete unit, and that "Acts was intended by Luke to be the climax and completion of his career as historian and epitomizer of earliest Christianity."[10]

There are many textual clues indicating that Luke was likely a Gentile Christian who composed Acts for a Gentile-Christian audience of God-fearers. The term *God-fearers* refers to Gentile participants in the synagogue who may not have been wholly converted to Judaism but participated in Judaism to the degree that they were able (see Acts 10:1-2; 13:43). When speaking of the Jews, he gives the impression that he is not one of them. For instance, he speaks of the "synagogue of the Jews" and "the Jews in Jerusalem" (Acts 13:5; 14:1; 17:1; 21:11). Moreover, the author appears to be from outside of Palestine, because his understanding of the geography and customs is limited. There is "the transformation of Palestinian local color and details into Hellenistic counterparts."[11]

Several ancient writers, including Josephus, Eusebius, and Jerome, mention that Luke was from Antioch in Syria. This would not require, however, that Luke was Greek. Based on the form of Luke's name, the New Testament passages that mention Luke, and the ancient tradition about Luke's origin from Antioch, Joseph A. Fitzmyer contends that "Luke was a native Syrian inhabitant of Antioch, a non-Jew from a Semitic cultural background, an *incola* of Antioch, a Gentile."[12] He maintains that Luke had an early acquaintance with the church at Antioch based on the references found in Acts that imply personal insight, thus giving credit to the ancient tradition (11:19-20; 13:1-4; 14:26-28; 15:1-3, 13-40; 18:22-23).

Some surmise, from the evidence within Luke-Acts, that the author is a person converted to Christianity from Judaism, familiar with the Old Testament scriptures and their phraseology. Luke's style and language indicate a sophisticated command of Greek. These two observations have convinced some scholars that Luke was a Hellenistic Jew. If Luke was a Gentile, on the other hand, then he was somehow steeped in the study of Old Testament scriptures and remarkably sensitive to the issues and needs of Jewish believers. For these reasons, Luke might have been a Hellenistic Jew, a convert to Judaism, or possibly a God-fearer.[13]

## LUKE'S AUDIENCE

Luke and Acts are both dedicated to Theophilus, the "most excellent" (Lk 1:3; see Acts 1:1).[14] Since this title is also used by the author to address the Roman governors Felix and Festus (Acts 23:26; 24:2; 26:25), Theophilus was likely a Gentile Christian or devoted sympathizer of some prominence. Lack of specification of a wider audience is unusual for ancient dedications. However, since the volumes give no indication that they are intended merely for Theophilus's personal use, Luke likely intended that through Theophilus, possibly a sponsor for Luke-Acts, he might convince literate Gentile readers and society's opinion makers, such as the governing classes.[15] Based on the following observations, Luke appears to be writing to a predominantly Gentile audience:[16] For instance, the prologue is Hellenistic in style (Lk 1:1-4; Acts 1:1-5), and Luke speaks of the Jewish people in the third person (Lk 7:3; 23:51; Acts 10:39; 13:5; 14:1; 17:1; 21:11). Acts is preeminently interested in the Gentile mission (Acts 10—11; 13:46-48; 18:6; 28:24-28). Luke's quotations from the Old Testament are mostly taken from the Greek Septuagint, and his use of the term *Judea* describes Palestine as a whole (Lk 1:5; 4:44; 6:17; 7:17; 23:5; Acts 2:9; 10:37).

By themselves, these and the many other Gentile indicators do not necessarily point to a Gentile audience, but they suggest a strong possibility that the author is a God-fearer who "stands at the crossroads" to embrace Christianity as the fulfillment of Judaism, who receives his Gentile identity while maintaining the best of Judaism. At the same time, the narrative indicates that certain Jews are suspicious of Christianity being a perversion of the truth about God.

## SETTING AND PURPOSE

The place of composition is uncertain. Syrian Antioch has traditional support because of Luke's detailed knowledge of the community in the Antioch church in Acts (11:19-20; 13:1-4; 14:26-28; 15:1-3, 30-40; 18:22-23), where the characteristics of the church correspond to those of Luke-Acts—the gospel preached to the Gentiles and a concern for the poor. However, early tradition in the Anti-Marcionite Prologues gives credence to Achaia as a possible site for the writing. Thus we cannot be sure where Luke wrote his two volumes. In modern times some of the intelligent guesses have included Asia Minor, Boeotia, Caesarea, Decapolis, Philippi, Rome, and Syria.[17] Rome is an attractive setting for the composition of Acts because Paul's arrival in Rome in the concluding chapter in Acts is a "we" passage (28:16) and because Luke treats the Roman government positively.[18] The majority of scholars give little space to this question and are reticent to elaborate; however, many would concede that Luke is cosmopolitan in scope.

Utilizing Robert H. Stein's four broad categories concerning the Lukan purpose,[19] the author may have written Luke-Acts to assure his Christian audience of the truthfulness of what they had come to believe; to clarify their understanding of their relationship with Israel; to correct the understanding of Christian concern about the parousia; and to provide an apologetic work for both Christians and non-Christians. Each of these categories, and many others, are explored in the chapters of this book.

### *Apologetic Aspect*

Luke's dual volumes are apologetic in their use of the Hebrew scriptures and approach to the Roman government. Luke-Acts is peppered with quotes and echoes from the Hebrew scriptures pointing to Jesus Christ as the suffering Messiah (Lk 3:4-6, cf. Isa 40:3-5; Lk 4:17-21, cf. Isa 61:1-2). This proof from prophecy includes the prophetic fulfillment of future events such as Israel's rejection of the Messiah, the death and resurrection of Christ as well as the Holy Spirit's coming and the destruction of Jerusalem (Lk 9:22, 44, 49-51). Stein also sees that Luke tried to assure his readers through the proof of miracles (Acts 2:43; 5:12; 6:8; 8:13; 14:3; 15:12), the greatest being the resurrection of Jesus (Acts 2:24-36), and the growth of the church in Acts (1:15; 2:41, 47; 4:4; 6:7; 9:31; 11:21, 24; 12:24; 14:1, 21; 16:5; 19:20).

In Luke-Acts the author presents a favorable view of the Roman government. It is not the Romans who thwarted the purposes of God but certain Jews. The

Jewish leaders pressured the Roman officials to crucify Jesus, although the government recognized his innocence (Lk 23:4, 14-16, 22, 24). Luke presents the death of Jesus as a miscarriage of justice.

The same thing happened to Paul in Acts. The Roman government wanted to release the apostle (24:23, 26-27; 25:18-19; 26:32), but Jewish leaders would not accept the decision. Repeatedly in the Book of Acts, Luke portrays the opposition to the messengers of the gospel coming from the Jewish community (4:1-22; 5:17-40; 7:1—8:3; 9:1-2, 23-25; 13:50; 14:19); the government officials giving favor or at least declaring Paul and the other Christians innocent of charges (13:7, 12; 16:37-39; 18:12-17; 19:31, 35-41; 24:22—25:25; 26:30-32; 28:30-31), and the Romans doing their best to protect the followers of Christ (18:12-17; 19:35-37, 40).

Why did Luke present the Romans in such a positive light? Some scholars argue that Luke-Acts was written to non-Christians as an apologetic for the Christian faith showing that they were not a threat to the Roman Empire.[20] For example, F. F. Bruce claims that at the time Luke wrote, Christianity was receiving widespread suspicion as a movement against the law and order of the Roman empire and that "Luke sets himself to deal with this handicap."[21]

Since Acts 1:8 lays out both the thesis and geographical outline for Acts, it follows that the overarching purpose of Acts is to explain the initiative of the Holy Spirit in the spread of the gospel throughout the Gentile world. Within this overarching purpose are many other subtopics, such as the unity of the flourishing movement within diversity, in spite of tensions and setbacks. Furthermore, Acts provided assurance to political leaders that Christianity was not a threat to Rome, and vice versa, that Roman rule was not a threat to Christians.[22] "Luke was most anxious to impress upon his readers that the Roman authorities treated the Christian missionaries with benevolence and acknowledged them to be politically harmless."[23] Ernst Haenchen observes the use of specific stories that demonstrate the "friendly and correct . . . behavior of Roman officials towards Paul."[24] We now move to several key approaches to the structure of Acts.

## THREE-PART STRUCTURE

The most important structural approach is the three-part structure laid out by the author of Acts in 1:8: "You will receive power when the Holy Spirit has come upon you; and you will be my witnesses

1. in Jerusalem,
2. in all Judea and Samaria,
3. and to the ends of the earth."

This passage (with the three numerals added) becomes the table of contents of Acts. Luke clearly follows this three-part geographical outline, reiterating and elaborating on it in the following verses:

1. 1:4 Jesus "ordered them not to leave *Jerusalem,* but to wait there for the promise of the Father."

2. 8:1b "That day a severe persecution began against the church in Jerusalem, and all except the apostles were scattered throughout the countryside of *Judea and Samaria.*"
3. 9:15 Paul is described as "an instrument whom I have chosen to bring my name before *Gentiles and kings* and before the people of Israel." Summarizing Paul's ministry in Ephesus, Acts 19:10 states: "This continued for two years, so that *all the residents of Asia, both Jews and Greeks,* heard the word of the Lord." Later, Paul says that Jesus told him, "Go, for I will send you far away to the Gentiles" (Acts 22:21).

This three-part outline indicates the heartbeat of Acts. The Holy Spirit dynamically empowers the early church in its infant stages in Jerusalem, then matures it and transforms it into a missionary force that extends to the ends of the earth, incorporating Jews and Gentiles into a universal and multicultural community. The church begins in Jerusalem with a *centripetal* mission, *attracting* people lovingly into its dynamic community, and then expands to Judea and Samaria with a *centrifugal* mission that *boldly ventures* into the Gentile world.

## SIX-PART STRUCTURE

Through six summary statements, Luke shows that the work of the Holy Spirit not only prevails but valiantly succeeds amid trials and persecutions as the church extends its mission to the world:

1. "The word of God continued to spread; the number of disciples increased greatly in Jerusalem, and a great many of the priests became obedient to the faith" (6:7).
2. "Meanwhile, the church throughout Judea, Galilee, and Samaria had peace and was built up. Living in the fear of the Lord and in the comfort of the Holy Spirit, it increased in numbers" (9:31).
3. "But the word of God continued to advance and gain adherents" (12:24).
4. "So the churches were strengthened in the faith and increased in numbers daily" (16:5).
5. "So the word of the Lord grew mightily and prevailed" (19:20).
6. "He lived there [the apostle Paul in Rome] two whole years at his own expense and welcomed all who came to him, proclaiming the kingdom of God and teaching about the Lord Jesus Christ with all boldness and without hindrance" (28:30-31).

If these statements on the growth of the church are studied carefully within their literary contexts, the reader discovers that such growth was not a goal but a byproduct of the work of the church empowered by the Holy Spirit. These are summary statements that serve to enhance the 1:8 thesis of worldwide mission in the power of the Holy Spirit. By beginning in Jerusalem and ending in Rome, the story emphasizes the centrifugal movement of the gospel. Rome, often interpreted as Luke's "ends of the earth," may not be the final intention of the narrative. The "ends of the earth" may be a symbolic reference to a universal mission that includes the Gentiles, that is, mission to the whole world. Here may be another case of Luke's theological use of geography (see "The Journey Motif" below).

Rome, in fact, is not necessarily the final place of mission. Paul describes his journey to Rome not as his final destination but as a stopping point on the way to Spain (Rom 15:23-24). Rome serves as another new point of departure for mission, much like Jerusalem and Antioch earlier in the narrative. Even within Acts, missionaries precede Paul to Rome. Paul discovered "believers" already in Rome when he arrived there (Acts 28:14-15). This believing community may have been established by the original visitors who had come from Rome at Pentecost (Acts 2:10). Thus Paul does not bring the gospel to Rome, reminding us that missionaries do not carry God in their suitcases. God is already at work before Paul arrives.

It is important to see Acts 1:8 not only as an outline of Acts but also as an indicator of God's missionary purposes within the narrative. The shape of the narrative is centrifugal, and the progression of the mission is theological within geographical terminology. There are many meetings in Jerusalem in which the witnesses return in order to explore further the theological rationale for a mission that includes those "at the end of the earth" (Acts 11:1-8; 15:1-2; 21:17-19; 22:21).

## TWO-PART STRUCTURE

1. Peter (chapters 1—12)
2. Paul (chapters 13—28)

The two-part structural approach focuses both on two key leaders and two geographical regions. In chapters 1—12 Peter is the leading character. Peter later makes an appearance in Acts 15 at the Jerusalem council to defend and validate mission to the Gentiles, then fades out of the picture completely. This final appearance is important, because he passes the baton to Paul, the missionary to the Gentiles, who becomes the leading character in chapters 13—28 and shares the gospel throughout wide regions of the world.

This two-part structure based on the main characters indicates two main locations of the story as well: Jerusalem, where Peter is the key leader and chief spokesman for the early church; and the Gentile world, where Paul pioneers the mission movement to vast regions. This two-part structure also signifies the spread of the gospel from Jerusalem to Rome, to Jews and then to Gentiles. This structure, like the other two, ties to the thesis of Acts 1:8, because it points to the geographical movement of the gospel from Jerusalem to the ends of the earth.

## THE STRUCTURE OF THE TWO VOLUMES, LUKE-ACTS

Since the structure of Acts must be understood in relation to its preceding volume, Luke-Acts may be viewed as one work with six parts. In Acts 1:1-2 the author reviews the first three parts of what he has said in his first account. Then, in Acts 1:8 he previews the second volume. Thus the following six parts of the book are based on: "In the first book, Theophilus, I wrote about *all that Jesus did and taught* from the beginning *until he was taken up* to heaven" (Acts 1:1-2, emphasis added) and "But you will receive power when the Holy Spirit has come upon you; and *you will be my witnesses in Jerusalem, in all Judea and Samaria, and to the ends of the earth*" (Acts 1:8, emphasis added).

Part 1: "All that Jesus did" (Lk 1:1—9:50).
Part 2: "And taught" (Lk 9:51—19:44).
Part 3: "Until he was taken up" (Lk 19:45—24:53).
Part 4: "You will be my witnesses in Jerusalem" (Acts 1:1—6:7).
Part 5: "In all Judea and Samaria" (Acts 6:8—9:31).
Part 6: "And to the ends of the earth" (Acts 9:32—28:31).

These six divisions come from Luke's use of summary statements throughout the two volumes to indicate narrative boundaries. In part one Luke emphasizes the deeds of Jesus in Galilee. This is followed by the "journey" of the Messiah and his disciples from Galilee to Jerusalem. On the way to the holy city, Luke focuses on the teachings of Jesus. In this second part there are eighteen scenes with Jesus' teaching central to all but four. As early as Luke 9:51[25] the author has Jesus moving toward his final destination. This is not his suffering in Jerusalem but his exaltation as Lord and Messiah "at the right hand of God" (Acts 7:55; see also Acts 2:33, 36). This occurs in part three of the gospel and carries over into the Book of Acts.

The mission of Jesus Christ through the early church continues in Acts. The end of part three and the beginning of part four duplicate the story of the disciples of Jesus waiting in Jerusalem for the power of "the baptism in the Holy Spirit" (Acts 1:5, 8). After his resurrection Jesus' final words in Luke serve not only as a conclusion to the gospel, but also as a precursor for Acts:

Thus it is written, that the Messiah is to suffer and to rise from the dead on the third day, and that repentance and forgiveness of sins is to be proclaimed in his name to all nations, beginning from Jerusalem. You are witnesses of these things. And see, I am sending upon you what my Father promised; so stay here in the city until you have been clothed with power from on high. (Lk 24:46-49)

After the disciples received the power of the Spirit to be Jesus' witnesses, Acts records the spread of the gospel from the capital of Judaism to the capital of the Roman Empire. The geographic expansion of the kingdom of God begins in Jerusalem (part 4). Following the death of Stephen, it then extends through the witness of the Hellenistic Jewish Christians to Judea, Samaria, and Galilee (part 5). The introduction of Paul in chapter 9 foreshadows the Gentile mission in part six of Luke-Acts.[26]

Supported by this six-part structural division, the overall thematic flow of Luke-Acts records the journey of God's people toward Jerusalem and then out from that holy city to the world. The author of the gospel of Luke stresses the characteristics that true disciples of Jesus must have on their journey to arrive at the heavenly destination in the kingdom of God. Similarly, in Acts, Luke underscores the characteristics that a true Christian community must have on its journey to arrive at the final destination that God has for it in the kingdom.

## THE JOURNEY MOTIF

Luke describes in the opening sentence of Acts how he begins to "trace out the continuation of and the continuities with the work which Jesus began (1:1-2)."[27] His chief concern is *"to identify the movement whose early history he describes as clearly as possible by its reference to Jesus."*[28]

In both Luke and Acts the journey is a central motif in mission. In Luke, Jesus journeys from Galilee to Samaria and into Jerusalem; in Acts, the church journeys from Jerusalem through Samaria and into the world. Thus, where Luke concludes with Jesus' journey *to Jerusalem*, Acts begins with the disciples' journey *from Jerusalem*. The ascension is the hinge that connects Luke-Acts.[29] It concludes Luke and begins Acts. Revealing Luke's key missiological themes, both ascension accounts focus on the Holy Spirit sending the church into the world (Lk 24:48-53; Acts 1:8-11).

Samaria serves as the halfway point between Jewish and Gentile mission in both Luke and Acts. In the gospel of Luke, the journey, or travel narrative, brings out Luke's "concept of salvation as a journey through time, the time of Israel, the time of Jesus and time of the Church."[30] In this overall journey through history in Luke-Acts, "Jesus journeys to Jerusalem, the message spreads out from Jerusalem to the end of the earth in Acts (Acts 1, 8) and Paul journeys to Rome (Acts 19, 21—28, 28)."[31]

In the travel-narrative section, beginning with Luke 9:51, Jesus resolutely faces his death, resurrection, and ascension. Being "taken up" likely refers not only to Jesus' ascension, but rooted in his death and resurrection, it speaks of his passion predictions and anguish occurring during his journey to Jerusalem (9:22-44; 12:50; 13:33; 17:25; 18:31-34). Therefore, the journey to Jerusalem is a travelogue of Jesus' death, resurrection, and ascension.[32]

A key transition in Jesus' journey through Samaria occurs when a Samaritan leper is the only one of ten healed lepers to return and gives thanks (Lk 17:11-17). In this account Jesus is described as walking along the border between Samaria and Galilee (17:11), a powerful depiction of Jesus' disregard for geographical boundaries.

Not only did Jesus cross into Samaria geographically, but Luke also crossed Samaria theologically. It is primarily "a journey to Jesus' death, resurrection, and ascension" that provides "an opportunity for teaching his disciples"[33] the basis of their faith and mission. Jesus both accepted Samaritans in spite of their enmity with Jews and utilized them to illustrate exemplary behavior. For instance, unique to Luke's gospel is the parable of the good Samaritan, a model of compassion for Jewish people (Lk 10:25-37).

In Acts, Samaria is again a key halfway point between mission to the Jews and Gentiles, thrusting the gospel into the Gentile world through the ministry of Philip (Acts 8:4-40). This Samaritan episode has two overlapping themes that propel God's people into the world: (1) The outreach to Samaria launched the second phase of the Acts 1:8 program. The Samaritan mission, as in Luke, represents the halfway stage of the movement of the gospel, the connecting link between mission in Jerusalem and mission to the world. The racially mixed Samaritans were midway between Jews and Gentiles. (2) The first encounter with non-Jewish theology through Philip's encounter with Simon the magician, in which Simon attempts to purchase the Holy Spirit (Acts 8:9-24).

W. Ward Gasque highlights what he considers the essence of the story:

> The Spirit is in charge. It is the Spirit that assures continuity with Jesus and is the source of the vitality of the Christian mission. Hence the theology of Acts is a mission-centered theology: The church exists not for herself but for the world, to bear bold testimony to what God has done and is doing in Jesus. . . . The accent is on the growth of the church through the proclamation of the word.[34]

The "mission-centered theology" described above might only be discerned through a careful and concerted interpretation process by the reader of Acts.

## THE NATURE OF THE READER

Gordon D. Fee and Douglas Stuart, in *How to Read the Bible for All Its Worth*, speak of two factors that prevent good biblical interpretation.[35] They are the nature of the reader and the nature of scripture. Whether we realize it or not, every reader of the Bible is also an interpreter. As we read a text, we tend to bring to that text our whole person, including our cultural experiences and prejudices. These may cause us to place words into the mouth of God and thereby interpret the Bible in ways that were not intended by the author.

The dilemma is that every interpreter approaches the text with presuppositions, because no interpreter can approach the text with an empty mind (although, unfortunately, some appear to!). Therefore, the task of the interpreter is to be aware of the presuppositions he or she brings to the text and allow those presuppositions to be changed—if the text deems it so. Such a task involves great effort because: (1) we are often as unaccustomed to our presuppositions as a fish is unaware of the water within which it is immersed, and (2) it is difficult to change the presuppositions to which we cling and which make up our very beings.

Therefore, there are no shortcuts to the process of interpreting scripture, called the exegetical process. Careful exegesis (to *draw out* meaning from the text) must precede any movement from the biblical world to the contemporary world. It is not our task quickly to carry the text over to our world, but rather to take ourselves first to the world of the text. We do not shape the text; the text shapes us through historical and literary study in which we explore the context and intention of the original author of the text.

Fortunately, God, in speaking to human situations, chooses to utilize the communication methods of the receptors in their particular culture. God's word to the original audience was meaningful to that audience. Thus, another aspect of good interpretation is to consider God's means of communication such as narrative, poetry, proverbs, parables, letters, songs, hymns, prayers, sermons, and riddles.[36] God's communication style differs from one genre to another. To interpret scripture properly, we need to have some understanding of these literary forms as well as the specific words and their meanings.

To plunge into the task of interpretation, one should seek maximum pre-knowledge or common ground with the text. For instance, the plays of Shakespeare may be initially obscure to students in an introductory course. But when the students begin to learn and adapt to Shakespearean vocabulary, style, genre, and historical background, they begin to establish common ground with the text. Whole new vistas open up.

Thus biblical interpretation begins with the two-step process of (1) understanding the biblical writer's original meaning within that writer's particular context, and (2) translating that meaning to today's setting. Anthony C. Thiselton explains plainly that "understanding takes place when two sets of horizons are brought into relation to each other, namely those of the text and those of the interpreter."[37] Relevant questions and issues brought to scripture pave the way for a new understanding of the Bible for the contemporary context. These questions arising from concrete situations allow for a reformulation toward a more adequate reflection of the biblical perspective. This requires a "continuous mutual engagement between the horizons of the text and the horizons of our culture."[38] Since we are grounded in this world, and since God inspires scripture, the community of believers may never bypass this process. Therefore, authentic biblical interpretation raises questions for both the text and context within any given situation.[39] For transformation to occur, the interpreter must be immersed equally in the world of scripture and his or her own world. James D. Smart explains that by living in "two worlds at one and the same time," interpreters become "aware that they are not two worlds but one in the same world":

> The two worlds come together so that the Scriptures are like a magic glass through which we look to see ourselves, our fellow-men, and our world as they really are. We look *through* it in order to see ourselves and our own world. It is fatal when that transparency is missing.[40]

The scriptures become a magic glass through which we see reality in a new way. We become aware of who we were and who we are. We become changed. In the words of M. Robert Mulholland, "The purpose of the Scripture is not information but transformation."[41]

This leads us to contemporary missiological application. We have not completed our study until we begin to explore how our new understanding of the Bible applies to our particular situation. Just as the legal historian applies the law today only after interpreting previous cases, so our understanding of the Bible relates missiologically to our real-world contexts.

Once our authors reached this point, they were able to compose their essays, which weave together their interpretations of the original texts and their implications and applications for our contemporary context. Fee and Stuart speak of the Bible being both eternally relevant and historically particular.[42]

In doing hermeneutics[43] for Luke-Acts, we need to use our sanctified common sense and try to be consistent throughout the process. This is more difficult than it may first appear because we unwittingly bring to the text our own cultural biases, denominational traditions, and personal prejudices. This inculturated baggage tends to impose restrictions on our common sense.

Our various traditions and cultural locations may restrict our understanding of leadership selection and equipping in the church. It is easy for contemporary Christians to support their own denominational power structure and educational style from one Lukan pericope. For instance, many churches go no further than the example of the Jerusalem church and its choice of the "seven deacons" (Acts 6:1-6) for their leadership selection process. In fact, Luke-Acts does not present one set procedure but rather a variety in leadership selection and equipping (for example, 13:1-3; 14:26-27).

However, many times there is no relation between what many Christians believe to be the pattern of God for the church and Luke-Acts, which has no single pattern for a local church, para-church group, or denomination. It is the Holy Spirit who sets the stage. In Jerusalem the Spirit moved among people in a particular way. In Antioch and Galatia the Spirit of Christ did the work of God in another way. From Jerusalem to Rome the Holy Spirit was made manifest in a variety of ways. If the contemporary church tries to fit its established patterns into the Book of Acts, it may distort the true function of the sovereign Spirit. In Acts, the people of God often discover what God is doing in the world and in its community, then cooperate with the manifestation of God in its particular situation. Thus, by resisting the temptation to read into the text what we already believe and how we already behave culturally, we might avoid reading our particular brand of Christianity into Luke's work.

In Acts we do not find any church buildings or church building programs. The early church community met in homes and public places. Neither do we find a professional religious hierarchy. All Christians are equal; all are priests before God. Certainly some were given special gifts that gave them leadership capacity. Yet unlike the surrounding Gentile religions, laity or clerical divisions were not evident in the early church.

There were no advertising crusades or billboards, newspapers, or tax-deductible giving. There were no denominational headquarters, annual conferences, seminaries, or Bible schools in existence. There were no Sunday bulletins or Sunday schools as we know them today. The atmosphere of Luke-Acts is altogether different from anything we experience as Christianity today. We are in a different time and culture.

There is nothing wrong with these activities. They are dynamically appropriate in our Western society to reach our generation for God. However, we should not expect to find the same forms of Christian expression in the Book of Acts that we practice today. Nor should we try to justify what we already do from the example of the early church.

What we do find in Acts is a company of people utterly convinced that Jesus Christ is alive and that he reigns in the present tense. The early church knew its spiritual roots. Prophecy was fulfilled in the church. God's Messiah had come, so it was inviting people to come and join in that kingdom experience. The kingdom had arrived on earth, and all could participate in that expanding kingdom through the power of the Holy Spirit.

## REFERENCES

[1] James D. G. Dunn, *The Acts of the Apostles* (Valley Forge, Pa.: Trinity Press International, 1996), ix.

[2] John Nolland, *Luke 1—9:20: Word Biblical Commentary,* vol. 35A (Dallas: Word Books. 1982), xxviii.

[3] Robert Maddox, *The Purpose of Luke-Acts* (Gottingen, 1982), 185.

[4] Arthur T. Pierson, *The Acts of the Holy Spirit* (Marshall, Morgan, and Scott, 1895), 141-142.

[5] F. F. Bruce, *The Book of Acts: The New International Commentary on the New Testament* (Grand Rapids, Mich.: Eerdmans, 1988), 6.

[6] Dunn, *The Acts of the Apostles,* x.

[7] M. Dibelius, *Studies in the Acts of the Apostles* (London: SCM Press, 1956), 135.

[8] Ernst Haenchen, *The Acts of the Apostles: A Commentary* (Oxford: Basil Blackwell, 1971), 72. Haenchen adds that if the Apocrypha were excluded, the figure would be 80 percent.

[9] Ben Witherington III, *New Testament History: A Narrative Account* (Grand Rapids, Mich.: Baker, 2001), 386-387.

[10] Dunn, *The Acts of the Apostles,* xv.

[11] Joseph A. Fitzmyer, *The Gospel according to Luke (I–IX): Introduction, Translation and Notes,* The Anchor Bible (Garden City, N.Y.: Doubleday, 1981).

[12] Ibid., 42-47.

[13] Gerhard A. Krodel, *Acts: Augsburg Commentary on the New Testament* (Minneapolis: Fortress Press, 1986), 15. On God-fearers, see Witherington, *New Testament History,* 208-209; see also Acts 10:1-2; 13:43.

[14] Joseph A. Fitzmyer states that "the same destination has to be maintained for Acts as well [as the third gospel]" (*The Gospel according to Luke,* 58).

[15] Dunn, *The Acts of the Apostles,* xi; Robert H. Stein, *Luke,* The New American Commentary (Nashville, Tenn.: Broadman Press, 1992), 26.

[16] Some of these reasons may be used to argue that the author is a Gentile.

[17] I. Howard Marshall states this suggestion, supported by Luke's use of Q (*The Gospel of Luke: A Commentary on the Greek Text* [Exeter: Paternoster Press, 1978], 35).

[18] The Roman context is also based on Luke's use of Mark. See Stein, *Luke,* 27.

[19] Ibid., 36-44.

[20] Haenchen in *The Acts of the Apostles* sees the purpose of Acts to be a political apology to Rome and a mission effort to the Gentiles who no longer live under the law.

[21] Bruce, *The Book of Acts*, 8.

[22] See Dunn for a similar approach to these themes (*The Acts of the Apostles*, xii-xiii).

[23] Haenchen, *The Acts of the Apostles*, 106.

[24] Ibid.

[25] Luke 9:51 says: "When the days drew near for him to be taken up, he set his face to go to Jerusalem."

[26] This parallels the introduction of the Hellenistic Jewish Christians at the end of part 4 as a foreshadowing of their influence in the spread of the gospel beyond Jerusalem.

[27] Dunn, *The Acts of the Apostles*, xi.

[28] Ibid., xi-xii.

[29] Michael Prior, *Jesus the Liberator: Nazareth Liberation Theology (Luke 4:16-20)* (Sheffield, UK: Sheffield Academic Press, 1995), 24.

[30] Thomas J. Lane, *Luke and the Gentile Mission: Gospel Anticipates Acts* (New York: Peter Lang, 1996), 96.

[31] Ibid.

[32] Ibid., 97.

[33] Ibid., 98.

[34] W. Ward Gasque, "A Fruitful Field: Recent Study of the Acts of the Apostles," in *Interpretation* 42/2 (1998): 127.

[35] Gordon D. Fee and Douglas Stuart, *How to Read the Bible for All Its Worth* (Grand Rapids, Mich.: Zondervan, 1982).

[36] The word *narrative* is preferred to *story* because the modern use of *story* often suggests the realm of make believe.

[37] Anthony C. Thiselton, *The Two Horizons* (Grand Rapids, Mich.: Eerdmans, 1980), 103.

[38] C. René Padilla, "Hermeneutics and Culture—A Theological Perspective," in *Down to Earth: Studies in Christianity and Culture*, ed. John R. W. Stott and Robert Coote (Grand Rapids, Mich.: Eerdmans, 1980), 76.

[39] Ibid.

[40] James D. Smart, *The Interpretation of Scripture* (Philadelphia: The Westminster Press, 1961), 34-35.

[41] M. Robert Mulholland Jr., "Sociological Criticism," in *New Testament Criticism and Interpretation*, ed. David Alan Black and David S. Dockery, 296-316 (Grand Rapids, Mich.: Zondervan, 1991), 309.

[42] Fee and Stuart, *How to Read the Bible for All Its Worth*, 19.

[43] We use the term *hermeneutics* to refer to the process of discerning the relevance of biblical texts for missiological practice in our contemporary world.

# 2

# *The Launching of Mission:*
# *The Outpouring of the Spirit at Pentecost*

## ACTS 2:1–41

## Eddie Gibbs

The Acts of the Apostles has had a personal fascination for me over the years for a number of reasons. First, as I reflected on my early Christian experience in a struggling evangelical Anglican church located in an increasingly multicultural context, I wondered whether we had missed an important element of the Spirit's work. Why, despite our belief in the central truths of the gospel and our attempts to bear a faithful verbal witness in the community, were we so ineffective in winning people for Christ?

Second, through my participation in the charismatic movement, which affected traditional denominations in the United Kingdom beginning in the mid 1960s, I struggled to understand the phenomena described in Acts 2 both theologically and experientially. If the powerful baptism of the Holy Spirit occurred at conversion, which is what I believed theologically, where was the evidence?

Third, my experience as a missionary with the South American Missionary Society, one of the oldest Protestant missions in that continent, exposed me to the vibrant Pentecostal movement in Chile. What lessons could we learn from its understanding of mission that might be transferable to the Western urban contexts?[1]

Fourth, as a professor of mission, evangelism, and church growth, how can the churches move from a bureaucratic, hierarchical institution to become the dynamic, decentralized, hub-and-spoke movement that it was during the period covered by the New Testament?

## THE NEED FOR EMPOWERMENT

At this juncture I am convinced that I need to revisit the Book of Acts to try and uncover important lessons that I may have overlooked. This task has become all the more urgent as Western cultures move from modernity to postmodernity.

Before studying the exciting narrative of the rapid expansion of the church through the witness of believers, beginning at Jerusalem and reaching out to the ends of the earth (1:8), I must understand the spiritual dynamic that both triggered and sustained this movement. Within the scope of this chapter I cannot answer all the questions I have raised, but I will address those issues that arise from the Pentecost account.

With the opening announcement that "the day of Pentecost had come," the text makes clear that a significant moment had arrived. This is in fact the first occasion when the Twelve, representing the new Israel, address the twelve tribes of Israel to testify to the risen Christ.[2] The launching of the community of disciples into mission occurs on an appropriate occasion, "the day of Pentecost." Fifty days had passed since Passover, when Christ was slain and rose from the dead as the "firstfruit." He was that single seed that had fallen into the ground so that many seeds might appear in due course (Jn 12:24). The feast of Pentecost heightened that expectation in that it was the feast at which the first ripe sheaves of wheat were presented before the Lord in anticipation of the harvest to come (Ex 23:16; 34:22; Lv 23:15-21; Nm 28:26-31).

The other significant association was the linking of Pentecost with the renewal of God's covenant with Israel.[3] That renewal had already begun in the lives of the disciples in the events surrounding the crucifixion when they, in their frailty, had denied and betrayed Jesus. The sorrow and lamenting after the passing of their Lord Jesus was soon turned into amazement when the Lord Jesus appeared to the women at the tomb and when Peter ran to the tomb and verified that it was empty. The Lord then walked with two disciples on the road to Emmaus and later stood among the gathered disciples (Lk 24:15, 36). No barred doors of fear could keep him out. Amazement was mingled with joy unspeakable as Jesus ate in their presence; the covenant renewal was well under way (24:43). He opened their minds to scriptural understandings about himself (24:27, 45) and gave them a mission mandate to all nations that would begin in Jerusalem where they would be empowered with the Holy Spirit from on high (24:47-49).

Their renewal consisted not of one isolated event but of a chain of occurrences. Jesus, after his resurrection, continued to make sudden appearances, leading to his mission mandate (Lk 24:47-48).[4] The mission with which they were then entrusted was that of making disciples of all peoples. Before embarking on that daunting task, Luke emphasizes that the disciples needed to wait in Jerusalem. There they would receive the promise of the Father, which consisted of being "clothed with power from on high" (Lk 24:49; Acts 1:4).

As I have reflected on the work of the Holy Spirit both in my life and in the church, Luke's writings occupy a central place. He alone writes a two-part work in which an account of the birth and subsequent ministry of Christ is paralleled by the narrative of the birth and ministry of the church. The author makes it clear that his gospel recorded that which Jesus *began* to do and to teach until his ascension into heaven. The Acts of the Apostles recorded the continuing work of the ascended Lord through his church on earth, which is now inspired and guided by his Spirit. The ministry of the Spirit cannot be separated from the work of Christ. The work of Christ at Pentecost was an overpowering experience in the Spirit.

There have been a number of times in my Christian life and ministry when I have been acutely aware of my own powerlessness. I remember being thrust into a situation in Chile for which I felt ill-prepared. I was to begin a new church in a strange town with no prior experience and virtually no training for the task. Nothing I attempted seemed to yield results. My anxiety resulted in a bleeding duodenal ulcer. While confined to bed, I was reminded of Paul in Corinth and the reassuring word of the ascended Lord to him: "Do not be afraid, but speak and do not be silent; for I am with you" (Acts 18:9, 10). I remembered that the early disciples were themselves renewed after having denied and deserted the Lord. It was following their failure that Jesus told them to wait in Jerusalem until they had received the promise of the Father (Lk 24:49; Acts 1:4-5).

I had to learn once again the important lesson that it was not in my power to make ministry happen. The work of Christ can only be effectively made known and its benefits applied by the working of the Holy Spirit. I needed the reassuring ministry of the Spirit that Christ was with me, as he had been with Paul in Corinth. This produced deep healing in my life, and there has been no reoccurrence of the ulcer from that day thirty-seven years ago. Since that time I have consciously asked for the empowering of the Spirit for witness (and for teaching in the classroom), which has brought a great sense of freedom and more abundant evidence of the risen Lord at work.

## THE NATURE OF THE EMPOWERMENT

The Acts account begins where the gospel concludes—in Jerusalem. Luke makes no mention of the Great Commission given in Galilee. His focus is on Jerusalem as the place of renewal and the starting point of the mission of the church.[5] Central to the concept of the covenant renewal was the giving of the Spirit to an unprecedented degree. Luke's term is "outpouring," language with which other New Testament writers would readily identify. The outpouring of the Spirit (cf. 10:45) leads not only to the filling of the believer (6:3-4),[6] but also to the overflowing of the Spirit to engulf those with whom he or she comes into contact (Jn 7:38-39). In other words, the outpouring does not result in the bottling and corking of the Spirit as a commodity to be preserved, but as a stream flowing through a reservoir that constantly needs to be replenished. F. F. Bruce comments, "Being filled with the Spirit was an experience to be repeated on several occasions (cf. 4:8, 31), but the baptism in the Spirit which the believing community now experienced was an event which took place once for all."[7]

Luke, in company with the other gospel narrators, never loses sight of the fact that it is Christ who is the baptizer in the Holy Spirit (Acts 2:38). The greatest evidence of that experience is that individuals are empowered to witness for Christ whose Spirit they have received (1:8; 4:31). Therefore, the Pentecost phenomena must be interpreted according to Luke's intention, which is distinctively missiological. For Luke, the baptism in the Holy Spirit is not primarily concerned with salvation, or even "a second work of grace," but with the essential empowerment of the church for its witness throughout the world. The disciples were not waiting upon the Lord primarily for their personal renewal, but rather to receive corporate empowerment for their mission.

It was as a missionary in Chile that I saw most dramatically the impact of the Pentecost event in the life of the contemporary church. Until that time I had not witnessed rapid church growth occasioned by the continuous witness of communities of believers. The movement had its origins in the Methodist missionary, Willis C. Hoover, who visited a pre-Pentecostal church in Chicago in 1895 while on furlough from Chile. On returning to Valparaiso, Hoover began to long for spiritual empowerment for his church. It was not until 1909, after prolonged periods of prayer, that his church experienced the empowerment it sought. This led to the rapid growth of the congregation.[8] Thus was born the Pentecostal movement in Chile, which today accounts for about one-tenth of the country's population. Sixty years later I saw abundant evidence that their spiritual intensity and evangelistic fervor had not abated. They continued to witness in the streets, plazas, and railroad stations of downtown Santiago, as well as in the shantytowns that ringed the city.

## THE SYMBOLS OF PENTECOST

The symbols of wind and fire were familiar depictions of the presence of God among God's people. That mysterious movement, unseen yet unmistakably felt, might be a gentle breath, but on this occasion it came with gale force to fill the house where the disciples were gathered. In Ezekiel's vision it was the wind that breathed life into dead bodies, so that they were able to stand and move (see Ez 37:1-11).

If the wind symbolized life and movement, the fire represented the holiness of the divine presence and the disciples' need for refining. As with the wind, the fire represented a corporate experience, yet it was also intensely personal in that the tongues of fire separated and came to rest on each of them (Acts 2:3). The description of the fire coming as "tongues" to each person may also suggest empowerment for verbal and contextual witness.[9] The tongue over their head released the tongue in their head! The two symbols combined anticipate the rapid expansion of the church recorded in Acts, for wind and fire together make an unstoppable combination.

These brief supernatural manifestations lead to an ongoing consequence— the irrepressible, joyful, bold to the point of foolhardiness witness of the Spirit-filled community. The baptism in the Spirit is not for us to splash playfully around in the company of those who share the experience, but rather for believers to communicate that experience. Through the witness of God's people the good news was proclaimed so that all who received the message could enter into the same essential experience. While the same phenomena may accompany the experience, as with those gathered in the home of Cornelius (10:44-46), the baptism in the Spirit is as real and as powerful without that phenomena being apparent. The essential evidence is that those who have received the gift will be humbled and equipped to witness boldly for Christ.

It is in this regard that the charismatic movement within the traditional denominations and the later Third Wave movement faltered through loss of nerve. These renewal movements provided a gathering point for Christians who had become frustrated by the lack of vitality in their traditions. They gathered together seeking personal and corporate renewal, but, in my view, suffered a loss of courage at a number of crucial points:

- We want the Spirit to meet out needs, but not to challenge our priorities.
- We want the Spirit to renew individuals, but not to upset congregations.
- We want the Spirit to empower the ministers, but not to challenge our ideas of ministry.
- We want the Spirit to restore our confidence in the church, but not to test our credibility in the world.[10]

The authentic witness of the church must be preceded by periods of separation from the world (Lk 24:49, 52-53; Acts 2:1) and thorough transformation of the community (Acts 2:2-47) before its bold witness can occur in the world (Acts 3:1ff.).

The "birthday" of the church and "launch day" for mission were thoroughly supernatural. Concerning the mighty acts of God declared by the early believers in other tongues or languages, we notice two important points: First, the tongues were recognizable languages, identified by the hearers.[11] They were not speaking gibberish, nor were they speaking in unknown tongues or the languages of heaven. They were the languages spoken on earth. Second, the content of their communication was the mighty acts of God (2:11), a Lukan way of speaking of God's saving acts in history. This latter point was important in a world that was open to accept supernatural phenomena uncritically.[12]

## THE CROWD'S RESPONSE

It was Peter, the one who had been living with the shame of having denied his Lord, who now emerged in his role as the rock on whom Christ would build his church. As he stands before the crowd in the Jerusalem courtyard, we see remarkable evidence of the Holy Spirit's empowerment. The boldness of Peter in "raising his voice" to address the crowd demonstrates the fulfillment of the prophecy that the Spirit will give inspired utterance (Acts 2:4; see also 4:8, 31).[13] The phrase used expresses the authority as well as volume.

Not only does Peter find confidence to speak, but he does so in the corporate context of Jesus' followers. We must not lose sight of the others who stood with him. He was not an isolated advocate; rather, he spoke for a community who identified with his witness. The witness of the early church was corporate before it was individual. And it was all the more powerful in that it was praise to God overheard by the crowd.

The feast of Pentecost attracted crowds to this most international gathering. Being later in the year, it was safer to make the sea journey from the northern and southern shores of the Mediterranean. Those in the crowd, both Jews and proselytes, citizens of the Mediterranean world and products of the Diaspora, could speak either Aramaic or Greek. Many were bilingual. Therefore, the miracle was not necessarily that the supernatural utterance was necessary for the hearers to understand what the disciples were saying.[14] The miracle revealed the contextual nature of the mission of the church, which could enter into any context and be heard and understood, taking root in the language and culture of particular people.[15] This became the vision of Henry Venn (1796-1873) who yearned for indigenous churches on the mission fields that were "sown with the seed of the Gospel" and with the Spirit "poured down from on high, as the flowers of a fertile field multiply under the showers and warmth of summer."[16]

## PROPHETIC UTTERANCE

Authentic God-inspired prophecy in the biblical records that inspired Mary, Zechariah, Elizabeth, and Simeon had been absent for more than three hundred years until the coming of Christ. Just as prophecy accompanied the birth of Jesus in Luke's account, so prophecy accompanied the birth of the Christian community and its propulsion into the world. The Jewish hearers could be forgiven for expecting that prophecy would be uttered in Hebrew, the language of the Torah. Instead, the languages of the Jewish Diaspora were made the vehicle for the word of God. As they were soon to learn, the promise of God was not only for themselves and their children, but also "for all who are far away, everyone whom the Lord our God calls to him" (Acts 2:39; cf. Eph 2:17). Once again, we must interpret Luke as the missionary, concerned for the spreading of the message beyond Israel.

Whereas Paul more frequently focuses on the inner, sanctifying work of the Spirit in reference to the baptism and filling of the Spirit, Luke places the emphasis on the extension of the empowerment of the Spirit. Roger Stronstad points out that the disciples' "forthcoming role as witnesses, not the profound and moving experience of tongue-speaking, is the key to understanding the significance of the gift of the Spirit on the day of Pentecost."[17] His observation is supported by Peter, who, explaining to the crowd the phenomenon of "other languages," described it as prophecy. People will serve as the mouthpiece of God to declare God's word, irrespective of age, gender or social standing (Acts 2:17ff.).

In the Old Testament the Spirit's empowering had been restricted to key people on specific occasions. But now the Holy Spirit is poured out on all humanity. When the crowd demands an explanation of the phenomena they had witnessed, Peter refers to the Hebrew scriptures to provide an antecedent.[18] However, he does not turn to any of the passages from Isaiah, Jeremiah, and Ezekiel that refer to the renewal of the Spirit in the heart of the individual. Instead, he turns to Joel, one of the minor prophets, to explain this outpouring of the Spirit. Joel may be recalling an incident in the life of Moses when, overwhelmed by the demands of his people, he asked God to relieve him of his burden. In response to his cry the Lord told him to bring seventy of Israel's elders to the tent of meeting, and "I will come down and talk with you there; and I will take some of the spirit that is on you and put it on them; and they shall bear the burden of the people along with you so that you will not bear it all by yourself" (Nm 11:16-17).

Even though two of the seventy elders for some reason did not make it to the meeting, the Spirit came upon them also, and they prophesied in the camp. When news of their activities reached Joshua, he appealed to Moses to stop them. In response Moses replied, "Are you jealous for my sake? Would that all of the Lord's people were prophets, and that the Lord would put his spirit on them" (Nm 11:29). Moses was not interested in restricting power and exercising control. The seventy were empowered to prophesy when Moses yielded some of the spirit that was on him to be shared among them. This cry of Moses becomes a prophetic word on the lips of Joel, which finds its fulfillment in the experience of the disciples and the witness of Peter to that event.

In my study on the mobilizing of God's people for ministry, the difficulty is not so much a lack of teaching on the subject of spiritual gifts, but rather a reluctance by leaders to empower people to exercise their God-given ministries. Where there is a heavy emphasis on control, the ministry of God's people is inhibited. In the vein of Moses, however, Peter affirmed the role of the Spirit in the lives of all believers. Peter's use of Joel validated the pouring out of the Spirit on young and old, male and female, slave and free, thus shattering the barriers of age, gender, and class.

In spite of the scriptural affirmation and accompanying supernatural manifestations, the crowd's response is mixed with amazement, perplexity, and outright cynicism. Miraculous phenomena do not guarantee a positive response to God's gracious initiatives. It was so even in the ministry of Christ himself, and it will be no different for his followers.

## THE TRIUMPHANT PRESENCE OF THE CRUCIFIED CHRIST

Peter begins his public witness with a rebuttal. No, their uninhibited joy is not caused by intoxication but by the irrepressible joy of the Spirit, which causes them to proclaim and celebrate. Somehow, I cannot imagine the 120 disciples going to the Temple Courts in solemn procession! At nine o'clock in the morning, when drunks are recovering from their hangovers from the night before, the believing community was emerging invigorated from its nocturnal experiences (Acts 2:15).

Peter's message quickly establishes the significance of what has happened for the hearers. Pentecost is never a curiosity to be observed but always an experience to be shared. It is the church living out its experience before the watching world. It is a saving event, not merely a scintillating one. It is an event to be embraced and not simply observed. Pentecost empowered the church to begin its worldwide witness to Christ. The "last days" represent the epoch between the first and second comings of Christ. The hearers of the message are invited to respond (Acts 2:17). The final words quoted by Peter from Joel are:

Then everyone who calls on the name of the Lord
shall be saved. (Acts 2:21)

That provides the foundation for the remainder of Peter's witness for Christ during which the listeners become "cut to the heart" (2:37) and after which Peter tells them to repent, be baptized, and receive the gift of the Holy Spirit (2:38).

The message itself represents the pre-Lukan kerygma of the church in Jerusalem. Peter begins by identifying Jesus as from Nazareth, the town where he had grown up. He was accredited by God through miracles, wonders, and signs. Peter knew that there were people in the audience from that region who had seen the events and thus bore the responsibility for their lack of response. Here we are reminded that signs and wonders, even when performed by the Lord himself, do not guarantee a positive response to the message (Acts 2:22; cf. Lk 10:13; 17:17). He then focuses his message on the responsibility that his hearers must carry for the timing and manner of Christ's death. Although they had given him over to the Roman authorities, God had worked out God's own purposes. The vindication of God's Son is evidenced by the resurrection and the empty tomb.

In the remainder of the address Peter draws on passages from Psalm 16:8-11 and 132:11 (quoting the LXX Greek translation) to support the resurrection of Christ. Peter argued that David's words could not find fulfillment in himself, because he died and his body was buried in a tomb, a well-known landmark in Jerusalem. Jesus also died and was buried, but his tomb now lay empty, with the stone rolled away for the entire world to see. Peter concludes by utilizing the coronation psalm, arguing that David could not be referring to his own exaltation to God's right hand when he said:

> The LORD said to my lord,
> "Sit at my right hand." (Ps 110:1)

This prophecy found its fulfillment in Jesus of Nazareth and in no one else. The resurrection of Jesus Christ was the cornerstone message of the early church.

Commentators have drawn attention to the different content found in sermons addressed to Jewish audiences compared with those preached to non-Jews. There are six evangelistic addresses to Jewish audiences (Acts 2:14b-35, 38-39; 3:12b-26; 4:8b-12; 5:29b-32; 10:34b-43; 13:16b-41), and two to Gentiles, one in Lystra (14:15-17) and one in Athens (17:22-31). On this occasion Peter could assume with his audience both a knowledge of Christ, who had ministered throughout Galilee, Samaria, the Transjordan, and Judea, as well as an understanding of the recent events in Jerusalem. They also had a detailed knowledge of the Hebrew scriptures, to which the preacher could refer to reinforce his arguments and illustrate points.

Different starting points are necessary when preaching to audiences without such background knowledge. In our contemporary society this means that what we assume in preaching to a churched audience can no longer be assumed when communicating with those outside the church. I write these words during Holy Week, when one of our local churches has hung a scripture selection on doors in the neighborhood. It is an attractive publication, with Bible verses about

Jesus, but there is nothing from the gospels quoting what Jesus said or did. The booklet assumes people already know the Jesus story.

But the church, and thus the Jesus story, is no longer dominant in many traditionally Christian societies. Jonathan R. Wilson tells of a person visiting a jewelry store in California and asking to look at some crosses. The clerk replied, "Would you like to see ones with the little man on them or ones without?"[19] For many, it is no longer Jesus on the cross but some nameless person. Thus the church must take pains, as Peter did, to explain the full Jesus story, including his life, death, and resurrection (Acts 2:22-36), in a manner in which the Christian faith may take root and spring up in particular cultural contexts.

## CONVICTING POWER

The work of the Holy Spirit not only empowers the preacher; by the conclusion of the message the Spirit has also been at work in the hearts of the listeners. They are "cut to the heart" as they realize that the one they crucified had been made by God both Lord and Christ, the Messiah. Their sense of guilt demands an appropriate response. In reply, Peter presents a clear, step-by-step process. They are to repent and be baptized, steps familiar to the audience through the renowned ministry of John the Baptist. But their baptism is to be in the name of Jesus and associated with the giving of the Holy Spirit, as prophesied by John. Their baptism is to be both into the person of Christ and the body of Christ, his church.

During the Mission England campaigns in 1984 I was present at all forty-six meetings. As at Pentecost, I witnessed the convicting work of the Holy Spirit. I sensed a special anointing on Billy Graham as he called on people to make a decision for Christ. Admittedly, some people came forward out of curiosity or moved by the emotion of the moment, but among them were many deeply moved by the Spirit of God. Their decision led to a redirecting of their life. I witnessed deep repentance, profound conversions, and lives transformed. If three thousand responded on the day of Pentecost, I witnessed three thousand to ten thousand people a night making decisive commitments. As on that first day, their turning to Christ also meant a separation from a "corrupt generation" that would continue to reject Christ (Acts 2:40).

We have no idea how many of the three thousand persons who responded at Pentecost were inhabitants of Judea and remained in the local church, and how many departed and scattered to their homes around the Mediterranean world. But we do know that the Pentecost experience was a multicultural event that sparked a multicultural movement, as the following chapters describe. The movement initiated at Pentecost began as a movement of incorporation.

## COMMUNITY INCORPORATION

Water baptism itself is an act of incorporation. The witnesses standing alongside Peter presumably took part in the mass baptisms that followed. They were also ready to welcome the new believers who were added that day. The apostles and disciples who undertook this monumental task were prepared to help others become followers of Christ because they themselves had been discipled by Jesus. It takes a disciple to make a disciple.

In preparing for Mission England and the citywide campaigns with Billy Graham, we realized that the follow-up must not be looked upon as a separate phase. Rather, the follow-up must be addressed before rather than after the meeting. Otherwise, follow-up becomes "chasing-up." For this reason we focused from the beginning on knowing the pre-Christian people before their commitment to Christ. Thus we would be following up individuals whom we already knew. Furthermore, follow-up had to begin promptly; otherwise the trail grows cold. To receive the inquirers, participating churches established "nurture groups" that provided a six-week course in basic Christianity.[20]

At the conclusion of this brief study let me return to the three questions I raised at the outset. I believe that in order to become more effective in winning people for Christ we need to recognize that the witness of the individual believer needs to be reinforced by the corporate witness of the community of believers. Second, I believe that I must regularly seek the in-filling of the Holy Spirit not only for my personal holiness but in order that I might be freshly empowered for day-to-day ministry. Third, this chapter of Acts provides a powerful reminder that failure in ministry need not be final. The "promise of the Father" to the disciples was not revoked by their denial and desertion but reinforced their need for the empowering of the Holy Spirit. Furthermore, the Spirit comes not to divide a community into the "haves" and "have-nots" but to unite them in their corporate prophetic witness, both male and female, and young and old, so that the word of God might be communicated around the world in languages appropriate to each constituency.

## REFERENCES

[1] I explore the implications in *Urban Church Growth: Clues from South America and Britain,* no. 55 (Bramcote, Notts.: Grove Books, 1977).

[2] Joseph A. Fitzmyer, *The Acts of the Apostles, The Anchor Bible* (New York: Doubleday, 1997), 232.

[3] See James D. G. Dunn, "Pentecost," in *Dictionary of New Testament Theology,* vol. 2, ed. Colin Brown (Grand Rapids, Mich.: Zondervan, 1986), 783-787.

[4] Many New Testament scholars believe that this was the occasion when Jesus appeared to five hundred followers at one time, as reported by Paul to the Corinthians (1 Cor 15:6).

[5] Fitzmyer draws attention to the pivotal role of Jerusalem to anchor the church in Judaism (see Fitzmyer, *The Acts of the Apostles,* 56).

[6] In 1 Corinthians 12:13 Paul described the Christian's experience of the Spirit in terms of an initial "baptism"—a total immersion in the Spirit leading to the continuous activity of drinking of the Spirit. Note that Paul here refers to that as a community activity.

[7] F. F. Bruce, *The Book of Acts: The New International Commentary on the New Testament* (Grand Rapids, Mich.: Eerdmans, 1988), 51.

[8] For an account of the origins of the Pentecostal movement in Chile, see Willis C. Hoover, *Historia del Avivamiento Pentecostal en Chile* (Valparaiso, Chile: Imprenta

Excelsior, 1948); and Christian Lalive D'Epinay, *Haven of the Masses: A Study of the Pentecostal Movement in Chile* (London: Lutterworth Press, 1969).

[9] See Fitzmyer, *The Acts of the Apostles,* 238.

[10] I identified these points in an address at the annual conference of the Fountain Trust, which represented renewal groups in many of Britain's traditional denominations (see Eddie Gibbs, "Has the Wind Dropped?" *Renewal Magazine* [United Kingdom], Fountain Trust [April/May 1979], 4-10).

[11] A distinction must be made between *glossolalia,* understood as ecstatic utterance, and *xenologia,* speaking in foreign languages (see Fitzmyer, *The Acts of the Apostles,* 239).

[12] For examples, see Acts 8, 13, 19, and 1 Cor. 12:1-3. The existence of *glossolalia* or any other ecstatic utterances is no evidence of the presence of the Holy Spirit. In apostolic times it was necessary to provide criteria for deciding whether such utterances were of God or not, just as it had been necessary in Old Testament times.

[13] F. F. Bruce, *The Acts of the Apostles: The Greek Text with Introduction and Commentary* (London: The Tyndale Press, 1951), 88; Fitzmyer, *The Acts of the Apostles,* 251.

[14] C. Peter Wagner highlights the missionary significance of this miracle in that people are more likely to respond to a message that is communicated to them in their heart language (see *Spreading the Fire: Acts 1—8* [Ventura, Calif.: Regal, 1994], 91).

[15] Pentecost initiated the concept that the story will "be told in every tongue" and that "the expanding church will be gloriously multicultural" says Darrell L. Guder (*The Incarnation and the Church's Witness* [Harrisburg, Pa.: Trinity Press International, 2000], 50).

[16] Quoted in Norman E. Thomas, ed., *Classic Texts in Mission and World Christianity* (Maryknoll, N.Y.: Orbis Books, 1995), 208-209.

[17] Roger Stronstad, *The Charismatic Theology of St. Luke* (Peabody, Mass.: Hendrickson, 1984), 61.

[18] Ibid., 56ff.

[19] Jonathan R. Wilson, *Living Faithfully in a Fragmented World* (Harrisburg, Pa.: Trinity Press International, 1998), 36.

[20] "In the South-West Region of the Mission England Campaign, a poll was taken twelve months after the Bristol meetings and replies were received from 174 churches. The replies to the questionnaire revealed that after six months 70 per cent of all referred back to the churches were still in contact. After twelve months that figure had dropped to 59 per cent" (Gavin Reid, *To Reach a Nation* [London: Hodder and Stoughton, 1987], 62-63).

# 3

## *Dismantling Social Barriers through Table Fellowship*

ACTS 2:42–47

## Santos Yao

In early January 1987, I first came to the United States. Having been involved in theological education in the Philippines for ten years, I enrolled in the Westminster Theological Seminary Doctor of Ministry program for further study. But I came unprepared for jet lag and the winter's cold. Nor was I emotionally ready to handle the stress of being separated from my close-knit family. The loss of my wallet during a connecting flight to Philadelphia further compounded my trauma. Loneliness and sleeplessness characterized my culture shock.

However, a few days after my arrival Professor Harvie Conn invited me for lunch. I was totally baffled by his gesture of kindness. As a Filipino Chinese who was reared with Confucian ethics, it was natural to expect that esteemed professors would remain aloof from their students.[1] Deeply moved by this act of inclusion, my world view went through an upheaval. That brief moment of table fellowship began a paradigm shift in my life that God used to transform my life and ministry.

### TABLE FELLOWSHIP IN SOCIAL PERSPECTIVE

Table fellowship is significant in every culture. There are always some meaningful inclusions and exclusions. In other words, some people are warmly welcomed, while others are rejected. Some foods are appropriate, while others are taboo. Yehudi A. Cohen observes:

In no society are people permitted to eat everything, everywhere, with everyone, and in all situations. Instead, the consumption of food is governed by rules and usages which cut across each other at different levels of symbolization.[2]

29

Partaking in a meal is neither a mere biological process nor a mundane act of satisfying one's nutritional requirements. Eating a meal in traditional societies, particularly in the context of a group, always assumes social and religious significance. Food and its consumption are often used symbolically "to reflect on the things that are essential to society's psyche."[3] From private hospitality to ceremonial festivities, a culture's eating rituals are mediums for social symbolism. Hence Mary T. Douglas postulates:

> If food is treated as a code, the message it encodes will be found in the pattern of social relations being expressed. The message is about different degrees of hierarchy, inclusion and exclusion, boundaries and transactions across boundaries. Like sex, the taking of food has a social component, as well as a biological one.[4]

Food has always been employed by human societies as a "social and economic barometer."[5] As ancient societies illustrated their wealth or poverty through the language of food, modern societies also flaunt their affluence or reveal their poverty by food menus. Such a categorization based on the variables of wealth or poverty leads to the construction of social boundaries and hierarchies within societies. Thus humans are arranged into "maps of people" or "sets" based on the "laws of order, selection, and congruence."[6] Those who are dissimilar to the dominant group are relegated to the periphery as "others." They are often marginalized as the non-elite or the outcasts. Those who are related to the dominant center, either by kinship or by other forms of association, are arranged as extensions of the family. They are counted as members of the in-group. Anyone who is cast within the boundary of the in-group can enjoy intimacy and acceptance through a shared meal. Those on the periphery will be excluded from table fellowship.[7] Hence, beneath the facade of sharing the meal lies the deeper level symbolization of exclusion or inclusion, acceptance or rejection, love or indifference. John H. Elliott has indicated that meals serve as social boundary markers distinguishing types and groups of participants and consumers: men/women, adults/children, human/gods/demons, kin/non-kin, upper/lower classes, insiders/outsiders.[8]

## BIBLICAL CONTEXT FOR ACTS 2:42-47

The early Christian community lived in the Judean hills where Jewish particularism and exclusiveness abounded. Attitudes toward non-Jews were almost always negative. Gentiles were considered godless, idolatrous, and unclean; dealings with them rendered a Jew unclean. Likewise, the view of fellow Jews on the social fringes was negative. The *'am-ha-aretz* ("people of the soil") who belonged to the lower strata of Jewish society were often despised because they did not have political or economic power.[9] Thus Luke, recording the remarkable growth of the Christian movement, detailed how the church overcame racial and social barriers as it spread from Jerusalem to Rome. A central theme was the table fellowship that Luke saw as the litmus test for transactions across social hierarchies and ethnic boundaries. In Acts 2:42—6:7 Luke specifically illustrates how social barriers are effectively hurdled by the new Jewish Christian community. Beginning with the Cornelius episode in Acts 10, he describes how the ethnic boundaries are gradually overcome as the apostles, particularly Peter, Barnabas, and Paul, extended their table fellowship to the Gentiles.

## TABLE FELLOWSHIP IN ACTS 2:42-47

In describing table fellowship Luke uses in 2:42 the designation, *klasei tou artou* ("breaking of bread").[10] This unique phrase is set in the wider context of 2:42—6:7, which describes the earliest days of the Jerusalem church and covers the first three to five years (ca. 30-35 C.E.). Through the use of "illustrative vignettes in the imperfect tenses" and "the portrayals of representative situations drawn from many experiences within the Jerusalem Church," Luke presents a succinct account of what God was doing by the Spirit through the witness of the Church.[11]

The first part of this unit (2:42-47) pictures the life of the Christian community immediately following the pouring out of the Holy Spirit at Pentecost. The church suddenly mushrooms from 120 to more than three thousand members after the preaching of Peter. In 2:42 Luke not only sketches the community life but stresses the continuing action of the first believers, *esan* ("they"), through the imperfect verb that forms a periphrastic construction with the present participle *proskarterountes* ("were devoting themselves"). They are represented as "continually adhering with strength" to the four activities (in the dative case) that characterize the Christian community in Jerusalem.[12]

The believers are devoted, first of all to *te didache ton 'apostolon* ("the teaching of the apostles"). This refers both to the pedagogical activity of the apostles and the instructions being taught. Although Luke does not specify the content of the teaching, it must have included the kerygma concerning the work, words, and promises of Jesus the Messiah.[13]

The believers are also committed to *te koinonia* ("the fellowship") through which they participate in the liturgical life and sharing of common goods. The *koinonia* is the venue where the believers express their communion with the apostles in worship and their unity with one another in Christian service. It expresses what the believers "share in together" and what they "share out together."[14]

While the specific meaning of their *koinonia* may be difficult to discern, these expressions highlight deep unity of thought and purpose. Luke depicts the actualization of the demands of Christian love and deep longing to be always together. Such harmony is the offshoot of Pentecost. It is the direct result of the work of the Holy Spirit in the lives of the early Christians.

The oneness of the believers finds tangible expression through the daily table fellowship of "breaking bread and the prayers" (Acts 2:42). In particular, the breaking of bread vividly demonstrated their essential oneness on a social level. As Gary L. Carver remarked:

Sitting at the same table, the universal symbol of friendship, signified that indeed in Christ there was no east and west, no bond or free, no male or female, no Jew or Gentile. All were one in him.[15]

At a glance, the description of the Jerusalem church seems parallel to contemporary Jewish sects, such as the Essenes. Closer examination, however, reveals its distinctiveness. The table fellowship of the Jerusalem church is uniquely inclusive. Sinners, tax collectors, and marginalized people on the periphery of Jewish society discovered their unconditional acceptance in the church's table fellowship. In the daily sharing of meals "from house to house" not only were the social barriers dismantled, but so were the economic barriers that once separated the affluent from the destitute (2:46).

## CHRISTIAN CARING IS CHRISTIAN SHARING

Daily table fellowship served as the primary source of food for the poorer members of the church. In addition, it operated as a vehicle for their love for one another where the provision of food was made available for those in need (cf. 4:32-37; 6:1-6).[16] John R. W. Stott aptly summarizes that Christian fellowship "is Christian caring, and Christian caring is Christian sharing."[17] Thus the community of goods practiced in the Jerusalem church should be no surprise (2:44-45). The inclusiveness of table fellowship, coupled with the unity among the believers, made the transition from sharing food to sharing goods a natural one. Hence, as needs arose, it became common for the Jerusalem Christians, from time to time, to sell possessions voluntarily and to give the entire proceeds to meet physical needs (2:45). The unity instilled by the Holy Spirit continued to move the believers to a deeper and greater commitment toward one another. What began as selling possessions and goods in the fellowship progressed in the narrative to some members selling lands and houses (4:34). Private ownership of goods and properties no longer took precedence as *philadelphia* ("community love") prevailed in their mutual relationships. As the church continues to meet each concrete need that arises, Luke distinctly highlights that the early Christian community truly experiences God's shalom. The deuteronomic promise is literally fulfilled in their midst, for "there was not a needy person among them" (4:34; cf. Dt 15:4).

Luke depicts the joy and openness that characterize the early church table fellowship (2:46). While drawn together at a common meal, the early believers truly enjoyed one another's company, rejoicing with generosity of hearts. Pretense was not necessary in such a context of mutual acceptance. They felt at ease. They could be themselves. They were even transparent about their assets and needs.

Moreover, their table fellowship permeated with joy because the resurrected Lord was present there. Such sharing of meals depicted a continuation of the table fellowship the disciples had with Jesus. It also anticipated the imminence of the parousia of Christ. Stephen C. Neill states:

The Christians knew themselves to be living in an interim; the feast that Jesus celebrated with his disciples led their thoughts to that other and greater feast to which he had referred when he had spoken of drinking of the fruit of the vine new with them in the Kingdom of God. . . . [Their] sorrowful recollection was more than swallowed up in joyful anticipation.[18]

The breaking of bread was thus a time when the eschatological hopes of the believers were stirred, prompting its celebration in an atmosphere of joy (2:46). The early Christians were fully aware that they were "the community of the last time constituted by the saving act of God."[19]

Illustrating the remarkable openness of the early Christians, Luke highlights that the believers shared their meals with sincere hearts. In the hosting and the sharing of meals, no one withheld any delectable item from another. Their "radical generosity" characterized every meal.[20] Simplicity, innocence, and the absence of guile marked their interpersonal relationships.

The Christian meetings in the temple courts and the joyful table fellowship in various households exerted an impressive evangelizing influence. Many Jews became favorably disposed toward the believers (2:47). The numerous wonders and miraculous signs (2:43) along with the *homothumadon* ("oneness") of the believers demonstrated the effectiveness of their communalism and Christian message (2:44-45; 4:32-35). The Christian "presence and witness" in Jerusalem were "infectious."[21] As a result, the Lord blessed the Jerusalem church with healthy growth (2:47; cf. 3:1-26; 4:4; 6:7) despite the problems of hypocrisy (5:1-11), miscommunication (6:1-6), and the increasing opposition of the Sanhedrin Council (4:1-31; 5:17-40).

The early Christians continued the patterns of table fellowship of Jesus found in the gospels. Following in his footsteps, they refused to discriminate against the marginalized. Their table fellowship was characterized by acceptance and egalitarianism in which they shared with one another according to specific needs (2:44-45; 4:32, 35). This inclusive community of Jesus, gathered around the table, rejected the usual stratification based on social class and status, thereby redefining the meaning of "otherness." Luke portrays the church as a responsible people that reached out to the marginalized in holistic mission. Furthermore, the church continually rejoiced and remembered God's mighty acts extended to God's people. Every table celebration functioned as a liminal period that separated the participants from a fixed social structure or cultural condition and transformed them into a new phase of reincorporation into the world and commitment to one another.[22] Table fellowship in Acts 2:42-47 illustrated that the church that eats together, grows together.

## CONTEXTUAL OBSERVATIONS AND CONCLUSIONS

Among Asian cultures, food and table fellowship are always significant. A famous Chinese proverb states, "People regard food as the most important thing in their life."[23] Thus, to a Chinese, the family is commonly defined as "those people who eat together." It is often in terms of food that a family expresses its relations with other people.

The fondness for food and festivities is likewise deeply imbedded within the Filipino culture. It is through the medium of food that friendship and loyalty to a person or group are developed and sustained.[24] Thus it is common within Filipino society for any occasion to involve a festive celebration around food.

Table fellowship in either Chinese or Filipino society often extends beyond the limits of one's friends and acquaintances but may at times be inclusive only on the surface level. The motive behind the hospitality is not prompted solely by the intent to bridge friendship or to convey an act of kindness. Its primary motivation is oftentimes rooted in the desire to generate a sense of personal well-being in the host. Among the Chinese, this desire is linked with the aggrandizement of *mian-tzi* ("face"), while among the Filipinos, it is tied to the core values of *pakikisama* ("smooth interpersonal relationship").

Consequently, beneath the veneer of inclusiveness and hospitality that one often finds in Asian cultures, exclusiveness may lurk unnoticed to the untrained eye. In a subtle way the "us" versus the "them" is still distinguished and maintained. Social boundaries and hierarchies continue to be constructed and retained through various means, such as the different menu items served, the utensils used, the time and the venue where the food is served, the occasion, the social atmosphere, and the degree of mutual interaction. To minister effectively within Asian contexts, it is imperative that serious consideration be given to the function of table fellowship and the intricacies nuanced by its practice.

Table fellowship always plays an important role in evangelism and church growth in Asian cultures. No meaningful relationship can be forged unless accompanied, sooner or later, by a meal. No lasting relationships can be sustained without a regular interval of eating together. It is clear that beneath the facade of a social gathering where people share a common meal, table fellowship can judiciously and concretely express kerygmatic accentuations on hospitality, oneness, brotherhood, equality, acceptance, intimacy, and love. In a tangible way, a person can experience the love of God as he or she participates in a meal where every pretension is dropped and mutual acceptance is unconditional.

Every table fellowship, hence, is a locus for the contextualization of the gospel. In the final analysis, contextualization does not consist merely in understanding cultural forms, meanings, functions, and significance, and learning to express the kerygma in a culturally appropriate form. Contextualization is in addition a praxis. It is essentially action oriented, the love of God in action (cf. 1 Jn 3:18; 1 Cor 13:1-3). My life and ministry have gone through a paradigm shift because God has used instances of brotherly love and unconditional acceptance, all in the context of a meal, to effect such a change. God's love became real to me as his messengers, despite their lofty positions and prestige, humbly extended to me some brief yet precious moments of an inclusive table fellowship.

I experienced this at the Leadership Training Institute in 1973 sponsored by Campus Crusade for Christ, Philippines. The event was held at San Fernando,

La Union, a city two hundred miles north of Manila. Like myself, the delegates to this conference were mostly university students. We departed from Tutuban train station in the morning, and after five hours of a nauseating, roller-coaster train ride, we finally arrived at San Fernando. However, the journey was not yet over. We were then jammed into mini-buses that wove through crater-like pot-holes along muddy roads on the way to the resort. It was already past 3 P.M. when we reached the beach resort. By that time, we were all exhausted and famished.

After checking into my room, I discovered that our instructor, an American missionary, was sharing the room with us. Following a brief introduction, he offered me his ham sandwich, which I quickly gulped down with gusto. The blessing of the meal and fellowship was indeed unexpected. It was like manna sent from heaven. It made the fellowship pleasant.

The days quickly passed by, and the conference soon came to a close. I must confess that I cannot even recall the lectures I heard, the people I met, or most of the things that I did. Even the name of the missionary who graciously broke bread with me remains foggy in my memory. Yet, I distinctly remember the love of Jesus that I experienced that week. Like the two disciples on the road to Emmaus (Lk 24:35), I had experienced the Lord's presence through an indiscriminate act of table fellowship.

## REFERENCES

[1] For a more detailed discussion of *li* and other Confucian ethical norms, see Francis L. K. Hsu, *Under the Ancestor's Shadow: Kinship, Personality, and Social Mobility in China* (Stanford, Calif.: Stanford University Press, 1971), 265ff.

[2] Yehudi A. Cohen, "Food: Consumption Patterns," in *International Encyclopedia of Social Sciences,* vol. 5, ed. D. C. Sills (New York: Macmillan, 1968), 508. John Dominic Crossan has similarly asserted, "Eating is the primary way of initiating and maintaining human relationships. . . . To know what, where, how, when, and with whom people eat is to know the character of their society" (John Dominic Crossan, "The Life of a Mediterranean Jewish Peasant," *Christian Century* 108/37 [1991], 1195).

[3] Raymond Bailey, "John 6," *Review and Expositor* 85/1 (1988), 95.

[4] Mary T. Douglas, *Implicit Meanings: Essays in Anthropology* (London: Routledge and Kegan Paul, 1975), 95.

[5] Richard I. Pervo, "Wisdom and Power: Petronius' Satyricon and the Social World of Early Christianity," *Anglican Theological Review* 67/4 (1985), 311.

[6] Jerome H. Neyrey, "The Symbolic Universe of Luke-Acts: 'They Turn the World Upside Down,'" in *The Social World of Luke-Acts: Models for Interpretation,* ed. J. H. Neyrey (Peabody, Mass.: Hendrickson, 1991), 279ff. See also Edward T. Hall, *The Silent Language* (Garden City, N.Y.: Doubleday, 1959), 144.

[7] Arthur P. Wolf has shown that in the Chinese context, friends and relatives are often asked to participate in the family's feast or celebration. Outsiders are never invited. A beggar may be given a bowl of rice or sweet potatoes outside the door but is never invited into the house to eat. It is "impossible for a farmer or a coal miner to eat with a ranking official," because "eating together implies intimacy and a certain degree of social equality" (Arthur P. Wolf, *Studies in Chinese Society* [Stanford, Calif.: Stanford University Press, 1978], 176).

[8] John H. Elliott, "Household and Meals Versus Temple Purity Replication Patterns in Luke-Acts," *Biblical Theology Bulletin* 21 (1991), 103.

[9] They are often referred to as the *'ochloi* ("multitude" or "crowd"), whose personal identities are lost in the multitudes of humanity. Some rabbinic traditions considered them "the rabbles who do not know the Law." Hence, a rule among the rabbis warns: "The disciples of the learned shall not recline at table in the company of the *'am-ha-aretz*" (William Hendriksen, *Exposition of the Gospel according to Luke: New Testament Commentary* [Grand Rapids, Mich.: Baker, 1978], 95).

[10] While most usages of *klasei tou artou* are found in Luke-Acts (Lk 22:19; 24:30, 35; Acts 2:46; 20:7, 11; 27:35), its verbal phrase, *klan 'arton,* occurs in Matthew 14:19-20; 15:36; 26:26; Mark 8:6; and 1 Corinthians 10:16; 11:24.

[11] Richard N. Longenecker, "Acts of the Apostles," in *Expositor's Bible Commentary,* vol. 9, ed. F. E. Gaebelein (Grand Rapids, Mich.: Zondervan, 1984), 288.

[12] I. Howard Marshall, *The Acts of the Apostles,* Tyndale New Testament Commentaries (Downers Grove, Ill.: InterVarsity Press, 1980), 83.

[13] Everett F. Harrison, *Acts: The Expanding Church* (Chicago: Moody, 1975), 65.

[14] John R. W. Stott, *The Spirit, the Church, and the World: The Message of Acts* (Downers Grove, Ill.: InterVarsity Press, 1990), 82-83.

[15] Gary L. Carver, "Acts 2:42-47," *Review and Expositor* 87/3 (1990), 476.

[16] Robert M. Shurden, *The Christian Response to Poverty in the New Testament Era* (Ann Arbor, Mich.: University Microfilms, 1980), 258.

[17] Stott, *The Spirit, the Church, and the World,* 84.

[18] Stephen C. Neill, *Jesus through Many Eyes* (Philadelphia: Fortress Press, 1976), 32.

[19] Rudolf Bultmann, "'agallisomai, 'agalliasis," in *Theological Dictionary of the New Testament,* vol. 1, ed. G. Kittle, trans. G. W. Bromiley (Grand Rapids, Mich.: Eerdmans, 1964), 20.

[20] John Koenig, *The Feast of the World's Redemption: Eucharistic Origins and Christian Mission* (Harrisburg, Pa.: Trinity Press International, 2000), 213.

[21] Ben Witherington III, *The Acts of the Apostles: A Socio-Rhetorical Commentary* (Grand Rapids, Mich.: Eerdmans, 1998), 163.

[22] For details, see Horst Rzepkowski, "Celebration and Evangelization," *Mission Studies* 7/2 (1990): 218-233; and Victor W. Turner, *The Ritual Process* (Ithaca, N.Y.: Cornell University Press, 1977).

[23] C. V. James, *Information China: The Comprehensive and Authoritative Reference Source for New China,* vol. 3 (Oxford: Pergamum, 1989), 1410.

[24] Marvin K. Mayers, *A Look at Filipino Lifestyles* (Dallas: SIL Museum of Anthropology, 1980), 87.

# 4

## Holistic Ministry and the Incident at the Gate Beautiful

### ACTS 3:1–26

### Evvy Hay Campbell

It happened hundreds of different times at our remote West African mission hospital. On this particular day a young boy stood quietly before me in front of his father. Weeks earlier his eye had been grotesquely drawn sideways by an enormous swelling from Burkitt's lymphoma that had invaded his facial bones on the left side. It was said when the boy first came that he had a devil. The boy's father, protectively at his side, had brought his son at intervals for several weeks to take the necessary drugs for treatment. Some patients that morning, seeing for the first time the boy almost restored to normalcy, gathered around and let out soft whispers of amazement . . . "way-aaah."

During the years I worked at Kamakwie Wesleyan Hospital in Sierra Leone, West Africa, I was deeply moved on many occasions by the expressions of gratitude, relief, joy, and amazement occasioned by events of restoration and healing. The healing might be for a patient whose vision was restored following the removal of dense cataracts or perhaps for a child who could move her neck and shoulder freely after the thick web of tissue that had been caused by burns was removed. Often the event was putting a squalling newborn, following an emergency C-section, into the arms of family members who had anxiously carried in by hammock a young woman who had been in labor for several days. Or it might be the cessation of wrenching coughs that brought up blood in a patient with tuberculosis who finally responded to multi-drug therapy.

It was not surprising that over a period of years thirteen churches had grown up as a result of the ministry of the hospital. It was natural that patients who had heard the gospel each morning during their months in the tuberculosis unit would share the good news in their village on their return. Three chaplains ministered daily to the fifteen hundred inpatients and up to seventy thousand outpatients that would come in a year's time. It was a ministry that integrated word and deed or proclamation and the compassionate meeting of physical needs. A prospective patient, once encouraged to go elsewhere for his elective surgery in light of the long waiting list at the hospital, declined to do so, saying, "There is a lot of God here."

Those who have lived and worked in the developing world know well that ministries of compassion and proclamation are inseparably related, with the first often preparing hearts for the second. Bryant Myers, in World Vision's *Together* magazine, defined holistic ministry as "one in which compassion, social transformation, and proclamation are inseparably related."[1] Far from being a modern ministry strategy, holistic ministry is evident throughout scripture. Christ's ministry was profoundly holistic, combining proclamation, deeds, and power. The Luke 4:16-21 passage, for example, in which Jesus revealed himself as the fulfillment of Isaiah 61:1-2, contains elements of each sphere: preach good news to the poor (proclamation); release the oppressed (deeds); and recover sight for the blind (healing power). Another example of holistic ministry is seen in the third chapter of Acts.

## THE HEALING INCIDENT

A glimpse into the daily life of the early church concludes the second chapter of Acts. Believers with glad and generous hearts, who are accorded the good will of "all the people" (Acts 2:47), are seen sharing things in common, selling possessions to distribute the proceeds to those in need, and spending a good deal of time together in the Temple and in homes. Further, their number increased as more were saved. The miracle of healing recorded in the third chapter is told in a way that is similar to the description of healing miracles recorded in the gospels. The interaction between the person healing and the person healed is described as well as the type of infirmity, the appeal for help, the healing itself, a demonstration that healing has taken place, and the effect of the miracle on bystanders.[2] With a change of location and characters, the third chapter brings readers further into the astonishing days of the early church when miracles abounded, evangelism could not be suppressed, and conflict with Jewish leaders who were deeply threatened by both was inevitable.

## THE APOSTLES AND SETTING

The drama opens with Peter and John going up to the Temple at the hour of prayer. They were a familiar twosome in Jerusalem. They had been partners as fishermen (Lk 5:10), companions at the Transfiguration (Lk 9:28), and present together during the agony of Jesus in Gethsemane (Mk 14:33). They had been charged with the preparation of the Last Supper (Lk 22:8), engaged in a foot race to the empty tomb (Jn 20:4), and received word regarding their future from the Lord after his resurrection.[3] In this vignette Peter was the spokesperson. John later, however, filled the role of the second required witness to Jesus when they stood before the High Council (Acts 4:1-15).[4]

In addition to their longstanding partnership, which may have accounted for Peter and John going to the Temple together, it was also customary for Jesus' disciples to go about in pairs (Lk 10:1). Indeed, throughout the ministry of the early church, believers worked together. Two were set apart for the first missionary journey (Acts 13:2), and Paul partnered with Luke (2 Tm 4:11), Timothy (2 Tm 4:9), and Mark (2 Tm 4:11).

In this regard, an aspect of missionary life in West Africa that was deeply satisfying to me was the strong bond of community with missionary colleagues. I never felt that work at our mission hospital was a job. It was a vocation, something God had called us together to do. After an exhausting day of work there would often be evening calls to the hospital and surgeries in the middle of the night. Our surgeon would come padding down the hill to the hospital, crank over the generator to provide electric lighting for the operating room, and offer me an extra chocolate chip cookie he had stuffed in his shirt pocket. As a single nurse, families invited me on their fishing expeditions and annual vacations. Those bonds of fellowship, of *koinonia*, have endured through the intervening years. My first housemate on the mission field, with whom I still correspond regularly, closed a recent email with "to my forever friend." Having grown up in the competitive and individualistic society of the Western world, it was nourishing to be in such a closely knit part of the body of Christ. Surely Peter and John enjoyed such fellowship, doubtless at an even more intimate level, given all they had experienced together.

Peter and John were described as going *up* to the Temple because it dominated the city and consisted of terraced courts that ascended to the Holy of Holies.[5] During morning and evening sacrifices, which occurred shortly after dawn and in the middle of the afternoon, incense was burned, symbolizing the worshipers' ascending prayers (Lk 1:9-10).[6]

## THE MAN LAME FROM BIRTH

The biblical description "lame from birth" (3:2) encompassed an immense sorrow, including that of the man as well as his family. From disappointed expectations at the time of his birth to the necessity of extended care, such a misfortune doubtless had an impact on many. I recall as a young college graduate taking a friend, confined to a wheelchair due to childhood polio, to a restaurant that was not handicap accessible. I carried her into the restaurant, and to this day, I recall the awkwardness of the effort combined with her eagerness to be there. The man lame from birth in Acts 3 was fortunate to have friends who daily carried him to a place where he could ask for alms. The Gate Beautiful where he was placed to beg was possibly the Nicanor gate, made of Corinthian bronze, leading from the Court of the Gentiles to the Court of the Women.[7] Surely, because he was at the Temple each day, he knew of Jesus.

Almsgiving was a responsibility for the Jews (Acts 24:17), and a distinctive of Judaism was the duty to care for the poor. There was to be justice for the poor (Ex 23:6), the needy (Ex 22:25-27), and widows and orphans (Ex 22:22-23). The Gate Beautiful was an excellent place at which to ask for alms. The Temple treasury was in the Court of the Women and thus those coming through the gate might already have coins close at hand. Further, worship at the afternoon prayers might be marred if those attending had just passed by a man in evident need. That provided a further motive to give alms.[8]

I had an experience that compelled me to give alms just a few months ago. A man with a young family in Sierra Leone, whom I had helped through school, concluded a letter requesting financial assistance with the following paragraph:

> Ya Campbell, please don't consider it a pest. This is God's way. I am sorry to bother. It is only God who knows why He brought us in contact with my school days. But I suppose it is because you are a visible presence of God. An instrument to rescue the starving, those without shelter. Please help. . . . I am very much in dire need. I call upon you on behalf of my family.

Those who live and work in the developing world regularly have face-to-face requests from those in need. Discernment and wisdom are needed in responding, but my experience has led me to believe that it is far easier to fall into the response of the rich man, who ignored the needs of Lazarus (Lk 16:19-21), than it is to respond with cheerful giving (2 Cor 9:7). A compassionate response to physical needs is a fundamental element of holistic ministry, and we are about to see how Peter and John responded to the need they encountered at the Gate Beautiful.

## THE HEALING AT THE GATE BEAUTIFUL

The interaction between the disciples and the man lame from birth began with the petition of the latter for alms. The disciples looked intently at him or "stared gravely,"[9] establishing an inner contact with him. A similar scenario occurred in Acts 13:9 between Paul and Elymas the magician. "Paul, filled with the Holy Spirit, looked intently at him," with the meaning of "to focus one's eyes upon."[10] In the account in the Book of Acts the lame man fixed his attention on Peter and John, expecting to receive something from them.

Peter then said, "I have no silver or gold, but what I have I give you; in the name of Jesus Christ of Nazareth, stand up and walk" (Acts 3:6). On his way to worship without money in his possession, what Peter *does* have to offer, healing in the name of Jesus, is in sharp contrast to what he does not have. Note that Peter did not beg Jesus for healing but rather released the power of healing though uttering the name of Jesus.[11] Importantly, the use of the name Jesus was not simply to evoke the memory of Jesus' past ministry. It was, rather, the symbol of his continued power and presence as the ascended Jesus "channeling God's life-giving energy to the poor and the lame just as he did before his departure."[12] This incident showed the continuity of Jesus' ministry and that of the church.[13] Furthermore, the identifier "of Nazareth" underscored Jesus' humanity.

Touch provided the channel for healing as Peter took the lame man by the hand and raised him up. The instantaneous strengthening of the lame man's feet and ankles was doubtless of particular interest to Luke as a physician. A similar pattern of healing is evident in the Luke 13:10-17 passage in which Jesus healed a woman who had been bent over for eighteen years. He saw her, spoke to her, laid his hands on her, and immediately she was made straight.

While numerous commentaries pass quickly over this section and delve into an in-depth analysis of Peter's explanation of the incident, it is the "jumping up, he stood and began to walk" portion of the story that is most arresting to me (3:8). Hours of helping the elderly to walk, steadying post-surgical patients as they get on their feet, and assisting post-trauma patients in initial steps have enabled me to catch the joy that must have filled the lame man as he exulted in his new skill. The Greek literally says, "Springing up, he set foot firmly to the ground" and "walked about."[14] "Walk" or "walking" is used four times in the passage. The second use of "leaping" in 3:8 refers not to the initial "springing up" but simply "leaping and praising God," fulfilling the prophecy of Isaiah 35:6, "Then the lame shall leap like a deer."

Having served in the field of medical missions, I have seen much human misery. Impressed on my mind is a man who died, slumped against the wall, while waiting in a long clinic line; the final hours of trying to get medicines into a small boy with pulmonary anthrax; and the last breaths of a baby with cerebral malaria. No less significant are the weary helplessness and hopelessness that often surround those attending the gravely ill. Having shared in the lives of those with debilitating limitations, I find it simple to imagine the immense joy of the man healed from his lameness.

I also understand, through one of our Wheaton College students, the experience of leaping for joy. During the 1995 revival that occurred on campus, a graduate student in the missions department experienced a deep inner cleansing. In describing the experience and her response, she told of asking God to forgive her sins:

> For the next few seconds I felt a burning in my heart; a literal burning. And I felt like something was being burned away. And two or three seconds later it just went away. . . . I felt free . . . clean on the inside. . . . All of a sudden I felt extremely happy, joy like I've never felt before. . . . Nobody was in the room. So I started leaping and jumping up and down thanking God that old things had gone and something new had happened.[15]

What a privilege and thrill for Peter and John to be channels of the healing power of Christ. What an extraordinary sight to see the man born lame leaping about in the Temple. What a crowd this miracle attracted! People were face to face with the indisputable. They could not doubt what they saw. The familiar figure of the man born lame had been transformed into a walking and leaping fountain of praise to God. To describe the astonishment of the people Luke used *ekstasis*, literally "standing out of oneself."[16] The unimaginable had happened. A compassionate deed had been done through the powerful name of Jesus.

## PETER'S EXPLANATION OF THE HEALING (3:12B-16)

Following this extraordinary miracle, the healed man apparently accompanied Peter and John into the Court of the Women, added his prayers to theirs, and still clung to the apostles as they made their way out to Solomon's Portico, a gathering place for believers along the eastern wall (Acts 3:11; 5:12).[17] The crowd that must have come running as word of the incident spread gave Peter an opportunity to explain what had occurred.

Doubtless the crowd hummed with excitement. Perhaps that prompted Peter's opening question. He asked why the people wondered at the event and stared at him, John, and the man now healed. Peter's first task was to explain the miracle and source of the power that occasioned it (3:12). The rebuke implied in his initial question served to clarify that the miracle was neither due to their power or any piety on their part that may have influenced God and thus indirectly resulted in the healing.[18] This was a serious effort on the part of Peter to deflect glory from himself and John. A similar effort was seen when Cornelius tried to worship Peter (Acts 10:26).[19]

Peter prefaced his explanation about the miracle with "the God of Abraham, the God of Isaac, and the God of Jacob." That title, underscoring the covenant faithfulness of God, was used on solemn occasions (Ex 3:6; 1 Kgs 18:36; 1 Chr 29:18),[20] in this case emphasizing the crime of handing over and rejecting Jesus. Peter's remarks give a vivid picture of the way in which the new faith was presented to the Jews.

Peter presented Jesus as "servant Jesus" (Acts 3:13, 26; 4:27, 30), as well as "the Holy and Righteous One" (Acts 3:14; 7:52; 22:14), an early messianic title for Jesus that originated in Isaiah (Is 53:11; 11:5; 42:6).[21] "The Author of Life," similarly an early messianic title for Jesus and variously translated as "Pioneer" and "Originator," conveys the idea of a champion whose victory involves those whom he represents. Surely as Peter uttered "rejected [or, disowned] the Holy and Righteous One," there were echoes of his own disloyalty to Jesus stirring in his heart.[22] The key emphasis in the verse, however, is that God raised Jesus from the dead. It was faith in the resurrected Jesus that gave the man born lame perfect health in the presence of so many witnesses. It was health restored both through the power and in the name of Jesus as well as the man's faith, which itself was given through Jesus. While the scripture does not clearly speak of the man's faith in Jesus, his faith is implied in his praise of God following his miraculous cure.[23]

## PETER'S APPEAL FOR REPENTANCE (3:17-26)

Peter next reached out to the Jews with the welcoming address of "friends." He was careful to point out that their part in the death of Jesus was carried out in ignorance. In the Old Testament, crimes were committed either "in ignorance" or "with a high hand" by those who knew but flouted the law.[24] Using this bridge Peter opened the door for repentance if his hearers would acknowledge their guilt and turn to God with a change of heart. The apostle who himself had "turned back" to Jesus (Lk 22:32) following his denial was now offering to his fellow Jews the mercy of God. Peter also told them that the Messiah would be a suffering Messiah, a concept the Jews resisted. Peter himself had resisted the idea when Jesus told him of that earlier (Mt 16:21-22).

Beyond the relationship of the individual with God there was a broader implication related to the turning of the Jews: their repentance and turning would clear the way for the return of Jesus, the time of refreshing. The rabbis taught that Messiah would come if Israel repented as a nation even for a single day. The church, on the other hand, taught "that God had not waited for national repentance before sending Messiah," but rather that the "blessings of the messianic age had already begun to be experienced on earth with the coming of Jesus."[25]

While conciliatory in tone, Peter still made abundantly clear the serious consequences for those who would not repent and turn to Christ: They would be rooted out and no longer members of God's people (3:23). Peter was nevertheless optimistic and encouraging in reminding the Jews that they were the beneficiaries of the covenant made with Abraham and through their descendants the families of the earth would be blessed. Indeed, the Book of Acts itself shares the story of Gentiles who hear of Jesus through believing Jews and thus enter into the blessings of the covenant.[26] Peter's explanation of the healing of the man born lame was a masterful proclamation of the gospel contextualized for his Jewish audience.

## IMPLICATIONS FOR PRACTITIONERS ENGAGED IN HOLISTIC MINISTRY

There are two key areas of application regarding holistic ministry that can be drawn from this eventful passage in Acts. The first relates to the nature of the ministry and the second to those engaged in the ministry.

First, holistic ministry must be truly holistic. Proclamation, deeds, and power (or gospel-as-word, gospel-as-deed, and gospel-as-sign) are present in both the Luke 4:16-21 and Acts 3:1-26 passages. In the past century, however, the three have respectively become the emphases of the evangelicals, liberals, and Pentecostals. In fact, all three are necessary: words to clarify deeds, deeds to verify the meaning of words, and power to announce the source of all good deeds.[27] Those lacking knowledge may respond first to the gospel through words. The ill or impoverished may respond to deeds. Those living in fear of demons may be attracted by an act of God's power.[28] A complete proclamation of the gospel, desiring that all who respond come under the Lordship of Christ, is vital as are compassionate deeds and ministry carried out in the power of the Spirit.

Second, those engaged in holistic ministry must be spiritually mature, capable of contextualizing their message for the intended audience, and astute in bringing biblical truth to bear on all aspects of their ministry. They must be willing to engage people in daily life experiences and shun any form of "people as projects." They must be those who see, call out to, touch, and serve as channels of God's power to those who do not yet have a personal knowledge of Jesus and

God's Lordship in their lives. And finally, they must be those who are willing for God to interrupt their daily lives with God's priorities and plans, so that even something as common as walking to a worship service can be an occasion on which God can break through and be glorified.

May we live and minister in such a way that those whose lives have been distorted by sin can be restored to the normalcy envisioned by our heavenly Father, so that those who see them will gather around and let out soft whispers of amazement . . . "way-aaah."

## REFERENCES

[1] Bryant Myers, cited in *Serving with the Poor in Asia: Cases in Holistic Ministry*, ed. T. Yamamori, B. Myers, and D. Conner (Monrovia, Calif.: MARC, 1995), 1.

[2] E. F. Harrison, *Acts: The Expanding Church* (Chicago: Moody Press, 1975), 68.

[3] Ibid., 69.

[4] Ernst Haenchen, *The Acts of the Apostles: A Commentary*, 14th ed. (Philadelphia: Westminster Press, 1971), 201.

[5] William Neil, *New Century Bible Commentary* (Grand Rapids, Mich.: Eerdmans, 1973), 83.

[6] Harrison, *Acts*, 69.

[7] Neil, *New Century Bible Commentary*, 83.

[8] Harrison, *Acts*, 70.

[9] J. Munck, *The Acts of the Apostles: Introduction, Translation and Notes* (Garden City, N.Y.: Doubleday, 1967), 25.

[10] Haenchen, *The Acts of the Apostles*, 199.

[11] Ibid., 200.

[12] F. S. Spencer, *Acts* (Sheffield: Sheffield Academic Press, 1997), 48.

[13] I. Howard Marshall, *The Acts of the Apostles: An Introduction and Commentary* (Grand Rapids, Mich.: Eerdmans, 1989), 86.

[14] Haenchen, *The Acts of the Apostles*, 200.

[15] "Wheaton Revival 1995." *Ephemera 1950-77* (Wheaton, Ill.: Billy Graham Center Archives, 1995), Audio Tape 40, Collection 514.

[16] James D. G. Dunn, *The Acts of the Apostles* (Valley Forge, Pa.: Trinity Press International, 1996), 41.

[17] Neil, *New Century Bible Commentary*, 84.

[18] Haenchen, *The Acts of the Apostles*, 205.

[19] Ajith Fernando, *The NIV Application Commentary: From Biblical Text to Contemporary Life* (Grand Rapids, Mich.: Zondervan, 1998), 139.

[20] Harrison, *Acts*, 72.

[21] Neil, *New Century Bible Commentary*, 85.

[22] Harrison, *Acts*, 73.

[23] Marshall, *The Acts of the Apostles*, 92.

[24] Harrison, *Acts*, 75.

[25] Neil, *New Century Bible Commentary*, 86.

[26] Harrison, *Acts*, 77.

[27] Bryant Myers, "Modernity and Holistic Ministry," in Yamamori, Myers, and Conner, *Serving with the Poor in Asia*, 180, 183.

[28] John Steward, *Biblical Holism: Where God, People, and Deeds Connect* (Burwood: World Vision Australia, 1994), 170.

# 5

## From "Doingness" to "Beingness": A Missiological Interpretation

### ACTS 4:23–31

### Robert L. Gallagher

Zeal for the church's mission nearly cost me my marriage. Ten years after being filled with the Holy Spirit, I entered full-time ministry in an Australian Pentecostal church. In less than five years, full of youthful energy and vision, I helped create numerous church programs: a Christian elementary school, an international magazine, a radio program, two Bible schools, leadership-training seminars, and various evangelistic outreaches. In a hurricane of activity my young family was swept aside by my all-consuming zeal for the local church to grow.

Ignoring the pleas of my spouse and friends, I believed that every single minute of my day should be spent working for God. There was little time for prayer and the study of God's word, let alone time for the family. There were no periods of rest and recuperation, no time spent playing with my two young daughters in the park, no afternoons of sitting with friends over a cup of coffee. The time was short, the mission immense, the laborers few, and too much work to be done for such frivolous activities. My imbalanced notion of God's mission dominated my life. Ministry, I believed, flowed from doing things for God, not from a relationship with God. I had uncritically accepted the corporate business model for church life as the norm. Western society, rather than the word of God, influenced my concepts of mission.

This paper chronicles some of my journey that brought correction to this distorted picture of God's mission. Over a period of two years God graciously brought scripture, people, and literature into my life that caused a paradigm shift in my thinking toward mission and ministry[1]—that God's mission does not come from doing a host of activities, but rather from a prayerful relationship through the empowering of his Spirit. In simpler terms, mission flows from being rather than doing.

## CONTEXT OF THE SCENE

In particular, this chapter examines Acts 4:23-31, one of the key scriptures that God used to cause this paradigm shift in my thinking about mission. This passage may be shown to be within the first section of Acts (Acts 1:1—6:7).[2] This part focuses on the witness of the church in Jerusalem through the Holy Spirit's empowerment. Within part one are a number of separate acts: the disciples waiting for the coming of the Spirit as promised by Jesus (1:1-26); the Spirit coming at Pentecost after the exaltation of Jesus as God and Messiah (2:1-47); the first persecution coming from the healing of the physically challenged person at the Gate Beautiful (3:1—4:31); a picture of early church life coming through Barnabas, and Ananias and Sapphira (4:32—5:16); the second persecution of the church coming from the Sanhedrin Council (5:17-42); and another example of church life coming from the conflict between the Hebraic and Hellenistic Jewish Christians (6:1-7). All of these acts are recorded by Luke to depict the significant events surrounding the proclamation of the kingdom of God in Jerusalem.

Moving from the structure and purpose in part one of Acts, we may now consider the context of the passage within act three (3:1—4:31). The act has three scenes: the healing of the man through faith in Jesus' name (3:1—4:4); the witness of Peter and John before the Sanhedrin Council (4:5-22); and the disciples' prayer and filling of the Spirit (4:23-31). This act is enveloped between two scenes that give a summary of early church life. In 2:42-47 the unified community proclaimed Christ with signs and wonders. This scene is also repeated in 4:32-35. Hence, from the universal examples in Acts 2, which tell of the many miracles that took place during the Jerusalem witness, Luke moves to a particular miracle in Acts 3 and the subsequent events that led to the believers' prayer. There were many miracles happening in the city, but only this one is recorded. Perhaps the reason for this is that the miracle involved the two apostles Peter and John and led to the first persecution of the church. The Lukan narrative unfolds as follows:

After the coming of the Holy Spirit at Pentecost, Peter and John continued in the Jewish ritual of daily prayers in the Temple (see Lk 24:53; Acts 2:46; 5:12, 20-21). On one of their afternoon pilgrimages they came upon a physically disadvantaged person seated in the Gentile court in front of the Beautiful Gate. As these trips were part of their ritual, it is reasonable to assume that the two apostles (as well as Jesus and the other disciples) had passed this spot, and possibly the man himself, many times before. Why God chose this time to heal the man is not known. As with other supernatural manifestations of the Spirit that seem so particular, as the man healed at the Pool of Bethesda (Jn 5:1-18), one can only assume that the guidance of the Spirit was paramount in the selection of whom to heal. Peter stopped in front of the disabled man, fixed his gaze upon him, and knew immediately that Jesus was going to heal him. Instantly, the disabled man was able to walk.

A crowd gathered in the Gentile court as the healed extrovert jumped and leaped about, elated that he could now walk after a lifetime of dependence on others. Addressing the amazement of the Jewish crowd, Peter spoke of the God whom they served. As Peter spoke, the Sanhedrin Council, the most powerful religious, social, and civil body in the world of Judaism at that time, gave orders to the Temple guard to arrest Peter, John, and the healed man.[3] Their reasons for doing this were twofold. First, they were jealous that the people were again following the teaching of the disciples of Jesus and not their own (Jn 11:47-53; Acts 5:17). Second, since the council, largely composed of the sect of the Sadducees (Acts 4:1; 5:17), did not believe in the resurrection of the dead (Acts 23:6-8), it sharply disagreed with Peter's theology. This is the same group of seventy scribes, elders, and leaders who, along with the high priest, Caiaphas, unlawfully tried Jesus in the Temple at Jerusalem only a few months earlier.[4]

After spending the night in jail, Peter, filled with the Holy Spirit, spoke boldly before the council about the resurrected Jesus of Nazareth. Peter declared that "there is salvation in no one else, for there is no other name under heaven given among mortals by which we must be saved" (Acts 4:12). The silence of the council concerning the resurrection of Jesus is stunning. Here was a prime opportunity for it to eradicate what it believed was false teaching, yet not a word of denial came from anyone's lips. The empty tomb, only hundreds of feet away, served as a reminder of their twisted ploys to silence the truth (Mt 28:11-15). The Sanhedrin was unable to refute the miracle of the healed man and merely ordered the two apostles not to teach about Jesus again. The apostles then returned to the other disciples and reported what had taken place. It is in this context that Acts 4:23-31 must be interpreted and understood.

## INTERPRETATION OF ACTS 4:23-31

The narrator does not record the location where Peter and John went to report all that the chief priests and the elders had said to them, nor does Luke state specifically to whom they reported. It is not clear whether the apostles reported to the whole church, to selected representatives, or to the other apostles. Also, Luke does not clarify how the prayer was executed. In other words, did Peter and John pray, or all the apostles, or all the disciples? Was the prayer said in unison, or did the community agree to choose selected representatives to pray? Fitting with the rest of Acts, Luke emphasizes the unity of the group (1:14; 2:44-46; 4:32; 5:12a, 15:25) and that the prayer is addressed to the Father.[5] Yet, Luke's interest does not lie in the details of the event but in the content that showed the mindset of the early church. This prayerful approach to mission was missing in my ministry. Prayer was not the center of my calling in God as it was for the disciples in Acts 4. What follows is a study of the prayer that shows this attitude of the early church and that also aided in my cognitive paradigm shift toward mission.

The prayer has three sections that acknowledge the sovereignty of God: first, over creation (4:24); second, over humanity (4:25-28); and third, over the present situation (4:29-30). Each of these sections will be discussed, followed by an analysis of the results of the prayer.

## SOVEREIGNTY OVER CREATION

The disciples' prayer begins with a quotation from Exodus 20:11, "Sovereign Lord, who made the heaven and the earth, the sea, and everything in them."[6] The context of the quotation is the covenant ceremony between the nation of Israel and Yahweh at Mount Sinai following the people's deliverance from slavery in Egypt. After God had given the invitation to come into covenant (Ex 19:4-6) and the nation had agreed to its terms, the ceremony began with the appearance of God before Israel, followed by the covenantal terms summarized in the Ten Commandments (Ex 20:2-17). The fourth term concerned keeping the Sabbath holy. No work was to be done on the seventh day of the week. To reinforce the importance of this command, God's creation week was used as an example: "For in six days the LORD made heaven and earth, the sea, and all that is in them, but rested the seventh day; therefore the LORD blessed the sabbath day and consecrated it" (Ex 20:11; see also Gn 2:2-3).

In quoting this excerpt from the Sinai covenant, the disciples are highlighting the sovereignty of God over all creation and over the covenant people. After being threatened by such an authoritative group as the Sanhedrin Council, the believers place God on the throne in the broadest terms. God the Creator is also in control of the Sanhedrin and the present circumstances. Moreover, God made a covenant agreement with Israel that it would be God's possession among all the peoples. Israel would be to God "a priestly kingdom and a holy nation" (Ex 19:6). In Exodus 19:5 this covenant possession of God's people is linked with sovereignty over the earth: "Now therefore, if you obey my voice and keep my covenant, you shall be my treasured possession out of all the peoples. Indeed the whole earth is mine." Thus, for the early church members living in the era of the new covenant (Jer 31:31-34; Ez 36:24-28), the age of the Holy Spirit (Acts 2:17-18; 1 Pt 2:9-10), their lives were in the hands of their sovereign God and not the council. They were heirs to God's new covenant promise and had nothing to fear.

## SOVEREIGNTY OVER HUMANITY

Having claimed God's sovereignty over all creation, the believers' prayer now focused on God's sovereignty over humanity. Again, the prayer quoted another section of the Hebrew scriptures, this time from Psalm 2:1-2. Before the quotation the church affirmed the Lukan motif that the Holy Spirit empowered the people of God to speak God's words (Lk 1:67; 4:18; Acts 2:3-4; 10:44-46; 11:27-28; 19:6; 20:23; 21:4, 11). Then, the prayer quoted David, who, by the Holy Spirit, said

> Why do the nations conspire,
> and the peoples plot in vain? (Ps 2:1)

The prayer continued,

> The kings of the earth took their stand,
> and the rulers have gathered together
> against the LORD and against his Messiah.
> (Acts 4:26)

In writing these first two verses of Psalm 2, it may be that David, when contemplating the powerful nations of Egypt, Assyria, and Babylon, thought of their rebellion against the Lord. Like highly strung horses, these nations were against God and the anointed Messiah, rejecting their fetters and cords of love, saying,

> Let us burst their bonds asunder,
> and cast their cords from us. (Ps 2:3)

However, the psalmist also foreshadowed another occasion, one thousand years into the future, when the nations would be against God's Messiah. This is what the disciples were so aware of in their situation when they said, "For in this city, in fact, both Herod and Pontius Pilate, with the Gentiles and the peoples of Israel, gathered together against your holy servant Jesus, whom you anointed, to do whatever your hand and your plan had predestined to take place" (Acts 4:27-28). Only weeks earlier the disciples had witnessed the fulfillment of this prophecy when they watched the passion of Jesus unfold before their eyes.[7]

In this correlation between David's psalm and their present circumstances, the disciples underlined the fact that the Messiah of Psalm 2 is Jesus of Nazareth. They did this by (1) using three messianic titles for their Lord Jesus—the holy one, the servant of God, and the anointed one; and (2) emphasizing the foreknowledge of God in the events of Jesus' death and resurrection (Lk 22:22; Acts 2:23-25; 3:18), which was an echo of section two of the psalm (Ps 2:4-6).

As we have seen from the Exodus quotation in the above section, the early church does not randomly use passages from the Hebrew scriptures to support its claims. With purposeful intent, the believers chose scripture whose context also buttressed their arguments. In simpler terms, the meaning of the exact words taken from the Hebrew text also included the audience's understanding of the context surrounding that quotation. Therefore, this section from Psalm 2 indicates that the whole of this messianic psalm is in the believers' minds as they pray. Evidence for this claim may be seen in the request of the church and the results of their prayer.

The main point about Psalm 2 is this: David prophesied the rejection and death of Jesus the Messiah, and the early believers had witnessed those very events. The defiance of the nations was a part of God's foreordained plan, and this would give God's Son kingly authority over the nations of the world. This would produce people from the nations who would willingly obey and worship God's king and judge. In all this God's sovereignty over humanity was foremost in the minds of the prayers of Acts 4 when they quoted Psalm 2.

## SOVEREIGNTY OVER THE PRESENT SITUATION

Not only did the disciples of Acts 4 recognize the sovereignty of God over creation and humanity, but they also fulfilled Psalm 2 by their prayer and worship. In acknowledging God's hand in what they were experiencing, the church also embraced God's promise that the nations of the earth would be his Son's inheritance. They requested it to come to pass through them. They understood that they were joined to the risen Messiah through the Holy Spirit, and that when they prayed, the Messiah himself was praying. The early believers understood that Jesus actually had a spiritual union with the church.

Without regard to their own discomfort or acknowledgment of spiritual warfare, the believers made three requests in their prayer:

And now, Lord, look at their threats, and grant to your servants to speak your word with all boldness, while you stretch out your hand to heal, and signs and wonders are performed through the name of your holy servant Jesus. (Acts 4:29-30)

The believers asked, first, to surrender to God's sovereignty; second, for boldness of speech; and third, for miracles of healing to be manifested through them in Jesus' name. These three requests will now be discussed in turn.

### *Surrender to God's Sovereignty*

In the first request it is important to note the yielding nature of the disciples. Rather than hold resentment, anger, or fear, they surrendered their feelings and the outcome to the Judge of all the earth. They simply asked God to take note of the threats of the Sanhedrin Council and trusted in him for the results. Peter and John, faced with submission to the council's authority, decided that they should obey the higher authority of God. "Whether it is right in God's sight to listen to you rather than to God, you must judge" (4:19). Hence, the believers' prayer was reminding everyone that God was the sovereign Judge.

### *Boldness of Speech*

Second, having been commanded by the council "not to speak or teach at all in the name of Jesus" (4:18), and knowing that they could not stop speaking about what they had seen and heard (4:20), the believers prayed that the Lord Jesus would give them boldness to speak his word. In the phrase "your servants" (4:29), the notion of submission to the sovereign God, who is over all, including the highest religious and civil authority in Judaism, is evident. In addition, here was a request for a supernatural impartation of the Spirit to enable a freedom of utterance that was beyond their natural abilities. Again we see the interrelationship between the Spirit and human proclamation, a strong mission motif in Luke-Acts. When the Holy Spirit came upon the followers of Jesus, they spoke his words with authority and God's mission was accomplished. This was a fulfillment of what Jesus had promised them.

When Jesus was teaching on prayer he had promised the disciples that the Holy Spirit would be available to them if they asked their heavenly Father for help (Lk 11:13). "When they bring you before the synagogues, the rulers, and the authorities, do not worry about how you are to defend yourselves or what you are to say; for the Holy Spirit will teach you at that very hour what you ought to say" (Lk 12:11-12). Then, in Luke 21:12-15, this same promise of inspired speech in the midst of persecution is repeated with assurance from Jesus that "I will give you words and a wisdom that none of your opponents will be able to withstand or contradict" (Lk 21:15). By comparing these two passages, it may be shown that Jesus equated the work of the Holy Spirit and his work. The Lord Jesus and the Holy Spirit are working as one within the church of the Messiah.

If the disciples of Jesus asked for boldness to speak God's word (see 2 Cor 3:12; Eph 6:18-20; 1 Thes 2:2), then how much more should the contemporary church do the same? Yet, in my church-based ministry in Australia, I had not recognized the importance of asking for boldness to speak about Jesus. I was far too busy with programs and had no time for petitioning prayer.

### Miracles of Healing

The final request of the disciples' prayer within the prayer is to see the power of God continue in miraculous wonders and signs. After the believers were filled with the Holy Spirit at Pentecost, "many wonders and signs were being done by the apostles" in Jerusalem (Acts 2:43). This was evidence that Jesus was alive and continuing his work through his followers. Thus, at Pentecost, Peter had stated, "Jesus of Nazareth, a man attested to you by God with deeds of power, wonders, and signs that God did through him among you . . . God has made him both Lord and Messiah, this Jesus whom you crucified" (Acts 2: 22, 36). In fact, the situation the believers in Acts 4 addressed was due to a miracle of healing that even the council could not deny. "For it is obvious to all who live in Jerusalem that a notable sign has been done through them [Peter and John]; we [the council] cannot deny it" (Acts 4:16). Yet, the disciples prayed that God would continue to extend a healing hand and that more signs and wonders would take place through the name of Jesus. They did not take for granted the power of God being manifested in their midst, but earnestly asked God for more miracles.

Furthermore, the believers recognized that the Father, Son, and Holy Spirit were simultaneously working to bring about the witness in Jerusalem of the messianic fulfillment of Jesus being raised from the dead and sending the Spirit to the earth. Luke reinforced this significance by repeating the reference to Jesus as the Messiah found in Acts 4:27, with the same messianic title again in Acts 4:30: "your holy servant Jesus." The believers requested that God would do miracles in the name of the Messiah, God's holy servant Jesus. This was the same name spoken during the healing of the lame man (Acts 3:16). The phrase "through the name of" relates to the Old Testament significance of naming. In the Hebrew scriptures, naming often had important significance in revealing either the psychological condition of the circumstances at the birth of a child (see, e.g., Gn 41:50-52; 1 Sm 4:21; Hos 1:4, 6, 9); or the character of the person (Jn 1:42; see also Mt 16:17-18; Lk 5:1-11); or the change in spiritual status, as in the case of Abram to Abraham and Sarai to Sarah (Gn 17:5, 15) and Jacob wrestling with God and being renamed Israel (Gn 32:24-32). Thus, the request for the continuance of miracles through the name of Jesus the Messiah indicated that the believers knew their prayer would be answered according to the will of the holy servant Jesus (see Jn 14:12-14; 15:7, 16; 16:23-24, 26-27).

In Peter's sermon in Acts 3, Luke notes a number of these messianic titles from the Hebrew scriptures that he gives to Jesus of Nazareth. For example, God's servant (vv. 13, 26), the Holy One (v. 14), the Righteous One (v. 14), the Author of Life (v. 15), the Messiah (vv. 18, 20), and the Prophet (vv. 22-23). The title God's servant, along with the Holy One, is again referred to in the believers' prayer in Acts 4.

In summary, the prayer of the disciples within the larger prayer of Acts 4 consists of three requests: first, they surrendered to the sovereignty of God and asked him, and not themselves, to judge the command of the Sanhedrin Council for them "not to speak or teach at all in the name of Jesus" (4:18); second, God's sovereign servants asked God to grant them the supernatural ability to continue to speak the word of God with boldness. This was an echo of the promise of Jesus in the gospels that the inspiring wisdom of the Holy Spirit would be available to them in their hour of trial; and third, they called for God to continue to heal through the work of God's holy servant Jesus. These messianic titles, Holy One and Servant of God, were references to the Isaianic servant who would invite the nations to be a part of God's new kingdom of peace, righteousness, and justice. The people of the Way[8] were aware that they were now living in this age of the new covenant of the Holy Spirit and the fulfillment of these messianic promises (2:16-21).

## RESULTS OF THE PRAYER

The answer to the prayer seemed to be immediate. "When they had prayed, the place in which they were gathered together was shaken; and they were all filled with the Holy Spirit and spoke the word of God with boldness" (4:31). After "they raised their voices together to God" (4:24a), there was a physical demonstration of God's affirmation when the building where they prayed shook.[9]

God then granted their prayer in three direct ways. First, their surrender to the justice of God was answered as "the whole group of those who believed were of one heart and soul, and no one claimed private ownership of any possessions, but everything they owned was held in common" (4:32). There was unity in the church. The Holy Spirit enabled them to be more concerned about others than about themselves. The threats of the council did not cause a division among the ranks of the believers, but being filled with the Spirit, they united around the purpose of their king.

Second, the Spirit gave them boldness to speak about Jesus as the resurrected God and Messiah. They had prayed for confidence to speak God's word, and they then went out into the streets of Jerusalem and did just that with "great power." God also gave them abundant favor with the people of the city to proclaim with power the resurrection of the Lord Jesus.

Third, the refilling of the Holy Spirit upon the believers brought healing to the city and miracles.[10] This becomes explicit in Acts 5:12-16 when "many signs and wonders were done among the people through the apostles." Also in Acts 5 Luke mentions the growth of the church alongside the healing of the sick and deliverance from demons. The witness had now gone beyond the walls of the city to include a "great number of people . . . from the towns around Jerusalem" (5:16). The mission to Judea and Samaria had begun (1:8). At this stage of the witness there were extraordinary miracles taking place, such as Peter's shadow falling on people, "and they were all cured" (5:16). So, even though no healings were mentioned immediately after the prayer, it might be assumed from the record in Acts 5 that there was a continuation of signs and wonders from 2:43.

Further, there were miracles of a social and economic nature that could only be the work of the Holy Spirit. As in the situation after Pentecost in 2:44-45, "all who believed were together and had all things in common; they would sell their possessions and goods and distribute the proceeds to all, as any had need." In subjection to the Lordship of the Messiah, the congregation who were owners of "lands or houses sold them and brought the proceeds of what was sold. They laid it at the apostles' feet, and it was distributed to each as any had need" (4:34-35). This resulted in a miracle—a sign and wonder to the Jerusalem community—that nobody could deny; the followers of Jesus conducted a voluntary social-service program whereby there was "not a needy person among them" (4:34). This was a powerful testimony that supported their spoken message, even more so after the debacle of the hypocritical Ananias and Sapphira.[11]

Hence, the results of the prayer were threefold, relating directly to their three requests: First, God took note of the threats of the council by causing the church to have unity of mind and purpose under his sovereignty; second, they immediately continued in witnessing "to the resurrection of the Lord Jesus" with boldness (4:33); and third, the healing of the sick and demonized, and miracles of communal care and sharing were performed in the city of Jerusalem.

In Acts 4:31 Luke also links prayer, the Holy Spirit, and speaking the word of God as a paradigm for the church to follow. This tripartite model of mission is mentioned first in Luke 3:21-23, at the installation of Jesus' mission. It was during the water baptism of Jesus by John the Baptist, when Jesus was praying,

[that] the heaven was opened, and the Holy Spirit descended upon him in bodily form like a dove. And a voice came from heaven, "You are my Son, the Beloved; with you I am well pleased." Jesus was about thirty years old when he began his work.

Here the narrator observes that it was while Jesus was praying that the Holy Spirit came upon him, enabling his ministry to begin. In Luke-Acts the prayer motif is connected with the accomplishment of God's salvation purposes. God's people in prayer allowed the Spirit of God to bring forth God's mission.[12]

Further, the divine affirmation of Jesus by God was composed of two separate quotations joined together. "You are my Son, the Beloved" comes from Psalm 2:7[13] and "with you I am well pleased" from Isaiah 42:1. Both quotations come from mission contexts. We have already seen that in the next verse the psalm says:

> Ask of me, and I will make the nations your heritage,
>     and the ends of the earth your possession. (v. 8)

Meanwhile, the Isaiah quotation says:

> Here is my servant, whom I uphold,
>     my chosen, in whom my soul delights;
> I have put my spirit upon him;
>     he will bring forth justice to the nations.

Thus, it is no coincidence that God's affirmation to the Messiah before he begins his mission comes from two messianic mission contexts.

Thus, as prayer and the filling of the Spirit accompanied the beginning of Jesus' mission, so did the beginning of the church's mission to Jerusalem. Before the feast of Pentecost there was a gathering of about 120 persons who "were constantly devoting themselves to prayer" (Acts 1:14). Then, at the fulfillment of Pentecost, they were filled with the Holy Spirit and began calling people to repent, be water baptized, and receive the gift of the Spirit (2:38). As the mission moved beyond the borders of the city to witness next in Judea and Samaria, the prayerful church once again was filled with the Holy Spirit to accomplish the task.[14] The pattern of the people of God praying and the filling of the Holy Spirit propelling people into mission is a Lukan motif that begins at the baptism of Jesus and continues throughout Luke-Acts (Lk 4:1, 14, 18).

## APPLICATION OF ACTS 4:23-31

It was this reoccurring Lukan mission paradigm that most influenced my understanding of ministry. My work in the church demanded more and more of my time. My family was patiently suffering from an absent husband and father. On top of an already overflowing church schedule of meetings, committees, and preaching, I accepted speaking invitations that took me away from my family for weeks at a time. And all the while I was completing graduate studies in education at the local university.

"This is God's call on my life" was my continual answer to my wife's pleas to spend more time at home. How could she respond to such a claim? After nearly eighteen months of trying to communicate to me that I needed to slow down, my wife reverted to the only avenue of communication left—she shared her heart with me in a letter and showed me some drawings from my two little girls that depicted how they missed me. Both vehicles opened my heart to feel the pain that I caused those whom I loved the most. But how was I to change? What was I to do?

It was then that God graciously showed me the prayer life of Jesus in the gospel of Luke and the continuing importance of prayer in Acts 4. Gradually a shift in my thinking occurred as I saw that the mission of Jesus himself, as well as the ongoing mission of his church, came from a relationship with God. Mission was not based on works. In union with the Holy Spirit, Jesus and the first believers ministered to people from a position of relationship—of *being with* God rather than *doing for* God. This was the most important ingredient in mission: that mission comes from being, not doing.

So began a lifestyle change in how I did mission. Slowly I learned to say no to good opportunities, delegated tasks that others could do, prioritized my work responsibilities, and sought balance in the intellectual, spiritual, physical, and social dimensions of my life.[15] I altered my weekly planner to include healthy blocks of time with my family and one day retreats with God each week, completely away from telephones and people. This change of focus aroused some concern from the church leaders, yet I knew that if I was to have a healthy relationship with my God, wife, and children, in the midst of an effective ministry, I needed to follow the Lukan pattern of prayer, spirit, and mission. Furthermore, I asked myself, What is success?

So often the church has accepted Western society's definition of success without critical evaluation. Multiple seminars and conferences promote steps to success for a healthy church body based on the social axiom that bigger is better. Yet this is the secular business model, found nowhere in the scriptures. Godly success is finding the will of God and doing it, whether this means a life of prosperity or hardship. What is often promoted as success in life may be illustrated by an industrial image. At the end of life we can measure our success by how many cups on the conveyer belt of life are filled to overflowing. A twelve-cup life of multiple gifts and activity is more successful than a two-cup life. There is much pressure to perform at our peak and to fill as many cups in pursuing life's journey as possible. "Doing" is promoted as essential to a Christian life well lived.

This hyper-Protestant work ethic affects our evangelical churches, mission agencies, and schools. All too often our attitude toward work is propelled toward workaholism and compulsivism as we attempt to follow these perceived norms of operation.[16] In the process, the development and well-being of the staff and faculty are sacrificed for the mission of the visionaries. Stress and fatigue, causing emotional and physical burnout, are all too common in our Christian institutions. There is little theology of play and practice of sabbath rest. Token offerings of spirituality are submerged in the bustle of program productivity.

Yet the life of Jesus in mission is not one of striving or struggling for bigger or better. The pattern of being with God is often missing in Christian circles today. "But now more than ever the word about Jesus spread abroad; many crowds would gather to hear him and to be cured of their diseases. But he would withdraw to deserted places and pray" (Lk 5:15-16). A rhythm of spirituality is evident in Jesus whereby every major event in his earthly life is saturated in prayer. Luke records the importance of prayer in the life of Jesus as no other gospel writer does. Luke sees Jesus in prayer at his baptism (3:21), in selecting the Twelve (6:12), at Peter's confession of faith (9:18), at the mount of transfiguration (9:28-29), before the teaching of the Lord's prayer (11:1-2), at Gethsemane (22:41), and at Calvary (23:34, 46). Prayer surrounds every important event in Jesus' ministry. Prayer is the means whereby God directs Jesus' mission of salvation to a yearning humanity. It is the way Jesus apprehends the dynamic power of the Spirit for salvation history. The Messiah's redemptive work flowed from his relationship with God in prayer, not from his many deeds.

In the same way, Luke records in the Book of Acts the early church's pattern of prayer, spirit, and mission. The believers' prayer in Acts 4 is just one example of the church praying and seeking the power of God before accomplishing mission. The prayerful disciples followed Jesus' paradigm of mission flowing from beingness. They prayed to their sovereign Messiah who refilled them with his Holy Spirit. Only then did they begin to advance to the next stage in the kingdom's mission of expansion from Jerusalem to Rome. Scripture teaches that mission flows from "beingness" rather than "doingness," but secular Western culture teaches that only by hard work can anything be accomplished. This attitude may be summarized using Benjamin Franklin's axiom: "God helps those that help themselves." The church today needs to reevaluate its methods of mission. Like the early believers in Acts 4, contemporary Christians need to follow Jesus' model.

## REFERENCES

[1] This chapter uses the words *mission* and *ministry* interchangeably to refer to God's work in this world.

[2] The discourse analysis of a biblical narrative may be subdivided into parts, acts, scenes, episodes, paragraph clusters, paragraphs, sentences, and words. This chapter only considers those parts and acts that are relevant to the scene in Acts 4:23-31.

[3] Acts 4:14 states that the healed man was present at the council's trial the next morning, which suggests that he had spent the night in jail with Peter and John.

[4] The same Sanhedrin Council tried Jesus (Lk 22:66—23:2); Peter and John (Acts 4:5-7); the Twelve (Acts 5:17ff.); Stephen (Acts 6:12ff.; 7:51ff.); and sent Saul to Damascus to persecute any Christians he found there (Acts 9:1-2). Led by Caiaphas, with his father-in-law, Annas, the power behind the scenes (Lk 3:2; Jn 18:12-13; Acts 4:6), the council had a number of opportunities to repent to God (Lk 22:69-70; Acts 3:17-20; 4:8-12; 5:29-32; 6:15; 7:51-53; 9:28-29) but chose repeatedly not to change its mind because of the desire to protect the Roman/Judaistic power it possessed (Jn 11:47-48).

[5] This is clear from the repetition of the phrase "your holy servant Jesus" (Acts 4:27, 30).

[6] F. F. Bruce states that the words reflect such Old Testament passages as Exodus 20:11, Nehemiah 9:6, Psalm 146:6, and Isaiah 42:5. Further, "the invocation of God as Creator here and elsewhere has been considered liturgical, from the stereotyped character of the wording" (*The Acts of the Apostles: The Greek Text with Introduction and*

*Commentary* [Chicago: Inter-Varsity Christian Fellowship, 1952], 126). I. Howard Marshall goes further in stating: "The prayer itself reflects the use of the Old Testament, not merely Psalm 2, which is explicitly quoted but also the prayer of Hezekiah in Isaiah 37:16-20 which has supplied the general pattern and suggested some phraseology" (*The Acts of the Apostles: An Introduction and Commentary* [Grand Rapids, Mich.: Eerdmans, 1980], 106). However, Marshall does not elaborate on this suggested connection with Hezekiah.

7 To clarify this point, the apostles saw that the "Gentiles" who raged against the Messiah were the Romans; the "peoples" who devised futile plots were his Jewish adversaries; the "kings" who took their stand were represented by Herod Antipas; and the "rulers" against the Lord and his Messiah were represented by Pontius Pilate (see F. F. Bruce, *Commentary on the Book of Acts: The English Text with Introduction, Exposition and Notes* [Grand Rapids, Mich.: Eerdmans, 1986], 106). It is interesting to note that I. Howard Marshall states concerning the peoples of Israel: "The inclusion of Israel among the foes of the Messiah marks the beginning of the Christian understanding that insofar as the people of Israel reject the Messiah they cease to be the Lord's people and can be ranked with unbelieving Gentiles" (*The Acts of the Apostles*, 106). This statement needs to be carefully weighed against Paul's comments in Romans 9—11. Furthermore, in Luke 23:7ff. is the only reference to Jesus appearing before Herod. See Bruce for further details on Herod Antipas, who was involved in the imprisonment and beheading of John the Baptist and had the prophet/teacher Manaen, from the church of Antioch in Syria, as his foster brother (Acts 13:1) (Bruce, *The Acts of the Apostles*, 127-128).

8 The early name for the followers of Jesus was people of "the Way" (Acts 9:2; 19:9, 23; 22:4; 24:14, 22). It was not until Gentiles began to follow the Jewish Messiah in Antioch of Syria that they were called by the term *Christians* (Acts 11:26).

9 Compare the following scriptures as signs of divine affirmation: Acts 2:2-3; Ex 19:18; Is 6:4. Other examples of God's power upon inanimate objects are found in Luke 8:22-25 (the stilled storm), Luke 9:10-17 (the multiplied bread), Matthew 21:18-22 (the withered fig tree), and John 2:1-11 (the water turned to wine).

10 Note that the early church received refillings of the Holy Spirit. Such was the situation with the apostle Peter. It could be argued that he first received the Spirit in the upper room (Jn 20:22) and was filled again at Pentecost (Acts 2:1-4), then before the council (Acts 4:8), and after the prayer in Acts 4:31.

11 Luke compares the encouragement of Barnabas (4:36-37) with the scheming hypocrisy of Ananias and his wife Sapphira (5:1-11); see also 5:13-14.

12 There are prayer parallels in Luke-Acts. Through prayer, the Holy Spirit equips and transforms God's people "on their way" toward accomplishing God's mission in the world. This is evident in the anointing of the Spirit at the baptism of Jesus and the church (cf. Lk 3:21 and Acts 1:14; 2:1-4; 10:1, 9, 44; 11:15-17); the appointment of Christ's and the church's apostles (cf. Lk 6:12 and Acts 6:5-6; 13:1-4); the approval of God through extraordinary miracles (cf. Lk 9:28 and Acts 4:31; 19:6, 11); and the anguish of the suffering Savior and the saints (cf. Lk 22:41 and Acts 7:59; 9:15).

13 I. Howard Marshall states that "the words 'Thou art my Son' (Ps 2:7), spoken to Jesus at His baptism by the heavenly voice, actually hailed him as this Messiah" (Marshall, *The Acts of the Apostles*, 106).

14 During New Testament times in Palestine there were many groups involved in mission of one kind or another. For instance, in Matthew 23:15 Jesus spoke of the scribes and Pharisees who would "cross sea and land to make a single convert," referring to a Gentile convert to Judaism as in Acts 2:10, 6:5, and 13:43 and to the Jewish revolutionaries

such as Theudas and Judas of Galilee mentioned by Gamaliel in Acts 5:36-37, who drew away some people after them.

[15] For Jesus' development in these four dimensions, see Luke 2:40, 52.

[16] This is not to advocate laziness or slothfulness (Prv 12:27; 15:19; 19:24; 21:25; 22:13; 24:30; 26:13-15). Work is a blessed opportunity from God to express human creativity after his image (Gn 1:26-27; 2:15). Yet, within many institutions of contemporary Western Christianity, there are unhealthy imbalances of work and play. Sadly, little space and time are devoted to developing life's rhythms of rest and relationships (Ex 20:8-11; 34:21-24; Lv 25:8-12).

# 6

## *Cross-cultural Mediation:*
## *From Exclusion to Inclusion*

ACTS 6:1–7; ALSO 5:33–42

## Young Lee Hertig

> The more we run from conflict,
> The more it masters us;
> The more we try to avoid it,
> The more it controls us.
> The less we fear conflict,
> The less it confuses us;
> The less we deny our differences,
> The less they divide us.
>
> —DAVID W. AUGSBERGER
> *Conflict Mediation across Cultures*

As long as humans walk the face of this earth, there will be conflict. It is universal and yet culturally particular. My interest in examining the dynamics of conflict mediation arose from two concerns: The first relates to the mainline denomination, and the second to violent eruptions in North American major cities. Too frequently, church disputes end up in civil court, nearly bankrupting the church's financial resources and scattering the body of Christ. This jeopardizes the church's public witness. The second concern stems from the recent, violent eruptions in various North American cities.[1]

The gridlock of human dialogue is extremely costly. September 11, 2001, manifested one of the worst forms of mass killing in a borderless war. Hegemonic policies and their global impact deplete economic, ecological, and human resources. A prime symbol of American power and world capital center, the New York World Trade Center, and the Pentagon, the sign of military power, were attacked without warning. While hell was unleashed in New York and Washington, the world was glued to the television screen as if it were all a Hollywood movie.

Skyscrapers, symbols of modernity, melted down as cultic leaders carried out their apocalyptic mission in the name of Allah. It was as if the gods were at war. Suddenly, out of a beautiful blue sky, three thousand innocent people disappeared; the fallout was the emotional bombshell that fell on loved ones left living. Most haunting, the attackers disappeared with their innocent victims. Amid the fear of the faceless war, however, the unyielding human spirit of the firemen and workers at Ground Zero reminded us of relentless human courage that shines in the midst of evil.

At the heart of this event lies an ancient conflict dressed in modern technological devices. On the surface, culture seems to change. Yet, at a deeper level, the ancient conflict still persists in the modern and postmodern eras. Likewise, the apostles in Acts experienced both mediated and mediating roles as the gospel of Jesus Christ collided with ancient Judaism in a radically Hellenizing world. Seen through the lens of conflict mediation, Acts provides insights into our contemporary, globalizing world.

Due to radical technological innovation, both domestic and international migration have reached their peaks. As revealed in the case of Hebraic Jews and the Hellenists, any immigrant community's differences in language, birthplace, and traditions can become sources of discrimination. Its application to contemporary immigrant communities stands strong despite vast time and cultural differences with New Testament times.

The immigrant community in the United States is my social location for this chapter. I have pastored and taught in immigrant churches in urban and suburban areas of Los Angeles and the Midwest for twenty years. Also, I have ten years of teaching experience in the academic discipline of missiology, which is multidisciplinary and multicultural in scope.

As a Korean-American woman I often find myself on the periphery of both cultures as I move to and from Korean and American contexts. The nature of multiplicity often accompanies continual oscillation between life experiences in the realm of the either/or, neither/nor, in between, and both/and. This constant journey exposes me to raw issues of power. Learning to accept the strength of this in-between state as an asset has liberated me to move beyond the false, dichotomous view of perceiving power from the perspective either of the powerful or the powerless.

## ACTS 6: DEALING OPENLY WITH CONFLICT

No one wants to be pushed to the periphery or excluded. It is fundamental human nature to yearn for social inclusion. Therefore, much of human conflict revolves around the roller coaster of inclusion and exclusion in the human social drama. The main thesis of this essay is that dealing openly and wisely with conflict can reduce the level of violence. Conflict mediation depends on the availability of the mediator, the nature of the conflict, and timing. This essay celebrates the mediated conflict that results in the vitality of the mission of the church. Yet it does not gloss over the chronic and perpetuating conflict in world view between the Hebrews and Hellenists.

The conflict in Acts 6:1 arises around a very basic human need: the daily food distribution. It is concrete enough to mediate. This concrete conflict is much easier mediated than the chronic and enduring conflict between Hebrews and Hellenists, which is deeply imbedded in history, resulting from unhealed memories that resurface repeatedly in Acts (see 6:1; 7:51-60; 15:1-2). The apostles' immediate and open decision-making process eliminated further conflict. They gathered the disciples together and selected seven Hellenists full of the Spirit and wisdom to wait on tables for the Hellenist widows. Regrettably, in many churches today conflict brews under the surface, which either paralyzes or splits the body of Christ. One of the signs of vitality in Christian churches is dealing with conflict openly and immediately across cultures.

The exclusion of Hellenist widows from the daily food distribution uncovered the existing tension between the Hebraic Jews and the Jewish Diaspora in a rapidly Hellenizing world. Thus, it has a significant parallel to our rapidly globalizing world today. In the twenty-first century we still face the ancient and universal group dynamics centered on exclusion and domination. The numerical makeup of a minority group constitutes power dynamics that challenge the way the pie is cut.

## GROWING PAINS AND INTERGROUP CONFLICT

Having gone through direct persecution in Acts 5, the apostles are confronted with an intergroup conflict in Acts 6. The apostles are confronted with their own group's exclusion of Grecian Jewish widows during daily food distribution. Only four chapters after the Spirit brought about unity in diversity at Pentecost, Luke records a contrasting event. Tension between Grecian and Hebraic Jews reached its peak. According to James D. G. Dunn the tension had been brewing and the timing of the confrontation by the Hellenists is telling. When the number of disciples *grew*, the Hellenists grumbled against the Hebrews (6:1).[2]

Empowered by numerical growth, the Hellenists address their widows' complaint against the Hebraic Jews' unjust treatment. For the Hebraic Jews the increasing number of Hellenists may have meant a drying up of the welfare system. An economic down time sharpens the existing differences and heightens competitiveness over mercy. In a tightly knit group the distribution of limited goods takes precedence in the "in group" and thus marginalizes the "other." Sadly, the Hellenists were treated as outsiders in their homeland after returning from their Diaspora experience in foreign lands. The idealization of the homeland among immigrants is shattered when facing contrasting realities of change both within human beings and within their own homeland.

## HEIGHTENED OTHERNESS DURING CULTURAL CHANGE

The backdrop of the concrete event of Acts 6 is the larger issue of cultural change and its persistence in Judaism's encounters with Hellenism. Scholars vary in their views regarding Judaism and Hellenism. The most common description of Hellenists is that they were born outside of Palestine but lived in Jerusalem. These were Greek-speakers, not the Aramaic-speaking Jews. However, Shaye J. D. Cohen asserts that Hellenistic culture comprised many different cultures expressed in Greek language and thus contained diverse forms. In other words, Hellenistic culture was a melting pot:

> The natives were Hellenized, and the Greeks were "Orientalized." Through intermarriage with local women and through veneration of the local gods, the Greeks often lost much of their Greekness. . . . In this conception "Judaism" and "Hellenism" are *not* antonyms, since, by definition, Judaism was part of Hellenism and Hellenism was part of Judaism.[3]

Cohen argues against the antithetical dynamic between Judaism and Hellenism. Opposing the notion of a "pure" form of Judaism, he asserts that the land of Palestine was not a cultural island. As in today's globalizing world, the forces of sweeping cultural change could not keep any culture from the dominant—in this case, Hellenistic—influence. Problematic in drawing dichotomous distinctions between Hebraic Jews and Diaspora Jews is the notion that one group remains fixed against the tidal wave of a Hellenizing world. Instead, "Hellenistic Judaism is only a chronological indicator for the period from Alexander the Great to the Maccabees or perhaps to the Roman conquests of the first century B.C.E."[4]

Furthermore, as Martin Hengel points out, Jerusalem was "not only a Jewish but also a 'Hellenistic' capital—surely *sui generis*—with its own Jewish Hellenistic culture." Greek-speaking Jews of the Diaspora introduced synagogues in Jerusalem with the Pharisees' support.[5] Hengel describes Hellenists in Jerusalem as follows:

> This special Jewish-Hellenistic milieu in Jerusalem and its environment was formed by the Jewish pilgrims, returning emigrants and students of the law from the Greek-speaking Diaspora, by the members of the Herodian court, Herod's family and their clientele, by some aristocratic priestly families like the Boetheusians, by merchants, physicians, architects and other technical specialists, teachers of Greek language and rhetoric, skilled artisans and also slaves from abroad. . . . From this Greek-speaking group came the Seven Hellenists in Acts 6, people like Joseph Barnabas, John Mark, Silas-Silvanus, and above all, Saulus-Paulus from Tarsus.[6]

The diversity of class among the Hellenists in Jerusalem is noteworthy. In addition to the intergroup conflict with Hebrew Jews, the intra-group conflict centered on class consciousness.

The Diaspora Jews from Asia Minor pilgrimaged to Jerusalem and brought with them *syncretized* customs and religions. This raised a question among the Hebraic Jews as to how far Judaism ought to adapt to Hellenism. The responses, of course, varied. Some took an all-or-nothing approach, and others took a partial adaptation position. Whereas some were prepared to relinquish all beliefs and practices, others had a merely rhetorical anti-Hellenistic stance. All such stances threatened the stability of Judaism.[7]

As in today's globalization, an unavoidable question that Jewish people confronted was centered around identity issues. How do Jews maintain Jewishness in a dominant Hellenistic culture? What is nonnegotiable and what is negotiable in such a changing world?

In this tumultuous time the Pharisees played a stabilizing role. Contrasting the common portrayal of Pharisees as rigid legalists, many scholars now believe that the Pharisees supported a new system, the synagogue providing space and structure for both Hebrew and Hellenist Jews. Nevertheless, tension around particulars and universals had to be overwhelming.

Responding to the tension, the synagogue structure utilized an integrationist approach, whereas the apostles' creation of a deacon structure for handling the exclusion of the Hellenistic widows utilized a cultural-pluralistic-resolution model. The apostles impressively drew clear role boundaries and offered a proposal that satisfied the whole group. They did not defend the Hebraic Jews or blame the victims. They listened to the problem and delegated the resolution to the insiders. Unlike Gamaliel's mediation of utilizing his fellow high priests to rescue the apostles in danger (5:33-40), in dealing with Grecian widows the apostles chose the wounded group, the Hellenists, to mediate. The apostles presented their proposal by making their communication channel and procedure clear and open. They took the leadership in presenting the proposal rather than leaving it up to the masses, and then they delegated their leadership authority.

Often conflict in the church snowballs because the leaders either take total control or choose a laisser-faire approach that lacks guidance. The apostles' procedure included, first, gathering *all* the disciples together and stressing their primary role as apostles—the ministry of the word of God (6:2). Second, they presented a proposal to delegate to the congregation the solution to the problem: "Friends, select from among yourselves seven men of good standing, full of the Spirit and of wisdom, whom we may appoint to this task" (6:3). Third, the proposal satisfied the *whole* group (6:5). It appears that the seven chosen men became official mediators for the proposed problem. This was followed by rituals of granting authority to the seven men with prayer and the laying on of hands (6:6).

Such differences in styles of mediation also stem from the nature of the conflict. In the former conflict between the apostles and the high priest in Acts 5, the core belief was threatened, while the conflict between the Hebraists and the Hellenists in Acts 6 involved discriminatory behavior by negligence. Mediating chronic world-view clashes cannot be resolved once and for all. They keep resurfacing throughout Acts and in the history of Christianity. The new wine in old wineskin bursts the wineskin. In fact, the key chosen leader of the seven, Stephen, who mediated for Grecian widows (6:8, 15), was stoned to death because he challenged "old wineskins." The conflict between the apostles and the high priests resurfaced despite Gamaliel's temporary mediation, and it resurfaces again with a global impact as we confront ancient conflicts today in the Middle East.

Although critiquing ancient narratives from contemporary perspectives renders injustice, I want to address modern implications for the sake of today's reader. Whereas the apostles' freeing themselves from having to exercise power over the victim deserves admiration, a lingering question relates to its effective yet separatistic solution to the problem. Did it reinforce a social and cultural distance in the treatment of the poorest as the utterly other? It is often the powerful who can afford to draw clear-cut role boundaries while the lives of the poor, represented in the Grecian widows' daily lives, revolve around simultaneous multiple tasks. Especially in earlier centuries, gendered time and space categories placed women in polychronic time in contrast to the more male monochronic time. In the private sphere, women's tasks demanded multiple and simultaneous dimensions.[8] While such boundaries diffuse control over, they also maintain social distance between the two conflicting groups. Although there is merit in delegating the job to the in-group members (Hellenistic Jews), bridging the social distance cannot be achieved indirectly. The otherness defined by language, place of birth, migration, and emigration remains pronounced when a separatistic rather than an integrationist approach is taken. Upon highlighting the guidelines of selecting leaders, the apostles drew clear role boundaries. They stressed that "it is not right that we should neglect the ministry of the word of God in order to wait on tables" (6:2).

What could have happened if the apostles had not delegated moral responsibility? If a dialectic approach were taken, they might have organized a joint task force. From an experiential perspective, the experience gap between the two groups appears to have persisted despite the numerical growth of believers: "The number of the disciples increased greatly in Jerusalem, and a great many of the priests became obedient to the faith" (6:7). Not mentioned is how the treatment of *the culturally other* improved. Grecian widows, after their complaint, remain silent in the text. The proposed problem has to do with Grecian widows, and yet it ends with addressing the triumphant numerical growth of believers, including priests. One of the implications is that the proposed problem is resolved and the end result is the expansion of Christianity, which then snowballs into a threat to the high priests, leading to the martyrdom of Stephen, one of the seven Hellenist leaders.

The cost of conflict impasse is enormous. In today's world it results in massive ecological, human, and financial destruction. The impact of heightened conflict lasts generation after generation. When accumulated, conflict brews to a boiling point and results in violent eruptions. Therefore, dealing with conflict openly and in an orderly way is significant, as demonstrated by the apostles and the Hellenists. The Hellenists' strategic moment of raising an issue "when the disciples were increasing in number" (6:1) is significant in dealing with discrimination. Much of the politics revolve around engineering issues, timing, and the right channel. Such discernment takes seasoned and wise leadership. Obviously, until the Hellenists brought up their widows' experience of injustice, they must have exercised silence. In such a case, not acting may serve as an active process, not an escape from conflict.

## HEBRAIC SUSPICION OF HELLENIZED JEWS

The numerical growth of the minority group sharpened group consciousness and thus resulted in intergroup tension, particularly when resources were limited. Seen through the dominant group's perception, its piece of the pie is shrinking; from the minority's perspective, it deserves a fair share of the pie. Thus, justice and mercy are in conflict due to differing competitive values and perceptions of the way the pie is distributed. Lee G. Bolman and Terrence E. Deal indicate the conditions under which such conflict arose:

> The political frame asserts that in the face of enduring differences and scarce resources, conflict is inevitable and power is a key resource. Scarce resources force trade-offs. Enduring differences ensure that parties will disagree on both what and how to decide.[9]

Economic down times fuel existing conflicts, splitting scarce resources. Luke exposes the intergroup conflict that makes a particular group—Hellenistic widows in the Hellenizing world—"other." Miraslov Volf defines others as "those who are oppressed and in need of liberation."[10]

The sources of conflict can be traced back to the rift between the Hebraists and Hellenists beginning with the Hellenistic reform in Jerusalem (175-164 B.C.E.), when the Jewish Hellenists attempted to "convert Jerusalem to a 'Greek' city."[11] This event sent shock waves through Palestinian Judaism during the Second Temple era. Hengel concludes that this radical reform ended as a failed attempt against "theocracy." It ideologically sought resistance by the majority of the Jewish people to pursue a violent break with ancestral law.[12] It resulted in the collapse of the Jewish internal system of authority, loyalty, and leadership due to the external pressure of Hellenization, which forced Judaism to modify.

Dunn interprets Acts 6 in light of the "residue of suspicion" from the Maccabean revolt among devout Torah Jews toward Hellenist Jews. The Maccabean revolt shook the core belief system of the Hebraic Jews as the Hellenizers challenged circumcision, food laws, and even the Temple sacrifices.[13] Consequently, Judea had to go through a major paradigm shift due to Hellenization, which turned a cohesively unified society into a complex one. Its ideology was no longer representative as it clashed with the "new wineskins" initiated by Hellenism.

As in any revolutionary time, response to the external forces of change emerges and is expressed in at least three ways: all or nothing, in between, both/and. The diverse responses inevitably accompany a power struggle within and without. Jewish history professor Ellis Rivkin offers an important insight regarding the internal conditions for such a revolution to occur:

> Revolutions do not occur gratuitously. They are set in motion by a pattern of change; they are not mechanically induced by any single thought

or a single event. Revolutions can occur only when the processes of
change have altered the perceptions of those who are experiencing the
impact and pressure.[14]

In other words, revolution is dependent on many external pieces that are much
bigger than the revolution itself. Internal differences in responding to the
forced Hellenism by Antiochus IV (175-163 B.C.) diffused structural cohesive-
ness; this, in turn, altered the old structure. This alteration was possible because there were enough in the elite class who were restless and frustrated by
absolute theocracy.

Dunn also attributes language differences to the tension between the Hebraic
Jews and the Diaspora Hellenists. One of the most visible signs in intercultural
contact is the language gap. And this just when the tool of communication is
needed most. The Hebrew Jews, who spoke Aramaic and had to learn the dominant Greek language, must have been irritated by Hellenists who were mono-
lingual.[15] The Hebraic Jews had reason to be suspicious of people from the
Hellenized Diaspora and to perceive them as diluting the Hebrew core belief
system.

The intense conflict between the Hebraists and the returning immigrants, the
Hellenists, calls to mind a similar dynamic occurring among immigrant communities today. The first generation's struggle to hold onto its indigenous belief system and the second generation's reaction against the parents in favor of
assimilation to American culture evoke strong emotions in both generations.
The conflict between the two groups mirrors current broader struggles related
to race, ethnicity, gender, and religions. Thus our cities are haunted by frequent
racial unrest.

## THE CHALLENGE
## OF PRESERVING HEBREW IDENTITY

Amid such epochal change the core beliefs of the Hebrews were challenged
from every direction. Noted scholar on Diaspora Judaism A. T. Kraabel writes,
"The need for community in a bewildering larger world affected people at
nearly every level of wealth and education. Jews began to form their own communities in the Greco-Roman world early in the Hellenistic period."[16]

In such challenging times the conflict caused by the visible "otherness" undoubtedly escalates more than the greater "commonness." Ethnicity, nativity,
and Diaspora become sources of conflict, pitching one group against the other.
Naturally, the Hebrews sought to hold back the tidal wave of sweeping Hellenization. In such a closed climate the Diaspora Jews in Jerusalem became an
easy target for suspicion. The suspicion of the "other" led to their exclusion
from the daily supplies needed for survival. Turning a fundamental need into
a tool of discrimination instigates from the excluded an emotional uproar. In a
potentially explosive situation, the apostles, in the wake of their conflict with
the high priests, handled the case wisely.

## THE MEDIATED MEDIATE

A role reversal takes place in Acts 6, where the mediated mediate. Earlier, the apostles went through their near-death experience and were freed by Gamaliel's intervention in Acts 5. Their success in preaching the gospel of Jesus threatened the high priest and endangered their lives. Now the freed apostles themselves face an opportunity to release the oppressed through their mediation. Unlike the direct mediation Gamaliel demonstrated, the apostles choose to delegate mediation to the "other," the Hellenists. First, they draw clear boundaries in their role as apostles: "It is not right that we should neglect the word of God in order to wait on tables" (6:2). Then they lay down criteria for choosing Hellenists to handle the problem created by the Hebraic Jews: "Therefore, friends, select from among yourselves seven men of good standing, full of the Spirit and of wisdom, whom we may appoint to this task" (6:3). We can see two different kinds of mediation taking place in Acts 5 and Acts 6. The nature of conflict seems to determine the style of mediation, although the qualifications of the mediator remain the same.

Due to conflicting perceptions and experiences that taint realities, creating consensus in conflicting situations can be a challenge. The apostles' immediate and open consultation served as an effective mediation. Often when conflict gridlocks an organization, communication is secretive and indirect. Conflict swept under the rug festers and increases. From the apostles' response, we can observe a very important process of conflict mediation.

1. They listened to the voices from the margins.
2. They drew healthy role differentiation.
3. They laid out open and clear guidelines for selecting leaders.
4. They delegated power to the Grecian Jews without strings attached.
5. Spirit-filled leaders, like Stephen and Philip, were chosen for the new leadership team.
6. They legitimized chosen leaders through public authorization.

The apostles' process is exemplary. They do not show signs of needing to control the situation. Although not selected by the apostles themselves, the seven leaders whom the apostles installed into office successfully met their criteria. However, if the delegation had been carried out blindly and carelessly, it would have intensified conflict rather than reduced it. Although the task force dealt with one concrete issue successfully, the fundamental identity conflict remained unresolved, as indicated by Stephen's death. While key leaders, like Stephen, were byproducts of Pentecost, the widening gap between the core Jewish identity and the gospel of Jesus Christ persisted. For this reason I prefer the term *conflict mediation,* not *conflict resolution,* in approaching complex human dynamics. Yesterday's hasty resolution can revisit as today's nightmare.

## PENTECOST AS SOURCE OF UNITY AND DIVISION

Pentecost transcended linguistic barriers through the miraculous work of the Holy Spirit (Acts 2). Everyone understood the others. The Holy Spirit miraculously bridged linguistic, regional, and ethnic disparities. After Pentecost the believers "were of one heart and soul" and "everything they owned was held in common" (Acts 4:32). Barriers of otherness no longer mattered, and reciprocity created a powerful community.

However, the powerful intervention of the unifying Holy Spirit is marred by persisting human discord. Human boundaries rooted in difference and otherness quickly resurfaced. The next chapter depicts how Ananias and Sapphira lied to the Holy Spirit and concealed part of the proceeds of their land, disrupting this ideal community. Confronted by Peter, they dropped dead on the spot, creating fear among the believers. The signs and wonders that were once sources of unity now became sources of tension between the Sanhedrin Council and the apostles. During Pentecost the Holy Spirit manifested reconciling differences that challenged the status quos. The conflict rose to the high priest and associates. Ultimately a party of Sadducees arrested the apostles, but in vain. The high priest declared, "We gave you strict orders not to teach in this name, yet here you have filled Jerusalem with your teaching and you are determined to bring this man's blood on us" (5:28). But Peter and the apostles replied, "We must obey God rather than any human authority" (5:29).

## GAMALIEL'S MEDIATION

Although Peter's level of defiance corresponds to the level of oppression by the high priest, his outright defiance against the high priests' authority worsened the conflict. Both the message and the messenger paralyze any dialogue. Meeting confrontation with confrontation cannot ease tension. Edward DeBono accurately stresses, "Disputants are in the worst position to solve their disputes."[17] It requires a third-party mediator, Spirit-filled, honored, yet neutral. Often the mediation hinges on the availability of mediators such as Gamaliel at the peak of tension. Gamaliel, honored by all the people, stood up during the peak of conflict and powerfully diffused the heightened emotion:

> So in the present case, I tell you, keep away from these men and let them alone; because if this plan or this undertaking is of human origin, it will fail; but if it is of God, you will not be able to overthrow them—in that case you may even be found fighting against God! (Acts 5:38-39)

A key quality of the mediator is shown in Gamaliel, who is respected—honored—by all the people (5:34). Bruce J. Malina and Jerome H. Neyrey differentiate ascribed honor and achieved honor in the Mediterranean world. Ascribed honor is more highly valued, whereas acquired honor occurs "in virtue of performance" and thus opens up room for challenge by the other performer.[18] His status granted, Gamaliel possesses both ascribed honor as an insider and achieved honor by his powerful speech. As an insider putting on the outsider's perspective, he rescued the apostles from being put to death. His seasoned character diffused rigidly bounded perceived threats in need of a reality check. Successfully modeling mediation, Gamaliel diffuses the high priest's charge after the defendant, Peter, aggravated the tension with his direct response. Thus, the role of the mediator in changing antagonistic perceptions is crucial in intergroup conflict mediation because everyone sees reality through his or her own tinted glasses.

Several key principles emerge for the role of mediator from Gamaliel's example of using his powerful position to empower the powerless:

- He utilized both ascribed and achieved honor.
- He utilized both emic (insider) and etic (outsider) perspectives of the conflict.
- He expanded the dichotomous either-or perception to a reciprocal both-and perception.
- He wisely transported the insider's fixed perception toward the higher purposes of God.

Important missiologically, once conflict is mediated it accompanies the vitality of the mission of the church. Immediately after Gamaliel resolves the conflict and they leave the council, it states that "every day in the temple and at home they did not cease to teach and proclaim Jesus as the Messiah" (5:42).

Likewise, when the Hellenist widows' conflict was resolved through the appointment of Hellenist leaders, Luke again describes the vitality of the church: "The word of God continued to spread; the number of the disciples increased greatly in Jerusalem, and a great many of the priests became obedient to the faith" (6:7). The exclusion of Hellenist widows was unjust, so vitality and justice issues were linked.

The ideal community of sharing and growth originating at Pentecost, however, comes and goes in the narrative. Barriers based on region, ethnicity, and language, though temporarily mediated, continue to resurface throughout Acts.

## CONTEMPORARY EMERGENCE OF CONFLICT

A tumultuous conflict results when ideals, rules, roles, and relationships no longer hold together. As in biblical times, conflict between groups in contemporary times emerges when the minority group's number increases. Racial tension in the major cities of the United States escalates as the majority group encounters increasing numbers of minority groups. For example, Los Angeles periodically experiences violence stemming from racialized policies in multicultural contexts. As in many political dynamics, discerning the right timing of raising the issues, and the right representatives, determines the outcome of the conflict. We will now examine the implications of Acts 6 in light of contemporary cultural conflict.

## IMPLICATIONS FOR THE IMMIGRANT CHURCH TODAY

Many immigrant churches today suffer from chronic conflict and leadership crisis. In fact, many leaders are embroiled in church conflict and breed conflict. A significant area of conflict within the immigrant church includes differences in worship between and within generations, polity, personnel, and decision-making procedures. The first generation's language barrier limits its social boundaries. Consequently, the immigrant church becomes the primary social milieu where the members bring all of their unmet social needs. The American-born second generation wants to worship God according to its own preferences rather than simply mimicking its parents' models; the parents want to make sure that their traditions continue through their offspring.

In the absence of honorable leaders like Stephen and Gamaliel, the contemporary immigrant church, without shared criteria for decision-making, often creates social chaos. More and more often church matters are brought to litigation, lowering the quality of the church. Therefore, the role of tradition in the immigrant community is stronger than the mainstream culture that was left behind; that is, cultural change takes place faster in the mainstream culture than in the "island" subculture of the immigrants.

> Tradition offers continuity in the midst of disruptive changes, and for this reason it is very important to immigrants. In the midst of surrounding changes, immigrants can easily cling to tradition—denominational, cultural, or familial—like a security blanket.[19]

The ongoing spiritual vitality of the immigrant church challenges leaders to be equipped for mediation and peacemaking. Trained in a highly mono-cultural seminary curriculum, many younger generation leaders graduate, return to the immigrant church with the same lack of indigenous leadership models, and repeat the first generation's leadership style, which they had vehemently resisted. Thus the perpetuation of dysfunctional leadership, rather than contextual leadership, is transmitted to the younger generation. Who is the healthy third party for handling the immigrant church's world-view clash? Perhaps theological education is the key to such a breakthrough. A variation from Western domination in theological education would enhance both Western and non-Western theological education. It is time that we practice reciprocity and mutuality—like the apostles, who provided an opportunity for the "others" to represent their own group—in theological enterprise and thus in ministry. Despite the current self-critique of the Christendom model of theological education, implementing an alternative will remain bleak until non-Western leaders come to the table.[20]

Furthermore, internalized Christendom is stronger among the non-Western leaders who want to maintain their status rather than experience loss through change. Thus stronger resistance among the folks at the center, on the one hand, and the mono-cultural Western theological curriculum, on the other, makes equipping multicultural leaders a persistent challenge. The sharp increase in the number of non-Western Christians should not be perceived as a threat but a reason for celebration. Without sanction by Western theological educators for equipping non-Western leaders, an inclusive theological paradigm in the cities of the United States will remain elusive.

If the seventeenth-century Enlightenment has contributed to the theological paradigm of the West and has had a global impact, then multicultural paradigms may contribute to charting out a theological discourse for the twenty-first century that moves beyond mere discussions about multiculturalism, mutuality, and reciprocity. Based on Acts 5 and 6, the either/or epistemology that fosters conflict can be reduced by adopting a both/and epistemology. It is time for the American immigrant church to exercise ownership of relevant paradigms without denigrating the West or idealizing its own paradigm, but rather balancing the Western extreme with newer paradigms through partnership for the sake of mutuality and reciprocity. Such a paradigm will allow differences to enrich. The apostles offering the Hellenists a voice and structural support provides a model.

Acts 6 clearly demonstrates that mediating conflict in the midst of diversity and immigration is directly linked to missional vitality. However, some post–September 11, 2001, responses cast fear and doubt on human diversity when lacking the mediation of conflict that contributes to wisdom, justice, and mission vitality.

## REFERENCES

[1] I happened to be living in Los Angeles during the 1992 uprising and in Ohio during the Cincinnati uprisings in 2001.

[2] James D. G. Dunn, *The Partings of the Ways: Between Christianity and Judaism and Their Significance for the Character of Christianity* (Valley Forge, Pa.: Trinity Press International, 1991), 61.

[3] Shaye J. D. Cohen, *From the Maccabees to the Mishnah* (Philadelphia: The Westminster Press, 1987), 36.

[4] Ibid.

[5] Martin Hengel, "Judaism and Hellenism Revisited," in *Hellenism in the Land of Israel*, ed. John J. Collins and Gregory E. Sterling (Notre Dame, Ind.: University of Notre Dame Press, 2001), 26.

[6] Ibid., 28.

[7] Cohen, *From the Maccabees to the Mishnah*, 45.

[8] Young Lee Hertig, "Without a Face: The Nineteenth-Century Bible Woman and Twentieth-Century Female Jeondosa," in *Gospel Bearers, Gender Barriers: Missionary Women in the Twentieth Century*, ed. Dana L. Robert, 185-199 (Maryknoll, N.Y.: Orbis Books, 2002), 193.

[9] Lee G. Bolman and Terrence E. Deal, *Reframing Organizations: Artistry, Choice, and Leadership* (San Francisco: Jossey-Bass Publishers, 1997), 164.

[10] Miraslov Volf, "Exclusion and Embrace: Theological Reflections in the Wake of Ethnic Cleansing," *Journal of Ecumenical Studies* 29/2 (Spring 1992): 235.

[11] Hengel, "Judaism and Hellenism Revisited," 17. The key leadership of the revolt stemmed from the assimilation of the upper class and concluded with the apostasy of a smaller splinter group led by Menelaus.

[12] Ibid., 19.

[13] James D. G. Dunn. *The Acts of the Apostles* (Valley Forge, Pa.: Trinity Press International, 1996), 82.

[14] Ellis Rivkin, *A Hidden Revolution* (Nashville, Tenn.: Abingdon, 1978), 211-212.

[15] Dunn, *The Acts of the Apostles*, 81.

[16] A. T. Kraabel, "Unity and Diversity among Diaspora Synagogues," in *Diaspora Jews and Judaism: Essays in Honor of, and in Dialogue with, A. Thomas Kraabel,* ed., J. Andrew Overman and Robert S. MacLennan (Atlanta: Scholars Press, 1992), 25.

[17] Edward DeBono, *Conflicts* (London: Harrap, 1985), 92.

[18] Bruce J. Malina and Jerome H. Neyrey, "Honor and Shame in Luke-Acts: Pivotal Values of the Mediterranean World," in *The Social World of Luke-Acts,* ed. Jerome H. Neyrey, 25-65 (Peabody, Mass.: Hendrickson Publishers, 1991), 47.

[19] Young Lee Hertig, *Cultural Tug of War: The Korean Immigrant Family and Church in Transition* (Nashville, Tenn.: Abingdon, 2001), 93.

[20] Douglas John Hall's *The End of Christendom and the Future of Christianity* is one book in a series entitled the Christian Mission and Modern Culture that gives a current critique of Christendom (Valley Forge, Pa.: Trinity Press International, 1997).

# 7

## *Dynamics in Hellenism and the Immigrant Congregation*

Acts 6:8—8:2

## Paul Hertig

I once escorted my students from a church-based graduate school of mission on an excursion into their neighborhood. As we walked outside of our classroom and rounded the corner, a neighbor spotted us and demanded, "What are you doing here?" My students turned their heads toward me, their professor. I gingerly replied to the man, "We are with the church around the corner, and we are observing our local community." The man immediately began to express his feelings in the tone of "let *me* tell *you* something":

> Your church people park in front of our driveways, and sometimes we have to call the police to get out of our own homes. If we have a birthday party in our home, our guests have to park eight blocks away because your cars take up every parking space. On Sundays you direct traffic on our streets. You walk right past us without saying hello. You drive expensive cars and wear three-piece suits. If you are so rich, why don't you buy some property and build a parking lot?

At this point some students became defensive, denying they are rich and claiming that the elderly people in their particular immigrant group could not speak English, making it difficult for them to say hello. The neighbor continued: "You don't give us eye contact when you walk past us, and you never bother to come to our community meetings. You don't care about this neighborhood!"

We thanked him for his helpful feedback and continued the walk, observing graffiti on apartment walls and homes that had been gutted with only hollow basements remaining. The neighborhood was deteriorating right before our eyes. Yet the church had responded by building high walls around its perimeters and posting a guard at the door. The guard treated anyone of a different ethnic group as suspect. This particular immigrant church built nationalistic walls to protect itself from uncertainty and change in a seemingly dangerous urban context far from its homeland.

## STEPHEN AND HELLENISM

Faced with a similar situation, Stephen spoke eloquently and powerfully in Jerusalem to certain nationalistic Jews who were dwelling in a Greco-Roman context that clashed with many of their Jewish spiritual and ethnic traditions (Acts 6:8-14). The Stephen narrative depicts a tension between two contrasting cultures: Hellenism and Judaism. Rodney Stark says that in exploring "the marginality of the Hellenized Jews, torn between two cultures, we may note how Christianity offered to retain much of the religious content of *both* cultures and to resolve the contradictions between them."[1] From the outset of both volumes the writer of Luke-Acts seeks to depict cultural continuity with Judaism, showing how Christianity is both its fulfillment and extension. However, Luke simultaneously validates aspects of the familiar world of Greco-Roman culture.[2]

In exploring tensions among Hellenists over issues of contextualization we examine the clash between Stephen, a Hellenist, and a hellenistic synagogue. Through Stephen's speech we explore tensions and changes within Hellenism and discover mission applications for first- and second-generation Christian immigrants.

The term *Hellenist* means "Greek speaker" (6:1). Since Greek was the international language of the first century, most people who lived in the major cities of Palestine spoke and understood Greek to some degree. Paul, for instance, refers to himself as a Hebrew, yet he spoke Greek (2 Cor 11:22; Phil 3:5). Thus Dunn surmises that the term *Hellenist* referred to those who spoke primarily Greek, in contrast to native Jews of Jerusalem, who spoke mainly Aramaic but who also could speak a limited amount of Greek.[3] Therefore, the contrast between "Hellenists" *(hellēnistōn)* and "Hebrews" *(hebraious)* in 6:1 indicates differences in language and thus cultural preferences. The Hellenists were Jews of the Diaspora with a particular hellenistic disposition who returned and became residents of Jerusalem. They were likely drawn to the Holy Land and the Temple and were more fervent for their Jewish heritage than their hellenistic culture.

The synagogue of the Freedmen (Acts 6:9) provides an example of such Jewish fervor. It was made up of Cyrenians, Alexandrians, Cicilians, and Asians (6:9).[4] These Hellenists engaged in a dispute with Stephen, another Hellenist. Unable to withstand the wisdom and the spirit of Stephen's words, they secretly instigated people to accuse him of blasphemy against Moses and God. Then they stirred up false witnesses, resulting in Stephen's trial before the Jewish council (6:10-15).

Stephen, possibly a youthful descendant of the Diaspora population, challenged the fervent traditions of the Diaspora community, making its members feel threatened in their very existence in Jerusalem.[5] Enthusiastic in his loyalty to Jesus, Stephen was viewed as disloyal to the Temple and may have "undercut their [the Hellenists'] whole reason for being in Jerusalem in the first place (6:13)."[6]

Such are Luke's broad brush strokes in setting the scene for Stephen's trial speech before the council. At first glance Stephen seems to be merely reciting Israelite history (7:2-50). But what is said and left unsaid in this broad sweep of history is crucial to the narrative and foreshadows the Lukan agenda. Stephen marked the starting point of the interaction between "the Jesus-tradition and the traditions of diaspora Judaism, the beginning of the process of translating and thus interpreting the gospel into hellenistic terms."[7] This put many Hellenists off guard. In his speech Stephen drew from the history of the beloved patriarchs, thus beginning with common ground, but then contrasted the traditionally Jewish and Christocentric interpretations. The contrast was harsh and the conflict inevitable, leading to the sudden martyrdom of Stephen.

The dynamics of change within Hellenism played a critical role in the conflict. Since Hellenism had been the international culture for three centuries, first-century Judaism had already been hellenized to varying degrees. Palestinian Judaism had a certain pluralistic quality. Craig C. Hill maintains that we must interpret Acts 6:1-8:3 without assuming that Judaism and Hellenism were opposites. It is not a matter of good Hellenists versus bad Hebrews.[8] In fact, as mentioned, in the story of Stephen we have a Hellenist versus other Hellenists. No individual fits his or her own culture uniformly, especially in a pluralistic environment. All cultures are in a constant state of flux. Stephen attempted to shift seemingly fixed, sacred traditions by reciting Israel's narratives for a new context. In reality, Israel's narratives come embodied in specific cultural contexts, and Stephen, recognizing this, contextualized the narratives for a hellenistic world. In the words of Lesslie Newbigin, "Something which is not expressible in any human language, which is not embodied in any human way of living, which is not located in any specific time or place, can have no impact on human affairs."[9]

The retelling of Israel's history through story is a process of reconsideration, refinement and redaction. Dunn describes Stephen's speech as "a somewhat unorthodox account of Israel's history."[10] It even counters Luke's typically positive assessment of the Temple (see Lk 1:8-23; 2:22-38, 41-52; 24:53; Acts 2:46-47; 3:1; 5:42). The wilderness emphasis of the speech is characterized by purity of worship, the congregation *(ekklesia),* and living oracles—all prior to the entrance into the promised land (7:38). This emphasis in retelling the story of the patriarchs was a prophetic challenge for Stephen's particular context.

Stephen sought to move Judaism from a static belief to a dynamic one, from the Temple to the world. He shattered the static walls of the Temple and opened the way for the contextualized mission of the church. The fusion of Hellenists and believers in Jesus was an explosive one. Stephen's contextualized approach, which no longer required the Temple, set off alarms for his listeners. "The larger community of Hellenists had invested too much in the Temple to allow any kind of radical criticism of the cult to go unchallenged."[11]

## CRUCIAL TURNS IN STEPHEN'S SPEECH
## AND THE IMMIGRANT CHURCH

Early in the narrative charges are brought against Stephen by the synagogue of the Freedmen (6:9). This synagogue was likely made up of former slaves or descendants of former slaves who were Jews from the Diaspora. Why would a group of hellenistic Jews be so intolerant of new ideas? Many Jews from the Diaspora were known to have Palestinian nationalistic zeal, because they had left their homes to migrate to Jerusalem. They showed a zealous interest in the holy city and the Temple.

I have witnessed a zeal for God's holy place in the United States as a youth pastor in an immigrant church. There I faced the imposition of a dress code on the second-generation youths by the first-generation leaders. Young people wearing shorts were refused admittance. The clear message to me, as the youth leader, was that these ex-gang members, who had been going through a life-changing program, were now being sent back to their gangs to continue perpetuating violence. The message given to the second generation was that the first generation's concept of spirituality was all about making oneself look holy in order to participate in God's holy place. In fact, the head pastor was so enthusiastic about this issue that he came to our youth service and explained the dress code. He said that Jesus wants us to look our best. He added, "I have special clothing, which I do not wear any other day. I wear it only for Sunday service." When a high school student said that he could not afford a suit and tie, the pastor replied, "If you can't afford it, come see me, and I will buy one for you."

The pastor was zealously proclaiming a form of spirituality from his homeland. That form lacked meaning to the second generation, which viewed such supposed holiness as unholy. In an advertisement of the church the pastor gave three reasons for attending his church: It had (1) a new sanctuary, (2) a new parking lot, and (3) air conditioning. Religious form had replaced religious meaning. The youth group felt a quenching of the Holy Spirit.

Stephen also felt such a quenching. At the conclusion of Stephen's speech, he says, "You are forever opposing the Holy Spirit, just as your ancestors used to do" (7:51). Thus Stephen distances himself from his audience and links the people with their disobedient ancestors. Stephen's speech, then, consists of two major sections: a selective rendering of Israelite history (7:2-50) and a parallel drawn between past and present conduct (7:51-53).[12]

## THE JOURNEYS OF LANDLESS ABRAHAM

Stephen begins his historical survey by emphasizing Abraham's call. Stephen implies from the outset of his speech that God directed the entire movement of Abraham (7:2-4). Stephen's emphatic statement that Abraham was not given any of the land as a heritage, not even one foot in length, indicates that Abraham never occupied the land of promise—and yet God was present. The promise of land for Israel was given to the "landless Abraham." Stephen reminds the audience that Abraham's descendants became sojourners in a strange land and were enslaved and mistreated for four hundred years. The point of God's promise to Abraham was not the land but the promise of a covenant that allowed worship of God anywhere, even by a community of resident aliens dwelling in a country belonging to others (7:6). Stephen is leading up to his own charge that the Temple is not being used for true worship of God.

## JOSEPH AND MOSES: ALIENS IN FOREIGN LANDS

Stephen then transitions from Abraham to Joseph through Abraham's descendants, the patriarchs (7:8). The patriarchs are introduced in a negative light: "The patriarchs, jealous of Joseph, sold him into Egypt; but God was with him" (7:9). Here two key themes of the speech surface: the rejection of God's servants by God's people, and the presence of God wherever those servants may be, even in the midst of adversity.[13] God "was with him [Joseph]" in Egypt "and rescued him from all his afflictions" (7:9-10). Joseph was thrust into the role of a public servant for the good of all people. God gave Joseph the wisdom to stand before Pharaoh, "who appointed him ruler over Egypt and over all his household" (7:10). Joseph distributed grain to a world in severe famine. This indicates God's universal and holistic perspective, widening Israel's understanding of the faithfulness of God. Furthermore, the Joseph story serves to warn that opposition to God's will or plan will fail.[14]

John B. Polhill observes that "all of God's special acts of deliverance in Stephen's historical sketch take place outside the borders of Israel."[15] For instance, Stephen's mention of Shechem, the burial place of Jacob and the fathers, is significant because it was beyond the holy land in the spurned region of the Samaritans (7:14-16).

In moving from Joseph to Moses, Stephen returns to the patriarchal theme of father Abraham and the promise made to him (7:17). The promise most likely refers to descendants and a new land for Abraham (7:5, 7). Abraham remained faithful to the promise, though he did not witness its fulfillment in his own lifetime. Might it be that Stephen viewed the promise as fulfilled in the wilderness, the place where the angel spoke to Moses and where living oracles were received (7:38)? Stephen passes over the story of Israel's life in the promised land, so it seems that he perceives the fulfillment of the promise in new terms, according to the promise of the Holy Spirit (7:51; cf. 2:38-39). Stephen next recalls the oppressive situation in Egypt before introducing the future deliverer, Moses (7:18-23). Stephen is building upon a theme of the presence of God outside of the holy land and among resident aliens.

## THE REJECTION OF MOSES
## AND GOD'S PRESENCE IN THE WILDERNESS

A bicultural theme surfaces early in the story of Moses. He is described as "abandoned" and then "adopted" by Pharaoh's daughter who "brought him up as her own son" (7:21). Stephen paints a positive picture of Moses in Egypt. He is "instructed in all the wisdom of the Egyptians" and "powerful in his words and deeds" (7:22). The bipolar opposites, his abandoned Israelite heritage and his adopted Egyptian heritage, come together in the progressing story line.

Stephen's description of Moses as a "resident alien" in Midian indicates that although Moses was forced to live as a foreigner in a strange land, God was present; Midian became the land of the revelation of God's holiness (7:29-33). This sojourner stood on "holy ground" beyond the borders of the holy land; God was thus bound to neither a particular place nor a certain people.[16] Stephen's detailed reference to God's demand for the removal of Moses' sandals on holy ground indicates that God's presence requires neither a temple nor a holy city; it can be experienced even far away in the wilderness or wherever God's revelation occurs (7:33).[17] In this way Stephen defended himself from the charge of "saying things against this holy place" (6:13).

Stephen portrays Moses as a mediator between two Israelites who are in a dispute (7:26). Moses' effort to "reconcile" them is not mentioned in the Exodus narrative. Thus Stephen is stressing the role of Moses as God's mediator. Stephen establishes Moses as God's chosen leader and shows the Israelites' rejection of him (7:25, 27, 39-43),[18] eventually tying it to the rejection of the Messiah (7:52).

In the phrase "It was this Moses whom they rejected" (7:35), the Greek verb *ernēsanto* is often translated "denied." By denying Moses or Jesus they are refusing them as rulers and deliverers sent by God (7:52). But the one whom they rejected as "ruler and judge" (7:27, 35) is the one "whom God now sent as both ruler and liberator" (7:35). Stephen stresses the recurring pattern of God sending leaders to Israel and the people of God rejecting them. But God is not hindered by those who reject the prophets sent to liberate them and continues to move ahead in compassion.

In first- and second-generation ministry there is often a tendency to reject those who take up the prophetic role in either generation. It is important for God's leaders not to overreact and blame one another for differing approaches, but rather to approach differences by seeking to understand, knowing that God operates with compassion, working within both approaches, not choosing one over the other. In the case of the immigrant church, it is not only the first generation that overreacts to differing traditions in the second. I remember a second-generation preacher who in the midst of his sermon began to mock the people of his homeland, saying they were "short" and "talk funny." Such an approach creates deeper rifts and makes reconciliation difficult. Mutual rejection is an unhealthy response to cultural clashes between generations.

Stephen's discourse next moves to God's signs and wonders performed in Egypt and the deliverance through the Red Sea (7:36). In the land of Sinai, God's presence was revealed to Moses; in Egypt, God's power was revealed to Israel and to Egypt.[19] The earlier descriptions of Moses' bicultural experiences now come to a climax, as the Hebrew-Egyptian performs signs and wonders among the Egyptians and leads the Hebrews out of bondage into the wilderness (7:36).

Even after the Exodus and the giving of the law, Moses is rejected again (7:39-43), a rejection that subsequently leads to idolatry. The molding of the golden calf has often been depicted in Jewish writings as "the national equivalent to the sin of Adam" and "archetypal of Gentile sins" linked with "unacceptable sexual license."[20] The golden calf, as "the work of their hands," echoes familiar terminology for idolatry (Dt 4:28; Ps 115:4; Jer 1:16). "The implication once again is that the people addressed by Stephen have more in common with the idolaters of Exodus 32 than with Moses the law-giver."[21]

The forming of the golden calf initiated a period of idolatrous worship during which Israel took pride in human works (7:48, 50).[22] Stephen indicates that in spite of God's presence in the wilderness, this era included a major fall into idolatry (7:38-43). However, Stephen also "idealized the wilderness period" and sought to return to the "relative purity" of the period before this apostasy (7:38, 44-46).[23] Thus, Stephen validated the spiritual traditions of the first-generation Hellenists by recalling times of purity, when God was worshiped, adored, and followed during the harsh wilderness experiences. Likewise, first- and second-generation immigrants can find common ground through sharing the narratives of their common heritage, remembering when God worked mightily, even in the midst of their suffering.

## THE TENSION BETWEEN OLD AND NEW
## IN HELLENISM

In the midst of the push and pull of Hellenists who sought to return to the past and those who sought a new future, Stephen opened up a new era of mission by a fresh and relevant interpretation of the law. In Dunn's words, *"Stephen speaks still as a Jew eager to live within the terms actually laid down in the scriptures of his people."*[24] In reciting the stories of the patriarchs, Stephen speaks positively about Moses and the law. True, Stephen's accusers claimed that he never ceased speaking against the holy place and the law, but Luke describes them as "false witnesses" (6:13). This sets the tone for Luke's portrayal of Stephen as one who is true to the law in a contextual, Hellenistic perspective. The new way was dependent on the old. Hans Küng and David Tracy point out that even in the midst of the most revolutionary changes in society, a fundamental continuity always remains.[25] In fact, the stimulus for the tension within the Hellenistic camps was their affinity.

## THE TABERNACLE AND THE TEMPLE

In the midst of the tension Stephen seeks common ground with the mobile Tabernacle, rather than the Temple, as the center of God's presence among the people of God in the wilderness. Stephen and those who were scattered in the wake of his martyrdom understood the "potentially universal reign and presence of God" that cut "across ethnic and social barriers."[26] Stephen's speech implies that the worship of God at the Temple in Jerusalem was only temporary:

God had appeared to the patriarchs in various lands, with the covenant first broached to Abraham in Mesopotamia and the law given to Moses in Sinai. The prophet had announced that no one could build a residence for God, but the present leaders insist on making it the central and exclusive ground of relationship to God.[27]

In other words, Acts 7:48 indicates that the erecting of the Temple was a deviation from the pattern of worship established by Moses.[28] Thus it is no surprise that the main charge against Stephen concerned the Temple (6:13-14; see also 6:11-12, 15; 7:54-60).

For Luke, Stephen is a representative of the holy congregation. Stephen's purity contrasts starkly with the impurity of the Temple defendants who put him on trial.[29] For Stephen, Temple worship was no longer essential for salvation. In answer to the false witnesses, Stephen charged his fellow Jews with making their Temple an idol rather than a place of worship. Stephen uses phrases such as "made with human hands" *(en tois ergois tōn cheirōn autōn)* for both the calf (7:41) and the Temple (7:48). This clearly links the idolatry in the wilderness to Temple worship. The ancestors had turned from God in the desert through the worship of a calf (7:41); later they built Solomon's Temple, even though God "does not dwell in houses made with human hands" (7:48).

Stephen supports his view that God does not live in a temple with the words of Isaiah, who explains that heaven is God's throne and the earth is God's footstool and therefore a human cannot contain the Lord in a house (7:49-50).[30] It is not merely the Temple that is opposed, but the idolatrous use and concept of the Temple.[31] God is everywhere, and Stephen's speech will ultimately lead to the scattering of the church everywhere (8:1).

Further, Stephen's speech implies that the Temple's existence is due to the rejection of Moses and the Mosaic pattern of worship given by God.[32] The mode of Tabernacle worship was rejected in the wilderness. Thus, Charles H. Talbert observes, in Stephen's speech "the entire survey of Israelite history is told as one of a dual rejection of Moses and of a changing of the customs he handed down (cf. 7:11, 14)."[33] This is an interesting paradox; Stephen in the midst of seeking *change*, does so through seeking *continuity* with Moses (7:35, 39, 44) and the law (7:38, 44). Newbigin has pointed out that authentic contextualization occurs through faithfulness to the scriptures alongside costly identification with people in concrete situations. In such cases, he says, the sovereign Spirit of God works in surprising ways.[34]

Indeed, Stephen metaphorically brought down the Temple walls by opening the way for mission beyond the holy place.[35] Stephen sought to transform the Temple from a narrow and confined "house" under human control to a community that submitted to the reign of God anywhere and at any time (7:49-51).[36]

We have thus far observed missiological implications in Stephen's descriptions of the mobility of Abraham and the congregation (7:2-4, 38), the revelation to Moses in Midian and Sinai, as well as the bicultural natures of Joseph and Moses. Missiological applications are found also in the aftermath of Stephen's martyrdom and in the scattering of the church as mission moved beyond the borders of Israel to Samaria, Antioch, and to the Gentiles (8:1-4; cf. 11:19-20).

## RESIDENT-ALIEN STATUS OF THE PATRIARCHS

Laying the foundation for this cross-cultural movement is Stephen's use of the phrase "resident alien" *(paroikos)*. From the time of Aristotle the Greek term used referred to "a resident alien living in a place not his or her home, having no civic rights, but enjoying the protection of the natives of that place."[37] Stephen uses this nuance in reference to Abraham's descendants as "resident aliens in a country belonging to others" (7:6) and to Moses, who "became a resident alien in the land of Midian" (7:29). In contrast, the Greek word translated "dwell," as in "the Most High does not dwell in houses made by human hands," does not have a temporary or alien quality (7:48). It means "to live, settle down, inhabit."[38] Thus David and Solomon could not confine God to a dwelling place, and neither should followers of God seek a settled life of permanence. The presence of God was embodied in the tent of testimony.[39] Therefore, the building of Solomon's Temple reflected a distorted understanding of God (7:47).

In the climax of his sermon Stephen weaves two themes together: the idolatrous perspective of the Temple and the rejection of Jesus.[40] Idolatry of the Temple is linked to the rejection of the Holy Spirit and failure to follow the Pentateuch (7:48-53). Dunn asserts that the appearance of the Holy Spirit and Christ during the climax of Stephen's speech in 7:51-52 reinforces "Luke's repeated emphasis that these two are the central features of the new Christian sect."[41] The new sect probably had traits similar to those of Stephen and the main characters of the speech—Abraham, Joseph, Moses, and Jesus (6:5, 8).[42]

Dunn believes that second- or third-generation Christianity viewed Stephen and the Hellenists as the origin of the parting between Christianity and "the predominant Temple-centered Judaism of the mid-first century."[43] Worship and the sacrificial system at the Temple eventually lost their meaning and ceased for Hellenist Christians. "The focus of their liturgical life was probably exclusively in the house churches, functioning as the Christian Hellenist equivalent or supplement to the synagogue of the Freedmen (6.9), where Greek alone was used."[44]

There is a parallel in this conflict over the Temple in Stephen's day and the sanctuary in the contemporary immigrant church. While I was engaged in second-generation ministry at an immigrant church in the United States, some of our gifted musicians put on an evangelistic concert in the youth chapel of the church. It just so happened that the first generation was having its own "revival" service in the main sanctuary of the church that same night. The head pastor sent his assistant pastor to the concert, just before it was to begin, demanding that I cancel the concert and send everyone to the service in the main sanctuary. This was an impossible request. We had a diverse audience at our event, many of whom did not know the language being used at the first-generation service. I refused to submit to the head pastor's demand. I was ostracized for not submitting to the will of the pastor and eventually had to resign from the church. The message was loud and clear: What goes on in the main sanctuary is a sacred event, while the contemporary worship style of the second generation is not acceptable. In reaction, what occurred in the main sanctuary became meaningless to the second generation.

## THE LIVING LAW

The issue of the law was a corollary to the Temple because the observance of the law related to Temple observances. The noteworthy aspect of the charge against Stephen is that he said "Jesus of Nazareth will destroy this place" (6:14). The charge affirms that the core of Stephen's message concerned Jesus. Furthermore, it affirms that a particular aspect of Jesus' teaching, the destruction of the Temple, was one of Stephen's key themes (7:47-48), which greatly offended this particular group of Hellenists.[45] However, Stephen deals with the Temple issue by reversing the charge against him and implying that the Temple had lost its proper spiritual function and was now an idol. While Stephen did not criticize the law, but rather declared that angels ordained it (7:53), his angelic qualities validated the law as the living words of God in the narrative.[46] Stephen referred to the law only in positive terms (7:8, 38) but claimed that his accusers were lawbreakers themselves (7:53).[47]

## THE RAMIFICATIONS OF STEPHEN'S MARTYRDOM

The tone and climax of Stephen's speech show that he knew that he was risking martyrdom. Yet the Spirit moved him, in contrast to his accusers, who resisted the Spirit (6:3, 5; 7:51). Stephen apparently sought to lead them to repentance without squandering words. However, his speech was cut short by their rage (7:54).[48]

By bearing false witness (Ex 20:16) that led to the killing of Stephen (Ex 20:13), his accusers violated the commandments they cherished—just as had been done at Jesus' death. Stephen had prophetically turned their accusation back on them as those who "received the law . . . but have not kept it" (7:53).[49] When disturbing the status quo, dissonance allows truth to emerge. Springs of energy that create turbulent interruption are paradoxically works of beauty. In this case Stephen initiated faith when reason closed its ears and wandered from truth, and it cost him his life.

Although the accusers put their fingers in their ears to avoid being consumed by God for listening to blasphemy,[50] Stephen's testimony was not wasted. He had a vision of Jesus standing at the right hand of God, prepared to receive him and to act on his behalf. Paul, eyewitness of the event, who watched Stephen's death with approval (8:1), would eventually complete Stephen's abruptly ended speech. Paul would initiate a worldwide mission movement, and his theology would eventually parallel Stephen's. On his missionary adventure in Athens, Paul says that the Lord of heaven and earth "does not live in shrines made by human hands, nor is he served by human hands" (17:24-25).

## THE JOURNEYS OF THE PEOPLE OF GOD

The expulsion from Jerusalem of those who were of one mind with Stephen opened the way for a new phase in Christian mission. "The God of glory" in 7:2 is an early indicator of the theme of God's sovereignty and presence, and also an inclusio with 7:55, in which Stephen saw the glory of God (7:55).[51] This sovereignty and presence shattered the confines of the Temple and the holy land, reminding the people of God that God was present in the midst of their journeys.

The speech of Stephen passes over the Canaan settlement and the subsequent monarchy and instead focuses on the purpose and presence of God among a sojourning people. Patriarchal faith was not anchored in a particular location but centered in mobility. The patriarchs and matriarchs did not need to return to the place of God's revelation in order to sustain their faith.[52] God accompanies the people of God in the midst of the journey. "They do not have to call a halt to the historical march in order to meet their God. Their God is on the road with them! They walk in God's presence as they journey."[53] Both first- and second-generation immigrants are also on a journey together, toward God and one another, guided by God's transforming presence through interaction with one another as they are thrust into mission in the world around them.

God did not send the covenant people on an escape from history; God encounters the people along the road as they forge ahead. God initiated their journey and accompanies them all along their way.[54] Luke, through the Stephen narrative, sought to move the people away from seeking stability in the holy land and seclusion in the Temple and into a dynamic, contextual journey into the world, empowered by the Holy Spirit.

## STEPHEN'S MESSAGE
## AND THE IMMIGRANT CHURCH

A possible generational split existed between the Hellenists whom Stephen confronted, who had returned from the Diaspora, and Stephen, who did not hold to the fixed traditions of some Hebraic Jews. Stephen's challenge of the old paradigm was viewed by some as overly confident and offensive.[55]

The immigrant church faces a similar kind of generation split. The first-generation Christians come from a strong spiritual heritage in the homeland and seek to transplant their spiritual roots firmly in American soil. Their common assumption is that the church site is a sacred escape from the world. This holy "Temple" is contrasted with the unholy neighboring community. The main mission of the church is to preserve that holiness represented by traditional forms. The second generation's response recalls Stephen's charge that his accusers are treating the Temple as an idol. By reciting the history of the patriarchs, Stephen sought to open their understanding of God to include God's presence with the people on a journey in the world rather than to continue to perceive God as contained in a holy place.

For this same paradigm shift to occur in the immigrant church, the leaders of the first generation must journey with God to the world of the second generation and begin building a bridge between the two groups. The second generation must do likewise.

In Switzerland there is a legend about a bridge that was built across the Rhine River between upper-class and lower-class communities. In this joint project the lower class built its half of the bridge with stone, while the upper class built its half with wood. If the peasants revolted, the logic went, then the upper class could burn down the bridge.[56]

This describes the present problem in the immigrant church. The first generation controls the power and often builds its half of the bridge with wood. It does not embrace the world view of the second generation and is ready to burn the bridge the moment the second generation challenges its rules of holiness. It is now time for the first generation to step out of its "sacred space" and build its half of stone, journeying with God across the bridge to discover the presence of God in the midst of the journey and even on the other side. The second generation, likewise, must participate in building the bridge of stone and journeying to the other side. As the two generations journey and build together, they will rediscover their public witness to the wider world and embrace their disgruntled neighbors.

## REFERENCES

[1] Rodney Stark, *The Rise of Christianity* (San Francisco: HarperCollins, 1997), 59.

[2] Ibid.

[3] James D. G. Dunn, *The Partings of the Ways: Between Christianity and Judaism and Their Significance for the Character of Christianity* (Valley Forge, Pa.: Trinity Press International, 1991), 61.

[4] Many Hellenists of the Diaspora who migrated to Jerusalem had an intense devotion to the Temple and to its activities; the leaders would have treated nonconformists with suspicion (6:13). Their loyalty—to the law and to the Jews over against Gentiles—may have been questioned simply because they were Hellenists. Their dependence on the Greek language likely restricted them from full participation in the Temple activities. Therefore, it is no wonder that Greek-speaking synagogues, such as the one mentioned in 6:9, were set up for the Hellenist Jews of the Diaspora. This allowed the use of Greek in the liturgy (and possibly other hellenistic elements) (ibid., 62).

[5] James D. G. Dunn, *The Acts of the Apostles* (Valley Forge, Pa.: Trinity Press International, 1996), 86.

[6] Dunn, *The Partings of the Ways,* 64.

[7] Ibid., 68.

[8] Craig C. Hill, "Hellenists, Hellenistic and Hellenistic-Jewish Christianity," in *Dictionary of the Later New Testament and Its Developments,* ed. Ralph P. Martin and Peter H. Davids (Downers Grove, Ill.: InterVarsity Press, 1997), 465.

[9] Lesslie Newbigin, *The Gospel in a Pluralist Society* (Grand Rapids, Mich.: Eerdmans, 1989), 144-145.

[10] Dunn, *The Acts of the Apostles,* 92; idem, *The Partings of the Ways,* 66.

[11] Dunn, *The Partings of the Ways,* 64. Furthermore, Dunn says, since the Jews of Jerusalem, particularly the leaders of the hierocracy, depended on the Temple economi-

cally, politically, and spiritually, they could not be passive in such a situation. The term *Hebrews* as representative of Jews who were believers in Jesus indicates who is in control (6:1) (ibid., 64).

[12] Charles H. Talbert, *Reading Acts: A Literary and Theological Commentary on the Acts of the Apostles* (New York: Crossroad, 1997), 77.

[13] The first theme is found in Acts 7:25, 27, 35-36, 39-43, 51-53; the second in Acts 7:2-4, 9-10, 30-34, 38, 44-45, 48-50.

[14] Ben Witherington III, *The Acts of the Apostles: A Socio-Rhetorical Commentary* (Grand Rapids, Mich.: Eerdmans, 1998), 267.

[15] John B. Polhill, *Acts: The New American Commentary,* vol. 26 (Nashville, Tenn.: Broadman Press, 1992), 192.

[16] Ibid., 197.

[17] Gerhard A. Krodel, *Acts: Augsburg Commentary on the New Testament* (Minneapolis: Augsburg Publishing House, 1986), 146.

[18] Polhill, *Acts,* 196.

[19] Howard Clark Kee, *Good News to the Ends of the Earth: The Theology of Acts* (Valley Forge, Pa.: Trinity Press International, 1990), 45.

[20] Dunn, *The Acts of the Apostles,* 95. In 7:38-39 Stephen claims that they "have been unfaithful to their own greatest hero" (ibid.).

[21] Ibid.

[22] The reference to God giving them over to worship the host of heaven indicates that God responds to idolatry by giving people to its enslavement (7:42). Furthermore, God sent an idolatrous people to captivity beyond Babylon (Krodel, *Acts,* 147-148). Thus God is free to be passionately involved in the community (7:34) and free to put it at a distance (7:42).

[23] Dunn, *The Partings of the Ways,* 69.

[24] Ibid.

[25] Hans Küng and David Tracy, eds., *Paradigm Change in Theology* (New York: Crossroad, 1989), 29-30.

[26] Kee, *Good News to the Ends of the Earth,* 45.

[27] Ibid., 46.

[28] Talbert, *Reading Acts,* 76.

[29] For a similar view, see Dunn, *The Acts of the Apostles,* 85.

[30] Thomas J. Lane summarizes: "Stephen is not against the Temple but against the idea that God dwells in something made by humans" (Thomas J. Lane, *Luke and the Gentile Mission: Gospel Anticipates Acts* [New York: Peter Lang, 1996], 199).

[31] Krodel, *Acts,* 150.

[32] Talbert, *Reading Acts,* 78.

[33] Ibid.

[34] Newbigin, *The Gospel in a Pluralist Society,* 154.

[35] Stephen did not reject the Temple but sought to transform its purpose and use. Luke uses Stephen's speech to declare that the true purpose of the gathered congregation is prayer and salvation (Lk 19:46), which is linked to Gentile mission (Lk 19:46; Is 56:7).

[36] The Temple had become the object of worship rather than a place of worship. Stephen argues that the Temple was not being used for pure worship of God but as "a hindrance to spiritual religion." (F. F. Bruce, *The Acts of the Apostles: The Greek Text with Introduction and Commentary,* 3d ed. [Grand Rapids, Mich.: Eerdmans, 1990], 190). Furthermore, for Luke, the destruction of the Temple, which probably occurred before the writing of Acts, was no hindrance to salvation (Lane, *Luke and the Gentile Mission,* 200).

[37] Frank R. VanDevelder, *The Biblical Journey of Faith: The Road of the Sojourner* (Philadelphia: Fortress Press, 1988), 86.

[38] Ibid.

[39] Dunn, *The Acts of the Apostles*, 90.

[40] Ibid., 91.

[41] Ibid.

[42] Witherington, *The Acts of the Apostles*, 267.

[43] Dunn, *The Partings of the Ways*, 68.

[44] Ibid.

[45] Dunn, *The Acts of the Apostles*, 87.

[46] Polhill, *Acts*, 200.

[47] Dunn hypothesizes that Stephen drew from a feature of Jesus' teaching that foresaw "the replacement of the Temple by the community gathered around the twelve" (Dunn, *The Acts of the Apostles*, 88).

[48] "Ultimately his speech was not a defense at all but a witness" (Polhill, *Acts*, 207).

[49] Talbert, *Reading Acts*, 79.

[50] Polhill, *Acts*, 208.

[51] Dunn, *The Acts of the Apostles*, 92.

[52] VanDevelder, *The Biblical Journey of Faith*, 32. God's words to Jacob, "Know that I am with you and will keep you wherever you go" (Gn 28:15) indicate the continual presence of God in the midst of the journey.

[53] Ibid., 50. Mobility helped shape the character and faith of patriarchal religion. "But that mobility did not create the people's faith! Not everyone who moved around and lived in tents in the second millennium B.C.E. in the Fertile Crescent had a faith like the faith of Abraham and Sarah, Isaac and Rebekah, Jacob, Leah, and Rachel" (ibid., 36).

[54] Ibid., 50.

[55] Dunn, *The Partings of the Ways*, 64.

[56] Thomas D. Minton, "In the Shadow of Cathedrals," *Missiology* 26/1 (January 1998): 67-85. The story of the bridge has been simplified. For the specific details, see ibid., 76.

# 8

## *Preaching for Mission:*
## *Ancient Speeches and Postmodern Sermons*

Acts 7:2–53; 13:16–41; 14:15–17

### Mary E. Hinkle

Nearly one-third of the Book of Acts is written in the form of speeches. Regularly throughout the book, perhaps as many as thirty-six times in twenty-eight chapters, the action stops and talking starts.[1] Some of us, especially during the longer speeches, may be tempted to reach for the remote. Who can listen to all those talking heads? Would it not be better to have more narratives of the apostles' ministry and not so many monologues from them? The stories draw us into the world of the first Christians. We are amused by the magician who offers to pay for a dose of the Holy Spirit, then maybe a little frightened when we hear Peter rebuke him, "May your silver perish with you, because you thought you could obtain God's gift with money!" (8:20). We blink at the flash of light that blinds Saul on his way to Damascus (9:3). We recoil as Paul shakes the viper off his hand, watching with others around the fire to see whether he will swell up and die (28:3-5). The stories draw us in. Can the speeches do the same?

I am interested in this question both because I am a preacher and because I teach people who will preach. Can sermons draw us into their world the way stories do? Sermons and speeches have at least one thing in common: When either of them occurs, one person is talking for a long time. The medium has the potential to be monotonous and dreary. In an essay on preaching Barbara Brown Taylor writes: "Much of our direct communication from the pulpit is like a travelogue to someplace our listeners have never been. We may do a masterful job of telling them about the various points of interest in God's country—the architecture, the museums, the geography, the politics—but when it is all over and the lights go up, they have been on our trip, not their own."[2] Most people who listen to sermons know the experience to which Taylor refers. We can hear that the preacher has done some homework, for which we are grateful, but the sermon is still dull. What is more, those of us who preach are as apprehensive at the prospect of delivering boring sermons as our hearers are at the prospect of having to endure them. In the first preaching class I took as a seminarian, the professor said to the preacher after a practice sermon, "Can you get us out of Palestine any sooner?" Preachers know that if the sermon is dull, we will lose our audience. What is the answer to such a problem?

In some quarters the answer has been to cut back on the homework. Preachers study biblical texts only long enough to extract a theme from them or a "moral of the story." Having found something useful in a biblical text, the preacher goes on to construct a sermon that gives voice to the text's theme or moral for the lives of contemporary hearers. Such communication is thankfully no longer as dull as a slide show of someone else's vacation, but in this scenario, the Bible plays the role of a curiously written self-help book and the preacher acts as the one who can break its code. Describing this approach to the Bible, Beverly Roberts Gaventa observes: "Self-help books appeal to the individual's hope that he or she can achieve success or happiness *if only* a particular problem is solved or a goal achieved. . . . Such a claim is utterly foreign to Scripture."[3]

As a preacher, I seek to resist turning the Bible into life's instruction book, and I avoid travelogue. Yet these two mistaken preaching moves are not just the result of a lack of expertise or inadequate preparation. Self-help sermons and travelogue are inspired in part by two values that I want to retain.

First, I value the acknowledgment that the world of the scriptures is different from the world in which I live. I want to take seriously that before the Bible was the book of my faith community, its writings existed for other communities and individuals. Christians are part of a movement that has occurred in history, not just in story. I do not want to offer a monologue on someone else's trip when I preach. My teacher may have been right to encourage us to "get out of Palestine" as we proclaim texts in that setting. Even so, I do not want to dispense with Palestine, or treat it as if it were just a generic backdrop for a universal truth. The Christian confession that "the Word became flesh and lived among us" (Jn 1:14) requires that we take time, place, and event—that is, history—seriously as the arena of God's self-revelation.

Second, I want my preaching to speak to people's lives. Gaventa is surely right when she says that the biblical writers have little in common with the aims of those who produce self-help literature. Yet one thing all these writers do have in common—and something I and other preachers share with them all—is the desire to engage an audience. To view a biblical text as merely a bit of wisdom for a happier life is surely to miss much of the meaning of that text. Nonetheless, the desire to connect with one's hearers and to speak in a relevant way to them is good. We cannot persuade our listeners of anything if we have not first engaged them.

For their part, the speeches in Acts are neither travelogue nor self-help material, and the alternative they offer to these two contemporary sermon forms is worth investigating. If we resist the temptation to "fast forward" through the speeches in the Book of Acts, we see that the speeches, like the stories that surround them, construct a narrative world and invite hearers to find their true life within that world. The speeches, no less than the stories, reach out to listeners and draw them into a reality that was previously unknown to them. My goal in this chapter is to show how the speeches do this and to discuss implications of their method for preaching in a postmodern context.

Before we turn to the speeches themselves, two historical aspects require comment. First, in Acts we do not have the apostles' own record of their speeches; we have Luke's account of what various apostles said. Acts tells the story of events that occurred between about A.D. 30 and about A.D. 60. Luke probably wrote Acts sometime around A.D. 85-90. The speeches tell us as much about Luke's interpretation of a good sermon as they tell us about what was actually said.[4] The second historical aspect is the use of the Old Testament in the speeches of Acts. Perhaps it goes without saying that reference to the Old Testament would not have made sense to Jesus, the first apostles, Luke, or the first readers of Acts. The phrase would only come to have meaning after a group of writings known as the New Testament had been collected, and of course, New Testament writings were still being produced. Instead of speaking of the Old Testament in Acts, I speak in this essay of biblical material or biblical themes in Acts, by which I mean Jewish biblical material known to modern Christians as the Old Testament.[5]

Since it is not possible within the space of a few pages to review elements of all the speeches in Acts, I have chosen to focus on a small but varied collection:

- Stephen to the Sanhedrin Council in Jerusalem (7:2-53);
- Paul to those at the synagogue in Pisidian Antioch (13:16-41); and
- Paul and Barnabas to those in Lystra who mistake them for gods (14:15-17).

Together these speeches provide a window on various aspects of preaching in Acts. The first speech is to a group of Jewish leaders before whom Stephen is offering a defense. His audience is knowledgeable about much of Stephen's subject matter but hostile to his message. The second speech is delivered in the context of sabbath worship and study. Again, the audience and the speaker have a great deal of background in common. This time, however, the audience is receptive to what Paul has to say. Both of these speeches quote biblical material directly.

By contrast, the third speech on the list is delivered to an audience unfamiliar with the God of Israel and Israel's scriptures. The audience is favorably disposed toward the apostles but for the wrong reasons, having mistaken them for gods. The third speech does not cite Israel's scripture directly, yet alludes to biblical themes. This small collection of speeches will allow us to look at how preaching in Acts changes or remains the same while elements of the preaching event change. These elements include the speaker, the setting, the audience, and the audience's familiarity with Israel's scripture.

Although it is common to divide the Book of Acts into stories and speeches, the distinction is misleading because the speeches of Acts also tell stories.

Writers contributing to the present collection of essays have set out to read Acts in and for our context. When the apostles deliver speeches in the Book of Acts, they are doing the same thing. In the apostles' case the ancient narratives come from Israel's scripture and intersect with their present-day experience of Jesus and people's reaction to news about Jesus. The speakers in Acts tell the story of God's interaction with Israel and with God's creation as a whole, and of the life of Jesus, and they do so to incorporate their hearers into this story. These two objectives deserve close examination: (1) What story are the speeches telling? (2) How is the story told in such a way as to include the audience?

## STEPHEN'S SPEECH TO THE SANHEDRIN
## IN JERUSALEM (7:2-53)

Stephen's speech to the Sanhedrin may offer the clearest example of a disciple's work to tell ancient stories in a new context. Stephen does not set out to preach in a synagogue or before the council of the high priest. Yet as a result of the signs and wonders he performs and the words he speaks, his adversaries stir up enough trouble that the deacon is brought before the council and interrogated by the high priest. The charge brought by the false witnesses is that "this man never stops saying things against this holy place and the law" (Acts 6:13). The high priest asks Stephen, "Are these things so?" (7:1), and Stephen answers with the longest speech in the Book of Acts.

Stephen builds his defense out of stories from the Torah, the very law he is accused of speaking against. His speech quotes scripture at least fourteen times, with most of the quotations coming from Genesis and Exodus, along with one from Deuteronomy and two from the prophets (Am 5:25-27; Is 66:1, 2). At points, Stephen's rehearsal of Israel's history combines material from various parts of the Bible. For instance, in Acts 7:6-7 Stephen fuses a promise spoken to Abraham with one given to Moses. In Genesis, God speaks to Abraham about the slavery that will befall his offspring, saying, "I will bring judgment on the nation that they serve, and afterward they shall come out with great possessions" (15:14). When God calls Moses, he confirms this call with a prediction of worship: "When you have brought the people out of Egypt, you shall worship God on this mountain" (Ex 3:12b). Speaking of God's promise to Abraham, Stephen puts together part of Genesis 15:14 with the reference to worship made in Exodus 3:12. Instead of talking about the Israelites leaving Egypt with great possessions, Stephen combines liberation ("they shall come out") and worship ("and worship me in this place") in the same sentence (Acts 7:7).

### *What Story Does Stephen's Speech Tell?*

In spite of a few curiosities like this scripture combination in Stephen's account of Israel's history, the deacon is not as interested in rewriting Israel's history as he is in highlighting parts of that history that help explain events unfolding in the lives of his audience. Stephen's storytelling focuses on the conclusion that (1) God is currently accomplishing the deliverance of God's people, just as God has done throughout history, and (2) God's people are currently rejecting God's agent of deliverance, just as they have done throughout history.

The stories of deliverance foreshadow this conclusion as Stephen speaks of God's call to Abraham and his nation's escape from Egypt after centuries of mistreatment. In this promise, made centuries before Israel would be subjected to slavery, God vows judgment upon Egypt and rescue for the Israelites. Moving through Israel's history, Stephen tells stories of deliverance related to Joseph: First "God rescued him from all his afflictions," then God made Joseph an agent of rescue for his brothers, even though their jealousy was the cause of his trouble in the first place (7:9-10). Moving on, Stephen speaks of Moses (7:17ff.) and God's announcement to Moses that, "I have surely seen the mistreatment of my people who are in Egypt and have heard their groaning, and I have come down to rescue them" (Acts 7:34; cf. Ex 3:7-8). This statement corresponds to Stephen's first point: God means to liberate God's people.

Stephen continues explaining that God's people have traditionally not recognized a liberator when one has been presented to them. This statement is the second point of Stephen's speech. Stephen tells the story of Moses and the Israelites in order to point out the people's failure. Stephen says that Moses "supposed that his kinsfolk would understand that God through him was rescuing them, but they did not understand" (Acts 7:25). As the story unfolds in Exodus, Moses tries to stop two kinsfolk from fighting well before he has any understanding of his own call and before he knows anything of God's plan for rescue (cf. Ex 3:12-13). Stephen gets ahead of his own story here, but he does so in order to emphasize the point that God's deliverance has traditionally gone unrecognized by God's people. Eventually, Moses learns what he is to do, yet the response of his people is the same: The people as a whole reject Moses' attempt to lead them through the wilderness, just as his two kinsfolk had rejected his attempt to break up their fight. Stephen reports that the people rejected Moses, even though God had sent him "as both ruler and liberator" (7:35). Again, "Our ancestors were unwilling to obey him; instead, they pushed him aside, and in their hearts they turned back to Egypt" (7:39). Finally, the people's rejection of Moses results in a rejection of God. The Israelites begin to worship a golden calf rather than the God whose law Moses had revealed to them. If the Jewish people listening to Stephen believed that God dwelt in human houses, even one as grand as the Temple that Stephen is accused of speaking against, they are making the same mistake that the Israelites made when they turned from Moses and "reveled in the works of their hands" (7:41).

This section of the speech is Stephen's rehearsal of Israel's history: God sends rescuers. The people reject them, and in rejecting them, they finally reject God. Their worship becomes idolatry.

### How Does Stephen's Speech Include His Hearers?

Stephen might have remained alive if his speech had maintained a safe distance between the past, as narrated in scripture, and the present, as lived by his audience. However, he is not content to leave the story in the past.

Stephen makes it clear from the start that his hearers belong in the story he is telling. One of the ways he does this is to use first-person plural forms throughout the speech. His defense is a rehearsal of Israel's history, but that history belongs also to Stephen and his hearers. "Our ancestors" Stephen says, acted out this story:

- "The God of glory appeared to *our ancestor* Abraham." (7:2)
- *"Our ancestors* could find no food. . . . He [Jacob] sent *our ancestors* there [to Egypt] on their first visit." (7:11-12)
- "He himself died there as well as *our ancestors*." (7:15)
- *"Our people* in Egypt increased and multiplied." (7:17)
- A new king "dealt craftily with *our race* and forced *our ancestors* to abandon their infants." (7:19)
- "The angel . . . spoke to him [Moses] at Mount Sinai, and with *our ancestors;* and he received living oracles to give to us. *Our ancestors* were unwilling to obey him." (7:38-39)
- *"Our ancestors* had the tent of testimony in the wilderness. . . . *Our ancestors* in turn brought it in with Joshua when they dispossessed the nations that God drove out before *our ancestors. "* (7:44-45) (italics added)

The first-person plural has the effect of connecting the speaker and hearers with each other and with those whose story Stephen is telling. It is as if he were saying, "These are our people; this is where we come from and how people like us behave."

Stephen also draws his hearers into the story by mingling references to "now" with references to events in the past. At the beginning of his speech Stephen describes the land God called Abraham to move to as "this country in which you are *now* living" (7:4, italics added). At the end of his speech, Stephen tells his listeners that their ancestors "killed those who foretold the coming of the Righteous One, and *now* you have become his betrayers and murderers" (7:52, italics added). Stephen is closing the distance between "then" and "now."

By incorporating direct address into his speech, Stephen further encourages the hearers to find themselves in the story. As the speech ends, first-person plural gives way to second-person plural. The people to whom Stephen refers are no longer "our ancestors," but "your ancestors" (see 7:51-52). The focus gets even more direct as Stephen accuses the audience: "You are forever opposing the Holy Spirit, just as your ancestors used to do" (7:51). Finally, the distance between "then" and "now" collapses altogether as Stephen concludes, "You are the ones that received the law as ordained by angels, and yet you have not kept it" (7:53). It is strange that Stephen does not say something here like "Your ancestors received the law as ordained by the angels, and yet you have not kept it." Rather, he says "You are the ones." Were the members of the Sanhedrin at Sinai when Moses appeared with the law? Did they receive the law yet not keep it? As strange as it may sound to our ears, Stephen locates his hearers simultaneously in the past and in the present.

The narrative of Acts that follows Stephen's speech tragically witnesses to the truth of his words. The people lived out the story that their preacher had told about them and thereby confirmed the truth of the story. Without giving Stephen a formal trial or sentencing, they drag him outside the city wall and pummel him with rocks until he dies; in so doing, they mark themselves as those who rejected a messenger of God and failed to keep God's law. This dynamic of the narrative confirming the speech occurs throughout Acts, thankfully not always with such tragic results.

## PAUL'S SPEECH TO THE SYNAGOGUE
## IN PISIDIAN ANTIOCH (13:16-41)

Like Stephen's speech to the members of the Sanhedrin, Paul's speech in Antioch of Pisidia is delivered to people familiar with the story of God's interaction with his people. The setting of this speech is the synagogue. Paul and Barnabas have just begun their mission work and on the Sabbath they visit the synagogue in Antioch of Pisidia. When they are invited by officials of the synagogue to speak, Paul offers the first of his recorded speeches in Acts. As Stephen had done earlier, Paul begins by summarizing Israel's history and then speaks about what God is doing in the lives of the audience.

### What Story Does Paul's Speech Tell?

With the broadest of brush strokes, Paul sketches Israel's history up to the time of King David. In the space of a few lines he covers centuries of events. Paul mentions God's election of "our ancestors," and God's actions to make them great in Egypt, to free them from slavery, to "put up with them in the wilderness," to give them the land, to appoint judges for them, and eventually to give them kings.

When Paul starts speaking of King David, the history lesson leads directly into a discussion of current events. "Of this man's posterity, God has brought to Israel a Savior, Jesus, as he promised" (13:23). Paul describes the work of John the Baptist[6] and then addresses his audience directly: "My brothers, you descendants of Abraham's family, and others who fear God, to us the message of this salvation has been sent" (13:26). The message has come both from those who saw Jesus alive after his crucifixion and from scripture, which itself spells out God's intention to fulfill promises made long ago to David. The rest of Paul's speech is a reading of scripture aimed at (1) demonstrating how God in Jesus is fulfilling what God promised long before, and (2) coaching his listeners about how they should respond to the news that he proclaims and scripture confirms.

First, Paul pulls together texts from Psalms with one from Isaiah that speaks about promises made to David. All three texts are about Jesus. Jesus, the posterity of David, is shown to be the Son of God (13:33; cf. Ps 2:7; Lk 3:22) through the words David speaks. Also, in Psalm 16:10 ("You will not let your

Holy One experience corruption" [Acts 13:35]), David's words come true when God raised Jesus from the dead.[7] A word from Isaiah, originally spoken by God to all Israel, supports applying these texts, which had traditionally been addressed to David, to Jesus. In Isaiah 55:3 God promised that Israel would be the recipient of the divine faithfulness promised to David. "I will give you the holy promises made to David" (Acts 13:34), God says to the returning exiles. In the synagogue in Antioch Paul spoke Yahweh's word according to the prophet Isaiah to imply that God had given David's promises to Jesus. By raising Jesus from the dead, God has kept the "no corruption" promise given by David centuries before.[8]

Scripture bears witness to what God has done by raising Jesus from the dead, and it also explains the rejection that led to Jesus' death. In his synagogue sermon Paul explains that the "residents of Jerusalem and their leaders did not recognize him [Jesus] or understand the words of the prophets that are read every Sabbath" (13:27). There is something ironic about this observation. The prophets had spoken of the rejection of God's Anointed, and those in Jerusalem listened to the words of the prophets each Sabbath, just like the Jews and Gentile God-fearers listening to Paul's speech. Nonetheless, those in Jerusalem did not know what they were doing (cf. Lk 23:34; Acts 7:60). It is almost as if their eyes were kept from recognizing him (cf. Lk 24:16). They failed to understand the exposure to their own scriptures and so became agents through which the scriptures were fulfilled.[9]

### How Does Paul's Speech Include His Hearers?

Will Paul's audience unwittingly fulfill scripture too? Remember Stephen's techniques for placing his hearers within the story: (1) the use of first-person plural forms, (2) the blending of events from the past with current events, and (3) the use of direct address. Paul uses these features also but produces a different result.

Paul makes it clear that the events of Israel's history and the contemporary events surrounding the life of Jesus have been accomplished for the benefit of those who are listening to him: "What God promised to our ancestors he has fulfilled for us, their children, by raising Jesus" (Acts 13:32-33). Paul does not understand himself to be proclaiming a new story to his hearers but rather a new chapter in the story they already know and participate in, the story of God's activity in Israel's history. The people themselves will receive the fulfillment of promises made to David. Just as Jesus received what was promised to David and did not experience corruption as a result of his death, so also those who believe in him will receive freedom from the corruption of sin.[10]

Luke reports that it was after the reading of the law and the prophets on the Sabbath that Paul was invited to speak (13:15). In his speech Paul highlights the fact that those in Jerusalem heard the prophets every Sabbath, just as his audience in Antioch did. The people listening "now" and those acting "then" are alike in this respect. Yet Paul does not completely identify his hearers with one group of characters in his story. The story, and the role in it that Paul's audience will play, is open-ended. In fact, the story is so open-ended that the people listening to Paul apparently have a chance to keep another word of the prophets from coming true. "Beware, therefore, that what the prophets said does not happen to you," Paul warns, and then points the people to the prophet Habakkuk, who tells of God doing something the people will not be able to believe.[11] Paul does not say that this is the truth about his hearers, that they will never believe. Rather, he says, "Beware, therefore, that what the prophets said does not happen to you" (13:40).

The story that follows Paul's speech proves that not everyone who listens to him in the synagogue can be grouped with those who reject God's will and messengers. Sometimes commentators regard the apostle's synagogue visits in Acts as little more than a literary device meant to communicate Israel's continued rejection of its Messiah and to justify expanding the mission to include the Gentiles. In this line of thinking Paul goes to the synagogue, is rejected by his kinsfolk, and then proceeds to preach to Gentiles (13:46), as if preaching to the Gentiles would not have occurred to any of the apostles if Diaspora Jews had been more receptive to the gospel. Such a view is simplistic and distorted. Luke's account of life in the early church, and of apostolic preaching and its results, is not so neatly divided along ethnic lines. In addition to stories of Jewish resistance to the gospel and Gentile acceptance of it, Acts includes stories of Jews who come to believe and follow the Way and stories of Gentiles who hear the good news but do not believe or follow.

Paul closed his speech in the synagogue, as noted above, by saying, "Beware, therefore, that what the prophets said does not happen to you" (13:40). The audience received his words favorably and asked Paul and Barnabas to speak again the following week. While there were some Jews who did stir up opposition (13:45), "many Jews and devout converts to Judaism followed Paul and Barnabas" (13:43). This latter group comprises both Jews and Gentiles about whom the statement "You will never believe, even if someone tells you" (13:41) is not true.

## THE SPEECH OF PAUL AND BARNABAS
## TO THE GENTILES AT LYSTRA (14:15-17)

The third speech is much briefer than the other two and delivered to a completely different audience. Instead of hostility from the audience (as on the occasion of Stephen's trial) or a polite invitation to speak (as on the occasion of Paul's visit to the synagogue in Pisidian Antioch), in this speech we have adoration for the apostles, adoration so zealous that it sends the apostles into a panic that they will be the occasion for idolatry. When a priest of Zeus prepared to offer a sacrifice to Paul and Barnabas after Paul performed a miraculous healing, the apostles ran into the crowd, shouting:

"Friends, why are you doing this? We are mortals just like you, and we bring you good news, that you should turn from these worthless things to the living God, who made the heaven and the earth and the sea and all that is in them. In past generations he allowed all the nations to follow their own ways; yet he has not left himself without a witness in doing good—giving you rains from heaven and fruitful seasons, and filling you with food and your hearts with joy." (14:15-17)

### What Story Does the Speech of Paul and Barnabas Tell?

Paul and Barnabas proclaim the Hebrew God without using the name of the God of Israel, even though they use Jewish biblical phrases and themes.[12] The apostles do not begin with God's call to Abraham or linger over stories about the patriarchs, Moses, and David; instead they begin with creation and God's role in it. In contrast to blocks of wood or stone that serve as idols, God is living and is the Creator of all that is.

The apostles have not tossed out their tradition simply because they are speaking to people unfamiliar with it. In fact, the tradition is exactly where the apostles turn for help as they run into the streets to stop people from offering sacrifices to them. When Paul and Barnabas speak of turning from idols to serve the living God, they are echoing the psalms and the prophets. For example, Psalm 96 contrasts the idols of the peoples with the Lord, "who made the heavens." And the prophet Jeremiah brings together elements that are also combined in this speech: (1) idols are nothing but wood or metal; (2) God is creator of all; and (3) God is living (cf. Jer 10:6-17). Hence a speech may be sensitive to a new mission context and still be part of an old, old story.

### How Does the Speech of Paul and Barnabas Include Their Hearers?

Paul and Barnabas do not say to the residents of Lystra, "Please don't offer sacrifices to us because our religion does not allow it." Such words might have forestalled sacrificing in the streets by inspiring the residents of Lystra to respect the difference between themselves and these two wonderworkers in their midst; however, it would not have joined the apostles and pagans in a common story. Thus the apostles do not say, "Please do not do this because our belief is different from yours." They say, "We are mortals just like you," and then they go on to announce that the God they know belongs to the Lycaonians also.

Paul and Barnabas argue that their story is the Lycaonians' story too, even if it sounds at first like new information to them. "We bring you good news," the apostles say, "that you should turn from these worthless things to the living God" (14:15). Like the other speeches we have looked at, this speech uses direct address to draw the hearers into its story. Also like the other speeches, this one provides an interpretive frame for the hearers' experience directly from Israel's scripture. It is as if the apostles are saying that whether those listening to them realize it or not, Israel's scriptures are telling the truth about them. Paul and Barnabas point to the experience of their hearers (fruitful seasons, enough food, joy in their hearts) and weave that experience into the larger story of God's care for all that God has made.

As in the other speeches in Acts, we see that the narrative following the speech demonstrated the truth of the speech. In the case of this interaction with the residents of Lystra, the speech restrains the people from offering sacrifices to Paul and Barnabas. At least for the moment, those who hear the apostles turn from the worship of idols.

## ANCIENT SPEECHES AND POSTMODERN SERMONS

We have seen that preaching in Acts is neither a dusty tour through Israel's past nor a tidy compendium of self-help for the audience. Instead, speakers in Acts tell the story of God's interaction with Israel, including God's vindication of Jesus, to provide hearers with a context, or interpretive frame, for their current experiences. Stephen places his listeners in the tradition of those who fail to recognize God at work in the world. Paul places his synagogue audience among those to whom God is keeping the promises made to David. Paul and Barnabas position their pagan adorers among those who know God not by name but by God's benefits. In every case the story of scripture expands to "absorb the universe."[13] The scriptural narrative does not merely inform or advise hearers. Instead, the scriptural story tells the truth about God and the people to whom it is addressed.

What does all this mean for contemporary preachers? Are the speeches in Acts exemplary for postmodern preaching? The speeches are different enough from one another that they resist attempts to develop from them a template for apostolic preaching, either in terms of form or content.[14] Yet they do shape our imagination for the task of preaching. In the Book of Acts to preach is (1) to tell the story of God's interaction with creation, with Israel and with Jesus, (2) so that hearers may experience in themselves their world in terms of that story and (3) respond in ways that bear witness to the promises God has fulfilled for them in Jesus.

### *Preaching Tells the Biblical Story*

Whether the speakers in Acts are addressing audiences who know the scriptures of Israel or not, the apostles tell the story of the living God who is the Creator of heaven and earth, the God of Abraham, and the Father of our Lord Jesus Christ. This is the only story the apostles know. They look to this story to make sense of their experience of Jesus and the reaction of others to him.

Of course, to say that the biblical story is the only story the apostles know is not in any way to preclude creative reading of that story. For the first apostles, portions of that story "come true" in ways they could not have imagined before Jesus' death and resurrection. Christians confess that the Holy Spirit continues to work throughout the world and in the church. Our doctrine of God, with its insistence that through the Spirit, God continues to call, gather, enlighten, and sanctify, is our best defense against views of the scripture's authority that insist that nothing new can or should be found within the ancient texts. Today as ever, because of what the Spirit is doing, portions of the story we tell from the Old and New Testaments may be coming true in ways that surprise us. In fact, if God is acting in character, perhaps we should expect that our expectations about what God can and will do are too small or otherwise mistaken. Perhaps we should expect to be surprised, lest God should say about us,

> I am doing a work
> a work that you will never believe, even if
> someone tells you. (13:41)

In "The Eutychus Factor" Nancy Lammers Gross uses material from both Acts and Romans to do in her sermon what I see happening in the speeches in Acts.[15] Gross tells the story of Paul preaching so long that one of those listening to him, Eutychus, falls asleep and then falls out of the window where he had been sitting (Acts 20:7-12). Gross lingers over the detail that even after Eutychus fell out of the window and after Paul revived him, everyone returned upstairs and listened to *more* preaching. Within her sermon she wonders aloud what could have been so captivating about Paul's message. She imagines what Paul's sermon might have been, adapting language from Romans as she does so.

> Perhaps he talked about the one whose *cross is our center* and whose life is our unshakable ground. Maybe he said something like, 'You know, Jesus *died* for you. Why, one will hardly die for a good person, though maybe for a good person one will dare even to die. But God shows his fantastic love for us in that while we were still caught and conflicted in our painful past, while we were mired in the double binds of our present lives, while we were as far away from God as east is from west, *Christ died for us!* Anchor your life in him, and no earthy force within or without will be able to tear you away!'[16]

Ostensibly, Gross is imagining the content of Paul's sermon in that stuffy upstairs room in Troas. Yet she has also offered a thumbnail sketch of the biblical narrative: God shows love apart from the deserving state of those who receive that love, a love that will always be stronger than the forces arrayed against it.

### Preaching Includes the Hearers

Modern preaching, like modern biblical interpretation, may have given up too soon on the ability of biblical texts to "create worlds of meaning and invite readers to enter them."[17] Contemporary preachers have often sought to translate the text's truth into the vernacular of a new time and place instead of seeking to incorporate hearers of our sermons into a world created by the biblical text.[18] The speeches in Acts demonstrate that mission can happen through sermons that construct the world of the text and invite readers to find their life within that story. Paul and Barnabas do not say to the people in Lystra, "Your reality is like what our scriptures speak about." Analogy and translation are not their preaching techniques. Instead, they tell of God in a way that their hearers can relate to, as the Creator of all things, witnessed to you by the simple things of life such as the rain on your fields and the joy in your hearts (cf. 14:17).

### Preaching with Truth-claims Connects Preacher and Audience

The apostles were not shy about claiming truth across cultures. This is so in spite of the fact that in their ancient context, as much as in any postmodern one, the questions of truth and how to obtain it were contested.[19] Apostolic sermons attempted to persuade hearers of the truth of a particular world view. Why? The apostles preached to inspire repentance and to impart a new understanding of the way God is acting in history.[20]

The making of truth-claims may seem for us more complicated than it was for those who made speeches in Acts. Many postmodern Christians, aware of how easily missionary preaching and cultural imperialism are linked and how limited are our understandings of truth, are more timid about making truth-claims than were the first apostles.

In the sermon I am offering here as an example of preaching after the pattern of Acts speeches, Gross uses the language of "wondering" as she makes truth-claims. Earlier in her sermon she has quoted a writer in pastoral psychology commenting that modern individuals "live on scraps" of meaning.[21] As she closes her sermon, she returns to the theme of cobbling together bits of truth and meaning into a coherent understanding of reality:

> Of course, we can't know that these are the things Paul said to those Christians in the upper room during that all-nighter so long ago. And if he did say these things, they are still just pieces, scraps competing with all the other scraps. Paul knew that. He knew we never quite get it all together. But I wonder. I wonder . . . because the Scripture tells us that when dawn came, Paul went on his way, and that house church, the small, intimate group of families and friends, the worshipping community left. They took dear Eutychus with them. He was alive and well. And they were each one greatly encouraged . . . I wonder.[22]

I myself wonder if Gross's rhetoric is not too tentative here, bordering on timidity with respect to her own confession. Yet, her own language notwithstanding, she leaves us with little doubt that she does not just wonder; in fact, she believes that Paul preached something like "nothing can separate us from God's love" to those in Troas, and that the statement about God's love is as true for us as it was for Paul's late-night listeners.

There is a way in which Acts may help us to make truth-claims in a climate that is suspicious of them. The combination of speeches and stories in Acts may offer help for those who resist deferring questions of truth, while allowing for human limitations in articulating the truth.

The stories in Acts bear witness to the truth being proclaimed in the speeches. This connection of word and deed suggests a new direction for Christians as we consider what it means to claim that what we are saying about God is true for all humanity. What if a Christian community's truth-claims came not in the form of philosophical propositions but in the form of a life lived for Christ? I have in mind here that congregations and other Christian communities attend to questions such as these: Does our community's story demonstrate the truth of our sermons? Is the narrative that accompanies our speeches offering evidence that what we say is true? If not, how does that accompanying story point to situations where we are fooling ourselves and lying to others? As Stephen dies in Acts 7, he looks very much like Jesus; they both die outside the city wall; pray for forgiveness for their murderers; and commend their spirit to the Lord. In Acts 13, as Paul preaches in the synagogue, he looks like Jesus preaching in the synagogue in Nazareth (cf. Lk 4); they both speak of the wideness of God's mercy and run into opposition to that message. Examples like this could be multiplied throughout Acts. In this narrative of life and mission in the early church, Jesus' story is being enacted by the apostles and the communities to which they preach. It comes true in their lives. To what extent can people viewing the common life of our Christian communities see a similar connection between word and deed? In the postmodern context, our most persuasive story may be the one we tell with our lives.

## REFERENCES

[1] The number thirty-six is from Marion L. Soards, *The Speeches in Acts: Their Content, Context, and Concerns* (Louisville, Ky.: Westminster/John Knox, 1994), 21; for summaries of other modern numbering and organizing systems for the speeches, see ibid., 18-22.

[2] Barbara Brown Taylor, "Preaching the Body," in *Listening to the Word: Studies in Honor of Fred Craddock*, ed. Gail R. O'Day and Thomas G. Long (Nashville, Tenn.: Abingdon, 1993), 207-209.

[3] Beverly Roberts Gaventa, "What Makes Preaching Biblical?" *The Christian Ministry* 15/4 (1984), 8. Gaventa rejects understandings of the Bible as either a self-help book or a collection of principles, suggesting instead that readers regard the Bible as a parable.

[4] When I speak of Stephen quoting Deuteronomy, or Paul alluding to anti-idolatry themes that are known to us from the prophets, I am employing a kind of shorthand for the more complicated reality that Luke and/or Luke's sources present Stephen as quoting Deuteronomy, Paul as echoing the prophets' words against idolatry, and so on (Max Wilcox, "A Forward to the Study of the Speeches in Acts," in *Christianity, Judaism and Other Greco-Roman Cults: Studies for Morton Smith at Sixty,* part 1, New Testament, ed. Jacob Neusner [Leiden: Brill, 1975], 206-225).

[5] I do not say the Hebrew Bible because New Testament writers, including Luke, generally did not read the Jewish scriptures in Hebrew but relied instead on a Greek translation of those scriptures, commonly known as the Septuagint (LXX).

[6] Paul has to proclaim Jesus but spends little time explaining John and his baptism and call to repentance. It looks as if he expects his audience to know of John, just as he expects them to know characters from Israel's scriptural history. While it is true that

Paul's speech here has been reproduced by Luke decades after any such speech would have been given, it is still interesting that Luke tells this story. See Acts 18:24-28 for an example of Apollos, who preached John's baptism in this period.

[7] This quote from Psalms appears also in Peter's speech at Pentecost. Peter makes the same point Paul does: David died and was buried, "and his tomb is with us to this day," so the promise that God's Holy One will not see corruption must apply to someone other than David himself. Both Peter and Paul proclaim that the promise comes true in Jesus, whom God raised from the dead (Acts 2: 25-31).

[8] Paul's synagogue audience may hear him saying even more than this with the quotation from Isaiah. In the Greek text of both Isaiah and Acts, the "you" in the phrase "I will give you the holy promises made to David" is plural. Paul's citation of the text is not exact; it is more a paraphrase than a quote from Isaiah. Yet he does not change the form of the second person pronoun so that it refers only to one person, Jesus. By leaving this pronoun in the plural form, Paul implies that the promise "You will not let your Holy One see corruption" and the other promises made to David are not just for Jesus alone but for "all of you" who believe (13:39).

[9] We may want to ask here, "Is not the fulfillment of scripture a good thing?" or "Did it not all work out for the best?" Although it is conjecture to reflect on how things might have been if the religious establishment had recognized Jesus as the one who would redeem Israel (see Lk 24:21), surely God could have worked with such a scenario. The prophets wanted their audience to turn from sin even when they were predicting that the people would not make such a turn and would bear God's wrath because of it (e.g., Jer 36:2-3; Ez 33:11, 14-16).

[10] See John J. Kilgallen on the significance of the language about forgiveness of sins in this speech, "Acts 13: 38-39: Culmination of Paul's Speech in Pisidia," *Biblica* 69/ 4 (1988), 480-506.

[11] In Habakkuk these words spoke of God rousing the Chaldeans to be agents in Israel's destruction. In Acts the "work that you will never believe, even if someone tells you" is God's work to raise Jesus from the dead.

[12] For the apostles, the fact that their audience may not recognize something as the language of scripture is not a reason to exclude such language from their speech. An example of this is that when Paul and Barnabas described God as the one "who made the heaven and earth and the sea and all that is in them" they borrowed a phrase found in Exodus 20:11 and Psalm 146:6.

[13] George Lindbeck, *The Nature of Doctrine: Religion and Theology in a Postliberal Age* (Philadelphia: Westminster, 1984), 117.

[14] The most widely known attempt to outline the points of apostolic preaching is found in C. H. Dodd, *The Apostolic Preaching and Its Developments* (London: Hodder and Stoughton, 1936), 21-24.

[15] Nancy Lammers Gross, *If You Cannot Preach Like Paul* (Grand Rapids, Mich.: Eerdmans, 2002), 137-147.

[16] Ibid., 144-145.

[17] This is a phrase taken from the foreword to the volumes in the Interpreting Biblical Texts series from Abingdon Press. For example, see Donald Senior, *The Gospel of Matthew* (Nashville, Tenn.: Abingdon, 1997), 11.

[18] For more on the distinction between translation and incorporation as ways of thinking about preaching, see Richard Lischer, "The Interrupted Sermon," *Interpretation* 50/ 2 (1996), 169-181; Mary E. Hinkle, "Exegesis for Textual Preaching," *Word and World* 19/1 (1999), 58-64.

[19] One is reminded of Pilate's question to Jesus, "What is truth?" (Jn 18:38).

[20] Indeed, repentance could have been the outcome of Stephen's speech, as it was the outcome of Peter's Pentecost sermon. On Pentecost, when people are accused of lawlessly having Jesus killed, they are cut to the heart and respond, "What should we do?" Unfortunately, Stephen's audience does not respond with repentance at the judgment Stephen pronounces but with rage that results in yet another murder.

[21] Gross, *If You Cannot Preach Like Paul*, 137, quoting Don S. Browning, *Religious Thought and the Modern Psychologies* (Philadelphia: Fortress Press, 1987).

[22] Gross, *If You Cannot Preach Like Paul*, 147.

# 9

# The Magical Mystery Tour: Philip Encounters Magic and Materialism in Samaria

## ACTS 8:4–25

## Paul Hertig

During my early Christian days as a university student I was attracted to Christians who had gifts that demonstrated the supernatural power of God. I longed for these gifts, reasoning that if I had this kind of power, I could convince anyone of God's existence. Was this a commendable motivation for faithful and effective witness or a subconscious ploy for power over people? This chapter explores the motivations of those who seek to tap into Christian power. It explores Philip's ministry in Samaria, with particular attention to Simon's motivation to buy the Holy Spirit. For some onlookers, including Simon, Philip's Samaritan visit appeared to be a magical mystery tour. However, Philip's phenomenal signs and wonders were rooted in the ministry of Stephen.

Acts initially introduces Stephen and Philip as a pair (6:5). Both were among the seven deacons who had the social responsibility of waiting on tables for the Hellenist widows (6:5). Both were evangelists who performed signs and wonders (6:8-10; 8:5-6). And both opened the door for Gentile mission. Stephen did so through his strong words against the Temple, law, and land, and his subsequent martyrdom, which led to persecution that scattered the church widely into the Gentile world. And Philip, a trailblazing missionary who traveled to new lands, radically enacted Stephen's theology.[1] As Hellenists, both were capable of bridging Jewish and Gentile worlds. Bicultural people are equipped to cross cultural borders, as indicated by Philip's bold evangelizing of the Samaritans and an Ethiopian leader. "The Hellenists were ideally suited to evangelize Samaria since Samaritans did not accept the Jerusalem Temple as the only place of worship."[2] The Samaritans opposed worship at the Temple in Jerusalem (Jn 4:20-21). After Stephen's critique of the Temple made by human hands (Acts 7:48), now Philip, "another of the seven and therefore probably a member of the same circle as Stephen, will be working among the Samaritans, who also reject worship in the Temple."[3]

Philip's bold witness in Samaria stems from the persecution of Stephen in Jerusalem, demonstrating that resistance to God's mission may only add fuel to its fire. Philip, among those scattered after Stephen's martyrdom, initiated a new Diaspora that fanned missionaries over a broad area to places such as Cyprus, Cyrene, and Antioch (11:19-20).

In laying the groundwork for the expanding mission to the Gentiles, the gospel first moves to the fringes of Judaism, then Samaria, and then to a pros-elyte from afar, an Ethiopian eunuch. Although Philip remains within the bor-ders of Israel, his ministry in the nation of Samaria (8:9) and with the Ethio-pian traveler (8:26-39) "locates him socially on the fringes of Judaism . . . and justifies his identity as one of the scattered" (8:4).[4] The term for "scattered" *(diaparentes)* is utilized widely in the Septuagint to refer to the "dispersion of Jews from Israel to the lands of Gentile nations."[5] The subsequent term of motion, translated "went from place to place" (8:4), refers in Luke to the coming and going of those engaged in such missionary activity. Philip is depicted as a wandering evangelist among those who, literally, "went from place to place proclaiming the word" (8:4) while "passing through" (8:40) particular regions.[6]

While Philip is scattering seeds of universal mission in new lands, we dis-cover fascinating adventures and power encounters in the narrative. Philip pro-claimed the Messiah (8:5),[7] cast out unclean spirits, healed the paralyzed and lame, and produced great joy in the city (8:7-8). Philip's preaching, exorcisms, and healings were mutually reinforcing; the signs were not random showcases of power, as in the case of Simon's magic, but affirmations of the word Philip preached.[8]

The duality of proclamation and signs (word and deed accompanied by hear-ing and seeing, 8:6) constitutes an important holistic theme in the Philip ac-count, characteristic of the wider missiological approach of Luke-Acts. Addi-tional missiological themes of Luke-Acts found in the Philip narrative include Christian superiority over magic (8:6-13), the work of the Holy Spirit (8:15-20), warnings about money (8:18-20), baptism accompanied by repentance (8:13, 22), the power of prayer (8:15, 22, 24), enthusiastic and exemplary response of the marginalized (8:5-6; cf. Lk 10:33), and the powerful movement of the gospel into new regions.[9] Philip's encounter with Simon is characteristic of a series of power encounters between missionaries and magicians in Acts.

## SIMON THE "GREAT"

The text shifts from a general description of Philip's ministry to a particu-lar individual who encounters Philip, Simon the "Great"*(megalē)* (8:9-11). Simon called himself someone great (8:9), and the people who were amazed by his magic also called him "great," literally saying, "This is the power called great of God" (8:10). This term for power *(dunamis)* here is the same used to describe the Holy Spirit in Acts 1:8. Simon is exalted by the Samaritans as a divine person with supernatural power. Thus the people appear to respond to

Simon with a mob mentality rather than a faith commitment. The text describes the Samaritans eagerly listening to *him* (8:11), captivated by Simon as a kind of cult figure; in contrast they "listened eagerly to what was *said*" by Philip (8:6).[10] The focus was not on Philip but on what he proclaimed, the good news about the kingdom of God and the name of Jesus Christ (8:12); however, 8:12 states that "they believed Philip." We will discuss later the argument that the Samaritans believed only intellectually, but at first glance it appears that the term used *(pisteuō)* implies genuine faith and that the occurrence of "great joy" complements "good news" and indicates receptivity (8:8). The phrase "Even Simon himself believed" does not specify what Simon believed but may link Simon's belief to the other Samaritans who "believed Philip" in the previous verse (8:12-13). In the words of Fitzmyer, *"Simon too came to believe, was baptized, and became a devoted follower of Philip."*[11] This link of Simon to the other Samaritans has caused many to postulate deficiencies in the Samaritans' faith, since Peter and John later arrive to lay hands so that they might receive the Holy Spirit, and Simon's impure heart is eventually disclosed.

The New Testament provides little on Simon, but since he is active in Samaria, he may have been a Samaritan. Depicted as "a practitioner of magic *(mageiais)*" in 8:11, he is eventually referred to as "Simon Magus" by Eusebius. *Magus* is associated with the Persian *magha*, meaning "power," and originating from a tribe of priests from the Medes who conducted a daily ritual of fire worship. This borrowed name in Greek referred to this Persian "fire priest" but also meant "teacher," "magician," and "quack."[12]

While Luke does not define "the power of God" or identify its source, the phrase parallels pagan gods such as the Anatolian moon god men, "the great power of the immortal god."[13] Attributes of greatness and power were often associated with ancient deities and "great" was often applied to gods in the Hellenistic era.[14] Luke describes the people as having been astonished for a long time by Simon's magical arts (8:11). They followed him out of fascination, not belief.

It seems that Simon joins the believing community to obtain Philip's amazing power. Ironically, just as the Samaritans followed Simon in amazement,[15] so Simon followed Philip in amazement (8:10-13). These particular Samaritans seemed easily drawn to personality cults. It is ironic that "Philip the least— friend of the poor, table-waiter, himself oppressed and homeless—becomes the greatest, overwhelming the 'great' Simon Magus revered by even the 'greatest' Samaritans (cf. 8.10)."[16]

Philip stands out as superior to the venerated Simon, who could not match Philip's miraculous signs. Philip's authority supplants Simon's without struggle; even Simon himself, the "Great Power," submits to the superior power manifested through Philip.[17] Characteristic of Acts, early church leaders win decisively in every battle against self-promoters who lay claim to divinity (cf. 12:22-23). Philip's "signs and great miracles" (8:13) indicate that Philip's ministry among the constituency of the "Great Power" was a power encounter. But Philip's priority was not on wonder working, self-aggrandizement, or even on head-to-head battle with Simon, but on declaring the good news about the kingdom of

God (8:12). Evil manifests itself while God's missionary people go about the daily work of proclaiming the good news of the kingdom. In power encounters in Acts, the missionaries do not search for the devil behind every bush but are prepared when evil manifests itself.

I once received a missionary's prayer letter that described his daily battles with the devil. The devil caused his suitcase handle to break, his computer to crash, and his visa problems at the airport. When the devil is everywhere, is the devil really anywhere? Rather than seek out the devil or attribute every inconvenience to the devil, authentic disciples expect the unexpected, knowing that evil will manifest itself in the course of authentic ministry (8:6-7, 12-13). God's missionaries in Acts do not chase down the devil. Yet when all is said and done, "the supremacy of Christian power *[dunamis]* and authority *[exousia]* over all competitive forces" dominates Luke-Acts.[18]

Simon seemingly becomes a disciple of Jesus through belief in Philip's message, baptism, and through following Philip (8:13). But we eventually learn of Simon's desire for power and possibly the economic gain that comes from buying the Holy Spirit. This is evidenced in his impure heart, the seat of sin (8:21-22), and Peter's direct challenge, "May your silver perish with you, because you thought you could obtain God's gift with money" (8:20). Simon apparently wants to buy the Holy Spirit so that he might make money. The nuance of Peter's response, "May your silver go to hell with you," is verified by the fact that the word translated "perish" has a nuance of "destruction which consists in the loss of eternal life, eternal misery, perdition."[19]

## FORM AND MEANING

Simon's response of belief and amazement was a strange concoction. Seeing that the Holy Spirit was given through the laying on of hands, Simon offered money to buy this ability: "Give me also this power so that anyone on whom I lay my hands . . . " (8:19). Simon's response to this new form of power contains the words *me, I,* and *my.* He seeks a power that he may own. He accepts a new form but gives it an old meaning: authentic spiritual power understood as magic. In Philip's ministry, both Simon and the Ethiopian eunuch are immediately baptized following belief, making spontaneity a seeming virtue (8:36b). However, the risky side of spontaneity is shown here as well. The quick response lacked what baptism signifies: repentance. This is evident in Peter's mandate to repent after Peter's "curse," "To hell with you and your money" (8:20a).[20] The inseparability of baptism and repentance is rooted in Peter's Pentecost sermon, in which he declared, "Repent, and be baptized" (2:38). Simon Magus is accustomed to power manifested through money and greatness. The power of the Holy Spirit prevailed over magic (13:4-12, 19:11-19).

What God gives freely cannot be bought or sold. Peter, a modest fisherman from Galilee, understood spiritual economics, having experienced at Pentecost the Holy Spirit as the equalizer, who was poured out on all humanity. But Simon Magus misunderstood the distinctions between the convicting power of the Holy Spirit and the power of magic.[21] Money, magic, and religion make strange bedfellows. Simon attempted to mix these three into a strange brew in order to obtain power over others.

Samuel Escobar challenges Christian overtures to power: "Are we really trying to cultivate the wealth and the privilege of unrepentant hearts among the powerful, guaranteeing for them that the gospel will produce laborers who do not strike, students who sing religious songs instead of painting graffiti with calls for social action, guardians of peace at the price of injustice?"[22]

Simon had become a baptized, believing follower (8:13). The implication is that even baptized, believing Christians must guard their hearts from evil motives that quench the work of the Spirit. Neither belief nor baptism magically removes all inclinations toward evil. Fortunately, a repentant response remains a possibility for Simon (8:22). And here the story ends, with Simon desperately asking Peter to pray that "nothing of what you have said may happen to me" (8:24). Luke does not seem concerned about finishing the account but with warning the reader. Peter's phrase that you have no part or share in this "word" is translated "ministry" in the NIV (8:21), an appropriate nuance that ties to Simon's request for power (8:19) and to Philip's ministry of word and deed (8:12). Peter's phrase suggests a form of excommunication and implies that Simon does not embrace authentic Christian faith.[23] Peter's response to Simon is an interesting mix of curse and a summons to repent. David Seccombe summarizes succinctly, "Without genuine repentance and a true heart there is no entry amongst the people of God, no matter what the apparent outward response or the sacramental symbols."[24]

## CONTEMPORARY BLEND OF FAITH AND MONEY

This text is not far removed from present-day life. Contemporary Christians easily slip into an unhealthy blend of faith and prosperity. One television preacher declared that he had a word from God in an envelope with a golden seal and appealed for a donation in order to send out a special word from God. On a talk show a pastor appeared in green attire from head to toe—his suit, tie, shirt, and shoes—declaring money as God's sign of blessing. The Simon Magus that Peter faced in the past continues to rear his eager head in the present. In fact, many similar shades of magical beliefs and practices continue to surface in Christian circles today. The following continuum allows us to examine further areas where Christianity might slide into popular forms of magic:[25]

| Christianity | Popular Magic |
|---|---|
| God-centered | Self-centered |
| Belief | Amazement |
| Submission | Control |
| Prayer | Formulas |
| Cross/resurrection | Instant success |
| Personal/communal commitment | Impersonal/lacking commitment |
| Organic | Mechanistic |
| God's authority | Human charisma |

A contemporary example that follows the sequence of the above chart from God-centered to self-centered is found in a seven-year-old girl's widely circulated letter to God. "Dear God, thank you for my brother, but don't you remember that I prayed for a puppy? I trusted you'd answer my prayer. If you turn my brother into a puppy I'll know you are God." An adult version of this attempt to manipulate God occurred when an evangelist declared that God never says "I *may* heal you," but God *will* heal you, as long as you meet the conditions for healing. "If it's not God's will for you to be sick, why go to a doctor?" he proclaimed. Along similar lines of sensationalism, a radio preacher moved from belief to amazement when he declared that he had never been sick and that none of his family members had ever even caught a cold. Here is an attempt to amaze people into the kingdom rather than encourage authentic belief through daily dependence on God.

A pastor demonstrated the temptation to move from submission to control when he urged parishioners to find a house that meets their interests and then "stand in front of it and claim it in the name of Jesus!" This is also an example of prayer becoming a formula. "In the name of Jesus" should indicate authentic reverence and submission to Jesus, not a magic formula. Popular forms of Christianity often move into the realm of magic when they misinterpret the basic tenents of Christianity by bypassing the cross and moving directly into a resurrection experience of instant success.[26] For example, a television preacher blessed several loaves of bread and threw them to the audience. As people fought for the blessing of the "holy bread," he told a woman in the crowd to feed a loaf to her non-Christian husband so that he might be saved. Suddenly the communion bread became a magic loaf.

In the medieval era the priest during communion announced "Hoc est corpus," meaning "This is my body." What some parishioners thought they heard was "Hocus pocus," which has become a popular term for magic. A sacrament that should deepen one's *personal* commitment to God and *communal commitment* to the body of Christ may become an *impersonal* form of popular magic. This movement from an organic to mechanistic approach was further illustrated by a radio evangelist who advertised a shower cap with the outline of his hand imprinted on the top. He claimed that purchasing and wearing the cap would provide periodic anointed blessings. These contemporary stories illustrate a lack of discernment and common sense that can occur in the name of Christ when people stray from faith and dependence, as Simon did, and gravitate toward the misuse of power and authority.

## THE MISUSE OF POWER

Parallel to Simon manifesting the attributes of a disciple through his belief in Philip's message and baptism, in my college days I sought to be a disciple of Christ and identified with the Christian community. But the "power" gifts I longed for were not given to me. The Gift Giver was gracious to humble me rather than exalt me at a time when I did not understand the dangerous side of power. In contrast to Simon, Philip seemed prepared to deal with power. He focused on the kingdom rather than on himself. This produced great joy in the city of Samaria (8:8), apparently referring "both to those who were healed and to the message itself, the good news that Philip preached."[27] The text indicates that it was not a deficiency in Philip's faith that caused Simon's downfall, but rather Simon mistaking the new form that Philip introduced as magic.

The narrative would be self-contradictory if Simon's faith and baptism were deficient due to a flaw in Philip's faith since, after describing the coming of the Spirit through the apostles, the text then recounts that this same "deficient" Philip led the Ethiopian to faith, baptism, and rejoicing (8:36-39).[28] In fact, Philip's initiatives to the Samaritans and Ethiopian eunuch chart new territory among people who could not participate in the Temple at Jerusalem. Rooted in Stephen's strong words against the Temple, his martyrdom, and the ensuing persecution, Philip's Samaritan mission widened the church's activity beyond the borders of Judaism. Philip demonstrated that authentic Christianity cannot be confined to a sacred place, but discovers itself when it reaches beyond itself. When God's people are guided into unfamiliar territory, God empowers them with fresh experiences of the Holy Spirit.

## THE SECOND PENTECOST

In the middle of the Simon Magus account the text explains that Peter and John are sent from Jerusalem to Samaria because they heard that the word of God was accepted there. This seeming interruption in the account is actually vital to the story because it is Peter who later declares Simon's need to repent. Although Philip's outreach was endowed with the work of the Holy Spirit, the two apostles discover that those who believed and were baptized had not received the Holy Spirit. This unusual post-Pentecost dilemma is quickly resolved when the apostles, with the laying on of hands, prayed for the Samaritans to receive the Holy Spirit (8:14-17). The initial absence of the Holy Spirit on the new Samaritan believers raises questions about Philip's ministry. Did the Samaritans, resembling Simon, lack an authentic faith commitment? Or are there normally two stages of initiation into Christ? There are at least three possible answers to these questions.

1. James D. G. Dunn postulates that the Samaritans accepted the word of God intellectually (8:14) but had not received new life in the Spirit. They had believed in Philip (8:12) but not in Jesus Christ.[29] Their baptism was, like Simon's, a form with no meaning. Thus the Samaritans participated in a mass movement but were not Christians until Peter and John came. In other words, what seemed to be their second stage was really their first. The Samaritans may have believed Philip in the same way that "Simon himself believed" (8:13), not with genuine faith. Thus the apostles Peter and John made haste to Jerusalem to minister to the new believers in Samaria and solve the deficiency. Dunn believes that Luke intended to show that the Samaritan response was defective by highlighting their extreme fervor, eschatological expectation, scarcity of discernment, lack of depth, and heightened mass emotionalism (8:9-11). Dunn also believes that just as Simon's belief was centered on one person, Philip, so was the faith of the

other Samaritans: "They all went through the form but did not experience the reality."[30] He notes that Luke highlights a distinction between true and false Christianity. Initially, each advance of the Samaritans parallels that of Simon: "They turn from magic to Philip, so does he; they believe Philip, so does he; they are baptized by Philip, so does he. Yet their paths diverge—*they* receive the Spirit, whereas Simon receives only a curse."[31] Thus the reception of the Spirit is the indicator of authentic Christianity in Acts.

It is interesting to note that Simon's story has no ending—he is backed into a corner, told to repent or else, pleads for prayer, then disappears from the scene. Luke has reached his objective and thus ends the story. The reader has been warned of the choice between two divergent paths—to submit to the Holy Spirit's authority or to suffer the dire consequences of submitting to self-centered interests.

2. Another common theory postulates that the Samaritans received the Spirit during their initial belief in Jesus. The purpose of Peter and John's visit was to give them charismatic manifestations of the Holy Spirit. Even John Calvin believed that the Samaritans had received the Spirit of adoption but "were not yet rich in the extraordinary gifts," and that "the extraordinary graces of the Spirit are added as a culmination."[32] According to this theory, "the Spirit had not come upon any of them" (8:16) referred to special gifts and graces. This is a common belief in Pentecostal and Holiness denominations, which believe in a baptism of the Holy Spirit as a second stage of initiation into Christ for empowerment to serve.

3. According to this interpretation, belief and reception of the Holy Spirit normally occur in one stage (1 Cor 12:13; Rom 8:9), but the Acts 8 episode is an exception to the norm, without parallels today. Merging with this interpretation is the belief that the apostles must continually "play catchup" with a mission initiated by others, a mission that progresses to new regions and peoples without the apostles' initiative or control.[33] This defies predictable principles of church growth and predictable doctrines of the Holy Spirit. Acts is first and foremost a historical document, not a doctrinal handbook. Whether what happened at Samaria is doctrinally correct may not matter to Luke, whose main goal is to show the mysterious and unpredictable power of the Holy Spirit at work among the nations.

No matter which of the above hypotheses one may choose (and each carries weight in various Christian denominations), there are other important reasons for the visit and laying on of hands by Peter and John. The "delayed" gift of the Holy Spirit is most likely related to Philip's ground-breaking mission beyond the region of Jerusalem. The outpouring of the Spirit ensured continuity with Pentecost and authenticated the work of God in Samaria. The laying on of hands by Peter and John (Jews actually touching Samaritans) was a sign of fellowship and solidarity so that Samaritan converts would know that they were bona fide Christians connected to the community of Jerusalem. The Samaritans' reception of the Spirit, through Peter and John, is repeated four times in 8:14-18. The two apostles, representatives of the Jerusalem church, needed a firsthand experience of blessing the Gentiles if the mission to the Gentiles was to fully begin.

Clearly, Peter and John needed this experience as much as the Samaritans, since they had to overcome their own prejudices by witnessing the Spirit's work beyond regional boundaries (cf. Lk 9:52-54; Gal 2:11-14). Thus, Luke may be portraying the healing of generations of hostility between Jews and Samaritans. The Jewish apostles' excursion from Jerusalem validates the mission in Samaria, fortifying a crucial narrative transition in the second phase of the Acts 8:1 program launched by Philip (8:1, 5). The Samaritan mission (see Lk 9:51-55; 10:25-37; 17:11-19) represents the halfway stage of the mission movement, linking mission from Jerusalem to the world. "Philip's missionary breakthrough in Samaria occupies a foundational position in Acts 8.4-25 on which the entire story builds" and leads directly into his encounter with the Ethiopian eunuch (8:26-40).[34] Furthermore, in Acts 1:8 Samaria is associated with Judea as an outer region beyond Jerusalem, linked in 8:1 and 9:31. This connects Philip's Samaritan mission geographically with his missions along the coastal plain of Judea (8:26-40) and again with Peter's mission in the same coastal areas (9:32-10:48). Philip's mission in the narrative represents a linchpin between the persecution following Stephen's death and the expanding Hellenist missionary activity in regions beyond Judea (8:4-5; 11:19-20).

Since they were of mixed ethnic origin, Luke portrays the Samaritans as people midway between Jews and Gentiles.[35] This midway point is no mere transition but a giant leap, considering that after the Babylonian exile, the Samaritan claim of a holy mountain for their temple produced antagonism with the Judean Jews. The animosity was heightened by the Samaritans' exclusive acceptance of the Pentateuch as their sacred scripture. By the first century racial hatred existed between Jews and Samaritans, who were viewed by Judean Jews "as, at best, half-breeds who had significantly intermarried with the pagan Assyrians."[36] While the Samaritans did not believe in a Messiah, per se, they had at least a shadowy messianic consciousness and expected a prophet like Moses who would restore authentic worship on Mount Gerizim.[37]

Philip's ministry in Samaria fits the structure of a sodality, a roving and independent missionary movement. The ministry of Peter and John, on the other hand, represented a modality, a more fixed structure of believers rooted in a particular place—in this case, Jerusalem.[38] Luke's account of Philip in Samaria depicts modalities and sodalities working together in harmony for the sake of God's mission (see 11:22-23). At times tensions occur, although resolvable, between sodalities and modalities (see 15:1-2). Since church and mission are one, and should not be at odds with one another, sodalities and modalities should work together in a symbiotic relationship for the sake of the wider mission of God.

## CONCLUSION

During my early Christian days as a college student, having not yet discovered the wider mission of God, I pursued the supernatural gifts that demonstrated the supernatural power of God. I impulsively focused on seeking power that would persuade people rather than on humility that would allow God's

Spirit to work through me and authentically attract people to God's power. I focused more on the form of the power rather than on the all-powerful One. I found myself surrounded by the believing, baptized Simon Magus's of the church, who gathered together in Christian fellowship, seeking more and more power. However, as I grew in my Christian faith, I began to discern a skewed focus. I asked questions. I heard these people describe their daily battle with the demons, babble as a pretense for tongues, and admit that sometimes their "prophecies" were simply messages they felt people needed, dressed up in the phrase "thus says the Lord." I became further uncomfortable when I saw these spiritual leaders strut around campus, disconnected from the world around them, as if they somehow lived in a dimension above ordinary people.

In my growing discomfort with this quest for spiritual power, I began to change my focus to passing on the power—sharing my faith. Here I discovered a more humbling but a more rewarding experience than trying to impress people with power. I discovered the joy of moving out of sacred spaces and into unfamiliar territory. I was humbled by seeking to make the gospel relevant, first on my own campus, then among international students on campus, and eventually on the other side of the world in Asia. I began to connect better with Philip, who moved the church out of its familiar and sacred spaces into a world where God was at work anywhere and at any time. The modalities are still vital to me—places for worship, prayer, sacraments, centering, and cultivating gifts. But the account of Philip reminds me of the importance of balancing these experiences with the sodality that represents engagement in the world where God is at work beyond my sacred spaces.

## REFERENCES

[1] John R. W. Stott, *The Spirit, the Church, and the World: The Message of Acts* (Downers Grove, Ill.: InterVarsity Press, 1990), 144.

[2] Raymond E. Brown, *An Introduction to the New Testament* (New York: Doubleday, 1997), 297.

[3] Justo L. González, *Acts: The Gospel of the Spirit* (Maryknoll, N.Y.: Orbis Books, 2001), 107.

[4] F. Scott Spencer, *The Portrait of Philip in Acts: A Study of Roles and Relations* (Sheffield, England: JSOT Press, 1992), 35.

[5] Ibid., 34.

[6] Ibid., 36. This fits the model of Jesus, who also enters Samaritan regions during his continual mission journey (Lk 9:51, 56; 17:11). In fact, mythological history referred to Ethiopia as both the ends of the earth and the extreme habitable region of the south, thus Philip's eventual encounter with the Ethiopian foreshadows wide mission expansion (Ben Witherington III, *New Testament History: A Narrative Account* [Grand Rapids, Mich.: Baker Books, 2001], 193). Many have noted that in this sense the gospel went to Africa before it went to Europe.

[7] Specifically, "good news about the kingdom of God and the name of Jesus Christ" (8:12).

[8] Susan R. Garrett, *The Demise of the Devil: Magic and the Demonic in Luke's Writings* (Minneapolis: Augsburg/Fortress Press, 1989), 63.

[9] This is a variation of the discussion in Spencer, *The Portrait of Philip in Acts,* 31.

[10] Spencer, *The Portrait of Philip in Acts*, 51.

[11] Joseph A. Fitzmyer, *The Acts of the Apostles*, The Anchor Bible (New York: Doubleday, 1998), 405.

[12] Ibid., 403.

[13] Ibid., 404.

[14] Spencer, *The Portrait of Philip in Acts*, 92, 93.

[15] "All of them, from the least to the greatest, listened to him eagerly . . . because for a long time he had amazed them" (8:10, 11).

[16] Spencer, *The Portrait of Philip in Acts*, 102.

[17] Ibid., 93-94.

[18] Ibid., 95.

[19] Joseph Henry Thayer, *A Greek-English Lexicon of the New Testament*, Being *Grimm's Wilke's Clovis Novi Testamenti*, trans., rev., and enl. (Grand Rapids, Mich.: Baker, 1977), 686; see Phil 3:19; 2 Pt 3:16; Rv 17:8, 11.

[20] J. B. Phillips, *The New Testament in Modern English: Student Edition* (New York: Macmillan, 1972), 250.

[21] By *magic*, I refer to the attempt to control supernatural powers for one's own benefit. For more on the deeper nuances of magic, see Chapter 15 n. 10.

[22] Samuel Escobar, quoted in González, *Acts*, 113-114.

[23] Ernst Haenchen, *The Acts of the Apostles. A Commentary*, 14th ed., trans., rev., and updated R. McL. Wilson (Philadelphia: Westminster Press, 1971; German original, 1965), 305. Philip is not the only early church leader who must deal with this problem; Peter also deals with a member of the early church congregation whose heart is "filled with Satan" (5:3).

[24] David Seccombe, "The New People of God," in *Witness to the Gospel: The Theology of Acts*, ed. I. Howard Marshall and David Peterson, 349-372 (Grand Rapids, Mich.: Eerdmans, 1998), 359.

[25] This chart has its roots in the teachings and writings of Paul G. Hiebert, for example, *Anthropological Reflections on Missiological Issues* (Grand Rapids, Mich.: Baker, 1994), 246-247.

[26] Jesus faced this temptation more than once (see Lk 4:5-8; 22:42-44).

[27] González, *Acts*, 106.

[28] James D. G. Dunn, *Baptism in the Holy Spirit: A Re-examination of the New Testament Teaching on the Gift of the Spirit in Relation to Pentecostalism Today* (Naperville, Ill.: Alec R. Allenson, 1970), 58.

[29] A counter-argument is that they had been baptized "in the name of the Lord Jesus" (8:16), implying faith in Jesus.

[30] Dunn, *Baptism in the Holy Spirit*, 63-66.

[31] Ibid., 66-67.

[32] John Calvin, *Calvin's Commentaries: The Acts of the Apostles, 1-13*, trans. John W. Fraser and W. J. G. McDonald (Grand Rapids, Mich.: Eerdmans, 1965), 236.

[33] Robert C. Tannehill, *The Narrative Unity of Luke-Acts*, 2 vols. (Philadelphia and Minneapolis: Fortress Press, 1986, 1989), 2:102.

[34] Spencer, *The Portrait of Philip in Acts*, 32.

[35] Thomas J. Lane, *Luke and the Gentile Mission: Gospel Anticipates Acts* (New York: Peter Lang, 1996), 102.

[36] Witherington, *New Testament History*, 189, 191; see Jn 8:48.

[37] Ibid., 191; Fitzmyer, *The Acts of the Apostles*, 402; see Jn 4:25.

[38] Ralph D. Winter, "The Two Structures of God's Redemptive Mission," *Missiology* (January 1974): 122-123.

# 10

## The Ethiopian Eunuch: A Key Transition from Hellenist to Gentile Mission

### Keith H. Reeves

The story of the Ethiopian eunuch has fascinated readers for generations. It has captured the pen of popular writers and academics alike. Part of this fascination derives from the character of the queen of Sheba, a popular topic of Hollywood during the last century. My interest in this story stems in part from my own family situation, since my wife was born in Ethiopia and lived there for the first seven years of her life. Her stories of early childhood in that beautiful country have been a source of interest to our children as we gather by the fireplace on cold winter evenings. This past year she was able to return to Ethiopia with a church group to work for several weeks as a nurse in a free medical clinic.

As she walked to work through the city of Addis Ababa, she tells of the innumerable polio victims that she observed on the streets. The fear of polio terrorized the United States in the first half of the last century, beginning with the New York outbreak in 1916. Yet polio has largely been eliminated in most parts of the world through aggressive childhood vaccination programs. Ethiopia, however, is one of five remaining nations where polio ravages largely unchecked. This disease has crippled even those who survived. Aggressive physical therapy at an early age can allow many of its victims to walk again. Yet without therapy, polio often causes deformation of the limbs. While some of the polio victims of Addis have family networks that help them survive, others are left to fend for themselves. Simple devices such as wheel chairs are too expensive for many of these people, and they are forced to drag themselves around using only their hands. Among Ethiopia's outcasts, they often live as beggars. Such stories continually lead me to revisit Luke-Acts, with its broad social concerns, and the narrative of the Ethiopian eunuch in particular, which challenges the church to move beyond boundaries set by ethnic origin or impediment.

114

My interest in the story of the Ethiopian eunuch also stems from my work of teaching Acts for the last dozen years. I have been engaged in the task of enjoying, understanding, and interpreting with sophomore readers this wonderful narrative we call Acts. The story of the Ethiopian eunuch serves as a window to some of Luke's concerns for the poor and outcast, those members of society who find themselves on the fringe through no fault of their own.

This story in particular has often been relegated to the backwoods of Acts research. In bringing it to the forefront again, I address two primary questions: (1) What is the ethnicity of the Ethiopian eunuch? (2) How does the story fit within the overall narrative of the Book of Acts? These questions are addressed in an effort to determine the literary and theological significance of the story within the narrative. The questions are not independent. I argue that the answer to the second question, the role of the story in the larger narrative, answers the first question, the Ethiopian's ethnicity. From this we can draw some implications for ministry.

Many treatments of the story of the Ethiopian eunuch in the secondary literature come to one or two conclusions: (1) the Ethiopian eunuch is a Gentile;[1] (2) the story disrupts the narrative, since Cornelius is clearly presented as the first Gentile convert (Acts 10:1—11:18).[2] I attempt here to demonstrate that Luke[3] presents the Ethiopian eunuch as a Jewish person on the fringes of Jewish society because of a disability that makes him unfit for worship in the Temple (cf. Dt 23:1), and that the story provides a powerful transition in Luke's developing narrative.

First, what evidence is there for the eunuch's ethnicity? Is he a Jew or a Gentile? Or might he be a proselyte? The story itself (8:26-40) provides only slight direct evidence. Luke identifies the man in the narrative as a man, an Ethiopian, a eunuch, a minister of Candace, queen of Ethiopia *(anēr Aithioph eunuchos dunastēs Kandakēs basilissēs Aithiopōn,* 8:27). Three terms are used to describe this man. One, translated "Ethiopian," signifies his homeland. Another "minister" *(dunastēs)* identifies him as a royal official of Candace, queen of Ethiopia. A third term *(eunouchos)* identifies his physical impairment. Each of these terms deserves further comment. It is noteworthy that Luke does not identify the man as a Jew, but neither does he identify him as a Gentile or as a God-fearer, both of which are applied to Cornelius (10:45; 11:1; 11:18 and 10:2, 22, 35).

## AN ETHIOPIAN

The man is first identified as an "Ethiopian." The Greek term for "Ethiopian" *(Aithioph)* is used twenty-nine times in the Septuagint. Generally, it is used to translate the Hebrew *Cush.* Throughout its history the term *Ethiopia* had no precise location.[4] In the Septuagint it could refer to Nubia, which adjoins Egypt to the south (Ez 29:10; Jdt 1:10).[5] The term was used during the Persian period to refer to the extreme southern edge of the empire.[6] Josephus, in referring to the queen of Sheba, notes that she ruled over Ethiopia and Egypt.[7] He apparently equates Ethiopia with Sheba in Southern Arabia (Yemen).[8] In the Septuagint, Sheba and Seba, the son of Cush, are spelled identically. This may be the source of the confusion.[9] Certainly in recent times the biblical word *Ethiopia* has been confused with the modern nation of Ethiopia. While the ancient term could certainly include the region of modern Ethiopia (Abyssinia), it was never restricted to that region.[10] Thus the term *Ethiopia* could refer to several different regions.

Luke, however, qualifies the term by reference to Candace, queen of Ethiopia. Pliny, in his *Natural History*, notes that Candace is a title.[11] It was used of the queens who ruled in Meroe, the capital city of Nubia.[12] We know three queens with this title from the ancient world. Pseudo Callisthenes mentions a Candace who visits Alexander the Great.[13] Strabo tells of a one-eyed Candace who led troops against Gaius Petronius.[14] Finally, Pliny mentions a Candace known to an expeditionary force of Nero.[15] According to Bion of Soli (as cited in Pliny), the title was given to the queen-mother, the real head of government.[16] In any case, it is likely that the eunuch is a minister in the court of one of the Meroitic queens.

### Gentile or Jew?

This being the case, there is no a priori reason to conclude that he is a Gentile. There is evidence of Jewish people living in Nubia long before the first century C.E. Isaiah 11:11 refers to scattered Jews living in Ethiopia. Zephaniah 3:10 refers to people, who, "from beyond the rivers of Ethiopia my suppliants, my scattered ones, shall bring my offering" (cf. Ps 87:4). In Esther 8:9 Ahasuerus issues a decree "to the Jews, and to the satraps and the governors and the officials of the provinces from India to Ethiopia." The Elephantine papyri also give evidence of Jewish settlements on the border of Nubia.

A fascinating tradition connects the Candace with the modern nation of Ethiopia. The Ethiopian national saga, the *Kebra Nagast* (Glory of the Kings) traces the first king of Ethiopia to Menelik I, the son of Solomon and the queen of Sheba.[17] This story is similar to the story in 1 Kings 10:1-13 and 2 Chronicles 9:1-12 but supplies many details where the biblical story is silent. It describes how Solomon serves a very spicy meal to the queen of Sheba and then out of courtesy invites her to spend the night. The queen agrees, but only if Solomon agrees not to take her by force, for she is a virgin. Solomon agrees with the queen's decision, but only if she does not take anything from his house. Solomon has a bed prepared for the queen on the other side of his bedchamber. He also instructs a servant girl to set a pitcher of water in the center of the room. During the night the queen awakes from dire thirst, due to the spicy foods that Solomon had served. Seeing the pitcher of water, she attempts to get a drink. Solomon, however, had been waiting for the moment. He grabs her arm, accusing her of taking something from his household without his permission. The deal is off, the king rapes the queen, and she eventually gives birth to Menelik.[18] Consequently from the middle ages until the time of Haile Selassie (225th in direct descent),[19] the Ethiopians have traced their royal line to Solomon and the queen of Sheba.

Though the *Kebra Nagast* dates from the fourteenth century, it no doubt contains earlier material, much of it pre-Christian. This is supported by various versions of the legend that are also found in Ge'ez, Arabic, Coptic, Syriac, Greek, and Jewish sources.[20] The specific version of the legend, which includes the birth of Menelik, probably arose sometime between the sixth century C.E. and the beginning of the second millennium.[21] We must conclude, then, that external evidence gives no indication of the man's ethnic background. What hints may we glean from the story itself?

## A MINISTER OF CANDACE AND A EUNUCH

The man is identified as both a minister *(dunastēs)* and as a eunuch *(eunouchos)*. The term used for "minister" is often used to refer to a high official or a ruler. Here Luke qualifies it; the man is in charge of the queen's entire treasury (8:27). Thus he is a man of some importance.

However, the operative term that Luke uses to refer to this man is the word for eunuch. Luke uses the term five times (8:27, 34, 36, 38, 39). In the Septuagint the term (used thirty-eight times overall) often refers to a high official (as in the case of Potiphar, Gn 39:1), but it is equally used to refer to a castrated male, typically related to work in the harem.[22] The only other occurrences of the term in the New Testament are three times in Matthew 19:12, where it clearly refers to a castrated male. I argue that the term here denotes a castrated male rather than merely an official, because he has already been adequately identified as a minister. Were "eunuch" simply understood as minister, it would be redundant. Indeed, the repetition of the term for eunuch emphasizes the man's physical defect. This is his dominant trait in the narrative.[23]

Thus the man is of some importance, as a minister to the queen, but the description of his physical defect dominates Luke's characterization. He had been to Jerusalem to worship, but would have been prohibited from entering the Temple because of his physical impairment (Dt 23:1).

### Ethnicity of the Eunuch

The strongest evidence for the ethnicity of the eunuch is in the larger narrative structure. The narrator makes a great effort to show that Cornelius is the first Gentile convert and that his acceptance into the community of faith is by direct intervention of God (Acts 10:1—11:18). The repetition of Peter's and Cornelius' visions (10:3, 9-16), the appearance of angels (10:3), the Spirit speaking (10:19), the presence of the Spirit and the evidence of tongues (10:44-47), all demonstrate God's acceptance of Cornelius into the community of faith and lead to the narrator's conclusion that "God has given even to the Gentiles the repentance that leads to life" (11:18; cf. 10:45). Thus, if Cornelius is the first Gentile convert, it is apparent that the eunuch is not.[24]

Nevertheless, the evidence of the larger narrative is often discounted or misunderstood. Ernst Haenchen, for example, recognizes the importance of the Cornelius episode but concludes that the Ethiopian story is one of two stories told of initial Gentile conversion, this one told by Hellenists.[25] According to this view, the Greeks and the Jews each have their story of initial Gentile conversion. Luke, for his part, makes no attempt to integrate the stories into the overall narrative. He simply places them side by side. This interpretation, however, requires that we see a huge oversight on Luke's part as narrator, as elsewhere careful arrangement of the narrative appears to further Luke's interests. In short, were the reader to understand the eunuch as a Gentile, the story simply would not fit within the apparent narrative structure.

Robert C. Tannehill takes a slightly different approach. For him, the story of the eunuch foreshadows the Gentile mission. Indeed, it is not a steppingstone between the Samaritans and the Gentiles but "a leap to the extreme."[26] Tannehill recognizes that the words of Jesus in Acts 1:8 drive the narrative forward: "and you will be my witnesses in Jerusalem, in all Judea and Samaria, and to the ends of the earth" (1:8). Prior to the Ethiopian story, Luke narrates the expansion of the gospel to the Samaritans (8:1b-25). Thus, the gospel has in some sense now gone to the "ends of the earth."[27] While it is true that Ethiopia was considered in the ancient world to be the ends of the earth[28] and that the conversion of the Ethiopian may foreshadow the expansion of the gospel to the ends of the earth,[29] it does not necessarily follow that the Ethiopian is a Gentile.

## THE ROLE OF THE STORY

How, then, does the story of the eunuch fit into the larger narrative? In the Book of Acts Luke demonstrates how Jesus' words in 1:8 are fulfilled. Thus the spread of the gospel is narrated within ever-expanding cultural and geographical circles: (1) devout Aramaic-speaking Jewish people (Acts 2:5); (2) Greek-speaking Jewish people (Acts 6:1); (3) people on the fringes of Judaism, such as Samaritans (Acts 8:4-25) and the Ethiopian eunuch (Acts 8:26-40); and finally (4) Gentiles (Acts 10:1—11:18). Even the Gentile ministry itself is narrated along expanding geographical lines: Judea (Acts 10:1—11:18), Cyprus and Asia Minor (Acts 13:1—16:8), Europe (16:9ff.), and ultimately Rome (28:16).

Let me briefly sketch this development. After the preface, the Book of Acts begins with the disciples receiving instructions from Jesus. They are to "wait . . . for the promise of the Father" (1:4), which Luke identifies as the coming of the Holy Spirit (1:8). This would empower them to be Jesus' "witnesses in Jerusalem, in all Judea and Samaria, and to the ends of the earth" (1:8). Luke carefully demonstrates in his narrative how the disciples are obedient to the command of Jesus and how this command is carried out. Thus, the disciples return to Jerusalem, which is but a "sabbath day's journey" from the Mount of Olives (1:12), and devote themselves to prayer (1:14). The reference to the "sabbath day's journey" confirms that the disciples are indeed "waiting" in Jerusalem as commanded (1:4).

In the next scene (1:15-26) the disciples choose a successor to Judas. This particular narrative, while having a function of its own, serves to separate the promise of Jesus in 1:8 from its initial fulfillment at Pentecost (2:1-4), thereby heightening the suspense.

In the following scene (2:1-42) Luke narrates the coming of the Holy Spirit on the day of Pentecost, followed by Peter's interpretation of the event (2:14-36). The original core of disciples receives the outpouring of the Spirit. This original core is composed of Galilean, Aramaic-speaking Jewish Christians who continue to be faithful Jews (cf. 1:12) and who engage in Temple prayers (2:46, 3:1; cf. Lk 24:53). To this original core is added "devout Jews from every nation under heaven living in Jerusalem" (2:5). These devout Jews hear the gospel in their "native language" (*glossalalia*, 2:8) and many of them believe and are baptized (2:41).

During the Pentecost event, then, the gospel comes to those devout Jews who are living in Jerusalem (2:5). As Peter quotes from the prophet Joel, God's Spirit has been poured out on "all flesh" (2:17). Even though these Jews are from every nation, it is only the first step in the spread of the gospel. Pentecost is a proleptic event, as the following narrative indicates.

After Peter's sermon Luke provides a summary (2:43-47). Several items are mentioned, but in particular Luke mentions the "many wonders and signs" being done by the apostles (2:43). In chapters 3 and 4 Luke gives a specific example of a "wonder and sign": the healing of the lame man. This event gives color to the narrative and serves to distance the early church from the central tenets of Judaism. Indeed, the disciples are confronted for preaching the resurrection of the dead in the name of Jesus (4:2). On seven different occasions the narrator, or one of the characters in the narratives, uses the term *name* (3:6, 16; 4:7, 10, 12, 17, 18), highlighting the discontinuance of the early church from Judaism and the Sadducees, the guardians of the name of God (cf. 1 Kgs 8:12-21). Thus the Temple is no longer merely a place where God's name will dwell; forgiveness and healing now take place in Jesus' name.

The events in the Temple are followed by the disciples' prayer for boldness (4:23-31) and another summary statement of early church life (4:32-35). This summary statement emphasizes that there was no economic need in the early church: "Everything they owned was held in common" (4:32). As with the earlier summary, Luke follows it with examples. Barnabas, a positive example, sells a field and lays the proceeds at the apostles' feet (5:36-37). Ananias and Sapphira, negative examples, sell a piece of property but withhold a portion of it, lie about it, and die for their deceit (5:1-11).

This series of stories reveals a tightly woven narrative of the preaching of the gospel along expanding geographical lines in and around Jerusalem. The disciples encounter opposition, but the gospel ultimately prevails.

At the beginning of chapter 6 we have a transition, since this is the first time that Luke mentions the Christian-Jewish Hellenists. In chapter 3 we notice how the early Jewish Christians begin to be distanced from Judaism by preaching in the Temple in the name of Jesus. Now the Hellenistic Christians are further distanced from the center of Judaism. The Sanhedrin Council charges Stephen with speaking "blasphemous words against Moses and God" (6:11). He spoke "against this holy place and the law" (6:13). Stephen's speech begins by reciting the patriarchal history and gradually moves to a climax in 7:48: "Yet the Most High does not dwell in houses made with human hands." It is this rejection of the Temple that results in the persecution of the Christian-Jewish Hellenists and their resultant expulsion from Jerusalem.

The narrative of the Hellenist controversy and the resulting persecution is followed immediately by the stories of Philip's ministry, first to the Samaritans, then to the eunuch. The Samaritans are not Jews, but neither are they Gentiles. Popular thought among the Jewish people in the first century regarded the Samaritans as unholy stepchildren of Abraham. They have second-class status among the Jewish people, and this status is legendary.[30] Luke's story of the good Samaritan is known beyond academia and Sunday School.

The story of the Samaritans leads directly into the story of the eunuch, who, I would argue, is in a similar condition to the Samaritans. Though he is a Jew, he is unfit to worship in the Temple. He too is a second-class citizen. The stories of the Samaritans and the eunuch function as transitions from the Hellenists to the Gentiles.

In the following episode, after the story of the eunuch, Luke narrates the call of Saul. For Luke, Saul, also called Paul, is the preeminent missionary to the Gentiles. Luke narrates his calling prior to the conversion of Cornelius in chapter 10, though his ministry to the Gentiles does not begin until after the conversion of Cornelius. Interestingly, Luke describes Saul at Damascus proclaiming "Jesus in the synagogues" (9:20). Later, in Jerusalem, Saul argues with the Hellenists (9:29), since his mission among the Gentiles must await the call of Cornelius. Only then does his ministry to the Gentiles begin. Paul's own ministry thus parallels the narrative of Acts as a whole. He preaches first to Jews, then to Hellenists, then to Gentiles.[31]

## CONCLUSION

In conclusion, the narrative of the Ethiopian eunuch demonstrates Luke's skill as a storyteller; he weaves his strands of material into a tapestry. Within this well-woven cloth, the eunuch highlights again Luke's concern for those who find themselves outside of the religious mainstream through no fault of their own. Luke's concern for the poor and oppressed, including women, the sick, and the ethnically impure is well known. The story of the Ethiopian eunuch is simply one more example of Luke's broad social concern.

The implications for ministry are profound. The narrative of Acts demonstrates the expanding circle of the people of God to larger and more diverse groups. Barriers once considered sacred, such as ethnic origin or physical impairment, are removed. The definition of the people of God is expanded to include all who trust in Christ.

While it may seem obvious to us today that we should not exclude people from the kingdom due to their ethnic origin or physical defects, this was not clear to the early church. These changes came slowly and painfully, forced the destruction of centuries-old taboos, and required a complete paradigm shift on the part of the early Christians. While Luke tends to minimize these struggles in order to show that all are accepted by God, a careful reading of his narrative reveals them. These struggles are far more pronounced in the letters of Paul, particularly in his letter to the Galatians.

The last chapter has not yet been written. Each generation must address again the same questions that the early church addressed. Are the people of God erecting barriers to the work of the kingdom? Are they the same old barriers, such as ethnic origin or handicap that the early church faced, or are they new barriers to ministry? Our question needs to be the same question that Peter addressed later to his more conservative constituency, "Can anyone withhold the water for baptizing these people who have received the Holy Spirit just as we have?" (Acts 10:47).

## REFERENCES

[1] F. F. Bruce, "Philip and the Ethiopian," *Journal of Semitic Studies* 34/2 (Autumn 1989), 377; Ernst Haenchen, *The Acts of the Apostles: A Commentary*, 14th ed., trans., rev.. and updated R. McL. Wilson (Philadelphia: Westminster Press, 1971; German original, 1965), 314; I. Howard Marshall, *The Acts of the Apostles: An Introduction and Commentary* (Leicester, England: Inter-Varsity Press, 1980), 160; Robert C. Tannehill, *The Narrative Unity of Luke-Acts*, 2 vols. (Philadelphia and Minneapolis: Fortress Press, 1986, 1989), 2:107. Conzelmann thinks Luke intentionally leaves the religious status of the eunuch vague because he does not want him to appear to be a Gentile (Hans Conzelmann, *Acts of the Apostles*, Hermeneia [Philadelphia: Fortress Press, 1987; German original, 1972], 68). For a reasoned argument that the Ethiopian is a Jew, see Luke Timothy Johnson, *The Acts of the Apostles*, Sacra Pagina, vol. 5 (Collegeville, Minn.: The Liturgical Press, 1992), 159.

[2] Haenchen, *The Acts of the Apostles*, 314; Bruce, "Philip and the Ethiopian," 377.

[3] Throughout the rest of this article I use Luke as the traditional name of the author, without drawing any conclusions as to who this Luke might be.

[4] F. D. Gealy, "Ethiopian Eunuch," *The Interpreter's Dictionary of the Bible* (Nashville, Tenn.: Abingdon, 1962), 177; Edward Ullendorff, *Ethiopia and the Bible: The Schweich Lectures of the British Academy, 1967* (London: Oxford University Press, 1968), 5.

[5] Herodotus uses the term this way: "Ethiopians inhabit the country immediately above Elephantine, and one half of the island; the other half is inhabited by Egyptians; . . . finally, you will arrive at a large city called Meroe: this city is said to be the capital of all Ethiopia" (Herodotus, II.29, cited in Ullendorff, *Ethiopia and the Bible*, 5; Strabo, I.2.25; Pliny, VI.185).

[6] In Esther 8:9 Ahasuerus issues a decree "to the Jews, and to the satraps and the governors and the officials of the provinces from India to Ethiopia." This reference indicates that Ethiopia was considered to be the extreme southern edge of the Persian Empire in the author's time, and it also indicates awareness of Jews living in Ethiopia.

[7] Josephus, *Antiquities* VIII, 6.5-6.

[8] In the Septuagint the people of Ethiopia are sometimes seen as a distinct people. At other times they seem to be identified with the people of Southern Arabia. In Isaiah 45:14 the Sabeans are listed as a distinct people from Egypt and Ethiopia. In an oracle describing the events after the coming of Cyrus, the prophet announces: "The wealth of Egypt and the merchandise of Ethiopia, and the Sabeans, tall of stature, shall come over to you and be yours" (45:14; cf. Dn 11:43). It appears that the prophet is referring to three distinct entities. In Isaiah 43:3, Ethiopia and Seba are listed together, but it is unclear whether they should be understood together or separately. In Habakkuk 3:7, Ethiopia and Midian are connected through parallelism: "I saw the tents of Cushan under affliction; the tent-curtains of the land of Midian trembled." In Numbers 12:1 Moses is criticized for marrying a Cushite woman. She is identified in Exodus 2:16 and 21 as a Midianite. Thus it appears that Ethiopia and Arabia were sometimes connected in the ancient world. Isaiah 18:1 refers to "a land of whirring wings beyond the river of Ethiopia." These people sent ambassadors to Judah. The prophet refers to them as "a nation tall and smooth" (18:2). Interestingly, in Isaiah 45:14 the Sabeans are referred to as a tall nation. Thus the prophet may be referring to Sabeans in Isaiah 18.

[9] A. H. M. Jones and Elizabeth Monroe, *A History of Ethiopia* (Clarendon: Oxford, 1968; 1935), 18.

[10] By the sixth century C.E. the kingdom of Axum (Abyssinia) regarded Ethiopia (Nubia) as a foreign country. In *A History of Ethiopia* Jones and Monroe quote the *Christian Cosmography* of Cosmos, who refers to an inscription of an Axumite king and his conquests of Ethiopia (23-24).

[11] Pliny, *Natural History,* 6.186.

[12] Herodotus, II.29.

[13] Pseudo Callisthenes, 111:18, in *The Ethiopic Versions of the Pseudo Callisthenes,* ed. Sir Ernest A. Budge (London: Oxford, 1933), 112.

[14] Strabo, XVII.820.

[15] Pliny, VI.186.

[16] Cited in Kirsopp Lake and Henry J. Cadbury, *The Acts of the Apostles,* vol. 4, *The Beginnings of Christianity,* part 1, ed. F. J. Foakes Jackson and Kirsopp Lake (Grand Rapids, Mich.: Baker Books, 1979), 96.

[17] Ullendorff discusses the fusion of the Candace traditions with the queen of Sheba traditions in the *Kebra Nagast* (Edward Ullendorff, "Candace [Acts viii.27] and the Queen of Sheba," *New Testament Studies* 2 [1955-1956], 53-56).

[18] *Kebra Nagast* 33.

[19] Kevin G. O'Conner, *The Ethiopian Eunuch,* master's thesis (Dekalb, Ill.: Northern Illinois University, 1969), 66.

[20] For a detailed discussion, see James B. Prichard, ed., *Solomon and Sheba* (London: Phaidon, 1974).

[21] The *Kebra Nagast* was translated from an Arabic translation of a Coptic original in 1225, and Greek writers of the sixth century do not know of the legend. They seem to think that the Abyssinians are a colony of Syrians transplanted to Ethiopia by Alexander the Great (Jones and Monroe, *A History of Ethiopia,* 18-20).

[22] We cannot exclude the possibility that the term *always* refers to a castrated male, even in those cases where the term is traditionally understood to refer to a person's official status. Potiphar may have been a high official in the Egyptian court, but he may have been a castrated male as well. The actions of Potiphar's wife, which are legendary, do not require this understanding. Yet her attempts to seduce Joseph take on new light if the reader understands that her husband is unable to fulfill his marital duties.

[23] Compare F. Scott Spencer, "The Ethiopian Eunuch and His Bible: A Social-Science Analysis," *Biblical Theology Bulletin* 22/4 (Winter 1992), 155-165.

[24] This is further supported by Luke's story of the centurion in Luke 7:1-10. In Luke's telling of the story the centurion sends "Jewish elders" (7:3) to see Jesus. In the Matthean account, however, the centurion comes directly to Jesus (Mt 8:5-13).

[25] Haenchen, *The Acts of the Apostles,* 314; Conzelmann, *Acts of the Apostles,* 67; Bruce, "Philip and the Ethiopian," 377.

[26] Tannehill, *The Narrative Unity of Luke-Acts,* 107.

[27] Ibid.

[28] Herodotus, III.25, III.114. For evidence from the Septuagint that Ethiopia represents "the ends of the earth," see Esther 8:9.

[29] Tannehill, *The Narrative Unity of Luke-Acts,* 107.

[30] Ben Witherington III says that "the Samaritans came to be viewed by Judean Jews as, at best, half-breeds who had significantly intermarried with the pagan Assyrians" (*New Testament History: A Narrative Account* [Grand Rapids, Mich.: Baker Books, 2001], 189).

[31] Paul's own ministry expands along geographical and cultural lines. It is beyond the scope of this chapter, however, to relate this movement.

# 11

## *Worshiping, Working, and Waiting: Exploring Paul's Call to Mission*

### Acts 9:1–22

### Nancy J. Thomas

Samuel Medina's[1] call to mission sounds likes a Barnabas-Paul story, straight from the Book of Acts. While yet in high school and just one year after his conversion to Christ, a local Bolivian pastor took this young man by the hand and said, "Come with me on a mission journey."

It was while traveling to remote villages located along the Amazon River that Samuel, along with a small group of high school companions, experienced God working through them cross-culturally to lead people to Christ and build up the church.

Samuel claims God called him to mission as he worked alongside this experienced missionary, saw his faith in action, observed human need, and tasted the fruits of ministry. He recalls one village in particular where the team held a campaign and six people became Christian. Only one of them could read. Samuel asked himself as they left, "Who will care for these people?" He returned after three years to find a stable, growing church in the village. The one man who could read had read the Bible aloud to the church during those years. "I realized that the work is God's," claims Samuel, and his sense of God's calling grew stronger.

Back home, the young disciples of the Bolivian Barnabas formed a missionary association for the purpose of awakening vision in local churches. They continued to organize short-term mission trips to various ethnic groups in the country. Working and praying together confirmed the call all these young people felt. Samuel's own local church, however, did nothing to encourage his call. To the contrary, leaders criticized him for neglecting them due to all these "outside activities."

During the following years Samuel attended a four-year seminary to prepare himself for mission, married, began a family, and entered upon a successful career as head of the public-relations department of a university, all the while pulled by his desire to participate in God's purposes in the world.

Some twenty years after his initial sense of call, Samuel found what seemed to be the perfect opportunity. A Bolivian missionary serving in Mexico invited him to join his team. Samuel and his wife, Silvia, tried unsuccessfully to elicit the support of their local church and, failing this, decided to go anyway, independently, trusting God.

After selling their possessions and quitting their jobs, Samuel, Silvia, and their two young daughters packed their bags and headed off for Mexico. Their adventure turned into seven months of frustration, suffering, and mounting confusion. The missionary who had invited them turned against them, the few people back home who had promised to send money forgot, and without the support of agency or church, they were forced to return to Bolivia, broken and embarrassed, to try to rebuild their lives.

Today Samuel is still working off the debts incurred by his missionary misadventure. Yet he continues to affirm God's call on his life. Analyzing his experience in Mexico, he notes that they were "invited, but not sent," and he is determined that any future work in mission involve the local church.

Samuel's experience is both unique and typical of that of the many Latin Americans God is calling to mission. It is unique in the fact that twenty years of preparation and waiting followed the initial sense of call. It is typical in the haste that precipitated the journey to Mexico. Unfortunately it is also typical in the lack of participation by the local church in confirming Samuel's call, in encouraging him, and in sending and supporting him.

A 1996 study of missionary attrition conducted by the Missions Commission of the World Evangelical Fellowship (WEF) shows the importance of both a sense of call and the participation of the local church, two aspects of Samuel Medina's story.[2] The extensive study sought to identify causes of missionary attrition, investigating missionary sending in some fourteen countries, divided between "old sending countries" and "new sending countries." In the category of the younger missionary sending force in the majority world, the investigation showed that the two top causes of missionaries prematurely coming home from the field are lack of home support and lack of a clear call.[3] Results also showed that sending agencies with a low "preventable attrition rate" consistently insisted that their candidates have a firm sense of call from God.[4] Sending agencies from Brazil, the country with the largest missionary deployment in Latin America, named "a clear calling to mission work from God" as one of the top three factors in preventing missionary attrition. The same Brazilian survey recommended more attention be given to the role of the local church in the personal life of the missionary; this would include the aspect of call and its confirmation.[5]

My husband and I are currently involved in equipping Latin Americans for mission, and the issue of the missionary call and its confirmation is current and often troublesome to our students, along with the problem of apathy in many local congregations. This chapter attempts to study the issue of call in the Book of Acts, taking the apostle Paul as a model. I compare the parallel passages that describe Paul's conversion and call, as well as other passages that detail Paul's response to God's call. This extends from the time he received the call to the beginning of his first missionary journey. Paul's model may provide guidelines for those God is raising up to go from Latin America to the uttermost parts of the earth.

## PAUL'S MISSIONARY CALL

The story of Paul's conversion and call to mission is recounted four times in the New Testament, something that in itself says, "Take notice. This is important stuff." The first account is Luke's version of the story told in Acts 9. This is repeated, as Paul himself speaks to the Jewish mob in Jerusalem in Acts 22 and again as Paul tells his story to the Roman court of Agrippa in Caesarea in Acts 26. The final version occurs in Paul's letter to the Galatians, written at the end of his first missionary journey. In this section I also explore related passages in Acts 11, 12, and 13. I look at the nature and description of the call, how God chose to communicate it, and how Paul responded.

First, it would be helpful to list and date the events between Paul's conversion and his first missionary journey. I base the following chronology on F. F. Bruce's conclusions after comparing passages in Acts with the epistles and other historical records.[6] Not all the facts are available, and the order and dating are therefore necessarily tentative (see table on following page).

## NATURE AND DESCRIPTION OF PAUL'S MISSIONARY CALL

The verb translated into English as "call" *(kaleo)* occurs 148 times in the New Testament with a variety of meanings, including the general call to follow Christ and live godly lives (e.g., Rom 8:28-30; 1 Cor 1:2; Eph 4:1; Col 3:15). I am looking specifically for references to a call to special service, to what is known in Christian circles as "the missionary call." The passages I study use a variety of words in describing God's call to Paul.

Only once in these passages is the general verb for call, *kaleo*, used, and that is in Galatians 1:15, where Paul writes that God "called me through his grace." Luke uses other, more specific terms. In Acts 9 the Lord tells Ananias that Paul is "an instrument whom I have chosen" (v. 15). The noun "choice" *(ekloge)* comes from the verb *eklegomai*, "to choose, elect, pick out for oneself," with the noun form "used unambiguously and exclusively for God's act of election."[7]

Luke uses the verb *proskaleo* (built on *kaleo*) in Acts 13:2, as the Holy Spirit speaks to the church at Antioch. This term connotes a call to service and the perfect tense "emphasizes the divine decision was made before it was announced."[8] In this same passage Luke uses a term translated as "set apart," repeated by Paul in Galatians 1:15 *(aforizo)* with connotations of being marked off from others with a boundary, set aside for special purpose.[9]

There are two other "calling verbs" in the passages under consideration that are translated as "assign" and "chosen." The word used in Acts 22:10 ("everything that has been assigned to you to do") comes from a military verb *(tasso)*

| Event | Date | Reference |
|-------|------|-----------|
| Paul's conversion on the road to Damascus; hears his missionary call for the first time through Ananias; testifies in Damascus | 33 | Acts 9:1-22; 22:3-16; 26:12-18 |
| Spends time alone in Arabia; goes back to Damascus | 33-35 | Gal 1:15-17; Acts 9:21-25 |
| First post-conversion trip to Jerusalem; call reconfirmed directly from God in a worship experience in the Temple | 35 | Acts 9:26-29; 22:17-21; Gal 1:18 |
| Travels to Syria, Cilicia, Caesarea, Tarsus | 35-45 | Acts 9:30; Gal 1:21—2:1 |
| Joins Barnabas for ministry to the multicultural church at Antioch | 45 | Acts 11:19-26 |
| Famine-relief visit to Jerusalem; call confirmed by church leaders | 46 | Acts 11:27-30; Gal 2:1-10 |
| Call conveyed by the Holy Spirit to the local chuch leaders; the church at Antioch sends Paul and Barnabas out on their first missionary journey | 47-48 | Acts 13:1-3 |

with a primary meaning of "command."[10] In both Acts 22:14 ("the God of our ancestors has chosen you"—*proxeirizomai*) and Acts 26:16 ("I have appeared to you for this purpose, to appoint you"—*proxeirizo*), the verbs combine the words "before" and "hand" and carry the connotations of "plan, purpose, and determine" with anticipation.[11]

In all these passages not only is the variety of verbs noteworthy but also especially significant is the emphasis on God's sovereignty. In each case God is choosing, commanding, planning, and appointing. The tone of divine determination is strong. For instance, Galatians 1 emphasizes this as Paul testifies that God set him apart even before his birth.

The passages also give insight into God's purposes. To what end did God appoint Paul? What was Paul's divine job description? In Acts 9 the Lord calls Paul "to bring my name" (v. 15), to carry and spread forth the person and message of Jesus. In Acts 26 the Lord appoints Paul to "serve and testify" (v. 16) in order that people repent, be converted, receive forgiveness, and join with the people of God, God's church (v. 18). In Galatians 1 Paul records his call to proclaim God (v. 16). These job descriptions are all presented in general terms, without specifics.

The version in Acts 22 gives additional insight when Ananias informs Paul that God has appointed him to know God's will and to see and hear Jesus (v.

14). It is a call first to relationship and intimacy with the result being that "you will be his witness to all the world of what you have seen and heard" (22:15). The Galatians 1 version demonstrates that Paul's proclamation flows from the revelation of Jesus.

Several of the passages provide brief glimpses of other aspects of the missionary call. In Acts 9 we find suffering mentioned as an aspect of the call to mission (v. 16), almost as though it is an integral part of the job description. In Galatians 1 the idea of grace is connected with call (v. 15). Both the concepts of grace and suffering and their connection with the missionary call open up areas for reflection and study beyond the scope of this chapter.

The passages, combined and compared, show the whole Trinity involved in calling Paul to mission. The Lord Jesus chooses him (Acts 9:15; 22:21; 26:16), the Father appoints him (Acts 22:14; Gal 1:15), and the Holy Spirit calls him forth (Acts 13:2). Paul's call to mission is the sovereign work of the triune God. God takes the initiative and calls Paul specifically and uniquely to be an agent of the divine purposes in the world.

The passages also show the destination of the call. All four narratives state that Paul was called to the Gentiles. Acts 9 gives a broader perspective as the Lord informs Ananias that Paul would bear the divine name "before Gentiles and kings and before the people of Israel" (v. 15). Acts 22 records the call "to all the world" (v. 15) and later adds the detail that Paul would go "far away to the Gentiles" (v. 21). In the aspect of destination Paul's call was both specific (to the Gentiles) and general (to political leaders, Israelites, and all people). God apparently did not supply Paul ahead of time with details of geography or the specifics of what he was to do. Paul would discover the details on the road, as he partnered with God in mission. The call provided wide-open boundaries, a panoramic vision.

## HOW GOD COMMUNICATED THE CALL TO PAUL

In the last section I looked at the nature and description of Paul's call to mission. In this section I explore the same passages to see the mode of communication of God's call to Paul. I take a chronological approach.

Both Acts 9 and 22 record that God first communicated the call through a human agent. Although the Lord Jesus spoke directly to Paul on the Damascus road in his conversion experience, he ordered Ananias to deliver the message of the missionary call. Two items of interest stand out: First, Paul's missionary call came straight after his conversion; and second, God chose to use another person to deliver the message rather than speaking directly to Paul.[12]

God's choice of Ananias as the message bearer is significant. This disciple of Jesus knew how to listen to and speak with the Lord, and he was apparently accustomed to obedience even in the face of risk (Acts 9). He was also a devout keeper of the Law and a person highly respected in the Jewish community at Damascus (Acts 22). This would give the call credibility, not only to Paul himself but also to the wider community.

Although his initial understanding of God's call to special service involved another human being, Paul himself emphasizes the personal nature of God's communication to him. In his letter to the Galatian Christians, he writes that after his conversion and call "I did not confer with any human being, nor did I go up to Jerusalem to those who were already apostles before me, but I went away at once into Arabia, and afterwards I returned to Damascus" (1:16-17).[13] We don't know what happened in Arabia, but Paul apparently was alone with God. The call to know God's will, to see and hear from Jesus, must have been part of the scene. God would have continued to reveal his person, message, and the role Paul was to play in a communication that was intensely personal yet intensely communal as well.

The next chronological reference to Paul's reception of his call takes place during his first visit to Jerusalem, recorded in Acts 22:17-21. Paul is alone, praying in the Temple, and, as he later testifies to a Jewish audience, he falls into a trance and converses with the Lord Jesus. In this encounter the Lord warns Paul of imminent danger, gives specific instructions for him to leave Jerusalem immediately, and confirms the missionary call: "Go, for I will send you far away to the Gentiles" (v. 21). It is important to note that it was during Paul's time alone in worship that God spoke to him.

Two other passages show God confirming to Paul the call to mission and both these events involve the community of faith. They take place approximately fourteen years after Paul's conversion and initial reception of the missionary call. In Galatians 2:1-10 we see the leaders of the church in Jerusalem (and of the whole early Christian movement) recognizing and affirming the calls of Barnabas and Paul to the Gentiles.[14] The next scene takes place in Antioch, where local church leaders are gathered, ministering to the Lord and fasting. The Holy Spirit speaks to these leaders, confirming the calls to Barnabas and Paul, and saying, in effect, "Now is the time" (Acts 13:1-3). Again, we note that God spoke as the church was gathered for worship.

It is significant to note that God communicated the call to special missionary service communally and personally. God spoke directly to Paul. Also, God spoke to Paul through other people. And God told the church, for its own sake, that Paul was to be set apart for his divine missional purposes in the world. God used different means, at various times, to communicate the missionary appointment to Paul and to the church.

## HOW PAUL RESPONDED TO THE MISSIONARY CALL

Having discussed the nature of Paul's call to mission and how God communicated that call to him, I now look at Paul's response. Three things stand out during the fourteen years between Paul's initial reception of the missionary call and the first missionary journey: obedience, active preparation, and growth in relationship.

Paul testifies to the Roman court that "I was not disobedient to the heavenly vision" in preaching to the Jews and Gentiles (Acts 26:19-20), and Luke notes that this response of active obedience to God's call was immediate (Acts 9:20).

Paul responded in obedience directly to God, but he also responded by submitting to God's agents. Ananias urged him not to delay for an instant but to be baptized and call on God's name (Acts 22:16). Paul followed the instructions of the church at Jerusalem in leaving that city and returning eventually to his hometown of Tarsus, effectively disappearing from the scene for some ten years (Acts 9:30). Barnabas mentored Paul, bringing him from Tarsus to Antioch for a time of team ministry. Paul then submitted his call and ministry to the elders of the Jerusalem church (Gal 2:1-10) and to the local church leaders at Antioch, not embarking on his first missionary journey until the church, through God's bidding, sent him (Acts 13:1-3). Paul responded to God's missionary call in obedient submission directly to God and to the faith community.

We do not know everything that happened during the fourteen years between Paul's call and his first journey, but the scriptures testify that he did not sit by idly, waiting for the green light. As we noted earlier, after becoming a follower of Jesus, Paul "immediately began to proclaim Jesus in the synagogues," and he "became increasingly more powerful and confounded the Jews who lived in Damascus" (Acts 9:20, 22). In his first visit to Jerusalem he was "speaking boldly in the name of the Lord. He spoke and argued with the Hellenists" (Acts 9:28-29). We don't have a record of the ten years Paul spent in the regions of Syria, Cilicia, and his hometown of Tarsus, but we know that during this time he developed a ministry among Gentiles and that his reputation among Christians in Judea was growing, sight unseen (Gal 1:21-24). In Acts 11—13, we get glimpses of Paul's ministry with Barnabas at the new Gentile church in Antioch. The picture is one of growth in active ministry. Paul probably would not have seen these years merely as preparation for future service; he was serving God and fulfilling his calling, even without travel to distant lands. He responded to his missionary call by entering into ministry from his context.

The other aspect of this time between call and fulfillment is Paul's obviously growing relationship with God and the church. The passages under study only indirectly hint at this growth. The time alone with God in Arabia, early in Paul's Christian life, certainly contributed to his intimacy with his Lord. The occasions spent with Barnabas and with church leaders in Jerusalem and Antioch show a man who had learned to work in a team, be part of a local church, and follow the leadership of those in authority. When Paul began his first missionary journey, he was not an isolated, heroic individual, bravely striking out alone to follow God's call. He was a person intimate with God and in close relationship with God's people. The intimacy and relationship were part of the call and part of the preparation for mission.

## APPLICATIONS TO LATIN AMERICAN INVOLVEMENT IN THE MISSIONARY MOVEMENT

Samuel and Silvia Medina, as well as a growing number of other Latin Americans eager to participate with God's mission in the world, have been given a helpful model in the apostle Paul. In conclusion, I draw applications from the biblical narratives to the Latin American missionary scene.

1. The bedrock of the missionary call is the sovereignty of God. In answer to the questions many young Latin Americans are asking, "Yes, God does call

persons forth to world mission." This is important to remember in the emotional appeal of the missionary movement. Call is more than emotion. It is the sovereign choosing of an almighty God who beckons.

2. We also learn from the narratives that God intends to communicate the call to missionary service without leaving us guessing. Many young Latins ask, "How can I know if God is calling me?" An excellent question and an important one, because it is crucial to be sure of a call before embarking on a missionary adventure. Paul's experience shows that God uses different means, even with the same person, and that after an initial communication of the call, God confirms and reconfirms. We need to be open to visions, words from mature Christian friends, the leading of our local church, as well as means not mentioned in these particular Pauline narratives, such as scripture and preaching. The passages suggest a connection between worship, both on a personal and on a community level, and the communication of the call. Paul's story lets us know that through whatever means, when God calls us to mission, God also communicates that call.

3. A missionary call, as experienced by Paul, can be a process, often taking considerable time. Paul's experience of his call took fourteen years. It involved many steps, and Paul's obedience along the way seemed to lead to new evidence of his call and fresh confirmations. The process involves God's communication to us and our response back to God. It's a process of growth in obedience, intimacy, relationship, and ministry. Preparation is part of the process, but preparation that involves active ministry.

It is a process that takes considerable faith, as the specifics of geography or job description aren't always revealed. The details seem to come as we are on the road, walking with the Savior in active ministry. The process calls for patience, something that challenges many Latin Americans, especially young people who want to get started now. The Mexican peasant asleep under a cactus, sombrero over his eyes, kept by a "mañana mentality," is a cliché that does not even approach reality. Impatience and fiery enthusiasm better characterize young Latins, and it is these characteristics that need to bend to the process of call.

4. God's call to mission is intensely personal. God knows each person individually and uniquely, even before birth, and communicates intimately with that person. Relationship with God is a part of the missionary call. Just as God called Paul into a personal relationship and understanding of the divine will, so servants of God are called today, first to intimacy and worship, and then, as a result, to witness and mission. A missionary call is a very personal experience.

5. God's call to mission is a call into a community of faith. This is the other side of the coin. As persons, we are part of a family, and God seems to delight in using other members of the family to communicate and confirm the missionary calling of its members. In Paul's experience, God used mature Christians who mentored Paul, the key leaders of the whole Christian movement, and leaders in the local congregation. Especially noteworthy in Paul's experience is the importance of the local church and the fact that, after waiting fourteen years, it was through the local church at Antioch that the recorded confirmation of the

call took place. It was the local church that, finally, sent Paul and Barnabas on their first missionary journey.

Latin American missionary candidates need to submit to local church authority in confirming their call, in preparation for missionary service, and for discernment as to the timing. Local church leaders need to be sensitive to the role God would have them play in shepherding the potential missionaries in their congregations. This was the missing link in the case of the Medinas, and it continues to be a general weakness in the Latin American missionary movement.

Samuel and Silvia have not given up. They continue to sense God's missionary call. They are currently part of a local congregation that is actively seeking ways to cooperate with other people in mission. The church's advocacy and mentoring are giving this couple new hope.

May this study of the experience of Paul, and of others throughout Scripture who received God's call to special service, lead to a theology of call that would help the church in the majority world participate wisely and effectively in God's mission among the nations.

## REFERENCES

[1] I have changed the names of the people involved in this story.

[2] The study considers preventable attrition and defines this as "premature or avoidable return from field service . . . attrition that could have been avoided by better initial screening or selection in the first place, or by more appropriate equipping or training, or by more effective shepherding during missionary service" (William D. Taylor, "Prologue," in *Too Valuable to Lose: Exploring the Causes and Cures of Missionary Attrition*, ed. William D. Taylor [Pasadena, Calif.: William Carey Library, 1997], xvii).

[3] William D. Taylor, "Introduction: Examining the Iceberg Called Attrition," in Taylor, *Too Valuable to Lose*, 10; Peter W. Brierley, "Missionary Attrition: The ReMAP Research Project," in Taylor, *Too Valuable to Lose*, 99. This data reflects a survey of 203 sending agencies in eight majority world countries.

[4] Detlef Blöcher and Jonathan Lewis, "Further Findings in the Research Data," in Taylor, *Too Valuable to Lose*, 118.

[5] Ted Limpic, "Brazilian Missionaries: How Long Are They Staying?" in Taylor, *Too Valuable to Lose*, 153-154.

[6] F. F. Bruce, "Acts of the Apostles," in *The International Standard Bible Encyclopedia*, 3 vols., ed. G. W. Bromiley (Grand Rapids, Mich.: Eerdmans, 1979), 1:33-47; idem, "Paul the Apostle," in Bromiley, *The International Standard Bible Encyclopedia*, 3:696-720.

[7] L. Coenen, "Elect," *The New International Dictionary of New Testament Theology*, vol. 1, ed. Colin Brown (Grand Rapids, Mich.: Zondervan, 1971), 540.

[8] Fritz Rienecker and Cleon Rogers, *Linguistic Key to the Greek New Testament* (Grand Rapids, Mich.: Zondervan, 1976), 291.

[9] Ibid., 502.

[10] Ibid., 324.

[11] Ibid.

[12] In the Acts 26 version the Lord appears to speak the call directly to Paul on the Damascus road. But in this version, as Paul recounts his experience to the Roman court of Agrippa, he purposefully leaves out details that would not be pertinent to his Roman

audience, including the whole incident with Ananias. His speech in this context synthesizes several events that took place at different times and in different places.

[13] F. F. Bruce places Paul's sojourn in Arabia after his conversion and before the first trip to Jerusalem. The Arabian trip, not mentioned in either Acts 9 or 22, would have taken place in the middle of the "many days" spent in Damascus (Acts 9:23). Paul's conversion, his time in Damascus and Arabia, and his journey back to Damascus correspond to the "three years" of Galatians 1:18 (see Bruce, "Acts of the Apostles," 41-42; idem, "Paul the Apostle," 709, 712).

[14] Bruce connects this passage with the trip for famine relief recorded in Acts 11:27-30 and 12:25 (see Bruce, "Paul the Apostle," 713).

# 12

## Peter's Conversion: A Culinary Disaster Launches the Gentile Mission

### Acts 10:1—11:18

### Charles E. Van Engen

Many of us in cross-cultural missionary and ministry activity have had moments—at the time, often seemingly insignificant moments—over the years that become important threads in the tapestry of who we are and how we do ministry. I experienced such a moment early in my missionary career in Southern Mexico.

In 1973 my wife, Jean, and I were sent to Chiapas, Mexico, as missionaries of the Reformed Church in America to serve the National Presbyterian Church of Mexico. Thankfully, in our new missionary context there were church members and pastors who took an interest in teaching us. One of them was Reverend Genaro Mendez. Genaro was pastoring a large church that also had some sixteen smaller worshiping groups spread over a sixty-mile radius. Some of these were quite distant, up in the Sierra Madre mountain range, accessible only by horseback.

A year after we arrived in Chiapas, Genaro invited me to join him in visiting all sixteen of his church congregations during the Christmas season, taking along a movie of the Christmas story. One of the congregations we would visit was 11 de Abril (11th of April). In that area many small villages and towns in the remote mountains use dates as the name of their town. The date-as-a-name commemorates the exact day that the town was chartered by the governor of the state. At that time, 11 de Abril was located at the end of a three-hour horseback ride up a steep, winding, narrow mountain trail along the edge of a deep precipice, during which the traveler rose nearly three thousand feet. The jumpiness of the horse I was given, the stirrups being too short for my long legs, and my own inexperience in riding these kinds of mountain trails combined to make me as nervous as my horse. Having an electric generator and a movie projector tied on top of pack animals to be pulled along with us made the journey seem even more challenging.

The next three hours were unforgettable. When the horse climbed up the trail, jumping over rocks and tree roots, I nearly fell off its back because of the short stirrups. When we came to a ravine or small waterfall and the horse began to slide downhill, I could barely keep from falling over its head into the mud. Seldom have I been so relieved to get to my destination—and off the back of a horse—as I was that day.

We arrived at 11 de Abril in the mid-afternoon. Pastor Genaro and I were invited to enjoy an excellent meal with the leading citizen of the small town. After a time of rest, we set up all the equipment for the evening worship. The singing, showing the sixteen-millimeter film of the Christmas story, Genaro's preaching, more singing, and spiritual counseling after the worship took over five hours. By this time it was around midnight.

After I packed up all the equipment, I was approached by a short, elderly woman who said that I was to sleep in her house that night. I'll call her Eunice. At her invitation I accompanied her to a small, one-room lodging. The walls were made of bamboo, with newspaper tacked on the inside to stop the cold air from blowing through the house. At one end was a small table and two chairs. The house had a dirt floor. A sheet divided the eating area from the sleeping area. The woman, a widow—one of the first believers in this town—showed me to the short, narrow bed with a thin blanket where she normally slept.

"Here is your bed," Eunice said with joy and a sense of pride. "I will sleep over with my daughter's family tonight. The leaders of the congregation chose to give me the honor of having you sleep in my house. Tomorrow early, before you leave, I will bring you breakfast. Sleep well—and thank you for honoring me by sleeping in my home."

I did not sleep well. The bed was made of rope strung inside a wooden frame. Besides being too short and narrow, the rope suspension scratched through my clothing. The blanket was too thin for the cool mountain air that blew through the house, despite the newspapers. By sunrise, I was grateful to hear the dogs barking and to have a rooster crow right next to my head outside my newspaper wall. But the Holy Spirit's work in me was still not complete.

Eunice came early with breakfast. There were corn tortillas, black beans, some hot, very thick black coffee—and an egg placed on a small metal plate. The egg was still in its shell—still uncooked. It had probably been laid by one of the woman's chickens the day before. Next to the metal plate was a large nail. I had been given an egg for breakfast: literally. The custom of the area was to use the nail to poke a small hole in one end of the egg. Having poked a larger hole at the other end of the egg, one was to suck out and swallow the contents of the egg in one gulp. I was glad for the coffee after swallowing the raw egg.

Having survived the breakfast that sister Eunice had given me that morning, I met Genaro by the corral. "Last night you slept in the house of a saint," Genaro told me. "Did you sleep well?" I mumbled a gruff reply. "Don't undervalue or underestimate that woman of God," Genaro told me, as I got up on that nervous horse to sit in the saddle with the short stirrups, wondering what the trip down the mountain would be like.

Just then Eunice came up. As I was already in the saddle, she could hardly reach me to shake my hand. I reached down to say goodbye. But instead of shaking my hand, sister Eunice handed me something. It was an egg, wrapped up in a dried cornhusk. I was to hold the two ends of the cornhusk together and the egg would dangle about six inches below in the fold of the cornhusk. "I don't have anything else to give you as a parting gift to thank you for coming," Eunice said with a wide smile. "My hen laid this egg just this morning, so it is fresh. Please take it for your breakfast tomorrow. And give my love to your wife."

What was I going to say? I was already up on my jumpy horse. I had no other place to put the egg where it would not get broken. So Genaro and I said farewell and began our trek down the mountain. And then my suffering began. Holding that egg in its cornhusk wrapping with one hand, it became a very real challenge for me not to fall off that horse, either over its head while going downhill or off the rump while going uphill. For the next three hours I held that egg in the air, trying not to break it. The situation seemed to be a new form of torture.

As I made my way down the mountain, trying desperately to stay on that horse, it seemed that every few minutes I would hear the echo of pastor Genaro's words: "Don't undervalue or underestimate that woman of God." Or, in the words of Acts 10:15, "What God has made clean, you must not call profane." Several hours later I walked into my home and Jean asked me how the trip had been.

"Unbelievable!" was all I could think to say as I handed her the cornhusk with the egg inside. It was still intact. And I went directly to my desk to reread Acts 10.

## THE RELEVANCE OF PETER'S CONVERSION

We must not underestimate the importance that Luke and the early church ascribed to the episode recorded in Acts 10. In total, this episode, with the three explanatory retellings of theological and missiological significance, comprise seventy-four verses in Acts. By contrast, Luke's narrative of the first Pentecost experience in Acts 2 involves only forty-six verses—and is not retold. Even Stephen's sermon and its surrounding narrative—the longest sermon in Acts— covers only sixty-one verses.[1]

In addition to the amount of space that Luke devotes to this episode, its importance for Luke is also signaled in at least three other striking ways. First, this episode is written in an Old Testament style for recording the acts of God. It apparently took an act of God for the first Jewish Christians to be willing to accept the Gentile converts over the objections of the Judaizer faction.[2] With Peter as the representative of the Jewish church, this change was so radical it can properly be called a conversion, a turning point. Thus, it would seem appropriate to talk of the story of Acts 10 as the story of Peter's conversion—or at least the third in a series of conversions in the life of Peter.[3] For the early

Jewish church, the Holy Spirit's coming to Cornelius and his household constituted a radical transforming moment, a major paradigm shift.

Second, the episode was understood to have clear theological and missiological significance for the life and mission of those early Christians. The meaning of the episode is clearly stated and often repeated: The gospel is for both Jews and Gentiles (9:15; 10:34, 36, 45, 47; 11:1, 15, 17, 18; 13:47-48; 14:27). Peter's report to the church leaders in Jerusalem in chapter 11 and the decision of the Jerusalem council in chapter 15 are focused on this episode in chapter 10. Peter's vision and the coming of the Holy Spirit to the household of Cornelius created a new reality for the Jewish Christians. If the gospel of Jesus Christ was for everyone, Jew and Gentile alike, then the nature of the church and its mission were something radically new. From this episode the entire Gentile mission flows. This includes Paul's ministry described in the rest of the Book of Acts, as well as the continuing Gentile mission of Barnabas and John Mark (15:36ff.), the worldwide ministries of other disciples and the early church, and the worldwide expansion of a multilingual and multicultural, global church of Jesus Christ as we know it today.

Third, Luke weaves the telling and retelling of this episode as one of the major threads that draws together the longer narrative from 9:32 to 15:35. The mission of God to the Gentiles in Acts is launched on the foundation of the word-deed narrative theology that flows from God's sending of the Holy Spirit to the household of Cornelius through the ministry of a converted Peter. This unified narrative progressively includes:

- Peter's story in Joppa (which began with his going to Samaria in 9:14-17, where he witnessed the Samaritan Pentecost);[4]
- the detailed telling of the story of the angel being sent by God to Cornelius, Peter's vision, and then Peter's experience of the Holy Spirit's coming upon Cornelius and his household (10:1-48);
- Peter's reporting of the episode to the Christians in Judea (11:1-18);
- reference to the predominantly Gentile church in Antioch (11:19-30; 12:25);
- the continuation of Peter's story in his escape from prison in Jerusalem (12:1-24);
- the Antioch church's involvement in sending Paul and Barnabas on their first Gentile mission (13:1-14:27);
- the decision of the Jerusalem council to accept Gentile believers in their midst, including the letter whose content is repeated twice—a decision based on what God had done in sending the Holy Spirit upon Cornelius and his household (15:6-29).[5]

## THE FOCUS OF PETER'S CONVERSION

Acts 10 appears to be focused on the life of Peter—it is part of Peter's life story (9:32—12:24). It is not fundamentally a story about Cornelius. The radical transformation and conversion here is ascribed to Peter, not to Cornelius.

The chapter begins by presenting Cornelius, a devout family man, a God-fearing Gentile (10:2, 22) who "gave alms generously to the people and prayed constantly to God" (10:2). True to Luke's narrative form of describing angelic appearances (Lk 1:11-20; 1:26-38), he tells how God sends an angel to Cornelius to tell him to send for Peter (10:5, 22, 31; 11:13).

Yet Peter is emotionally charged and initially unwilling to follow God's initiative. "I replied," Peter says, "'By no means, Lord, for nothing profane or unclean has ever entered my mouth'" (11:8).[6] In the story Peter presents himself as the one who needs changing. Reference to this change of perspective can be found at least five times throughout the narrative. "But God has shown me" (10:28); "I truly understand" (10:34); "God . . . shows no partiality, but in every nation anyone who fears him" (10:34-35); "Can anyone withhold the water for baptizing these people?" (10:47); and "Who was I that I could hinder God?" (11:17).

## THE DISCOURSE-LEVEL NARRATIVE STRUCTURE

Modern-day writers are not the only ones who have known how to use the "meanwhile, back at the ranch" device for good storytelling. Luke uses it masterfully in this part of Acts. In 8:14-25 Peter is sent to Samaria by the apostles in Jerusalem. There he witnesses the Samaritan Pentecost, the Holy Spirit coming upon the Samaritans. In 8:25 he and John return to Jerusalem, "proclaiming the good news to many villages of the Samaritans" (8:25) on the way. At this point Luke inserts the story of Philip and the Ethiopian (8:26-40) and recounts the manner of Saul's conversion (9:1-31).

Luke returns to Peter's story in 9:32, with Peter being drawn closer and closer to Joppa. "Now as Peter went here and there among all the believers, he came down also to the saints living in Lydda." There he heals Aeneas the paralytic (9:33-34). In Joppa, Tabitha (Dorcas) dies, the poor set up an outcry over her death, God hears their prayers, and the believers in Joppa send two men to get Peter. Peter then accompanies them to Joppa and raises Tabitha from the dead (9:36-42). Peter stays in Joppa at the home of a tanner named Simon (9:43). One half of the stage is set.

While Peter is in Joppa, God speaks to Cornelius in Caesarea (10:1). Located thirty miles from Joppa, Caesarea was named in honor of Augustus Caesar and was the headquarters of the Roman occupation forces. It is 3:00 in the afternoon in Cornelius's house. As the curtain rises on this next major scenario, we see Cornelius the Gentile centurion experiencing a vision in which he sees an angel who blesses him and tells him that he needs to send for Simon Peter who is at the tanner's house by the sea. Cornelius, a God-fearer,[7] obeys, sending two servants and a soldier to Joppa. The second half of the stage is now set.[8]

The next day about noon, while the three messengers are approaching Joppa (meanwhile, back at the ranch), the second act of the play takes place while Peter is up on the roof of the tanner's house. While he is praying, he experiences a trance. Then, "while Peter was still thinking about the vision [and the messengers are at the door of the tanner's house] the Spirit said to him, 'Look, three men are searching for you'" (10:19). Peter goes down to meet them and invites them in to stay the night, an unacceptable association for a Jew.

On what would then be the third day of the story, Peter goes to Caesarea with the three men. When Peter gets there, he finds a large group of people gathered at Cornelius's house, waiting for him to arrive. At their request Peter begins to preach one of his three sermons recorded in Acts. And, amazingly, "While Peter was still speaking, the Holy Spirit fell upon all who heard the word" (10:44). The new Gentile believers were baptized, and Peter was asked to stay with them for several more days.

Meanwhile, "the apostles and the believers who were in Judea heard that the Gentiles had also accepted the word of God" (11:1). So Peter finds it necessary to go up to Jerusalem and explain the situation. Once there, he retells the entire episode in great detail, stressing that this is something God has done through the Holy Spirit, not something that Peter had sought. This story then leads naturally to Luke's description of the scattering of the Jerusalem church due to the persecution there, the development of the church in Antioch, and the sending of the offering from Antioch to Jerusalem. "About that time" (12:1) Herod arrests Peter, Peter experiences the miraculous escape from prison at the hands of yet another angel, and Herod is judged by God and dies (12:1-24).

About the same time Barnabas and Saul return to Antioch where the Holy Spirit has been raising up a new cadre of leaders. And "while they were worshiping the Lord and fasting, the Holy Spirit" directs the believers in Antioch to set apart Barnabas and Saul for what would become the first of several journeys throughout the Roman world (13:2). The Gentile mission is thus launched. What a story! Are all these events simply coincidences? Clearly Luke was seeking to describe a well-orchestrated, carefully designed chain of events that could only be the work of God.

## THE HEART OF THE STORY

Now let's return to the beginning of the story. Like a bell curve, Luke's narrative slowly builds to a major climactic moment after which there flows a rather long series of implications and consequences that will extend to the end of the Book of Acts. The very peak of the mountaintop is this:

> While Peter was still speaking, the Holy Spirit fell upon all who heard the word. The circumcised believers who had come with Peter were astounded that the gift of the Holy Spirit had been poured out even on the Gentiles, for they heard them speaking in tongues and extolling God. (10:44-46)

This is the moment that becomes the hermeneutical, theological, and missiological key to the eventual acceptance by the Jewish Christians of the Gentile Christians in their midst.[9] Peter's vision on the rooftop of the tanner's house is the springboard from which the Gentile mission will be launched.

A number of commentators mention that Luke tells us that Peter stays at the home of Simon the tanner, someone whose occupation of curing the hides of dead animals would be considered unclean for a Jew.[10] Yet it seems to me that we miss the pathos and humor of the story if we neglect the smells implied in the story; Luke seems to go to great lengths to give us all the necessary details of a wonderfully humorous story, and additional details can easily be assumed, knowing the cultural and historical context of the story.

- Peter is in Joppa (9:43).
- Peter is at the house of a tanner (9:43).
- It is reasonable to assume that the tanner has his business in his house, as that was very common at that time, and in that culture.
- It is noon (10:9).
- It is the Middle East, on the coast of the Mediterranean, and the sun is burning.
- Peter goes up to the roof. We can assume it was one of the standard flat roofs of the area (10:9).
- Peter is hungry and wants something to eat. Notice the parallel with Jesus in Luke 4:2 (10:10).
- The meal is being prepared (10:10).

Now, I invite the reader to imagine the scene. God is going to get to Peter, the large, burly fisherman, not through his head or his heart but through his stomach. Anyone who has been in a tannery will know what I am talking about. I don't think there is a worse smell than that of a tannery. There would be a number of large vats containing different kinds and concentrations of acids. The animal hides are allowed to soak and ferment in the vats in order to remove the hair and cure the leather.

So you and I can picture Peter. He is up on the roof at midday, the sun is beating down on him, he is hungry, and up from the inner courtyard of the house is wafting the terrible stench of a tannery! It does make us smile! And just at this point he has a vision! God has quite a sense of humor. In the vision God lowered a large sheet with things to eat and offered them to this hungry man. Here is food from heaven (10:11; 11:5). Except that in the sheet are "four-footed creatures and reptiles and birds" (10:12). Peter is being offered a mixture of what for a Jew would be clean and unclean foods (Lv 11:28, 43).[11] Then, to add insult to injury, Peter hears the divine voice speaking to him.[12] God tells him to "kill and eat" (10:13).

Peter is incensed at this seeming temptation. "By no means, Lord," he exclaims. But, remember, he is hungry—and he is smelling the stench of the tannery rising in the noontime heat of the day up to the roof where he is sitting. Peter's stomach is turning over in revulsion at the unclean animals. All his life he has been taught to despise them. Now he is being told by God to kill and eat them. Even more disconcerting is the fact that the divine voice repeats this gastronomical horror three times (10:16).[13] This is such a stomach-turning experience that Peter will remember later that it happened to him three times (11:10).

"I have never eaten anything that is profane or unclean!" Peter exclaims, echoing his earlier vociferous self-justifications. "What God has made clean, you must not call profane," comes the reply. And just as Jesus had earlier asked Peter three times "Do you love me?" (Jn 21:15-19), so now Peter must be told three times, "What God has made clean, you must not call profane" (11:9). Would Peter have remembered Jesus' words?

> There is nothing outside a person that by going in can defile, but the things that come out are what defile. He said to them, "Then do you also fail to understand? Do you not see that whatever goes into a person from out-side cannot defile, since it enters, not the heart but the stomach, and goes out into the sewer?" (Thus he declared all foods clean.) (Mk 7:15, 18-19; see also Mt 15:11; 1 Ti 4:3-5)

### THE IMPLICATIONS OF THE STORY

> Now while Peter was greatly puzzled about what to make of the vision that he had seen, suddenly the men sent by Cornelius appeared. They were asking for Simon's house and were standing by the gate. They called out to ask whether Simon, who was called Peter, was staying there. While Peter was still thinking about the vision, the Spirit said to him, "Look, three men are searching for you. Now get up, go down, and go with them without hesitation; for I have sent them." So Peter went down to the men and said, "I am the one you are looking for." . . . So Peter invited them in and gave them lodging. (10:17-23)

In constructing his narrative at this point, Luke makes it very clear that the vision has a profound theological significance.[14] The vision is itself the theological explanation—the "word," if you will—that will provide the revelatory foundation for the "deed" that will soon occur, the coming of the Holy Spirit to Cornelius and all Gentiles. That Luke clearly sees it in this way is evident in how closely he associates the coming of the three Gentile messengers with Peter's wondering about the meaning of the vision.

Peter also closely associates the vision with its missiological meaning when he re-tells the story in Acts 11:5-17. He concludes, "If then God gave them the same gift that he gave us when we believed in the Lord Jesus Christ, who was I that I could hinder God?" (11:17). Later Peter will tell the Jerusalem council:

> "God made a choice among you, that I should be the one through whom the Gentiles would hear the message of the good news and become be-lievers. And God, who knows the human heart, testified to them by giv-ing them the Holy Spirit, just as he did to us; and in cleansing their hearts by faith he has made no distinction between them and us." (15:7-9)

So Peter's vision is an integral part of God's action and the work of the Holy Spirit in moving the Jewish church to accept the Gentile mission.[15] F. F. Bruce calls Acts 10 the "test case" of the gospel being also for the Gentiles.[16]

"I truly understand," Peter exclaims, "that God shows no partiality, but in every nation anyone who fears him and does what is right is acceptable to him" (10:34-35). And the Holy Spirit confirms Peter's discovery by coming once again in the Gentile Pentecost (10:44-46).[17] "Peter interprets the experience as a unified story with divine purpose."[18] Jesus Christ is Lord of all—Jews and Gentiles alike (10:36).[19]

## CONCLUSION

Reading Luke's story in Acts 10 opened my eyes so I understood more fully my experience with Eunice. "Do not despise what I have called clean" was God's message for me as well. As I held that cornhusk with the egg inside all the way down that mountain, I had many rather unpleasant thoughts about the widow who had given it to me. But our Lord would say, "You will not call unclean what I have called clean."

Some weeks later I saw Genaro again at a gathering of pastors. He had the gall to tell the story of the egg-in-the-cornhusk to those gathered. They nearly died laughing at me. The mirth having subsided, Genaro said again to me, "Do not undervalue or underestimate that wonderful woman of God."

Then Genaro began to tell us about the elderly widow in whose house I had slept. Eunice and her husband had been the first believers in the area. Having become Christians, they began sharing their faith with their family members and with the people of their town. Because the area was so remote and a pastor's visit so infrequent, Eunice and her husband became the Bible teachers and functioning shepherds of the new flock. After her husband died, this woman had continued guiding, teaching, preaching, and essentially pastoring that congregation. Through her efforts, the 11 de Abril congregation had been able to start two other congregations in towns further up the mountain. This woman was the spiritual mother of several hundred believers.

"Whom God values . . . " I have learned to see people with new eyes: God's eyes. I am learning to accept, gladly and freely, the love and value of those whom the Holy Spirit calls to be part of Christ's church.

## REFERENCES

[1] I. Howard Marshall, *The Acts of the Apostles,* Tyndale New Testament Commentaries (Grand Rapids, Mich.: Eerdmans, 1980), 181.

[2] Ibid.

[3] Peter's faith development can be seen to involve a three-part conversion as recorded in Matthew 16:13-20; John 21:15-17 with Acts 1:4-8; 2:1-4, 14; and Acts 10:9-16. We might think of Peter's threefold conversion as given below. In this case, the episode in Acts 10 could be considered the crowning, fulfilling, and completing episode in Peter's spiritual formation: (1) conversion to Jesus the Christ as his Messiah and Lord (Mt

16:16); (2) conversion to the church as Christ's sheep, the body of Christ (Jn 21:15-17); and (3) conversion to the world for whom Christ died (Acts 10:15).

[4] F. F. Bruce, *The New International Commentary on the New Testament: The Book of Acts* (Grand Rapids, Mich.: Eerdmans, 1983), 180-184.

[5] With reference to the importance of this narrative in the framework of the Book of Acts, see Marshall, *The Acts of the Apostles*, 180; C. Peter Wagner, *Living the Word: The Acts of the Holy Spirit Series, Acts Nine through Fifteen* (Ventura, Calif.: Regal, 1995), 68; and William Sanford LaSor, *Layman's Bible Commentary: Church Alive, Acts* (Glendale, Calif.: Regal, 1972), 151.

[6] Compare the parallels to this vociferous bravado of Peter's in, for example, "Even if I have to die with you, I will never disown you" (Mt 26:35, 33; Mk 14:31; Lk 22:33) and "You shall never wash my feet" (Jn 13:8) (see R. J. Knowling, *The Knowling Greek Testament: The Acts of the Apostles* [Grand Rapids, Mich.: Eerdmans, 1970], 254).

[7] J. W. Packer, *Acts of the Apostles* (London: Cambridge University Press, 1966), 82; Robert C. Tannehill, *The Narrative Unity of Luke-Acts: A Literary Interpretation*, vol. 2, *The Acts of the Apostles* (Minneapolis: Fortress Press, 1990), 133; Wagner, *Living the Word*, 68; and LaSor, *Layman's Bible Commentary: Church Alive, Acts*, 152-153. For a parallel of Luke's narrative of Jesus' encounter with a centurion, see Lk 7:1-10; Marshall, *The Acts of the Apostles*, 182; Knowling, *The Knowling Greek Testament*, 251.

[8] Luke's recounting of Ananias's vision in which he is sent to bring new sight to Paul has many parallels to Cornelius being told by the angel to send for Peter in Joppa (see Acts 9:10-12; John Calvin, *Commentary on the Acts of the Apostles* [Grand Rapids, Mich.: Baker, 1979], 415; R. C. H. Lenski, *The Interpretation of the Acts of the Apostles* [Columbus, Ohio: Lutheran Book Concern, 1934], 395).

[9] LaSor, *Layman's Bible Commentary; Church Alive, Acts*, 158; Robert C. Tannehill, *The Narrative Unity of Luke-Acts*, 137.

[10] Lloyd J. Ogilvie, *The Communicator's Commentary: Acts* (Waco, Tex.: Word, 1983), 180; Knowling, *The Knowling Greek Testament*, 249, 252; Calvin, *Commentary on the Acts of the Apostles*, 404; John Stott, *The Message of Acts: The Spirit, the Church, and World* (Downers Grove, Ill.: InterVarsity Press, 1990), 184; Lenski, *The Interpretation of the Acts of the Apostles*, 387; Paul Pierson, *A Bible Commentary for Laymen: Themes from Acts* (Ventura, Calif.: Regal, 1982), 90.

[11] Calvin, *Commentary on the Acts of the Apostles*, 419; Bruce, *The New International Commentary on the New Testament: The Book of Acts*, 218; Wagner, *Living the Word*, 76; Lenski, *The Interpretation of the Acts of the Apostles*, 397.

[12] Calvin, *Commentary on the Acts of the Apostles*, 421; Marshall, *The Acts of the Apostles*, 184; Lenski, *The Interpretation of the Acts of the Apostles*, 397, 399; Stott, *The Message of Acts*, 187; Packer, *Acts of the Apostles*, 79; Wagner, *Living the Word*, 84. This parallels the divine voice speaking to Saul in 9:4.

[13] Calvin, *Commentary on the Acts of the Apostles*, 423; Bruce, *The New International Commentary on the New Testament: The Book of Acts*, 218; Lenski, *The Interpretation of the Acts of the Apostles*, 399; Packer, *Acts of the Apostles*, 83; LaSor, *Layman's Bible Commentary: Church Alive, Acts*, 155-158.

[14] Robert C. Tannehill mentions E. Haenchen, *The Acts of the Apostles: A Commentary* (Philadelphia: Westminster, 1971), along with Richard I. Pervo, *Profit with Delight* (Philadelphia: Fortress Press, 1987), as criticizing Luke for a kind of naive approach to God's guidance as evidenced in the narrative of Luke 10-11. Tannehill is right in stating that "The story of Peter and Cornelius . . . is considerably more subtle in tracing the process of discerning the divine will than Haenchen recognizes" (*The Narrative Unity of Luke-Acts*, 128).

[15] Ogilvie, *The Communicator's Commentary,* 182-183; Calvin, *Commentary on the Acts of the Apostles,* 419; Stott, *The Message of Acts,* 187-189; Bruce, *The New International Commentary on the New Testament: The Book of Acts,* 222-223; Lenski, *The Interpretation of the Acts of the Apostles,* 408-409, 413; Packer, *Acts of the Apostles,* 84; Wagner, *Living the Word,* 83.

[16] Bruce, *The New International Commentary on the New Testament: The Book of Acts,* 215.

[17] E. M. Blaiklock, *The Acts of the Apostles,* Tyndale New Testament Commentaries (Grand Rapids, Mich.: Eerdmans, 1959), 97; Wagner, *Living the Word,* 81.

[18] Tannehill, *The Narrative Unity of Luke-Acts,* 145.

[19] Ibid., 139.

# 13

## The Church at Antioch:
## Crossing Racial, Cultural, and Class Barriers

### ACTS 11:19–30; 13:1–3

### Norman E. Thomas

Can a local church be both a place to feel at home and a multicultural church? During my fifteen years of mission in Zimbabwe and Zambia this was a recurring question. I find this to be a burning issue both for student pastors in seminary and in my local church. The Antioch model has been my inspiration and my guide.[1]

Forty years ago Fairview Church served a homogeneous white neighborhood in northwest Dayton, Ohio. Most members were homeowners living within two miles of the building. They prided themselves on being a *family* church and a *friendly* church. Then came busing for integration of schools and increasing white flight to the suburbs. Today Fairview, my home church, has many new neighbors. A majority are African Americans; others are whites from rural Appalachia. Many rent houses formerly owned by Fairview members and neighbors. Some are clients of Fairview's community outreach programs—thrift shop, food pantry, before- and after-school care, and the weekend Sunshine Club for children. Meanwhile, most members commute four to eight miles from the suburbs to their family church. They refer with affection to Fairview as "our" church and call it "a place to feel at home." Many local neighbors shop at the busy drive-in and drug store across the street. Others catch the bus to downtown Dayton at the corner. Many children walk past on their way to and from school. Only a few come for Sunday school, or their parents for worship. Very few neighbors call Fairview their "home church."

### A GLOBAL CHALLENGE

Donald A. McGavran observed this phenomena in 1970. He saw that the rush to cities was on. He wrote: "Discipling urban populations is perhaps the most urgent task confronting the Church." He continued: "Now is precisely the time to learn how it may be done, and to surge forward actually doing it."[2] When McGavran wrote those words the earth contained twenty-four hundred cities with populations of more than 100,000. There were 161 metropolitan areas populated by more than one million persons. Each day 51,500 additional persons were born in or moved to those cities; most did not know Jesus Christ as Savior and Lord.

In 1970 I was serving as the first Urban Evangelism Secretary of the Christian Council of Rhodesia (now Zimbabwe). Leaders of the capital's African Ministers Fraternal, knowing of my passion for urban ministry, hired me for this position. The historic mission centers in that country were in rural areas. Could a predominately rural church develop effective new models for urban ministry? Five years earlier, while living in a rural village, I had watched as each weekend the bus from the city brought the fathers and sons and daughters back to their home village. Those buses brought more from the city than new radios, bicycles and fashionable clothes. They also brought people with changing values and lifestyles. Meanwhile, most city churches remained islands of comfort for rural migrants to town. Women's groups met Friday mornings, just as back home in the village, although the younger women were at work at that time. Some townships had "church rows"—buildings often closed and locked except for Sunday when each opened to serve mostly rural migrants to town with their particular regional and denominational subcultures.

More than thirty years after McGavran's challenge, the need for creative urban ministry is more urgent. By 2001 more than forty-one hundred cities counted more than 100,000 residents. Megacities had almost tripled in number to 410. The increase in new non-Christian urban dwellers had increased proportionately to an estimated 131,300 per day.[3] "Mission frontiers are no longer geographically distant but culturally distant," declared Ray Bakke, who specializes in global urban mission. The British used to rule fifty-two nations. Now fifty-two nations are in Britain. France used to rule forty-two nations. Now Paris is 14 percent Algerian, and Marseilles 31 percent African. Sao Paulo, Brazil, now has more than one million ethnic Japanese among its population. In Buenos Aires, 10 percent of all worship services are conducted in Korean. One center-city Lutheran Church in Oslo, Norway, has attendants of 97 nationalities. This same new multicultural reality can be found in urban United States. "The nations are in the neighborhoods," Bakke continued. In Chicago 15 nationalities live side-by-side in one neighborhood. Pittsburgh is the new capital for fifty thousand Serbs. In St. Paul, Minnesota, 25 percent of school children are Hmongs from Southeast Asia. In metropolitan Seattle 42 percent of the population is foreign-born.[4]

We cannot ignore these realities. We cannot turn our backs on the city. Charles Van Engen expressed the urgency well: "Christians can no longer ignore the enormity, complexity, and urgency of urbanism. The foremost agenda of the church's ministry and mission into the next century will need to be ministry in the city."[5] But what shall be the models for ministries in multicultural cities? Every context of ministry is unique. I believe that we should seek relevant contextualized models and not slavishly imitate those of others.

Yet despite this caution, I wish to introduce a model. It is thoroughly biblical. It has stood the test of time. It comes from the city where the followers of Jesus were first called Christians—Antioch of Syria.

## THE ANTIOCH MODEL

There is a tradition that Alexander the Great desired to build a city at Antioch. In fact, it was founded by his Macedonian general, Seleucus I, about 300 B.C.E. Situated about three hundred miles north of Jerusalem and twenty miles inland from its port, it had an estimated population of about 500,000.[6] Antioch thrived because of its strategic position. At the crossroads of trade routes south to Palestine and Egypt, west to the Asia Minor peninsula, and east to Persia, Antioch was a cosmopolitan city. A melting pot of Western and Eastern cultures, Greek and Roman traditions mingled with Semitic, Arab, and Persian influences.[7] Antioch was more like today's Singapore or Sydney, London or Los Angeles, than any other city in the Roman world.

Antioch had everything to offer. It had political prestige. Under Roman rule it was the third city of the empire. It was a provincial capital city for Syria.[8] In Antioch, Roman officials met political leaders from states to the east that acknowledged Rome's political supremacy. Known as Antioch the Beautiful, theaters and sports stadiums had been built there under Augustus and Herod. With such facilities Antioch could have hosted the Olympic games.

But Antioch also had its dark side. It was known for its immorality. Tourists came to see the dancing girls of Antioch. The city rivaled Corinth as a center for vice. Corruption was the game to be played in Antioch politics and business. The Roman poet Juvenal wrote about Antioch at the end of the first century. He charged that Antioch was one of the sources of Rome's corruption.

Yet Luke wrote nothing about Antioch's wickedness. Instead, he told only the news of great spiritual events that took place there, providing a wonderful biblical model of urban mission. At Antioch the gospel was preached for the first time to Gentiles. Furthermore, it was the Antioch church that commissioned and sent out some of the first missionaries to the Gentiles. It became the mother church of the Gentile churches. It was the apostle Paul's home church. Antioch Christians nurtured him and allowed him to experiment with new patterns of urban ministry. Antioch sent him forth to be the great urban apostle of the first century.[9]

In Acts 11 and 13, the Antioch story, I find an *eight-part model of urban ministry*. I commend it to you. It has been tested thoroughly. Follow it and your urban ministry will be more creative and more effective.

## EVANGELISM THROUGH LAY LEADERSHIP

Luke began his account of the church in Antioch with the scattering of the first Christians following the stoning of Stephen (11:19).[10] The areas mentioned are up the coast from Palestine—Phoenicia (present-day Lebanon), the offshore island of Cyprus, and Antioch (just north of present-day Syria). No passports were needed, as all were part of the Roman Empire. Indeed, it was the crossing of cultural barriers that made the Antioch church the breakthrough to Gentile mission.

At first the believers witnessed only to Jews (11:19), who were at the time a large and vigorous community of an estimated twenty-two thousand persons. The witnesses, however, included Greek-speaking Jewish Christians from Cyprus and Cyrene. They crossed a cultural bridge as they shared the good news with Gentiles. Luke's contrast of Hellenists with Jews suggests that the former had adopted the Greek language and culture in that cosmopolitan city.[11]

In Antioch there were statues to many gods. Antioch was known as a crossroads not only of trade but also of religions. That is another reason the Antioch model is also a twenty-first century model. If Antioch was his missionary training ground, it was there that Paul learned to "proclaim Christ crucified" (1 Cor 1:23). It was a stumbling block to many Jews. As for the Greeks, many shouted "foolishness!" But others responded. They found in the gospel God's wisdom and power for salvation.

We read that unnamed Christians in Antioch began "proclaiming the Lord Jesus" (11:20). Although some later writers named Peter as the founder of the church at Antioch and its first bishop, Luke does not name a founder.[12] This is significant because later churches vied to name an apostle as their founder. Luke reported that "all except the apostles were scattered" in the first Jerusalem persecution (8:1). Why not the apostles? Could it be that in the eyes of the authorities they were less a threat than the laity? The first Christian martyr was a Hellenist, Stephen, a layman—not Peter, or James, or John. When the Antioch church began to grow the apostles sent Barnabas, a layman. That church was founded, led, and spread by laypeople. Thus the missionaries from Cyprus and Cyrene were rooted in the Hellenist mission sparked by the stoning of Stephen (Acts 8:1; 11:19-20).

Will lay leadership be the secret of the church's renewal in our century? Reflecting on the Antioch model, E. Stanley Jones wrote:

> Hitherto, the center of gravity has been on the minister; now the center of gravity has to be shifted to the laity. We ministers, missionaries, and evangelists are never going to win the world. We are too few to do it and if we could do it it wouldn't be good, for it would take away from the laity that spiritual growth and development which comes through sharing one's faith.[13]

Another remarkable feature of the Antioch church was its ability to cross successfully what has been called "the most fundamental division in the Roman Empire—that between rural people and city dwellers." Within a decade of Jesus' crucifixion, the people of the Way had left behind rural Galilee and established new faith communities in a cosmopolitan Greco-Roman city.[14]

All the other marks of the Antioch model fail without this: "The hand of the Lord was with them, and a great number became believers and turned to the

Lord" (11:21). Later the Antioch church would reach out in mercy to the needy. Later it would commission two of its own leaders as missionaries. But first it learned to evangelize with power in its own city streets.[15]

## EVERY MEMBER A MINISTER

Do new Christians want to be inactive Christians? Certainly not! We read that news of the Antioch revival reached Jerusalem. And the Jerusalem church sent Barnabas to Antioch. Luke described him as "a good man, full of the Holy Spirit and of faith" (11:24). Earlier he had been introduced as a Levite, a native of Cyprus, and a generous giver (4:36). Barnabas had the complete trust of the Twelve.

Why did the Jerusalem church send Barnabas to Antioch? Was this an inspection by the mother church? Today we would call it quality control. But Barnabas liked what he saw and rejoiced. Notice that he "exhorted them all to remain faithful to the Lord with steadfast devotion" (11:23). He did not just gather the leaders for motivational training. Barnabas "exhorted them all." And the Antioch church grew like wildfire because every Christian had a ministry to do.

Two generations ago in India the Anglican diocese of Dornakal grew like that. Its leader was Bishop V. S. Azariah. He followed the Antioch model of ministry. His duty as Anglican bishop was to travel from parish to parish to baptize new Christians. The ceremony began as the bishop questioned each candidate upon the six to eighteen months of training received from local clergy. Next, the bishop baptized the new believers by immersion in a nearby river or pool. The climax came as new Christians placed their hands on their heads and repeated after the bishop this solemn vow: "Woe unto me if I preach not the gospel!" Baptism became a commissioning for grass-roots lay evangelism. Every new believer was to be a witness. It is no wonder that the church in Dornakal, India, grew rapidly. It grew for the same reason that the church in Antioch grew. Every member was called to be a witness for the Lord.[16]

I shall never forget Faith Methodist Church in Singapore. There I preached to hundreds of new young Christians. Across the street were tall apartment houses. Almost everyone in Singapore lives in buildings like that. After worship I saw 150 young people go out two by two to witness door to door in those apartment houses. They do this every Sunday. In fact, 75 percent of their one thousand members were trained for such witnessing.[17]

The seventy-five-hundred member Frazer Memorial Church in Montgomery, Alabama, practices this Antioch model of every-member ministries. More than 83 percent of its resident members are involved in 190 different lay ministries. Every November members respond to a "ministry menu." It lists 190 ministries with space to add another. At number 191 members write new ministries that they would like to start. The church staff members are not hired to carry out those ministries. Their goal, instead, is to facilitate every member in ministry.[18]

## CARE FOR NEW BELIEVERS

The third quality of the Antioch model was caring for new believers. Barnabas knew that he needed to do more than urge persons to be good Christians. He recruited the best trainer he knew—Saul of Tarsus (11:25). What followed was more than a weekend retreat for new Christians. It was more than a four-week new members' class on Sundays. We read that Paul and Barnabas met with the church "for an entire year." They taught "a great many people" (11:26).

While Christian witness was the initial priority, instruction became an essential part of the church's life. Those who came out of non-Jewish traditions needed solid grounding in the faith if they were to become strong disciples.[19] It was in Antioch that Paul had time to develop his strategy of mission to Gentiles. Antioch became the center of mission activities for the next twelve to fourteen years that he spent "in the regions of Syria and Cilicia" (Gal 1:21).[20]

Roman Catholics in the United States follow this Antioch model. They call it the Rite of Christian Initiation for Adults. New believers meet weekly along with a sponsor, who attends also. They study what Christians believe and consider how the early church grew. They share both their joys and problems in their new life in Christ. Through listening and sharing each week for almost a year they grow in caring love for each other.[21]

"When did you feel like you really belonged?" George Hunter asks new Christians. Often they respond: "I felt that I belonged before I believed." That was also John Wesley's experience. He invited seekers to join Methodist weekly class meetings. Each week they shared the highs and lows of their lives. They also encouraged one another and prayed for each member of the class. They knew that they were accepted as valued class members even before they believed or had a conversion experience.[22] This is the Antioch model.

## WITNESS TO ONENESS IN CHRIST

A fourth quality was their witness to oneness in Christ. We read: "It was in Antioch that the disciples were first called 'Christians'" (11:26). How did the name Christian come to be used? We do not know for sure, but we have important clues.[23] Luke, up to this point in Acts, called the followers of Christ disciples, brothers, believers, and saints (Acts 6:1; 9:13; 10:45; 11:12). None of these terms suggested any difference from the Jews. What made for the change in Antioch?

Secular history provides important clues. Malalas relates that in the third year of the reign of Emperor Gaius, 40 C.E., non-Jews fought against Jews in Antioch, killing many and burning their synagogues. These riots occurred possibly at the very time that Christians turned from preaching exclusively to Jews and began to witness to non-Jews. If Christians were blamed for the riots, then the name Christian was associated with sedition. That would help to explain why it was not used in other New Testament writings, except as a term of derision.[24]

"You are not your own. . . . For you were bought with a price," Paul wrote (1 Cor 6:19-20). Later he called the Corinthian Christians "slaves of Christ" (1 Cor 7:21-24). Could he first have used those words in his Antioch ministry? I believe so. Later, Paul must have longed to return to the Antioch model of Christian unity. The church in Corinth had no such unity. We read that divisions sprang up. Members claimed that their first loyalty was to Paul, or Apollos, or Peter (1 Cor. 1:10-17). Was this an early form of denominationalism? Certainly it was an early fracture of Christian unity.

Do you long to return to the Antioch model of witnessing to oneness in Christ? I do. You and I participate in churches where denominationalism is taken for granted. We are born, grow up, and die within our divisions. We do not pray fervently for unity. We more often call ourselves Presbyterians or Baptists than Christians.

In 1959 the capital city of the Congo erupted in violence. It was a foretaste of those tribal conflicts that have racked that nation for more than forty years. In a nation of strong, growing churches, did denominationalism add fuel to the partisan fires? "Yes," answered Hank Crane, a Presbyterian missionary. Crane's vision was for the church to become the new tribe, with Jesus Christ as the great new chief. Christ is "the mediating personality" by whom persons of all races and conditions of life are "drawn into one Holy Commonwealth, the New Tribe of the Church," he wrote. Crane's inspiration was the community *(ekklesia)* and fellowship *(koinonia)* of the early church as found in Antioch.[25]

Is a post-denominational Christianity possible? I believe so. In China I experienced it. Chinese Christians did not introduce themselves as "a former Methodist" or "a former Baptist." Instead, they had put on Christ as their new identity. Rather than wait for the decline of denominational loyalties to "put on Christ," you can live out the Antioch model in your ministry right now. Consider the need to minister more creatively to an entire neighborhood or city. Rarely will a denominational approach succeed. Ecumenical coalitions are a better way of urban ministry. That is the finding of urban church leaders in the United States. The problems of the city are too large for congregations to address alone. Effective community-organizing projects require coalitions of congregations. These are critical components of "a holistic metropolitan church strategy and structure."[26]

## COMPASSION FOR THE POOR

The fifth quality of the Antioch model of urban ministry is compassion for the poor. In Acts we learn that global famine is not just a modern phenomenon. Citing evidence from a first century Asia Minor inscription, one scholar contends that the statement about "a severe famine over all the world" (11:28) was a literary hyperbole used to refer to a severe famine or shortage of food. Since Egypt was the Roman Empire's breadbasket, crop failures there would have resulted in famines in Judea and other lands of the eastern Mediterranean area.[27]

What could a younger church in Antioch do? A key Antioch principle for urban ministry emerged. Each person gave according to his or her ability

(11:27-30), as earlier Jerusalem Christians, including Barnabas, had given "to all, as any had need" (2:45; cf. 4:35). Believers were free to give as their consciences directed them. This was the pioneer Christian relief effort. Rooted in Acts 2 and 4, it may have been the origin of all later relief and development efforts.[28]

Note another key Antioch principle here. Who controls the relief effort? Although Barnabas and Saul carried the gifts, they were sent to the elders. The Jerusalem church did not beg for help. The gift enhanced its feelings of self-worth. It empowered the church to go on. World Vision International focuses its outreach on ministries among the urban poor. Empowerment is the primary objective: "Any urban ministry which does not enable the poor to deal directly with their own problems will not really deal with the city's overwhelming needs."[29] Is this consistent with the Antioch principle? I believe so.

## BALANCED LEADERSHIP

A sixth quality of the Antioch model was balanced leadership. In Antioch there were both "prophets and teachers" (13:1), as well as members ready for action. Luke, in his account of Pentecost, included the conviction that Christian prophecy is a possibility for every Christian (2:17-18, 38). Nevertheless, there emerged persons with special gifts to interpret the purpose of God for particular situations.[30] Prophets were gifted to speak God's truth. In cosmopolitan Antioch they spoke both to faithful Christians and to inquirers. It took sensitivity and courage to speak God's truth in love. Those from Jewish backgrounds must have heard the gospel differently from those of Gentile backgrounds.

But there were also teachers. Their task was to deepen the understandings of new believers. Later Paul would write, perhaps out of his earlier Antioch experience: "Speaking the truth in love, we must grow up in every way . . . into Christ" (Eph 4:15).

Earlier in Acts, Luke presented persons who could be both prophets and teachers. Stephen, "full of grace and power, did great wonders and signs among the people" (6:8). Although he was not designated a prophet, his speech to the council displayed his ability to interpret Jewish tradition. Therefore, it is not surprising that Luke did not try to designate certain Antioch leaders as prophets and others as teachers.[31] Does your church have balanced leadership? Does your ministry include both evangelistic proclamation and thorough instruction? Do prophets and Bible teachers both feel at home? If so, then you have embraced the Antioch model of leadership.

## ELIMINATION OF RACIAL AND ETHNIC BARRIERS

A seventh quality at Antioch was overcoming racial and ethnic barriers. Luke recorded in Acts 11:19 the results of the Jerusalem persecution. Disciples of Jesus were scattered as far as Phoenicia, Cyprus, and Antioch. But as they fled, they witnessed only to Jews. Thus the breakthrough to a more inclusive church came at Antioch. Christians from Cyprus and Cyrene began to tell the good news to Gentiles. The Spirit could not be walled up in homogeneous Christianity.

Picture the table fellowship of the Antioch ministry team (13:1). Barnabas was there, a Cypriot landowner and Levite. Beside him sat Simeon "who was called Niger"—meaning " black," possibly from Africa.[32] Next sat Lucius of Cyrene, also from Africa. Beside Lucius sat Manaen—an aristocrat of the court of the ruler, Herod.[33] Saul, that fiery intellectual from Tarsus, completed the table fellowship. I do not imagine that it was easy for them to live together in peace. But they must have achieved it. How else would joint leadership have been possible?

Eight years ago I received communion at a remarkable ecumenical worship in Rome. Clergy from six *continents concelebrated* as together they spoke Jesus' words, "This is my body, which is given for you" (Lk 22:19). One was a Catholic bishop from Africa. Beside him stood an Anglican priest from England. Next was a Presbyterian woman minister from Australia. A Baptist pastor from Argentina, and a Disciples of Christ minister from the United States completed the celebrants. The setting was deeply moving. We worshiped together in the catacombs of saints John and Paul near to the Colosseum in Rome. There we heard a remarkable story. In Roman times pagans threw the bodies of the poor and the unwanted into horrible *puticoli*—pits for mass burials.[34] But Christians were different. In the catacombs are included the bones of slaves. In death, as in life, the early Christians broke through the prejudices of their day. They lived as Paul had taught: "For in the one Spirit we were all baptized into one body—Jews or Greeks, slaves or free—and we were all made to drink of one Spirit" (1 Cor 12:13).

Kim Chi-Ha, Korea's noted poet, expressed that quality of fellowship when he wrote: "Bread is heaven. As heaven cannot be monopolized, bread should be shared and eaten by all." Reflecting on that poem, Jae Soon Park interprets Jesus' ministry among the poor in the light of Korean *minjung* theology. Jesus was criticized for eating with tax collectors and sinners (Mk 2:16). He befriended the *minjung*, but he did more. He sat and ate with them. "Will the Korean church become a table community like that?" Park asks. Most urban churches are rich churches. "There is a high wall between the churches and the poor *minjung*," he writes. He calls for a true table fellowship like that of the Antioch church.[35]

## MISSION FOR OTHERS

Now note one final quality of the Antioch model of ministry. The church looked beyond itself to mission. The Antioch church was itself a mission. This young church owed its start to informal missionaries. Growing rapidly, it flourished with new Christians—undoubtedly fragile new followers of Jesus. But the church was blessed by the strong leadership of a cross-cultural ministry team. It had the best of teachers, Saul and Barnabas, who stayed and taught for the entire year. The church grew strong under their leadership.

Then the Spirit issued a new call: Antioch sisters and brothers, thousands more have not seen the light of Christ. They have not experienced self-giving love. They yearn for the reconciliation you have received. Who will go as missionaries to them? And the Spirit said: "Set apart for me Barnabas and Saul for the work to which I have called them" (13:2). And the Antioch church responded. It did not send a junior team. Instead, it sent its best leaders—Saul and Barnabas. It sent them not knowing where they would go or whether they would ever return.[36] The Antioch church both received and sent missionaries. It recognized its own needs and responded to the needs of others.

Note the three components of the church's response to the Spirit's call to mission (13:3). First, the members fasted. This was not their weekly custom. In fact, fasting is rarely mentioned in Acts (only in 13:3 and 14:23), and never in the letters of Paul. Clearly this call required a solemn preparation for decision-making and action. Second, they prayed. Earnestly they sought for divine guidance. They desired God's blessing on the commission about to be given to Saul and Barnabas. Third, they "laid their hands on them." It was both a recognition and endorsement of the call of God in this matter and an act of commissioning by the church. Here was the prototype of future acts sending forth Christians for mission.[37]

The lesson of the Antioch model is clear. The church that gives sacrificially in mission for others is the most vital church. That is the witness of the Methodist Church in Luanda, Angola. In 1978 I went as one of the first official United Methodist visitors after the country's independence from Portugal. When the liberation struggle began in 1961, twenty-three Methodist pastors were killed. Others were jailed. Many fled and became refugees. Missionaries were jailed and then deported. Outside funds were cut off. No new churches could be built. Would we find the church still alive in Angola? I wondered as our plane flew into Luanda, the capital. To my surprise I found it to be the most vital of the churches I visited that year among thirteen countries of Africa. In colonial Luanda the Portuguese permitted Methodists to have just three church buildings. Undeterred, they gathered in thirty-three house churches for prayer and Bible study. When national independence was won, each house church became a growing congregation. Each hoped to build both its own church building and a home for its pastor. If ever a church had reason to be self-concerned, it was the Luanda church. Instead, each of the thirty-three local churches supported a missionary evangelist to open new churches in resettlement areas. Why were the churches fired up for evangelism? They lived the Antioch model. They looked beyond themselves in mission.

## RADICAL CHRISTIANS

What can we learn from the early church in Antioch? In his now classic study of why the early church grew, Michael Green concluded that people "will continue to believe that the Church is an introverted society composed of 'respectable' people and bent on its own preservation until they see in church groupings and individual Christians the caring, the joy, the fellowship, the self-sacrifice and the openness which marked the early Church at its best."[38]

Fairview, my home church in Dayton, Ohio, has begun this risky yet essential transition. Last year we began a new ministry called People Taking Charge. Single mothers who participate desire to break the welfare cycle of poverty. In a twelve-week, thirty-six-session course they learn life skills (parenting, financial planning, computer-use, job interviewing). Together they become a spiritually growing and caring fellowship. Increasingly they move from being clients of the church's outreach ministries into active membership. "Everyone treated me with respect," Anita declared. "I liked everyone. I felt I belonged—that I was part of the family." Bonnie Maloney, recruited to be their mentor, is now their close friend. "We're very close," Bonnie confided. "I love them. They've given me more than I've given them."[39] Anita and Bonnie are what I call *radical Christians*. Doing so, I return to basic meanings. *Radical* originally meant not "extreme," but "basic." The Latin word *radix* means "root." Radical Christianity is essential, Bible-based, Spirit-filled Christianity. Such Christianity has power both to renew the church and to bring salt and light to a needy world (Mt 5:13-14).

"This simple account of the church at Antioch has enough constructive revolutions in it to remake the present structure of the church of the world." That was the judgment of E. Stanley Jones at the end of his long life of mission service. He continued: "Touch it anywhere and it pulsates with vitality, and not ancient but up-to-date vitality. . . . It is real and therefore universal and applicable for now."[40] I commend this Antioch plan to you, as Luke did to his readers. It is the best model available for urban ministry and mission.

## REFERENCES

[1] For two adaptations of the Antioch model for contemporary church renewal, see Michael Green, *First Things First: Whatever Happened to Evangelism?* (Nashville, Tenn.: Discipleship Resources, 1979), 14-28; and E. Stanley Jones, *The Reconstruction of the Church—On What Pattern?* (Nashville, Tenn.: Abingdon, 1970).

[2] Donald A. McGavran, *Understanding Church Growth* (Grand Rapids, Mich.: Eerdmans, 1970), 295.

[3] David B. Barrett and Todd M. Johnson, "Annual Statistical Table on Global Mission: 2001," *International Bulletin of Missionary Research* 25/1 (January 2001): 25.

[4] Ray Bakke, "The Context of Evangelism and Mission in World Cities," lecture to the Academy for Evangelism in Theological Education, Princeton, N.J., October 5, 2000.

[5] Charles E. Van Engen, "Preface," in *God So Loves the City,* ed. Charles E. Van Engen and Jude Tiersma (Monrovia, Calif.: MARC, 1994), x.

[6] Glanville Downey, *A History of Antioch in Syria from Seleucus to the Arab Conquest* (Princeton, N.J.: Princeton University Press, 1961), 54-60; Ben Witherington III, *The Acts of the Apostles: A Socio-Rhetorical Commentary* (Grand Rapids, Mich.: Eerdmans, 1998), 366.

[7] William J. Larkin Jr., *Acts* (Downers Grove, Ill.: InterVarsity Press, 1995), 176.

[8] Ben Witherington III, *New Testament History: A Narrative Account* (Grand Rapids, Mich.: Baker Books, 2001), 224-225.

[9] Roger S. Greenway, "Antioch: A Biblical Model of Urban Church Development," in *Cities: Mission's New Frontier*, ed. Roger S. Greenway and Timothy M. Monsma (Grand Rapids, Mich.: Baker Books, 1989), 31-32.

[10] The Greek verb *diasparentes* is the root from which "dispersion" and "diaspora" derive (Howard Clark Kee, *To Every Nation under Heaven: The Acts of the Apostles* [Harrisburg, Pa.: Trinity Press International, 1997], 146).

[11] Wayne A. Meeks and Robert L. Wilken, *Jews and Christians in Antioch in the First Four Centuries of the Common Era* (Missoula, Mont.: Scholars Press, 1978), 8, 14; Gerhard A. Krodel, *Acts* (Minneapolis, Minn.: Augsburg, 1986), 206. A variant in the Greek text allows "Hellenists" to be translated "Greeks." The nuance of "Gentiles" is preferred by Haenchen because, in this verse, it contrasts with "Jews" (Ernst Haenchen, *The Acts of the Apostles: A Commentary* [Oxford: Basil Blackwell, 1971], 365 n. 5).

[12] For a refutation of this claim, see Downey, *History*, 281-287.

[13] Jones, *The Reconstruction of the Church—On What Pattern?*, 42-43.

[14] Wayne A. Meeks, *The First Urban Christians: The Social World of the Apostle Paul* (New Haven, Conn.: Yale University Press, 1983), 11; Krodel, *Acts*, 207.

[15] Greenway, "Antioch," 34.

[16] Susan Billington Harper, *In the Shadow of the Mahatma: Bishop V. S. Azariah and the Travails of Christianity in British India* (Grand Rapids, Mich.: Eerdmans, 2000), 192-193.

[17] For a detailed analysis of the challenges and opportunities for Christian witness in that city, see Keith W. Hinton, *Growing Churches Singapore Style: Ministry in an Urban Context* (Singapore: Overseas Missionary Fellowship, 1985).

[18] George G. Hunter III, *Church for the Unchurched* (Nashville, Tenn.: Abingdon, 1996), 124-127.

[19] Kee, *To Every Nation under Heaven*, 149.

[20] Meeks, *The First Urban Christians*, 10.

[21] See Maxwell E. Johnson, *The Rites of Christian Initiation: Their Evolution and Interpretation* (Collegeville, Minn.: Liturgical Press, 1999), 307-318.

[22] Ibid., 166.

[23] For a detailed analysis of explanations see Justin Taylor, "Why Were the Disciples First Called *Christians* at Antioch?" *Revue Biblique* 101 (January 1994): 75-94. For a full bibliography of articles on the issue, see Joseph A. Fitzmyer, *Acts of the Apostles* (New York: Doubleday, 1998), 478-479.

[24] Downey, *History*, 194-195, 198; Taylor, "Why Were the Disciples First Called *Christians* at Antioch?" 94. The term *Christian* appears in only two other New Testament passages: in Acts 26:28, as a derogatory term on the lips of King Agrippa, and in 1 Peter 4:16, where it is linked with impending persecution.

[25] Hank Crane, "Revolution and the New Tribe of Africa," paper presented to the Africa Committee, Division of Foreign Missions of the National Council of Churches of Christ in the USA, September 16, 1959.

[26] Clifford Green, "Seeking Community in the Metropolis: Reflections for the Future," in *Churches, Cities, and Human Community: Urban Ministry in the United States, 1945-1985*, ed. Clifford J. Green (Grand Rapids, Mich.: Eerdmans, 1996), 288.

[27] Fitzmyer, *Acts of the Apostles*, 481.

[28] Greenway, "Antioch," 38-39.

[29] Robert C. Linthicum, *Empowering the Poor* (Monrovia, Calif.: MARC, 1991), 2.

[30] Krodel, *Acts*, 226.

[31] Although some scholars have tried to distinguish who was a prophet and who a teacher in this passage, there is no textual support for such a distinction.

[32] Some writers have sought to link Simeon with Simon of Cyrene, the father of Rufus and Alexander, who carried the cross (Lk 23:26). Because Luke spells the names differently, he probably was trying to distinguish the two men (Witherington, *The Acts of the Apostles*, 392).

[33] The Greek text means that he was an intimate friend of Herod Antipas, a friend in court, and therefore of high social standing. Lucius is literally referred to as his "foster brother" *(suntrophos)* in 13:1.

[34] J. Stevenson, *The Catacombs: Rediscovered Monuments of Early Christianity* (London: Thames and Hudson, 1978), 9.

[35] Jae Soon Park, "Jesus' Table Community Movement and the Church," *Asia Journal of Theology* 7 (1993): 63, 71, 78.

[36] Michael Green, *First Things First,* 24.

[37] Witherington, *The Acts of the Apostles*, 393-394; Fitzmyer, *Acts of the Apostles*, 497. See also Acts 6:6b.

[38] Michael Green, *Evangelism in the Early Church* (Grand Rapids, Mich.: Eerdmans, 1970), 275.

[39] Interview, Dayton, Ohio, December 19, 2001.

[40] Jones, *The Reconstruction of the Church—On What Pattern?*, 40-41.

# 14

## *Hope in the Midst of Trial*

### Acts 12:1–11

### Robert L. Gallagher

"I have colon cancer." My wife's words numbed my mind. I stood looking at her, unable to speak. What did this mean for my dear wife and two daughters? Suddenly our blessed life together was under threat and my best friend of thirty years had a cursed disease. The future was uncertain and full of darkness. I asked myself why the innocent should suffer. My wife, Dolores, was a godly woman who had dedicated her life to the service of God and others. She had looked after her body with proper nutrition, exercise, and regular health exams; and her family had no history of such a cancer.

From the first diagnosis my wife was bathed in prayer. As a family we asked God's grace for healing every step of the way. Christian people near and far rallied on her behalf, falling to their knees beseeching God's hand of healing upon her life. Dolores felt that the church's prayers gave her a "buoyancy of faith" that strengthened her throughout her journey. Even in the midst of this dark prison of suffering, she knew a peace that was beyond this world. While continuing to pray for God's healing mercy, she also embraced the reality of death and the hope of eternal life with Jesus.

Dolores was not afraid to die. In the early 1970s she had radically submitted her life to Jesus. She had been filled with the Holy Spirit in such a dynamic way that she said she had experienced a little taste of heaven on earth. At that moment of receiving the Spirit of God, her cultural bondage of fearing death had been broken.

How was God going to deliver my wife from this disease that had imprisoned her body? Would God miraculously heal her, or did God have another plan of deliverance? Just like Peter innocently suffering under the imprisonment of Herod in Acts 12, Dolores was innocently suffering under the imprisonment of cancer; both needed God's intervention.

This chapter will take the parallel between Peter and my wife, Dolores, and explore the meaning behind Luke's inclusion of this narrative. After a brief

157

historical background, I exegete the persecution of the Jerusalem church in Acts 12:1-5 and then God's intervention for Peter in 12:6-11.

## BACKGROUND OF ACTS 12

In Acts 11 the Jerusalem church moved beyond the borders of Judea and Samaria and continued to spread "to the ends of the earth." The first regions to be evangelized by the Hellenistic Jewish Christians (scattered from Jerusalem after the death of Stephen) were Phoenicia, Cyprus, and Antioch in Syria. It was in Antioch that the first Gentile mission was purposefully begun. This city with a population of about half a million then became a new mission center for the church. Antioch was a political, economic, and cosmopolitan center, and the church in this city reflected its character in its cultural and socioeconomic diversity (13:1). The church in Antioch was different from the church in Jerusalem not only in character but also in name (11:26) and mission. Antioch became the new center of mission to the world (13:2-4).

Although the church was moving its message out from Palestine, God had not left the church in Jerusalem. Between Acts chapters 11 and 13, describing the church in Antioch, Luke inserted a narrative depicting a crisis in the Jerusalem church at that time. It seems that he chose to close his picture of the Christian mission among the Jewish people with two narratives showing God's continued activity in the church of Jerusalem, in particular, to demonstrate the faithfulness of God in the midst of persecution. This chapter illustrates that Christian service entailed suffering (12:1-19) and judgment on those who caused the pain (12:20-25).

In addition, chapter 12 is an example of the power of prayer. Yet this was not all that Luke had in mind when he included the story of Peter's release from prison. By placing this story here in the narrative, Luke explained why Peter no longer dominated the narrative as he had up to this point. The text records that Peter "left and went to another place" (12:17b). This story is a transition between the mission of Peter and that of Paul. It provides a vehicle to make way for the journeys of Paul and the mission to the Gentile peoples.

## PERSECUTION OF THE JERUSALEM CHURCH: ACTS 12:1-5

Herod[1] attacked the church in Jerusalem during the stay of Barnabas and Saul as they distributed the collection.[2] So the events of chapter 12 are between the prophecy of Agabus and Barnabas and Saul's return to Antioch in Syria.[3] Richard N. Longenecker argues that the Peter vignette was happening simultaneously with Luke's account of the church in Antioch. He states: "If we were to seek more chronological exactness, we might say that the events of chapter 12 occurred between those of 11:19-26 and 11:27-30."[4]

The enemy of Christians, Herod Agrippa I (10 B.C.E.-44 C.E.)[5] was the son of Aristobulus and Bernice and the grandson of Herod the Great and the Hasmonean princess Mariamne. After a turbulent life in Rome, he became friends with Emperor Gaius (also known as Emperor Caligula) who in 37 C.E.

gave him authority over the Palestinian tetrarchies of Philip and Lysanias in southern Syria (cf. Lk 3:1). Two years later he acquired the title of king and the territories of Galilee and Peraea. In 41 C.E. the new emperor, Claudius, also gave him Judea and Samaria.[6] These last territorial additions gave Agrippa a kingdom as large as his grandfather's. Even though Herod descended from the Edomites, the people of Jerusalem (including the Pharisees) viewed him as one of their own because of his Hasmonean lineage and observation of their customs. Luke probably saw Herod as the first adversary of the church, and his miserable death served as a warning to the enemies of Jesus and an encouragement to the believers (Acts 12:23).[7]

As an enemy of the Christians, Herod arrested James. Luke does not say if there were any other leaders arrested. This James, son of Zebedee, and his brother John were two of Jesus' closest disciples.[8] He was the first of the Lord's apostles to be martyred and thus fulfill the words of Jesus that the sons of Zebedee would drink from the same cup of suffering as he did (Mk 10:39).[9]

King Herod, holding the powers of life and death in his hands, had James beheaded by the sword. According to Mishnaic law, only murderers and worshipers of idols were to be executed by beheading; thus, for James and the other Christians, this was an illegal action.[10] This may indicate that the charge against James was political and that Herod saw the church as a political threat to his rule. The Christians were now more than a religious imposition; Herod now regarded them as apostates and idolaters.

We are not sure why the persecution against James occurred. Herod knew how intensely the Jewish people hated his family, and he took every opportunity during his administration to win their favor.[11] Pax Romana was Agrippa's policy, meaning he supported the majority and suppressed the minorities when they disturbed the status quo. Perhaps the king, in support of the Pharisees, persecuted the church because the apostolic council had agreed to the Pauline mission. As a "good Jew" he would be concerned with abolishing any heretical sect. "He viewed Jewish Christians as divisive and felt their activities could only disturb the people and inflame antagonisms."[12] After Agrippa received popular support for the execution of James, he imprisoned the apostle Peter, who was the recognized leader of the Twelve and the instigator of the Gentile mission.[13]

When Peter was arrested, it was at the beginning of the seven-day festival of Unleavened Bread. Thus he was kept in prison for the duration of the festival and was to be executed after the Passover.[14] The reference to the Passover in 12:4 is used to describe the whole festival season. The parenthetical note that "this was during the festival of Unleavened Bread" introduces the time of the year (12:3b).

Luke identified the Passover week with the days of Unleavened Bread from Nisan 14 to Nisan 21.[15] The two festivals were seen as one since the feast of Unleavened Bread started immediately after Passover. William H. Willimon points to the ironic parallelism between the deliverance of God's people from Egyptian slavery and Peter from Herod's hands, both of which occurred during the celebration of Passover and the feast of Unleavened Bread. He contends that "the people who once saw God deliver them from slavery now make prisoners of their own kin during the feast of liberation—a bitter irony Luke does not want us to miss."[16]

Peter is guarded by four teams of soldiers, who guard the prisoner four men at a time. Each watch was shared by these quaternions (a team of four soldiers) and relieved in accordance with Roman army regulations every three hours. Peter had a guard on either side of him and two positioned outside his cell door. These precautionary measures emphasize the miracle of the imminent escape. Evidently Herod's plans were to make a public example of Peter in a forthcoming trial. Luke does not indicate where Peter was imprisoned, yet most commentators believe it was the Fortress Antonia, northwest of the Temple area.[17]

Perhaps these extra measures were taken because Peter had previously escaped (in Acts 5:19ff.) and because the church had many supporters who might try to free him. It would seem that ordinary citizens had no rights in the legal process, which is reminiscent of the arrest of Jesus. Jesus also died at the Passover (Lk 22:1), and there seems to be an intended symbolic parallelism. The delay of Peter's execution builds tension for the reader and allows the audience to see God at work on behalf of the church.

While Peter was under strong guard in prison, and all seemed humanly hopeless, "the church prayed fervently to God for him" (12:5b). The Christian community was in a crisis of immense proportions. Continuous prayer was being offered for Peter by the church in Jerusalem during the time of his imprisonment. Special emphasis is made by Luke regarding this continuous prayer. For him, prayer was extremely important as the means through which God's mission of salvation history was accomplished.[18]

Luke does not offer any speculation over why Peter was rescued and James lost his life. To deduce from 12:5 that the church prayed for Peter but not for James would be inconsistent with early church life. The church in Jerusalem had been enjoying peace since the persecution of Acts 8 had ended. James's death "signals the end of the short period of tranquility enjoyed by the Jerusalem leadership following the persecution of Stephen."[19] The majority of the Jewish people were appreciative of the early church with the exception of the Sadducean leaders of the Sanhedrin Council, who reacted with hostility. That Agrippa should target the leaders of the church in Jerusalem was evidence of a change in attitude toward them. Most of the action against the church in Acts comes from the Jewish religious authorities rather than the Roman government.

Thus one of the major lessons of the narrative is found in 12:5. The church was most likely praying for Peter's release, or perhaps emulating Jesus' prayer of "not our will, but yours be done." The fervency was a reflection of Jesus' prayers in Gethsemane (Lk 22:44) and was motivated by the church's concern for the apostle, not by the belief that God would be persuaded to answer prayer due to the intense devotion of the believers. C. K. Barrett notes the absence of any recorded prayer for Paul when he was arrested and imprisoned in Acts 22-28,[20] yet there was obvious concern for Paul even before he arrived in Jerusalem (21:4, 10-14).

## PETER RELEASED FROM PRISON: ACTS 12:6-11

During what Agrippa intended to be Peter's last night on earth, the church members were praying earnestly, not realizing that their prayers for Peter were being supernaturally answered at that very moment. Peter had been in custody for a week because the king did not want to violate the Jewish customs of Passover. The night before the execution Peter was sound asleep between two guards, bound by two chains, and guarded by men at his cell door. Usually a prisoner was chained to one guard only,[21] and the area between his cell door and the outside iron gate remained unguarded.[22] Herod doubled the guard to ensure that there would be no embarrassing escape. Humanly speaking, it was an impossibility.[23] The elaborate details of Herod's security procedures underscore the awesomeness of the miracle. Only a few hours before his intended death, Peter was in a deep sleep and had no thought of trying to escape.

What follows is direct intervention by God. "Suddenly an angel of the Lord appeared and a light shone in the cell" (12:7).[24] The entire escape from prison was attributed to this "angel of the Lord." The phrase "angel of the Lord" signifies that God was taking charge of affairs.[25] It happened in such a manner that there was no way Peter could be involved in the escape; he had no powers of self-preservation. The entire prison cell shone with a supernatural light while Peter slept.[26]

The angel is not gentle with Peter, prodding him awake. The word translated "tapped" *(pataxas)* actually means a rather violent blow.[27] F. F. Bruce describes the sleep of Peter as a "calm sleep that springs from a good conscience and quiet confidence in God."[28] Further, I. Howard Marshall states: "Peter was asleep, untroubled by the thought of what he expected to happen the next day, and had to be awakened by a nudge on his side."[29] Peter is in such a deep sleep that even after a firm strike to the side of his body, he simply followed the directions of the angel without question, as if still in partial slumber. The angel directed Peter in five stages to get up quickly, fasten his belt, put on his sandals, put on his cloak, and follow him. "The angel, like a parent with a child awakened from sound sleep, carefully instructed the groggy apostle to get dressed."[30] Luke's idea was that the sleep of the condemned Peter, rather than being a supernatural inducement, was a result of a riveted hope of eternal life and knowledge of his coming death, which Jesus had predicted for him in John 21:18-19. His purpose in the story was to demonstrate that God is at work, directing every aspect of the escape, even if the instructions were common sense.

The chains fell off and the gates opened of their own accord as Peter followed the angel and walked past the two guards between the cell door and the iron gate to the outside world. These soldiers made up the final two guards of the squad of four on duty. "There were three gates to be traversed before Peter reached freedom."[31] The mention in the text that the gate was made of iron only adds to the drama of the story.

Luke does not mention the specifics of how this miracle of liberation took place (for example, how Peter and the angel walk through the prison corridor undetected).[32] W. M. Ramsay in *St. Paul the Traveller* was typical of the commentators that present an explanation of the events in a natural way. Yet even he finds it difficult not to revert to the miraculous:

> There were obviously three gates and three wards to pass. Peter was allowed to pass the first and the second, being taken presumably as a servant; but no servant would be expected to pass beyond the outermost ward at night, and a different course was needed there.[33]

The writer acknowledged that Peter did not know what was happening and thought that he was "seeing a vision" (12:9) and then later "came to himself" (12:11). Perhaps Peter suspecting it was all a dream, thought he would wake up in the cell again, chained to the two guards and facing execution that day. "In fact, Luke manages to convey a remarkable dream-like quality to the entire sequence, including the angel's precise directions for putting on clothes!"[34] Outside the prison the two walked along a lane until suddenly the angel disappeared as mysteriously as he had come.[35]

It is only after the angel had gone that Peter realized what had happened. Peter "came to himself," or literally "in himself," since before that he has been "outside himself." This experience is similar to the one Peter had on the housetop in Joppa (10:10) when "he fell into a trance." The angel and the trance left him at the same time (cf. Lk 15:17). Peter was now able to look after himself. "Now I am sure that the Lord has sent his angel and rescued me from the hands of Herod and from all that the Jewish people were expecting" (12:11). The Jews had expected Peter to be condemned to death. Herod's execution of James had pleased the Jewish leaders, so, to please them further, he arrested Peter and sentenced him to suffer the same fate. Their calculated plans had failed.[36]

How are we to account for Peter's escape from prison? Was it a human "inside job," or a superhuman messenger from God that released him? Certainly both Peter and Luke recognized the event as divine intervention (cf. Lk 2:9 with Acts 12:7). "This was the finger of God: it was an angel of the Lord who had come to snatch him from his imminent fate."[37] Peter's deliverance was entirely the work of God. Neither the Christian community nor Peter was involved, with the exception of the prayers of the saints. "Many had gathered and were praying" (12:12). By linking this amazing escape with the church's prayer, Luke suggested the source of the power at work. Even so there was much doubt among the believers about the effectiveness of their requests to God (12:14-16); they accused the maid Rhoda of either seeing a vision or of being mentally unstable[38] when she reported that Peter was standing outside the gate to the house of Mary.[39]

With philosophical skepticism it has been argued that this event might be legend, because several of the motifs in the narrative appear in ancient stories circulated at the time.[40] Longenecker states confidently that "stories about prison doors opening of their own accord and of miraculous escapes from imprisonment were popular in the ancient world, and the form of such legends undoubtedly influenced to some extent Luke's narrative here."[41] Certainly it is possible that the early believers could have embellished the story of Peter's release from prison by human means, but it seems highly unlikely given the role of the supernatural in the Book of Acts and the style of the Lukan narrative. As Willimon so colorfully states: "The light, the angelic command, the chains falling away are all meant to be dramatic evidence that nothing can prevent the movement of God—even the chains and the prisons of Herod."[42]

A contemporary example of a miraculous escape from imprisonment is told of the Indian Christian mystic Sundar Singh. While a missionary in Tibet, the chief lama of a village threw Singh into a dry well and locked him in for preaching the gospel. There he was left to die like others before him upon whose bones he sat at the bottom of the well. After three nights in this Tibetan prison, and after much beseeching of God, he heard someone unlock the top of his prison cell and direct him to take hold of the rope that had been lowered. He was then drawn out of the well, and the lid replaced and relocked. Looking around, he did not see his rescuer. When morning came, he proceeded to preach to the village again. The lama, on hearing of the prison escape, had Singh brought before him and questioned. On listening to the incredible story of his release, the lama declared that someone had taken the key and let him out. Upon searching for the key, it was found on the lama's belt.[43] It would seem that both the rescue of Peter and Sundar Singh were miraculous interventions of God. The only marked difference is that Singh thought the rescuer a person until he disappeared, while Peter thought it was a vision until he was safe outside the fortress.

The Acts 12 narrative is a testimony to the delivering grace of God and to the power of earnest prayer. The sovereignty of God remains even while James was executed and Peter was released. To explain the mystery of this divine providence by saying the church did not pray for James as they did for Peter, or Peter had more faith than James, or James lacked faith, is a perversion of biblical truth. Yet, what would we say to the family of James (and perhaps others in the Jerusalem church) that had suffered under the "violent hands" of Herod Agrippa I? Although not promising freedom from persecution and death, at crucial moments God sometimes intervenes to demonstrate power and protection for God's people.

Peter was aware of the relationship between suffering and mission. In his letters he spoke about the suffering of Christ for us. Indeed, Peter tells the believers in 1 Peter 2:18-21 that we have been called to suffer for Christ. "For you have been called for this purpose, since Christ also suffered for you, leaving you an example for you to follow in his steps" (NIV) (see also 1 Pt 3:8-9). By this Peter did not mean that we are asked to atone for our sins, which have been forgiven through the substitutionary work of Christ, but that the followers of Jesus need to be willing to suffer for doing what is right, as he did. Since he suffered for us, we have the privilege of suffering like him. Peter then continued to describe the manner in which Jesus withstood the unjust suffering of crucifixion.

## CONCLUSION: THE PROGNOSIS

This biblical tension between suffering and the miraculous has been repeated many times in Christian history from its inception to the present day. The story of my wife's battle with cancer is an example. After the initial shock of the diagnosis, we prayerfully sought the best available medical treatment. Initially this meant Dolores underwent five weeks of chemotherapy and radiation in an attempt to shrink the cancer. When this failed, the cancer blocked the colon. She went through two major surgeries in an attempt to remove the disease. Unfortunately, it had spread, and the forecast was not optimistic.

Yet God was there in the prison with Dolores and our family through her journey. As I mentioned in the introduction, people from all over the world placed her on their prayer list; from Australia to Malaysia God's people gathered for prayer and fasting in her behalf. Strangers and friends alike sent cards and emails of support and encouragement, made meals, sent flowers, raked fall leaves, shoveled winter snow, and supplied listening care and concern along every step of the way.

For example, in the midst of a particularly painful recovery from one of the surgeries, Ruth, our next-door neighbor, came to the inner-city hospital where Dolores was in recovery. We were new in the area and had only met Ruth a couple of times, chatting over the back fence, but nothing more. Yet one stormy Thursday afternoon Ruth drove her car through flooded streets during peak rush-hour traffic to arrive at Dolores's hospital room at the precise moment she was recovering from the anesthetic, discovering as she awakened that the epidural was not working. She was in excruciating pain. So it was that this Christian nurse with more than thirty years of experience was able to comfort my wife through this horrible ordeal. Later I asked Ruth why she had come that afternoon in the midst of the storm and traffic. Her answer was simple: "God told me to."

How did God answer prayer for my Dolores suffering with cancer? Certainly, prayer brought about a manifestation of love through God's people that was breathtaking in its splendor and scope. Was she delivered from her prison as Peter was from his? Or did she follow the path of James and finish the race well, meeting our eternal King and Lord face to face? After eight weeks of hospitalization and seven weeks of home hospice care, Dolores ran into the outstretched arms of Jesus in March of last year. As in the case of Peter, there was no deliverance this side of the veil. Following the example of James, Dolores showed us not only how to live rightly but also how to die with dignity and grace. My wife finished well. So did both Peter and James.

## REFERENCES

[1] This is now the third Herod to be introduced to the text of Luke-Acts. The first was Herod the Great (Lk 1:5); the second was Herod the Tetrarch, who was involved with Jesus' ministry and death (Lk 3:1, 19; 8:3; 9:7-9; 13:31; 23:7-15; and Acts 4:27).

² The resumption of Acts 11:27-30 in 12:25 may imply that this period of persecution in Jerusalem was at the time of the visit of Barnabas and Saul to Jerusalem.

³ The death of Herod in 44 C.E. sets the time period.

⁴ Richard N. Longenecker, *The Acts of the Apostles*, The Expositor's Bible Commentary, vol. 9 (Grand Rapids, Mich.: Zondervan, 1981), Acts 12:1-4.

⁵ Also known as Julius Agrippa I; he bears his family name of Herod only in Acts. The Agrippa of Acts 25:13-26:32 is his son, Agrippa II; in addition, his two daughters are also mentioned in Acts: Drusilla (24:24) and Bernice (25:13).

⁶ F. F. Bruce, *The Book of Acts*, New International Commentary on the New Testament (Grand Rapids, Mich.: Eerdmans, 1954), 246-247; idem, *The Acts of the Apostles: The Greek Text with Introduction and Commentary* (Grand Rapids, Mich.: Eerdmans, 1968), 242-243.

⁷ A detailed account of the history of Herod Agrippa I is found in Josephus, *Antiquities of the Jews*, Books 18-19, and Longenecker, *The Acts of the Apostles*, Acts 12:1-4.

⁸ This James must be seen as different from the James mentioned in 12:17, 15:13, and 21:18, who is usually accepted as the Lord's brother. See Luke 6:14, Acts 1:13, and Mark 3:17 for mention of the brothers James and John. James enjoyed a close relationship with Jesus (Lk 8:51; 9:28, 54).

⁹ James's brother John suffered for the gospel (Rv 1:9) but outlived all the other apostles. In Acts there is no reference to John's death.

¹⁰ *Mishnah Sanhedrin* 9:1.

¹¹ Longenecker mentions some of the actions that Herod (and his wife Cypros) took to win the favor of the Jewish people: They followed the Jewish customs regarding the festivals; persuaded Caligula not to erect the emperor's statue in the Jerusalem Temple; intervened on behalf of the Jews in Alexandria who were suffering under Roman injustice; moved the seat of government from Caesarea to Jerusalem; and rebuilt the city's walls and fortifications.

¹² Longenecker, *The Acts of the Apostles*, Acts 12:1-4.

¹³ Agrippa was undoubtedly in Jerusalem for the Passover festival (see Lk 23:7).

¹⁴ This was similar to the problem the Jewish leaders had when they arrested Jesus (Mk 14:1ff.).

¹⁵ Ex 12:6-18; Lk 22:1. Nisan 14 in 44 C.E. occurred on May 1.

¹⁶ William H. Willimon, *Acts*, Interpretation (Atlanta, Ga.: John Knox Press, 1988), 111-112.

¹⁷ C. K. Barrett, *Commentary on Acts*, The International Critical Commentary (Edinburgh: T. & T. Clark, 1994), 577. Compare Acts 21:31, 35, 37, when Paul was about to go into the Fortress Antonia (Acts 21:34—23:30).

¹⁸ The relationship between prayer and mission may be seen in the following scriptures: Acts 1:14, 24; 2:42; 4:24-31; 6:4, 6; 9:40; 10:2, 4, 9, 31; 11:5; 13:3; 14:23; 16:25; 22:17; and 28:8.

¹⁹ Luke Timothy Johnson, *The Acts of the Apostles* (Collegeville, Minn.: The Liturgical Press, 1992), 211.

²⁰ Barrett, *Commentary on Acts*, 578.

²¹ Cf. Seneca, *Epistulae* 5.7.

²² Ernst Haenchen, *The Acts of the Apostles: A Commentary* (Philadelphia: The Westminster Press, 1971), 383.

²³ Agrippa knew what it was like to be bound in prison. He had been imprisoned by Tiberius in Rome and then released by Gaius on Tiberius's death.

²⁴ For sudden appearances of angels, see Lk 2:9; 24:4; Acts 27:23-24. Also, Jesus suddenly appeared to Paul in Acts 23:11.

[25] See the following biblical references to angels and their interaction with humanity: Lk 1:11; 2:9; Acts 5:19; 8:26; 12:23. Angels are also mentioned in Acts 7:30, 35, 38; 12:11; 27:23.

[26] For light as an accompaniment to the supernatural, see Lk 2:9; Acts 9:3; 22:6; 26:13.

[27] Johnson states that the choice of the Greek word *pataxas* translated as "tapped" in the NRSV was unusual because it was most often used in the Septuagint for the "smiting" of God's enemies (Ex 2:12; Jgs 1:5; Ps 3:7; 77:66) and as such was used by Luke in the same fashion (Lk 22:49-50; Acts 7:24) (*The Acts of the Apostles*, 212). Compare the blow by the angel to Herod in Acts 12:23. Perhaps this is why the NRSV chooses to use the gentler word, "tapped."

[28] Bruce, *The Book of Acts*, 248.

[29] I. Howard Marshall, *The Acts of the Apostles*, Tyndale New Testament Commentaries (Grand Rapids, Mich.: Eerdmans, 1980), 209.

[30] Longenecker, *The Acts of the Apostles*, Acts 12:6-9.

[31] Marshall, *The Acts of the Apostles*, 209.

[32] Compare the liberation of the apostles from prison by an angel of the Lord in Acts 5:19 and of Paul and Silas by an earthquake in Acts 16:26.

[33] W. M. Ramsay, *St. Paul the Traveller* (London, 1920), 28.

[34] Johnson, *The Acts of the Apostles*, 212.

[35] The Western text informs us that Peter and the angel descended "seven steps" to the outside street (see Barrett, *Commentary on Acts*, 581-582).

[36] Compare another Passover deliverance: the escape of the three Hebrew youths from Nebuchadnezzar's furnace (Dn 3:19-30).

[37] Bruce, *The Book of Acts*, 249.

[38] Compare this with the women in Luke 24:10-11 trying to convince the disciples that Jesus had risen from the dead.

[39] Mary was called "the mother of John whose other name was Mark." This home was obviously one of the meeting places for the early Christians. It must have been of considerable size to have an intervening court and living quarters at the back. (For other households run by women, see Lk 10:38-42 and Acts 16:14-15). The fact that Luke referred to Mary as the mother of Mark (cf. Mk 15:40; Lk 23:49) may suggest that John Mark (John is his Jewish name and Mark his Latin name) was better known to his readers than his mother. This John was the one who was a cousin of Barnabas (Col 4:10) and accompanied Barnabas and Saul on their first mission journey before turning back at Perga in Pamphylia (Acts 13:5, 13). After the argument over whether John Mark should accompany Paul and Barnabas on their second mission journey (Acts 15:36-41), he returned to Cyprus with Barnabas (Acts 15:39) and later became a companion of both Paul (Col 4:10; 2 Tm 4:11; Phil 24) and Peter (1 Pt 5:13). He was also the writer of the gospel of Mark.

[40] Barrett identifies other miraculous escapes recorded in ancient writings: Homer, *Iliad* 5.749; Virgil, *Aeneid* 6.81f.; and Eusebius, *Praeparatio Evangelica* 9.27.23 (Barrett, *Commentary on Acts*, 581). Johnson adds the following accounts of prison escapes: Lucian of Samosata, *Toxaris* 28-33; Achilles Tatius, *Clitophon and Leucippe* 3:9-11; Ovid, *Metamorphoses* 3:690-700; Artapanus, *On the Jews*; *The Acts of Paul* 7; and *The Acts of Thomas* 162-163; and Euripides, *Bacchae* 346-357, 434-450, and 510-643 (*The Acts of the Apostles*, 217).

[41] Longenecker, *The Acts of the Apostles*, Acts 12:10-11.

[42] Willimon, *The Acts of the Apostles*, 112.

[43] B. H. Streeter and A. J. Appasamy, *The Sadhu* (London, 1921), 30ff.

# 15

## *The Cursing Paul:*
## *Magical Contests in Acts 13*
## *and the New Testament Apocrypha*

### Acts 13:6–12

### Clark A. Walz

My interest in the events described in the first half of Acts 13 results from the convergence of three scholarly and pastoral concerns with both place and topic. For more than twenty years, my archeological interests have focused on Cyprus. My first exposure to field work was at a Bronze Age site on the island's south coast. On that first visit, I saw the pillar at Paphos where, according to Cypriot church tradition, Saint Paul was flogged as a result of his confrontation with the Roman proconsul's magician. When I reentered the church after a long absence, my continuing love for Cyprus and its history drew me to consider its Christian experience.

Second, while preparing for doctoral examinations in Mediterranean archeology and the anthropology of religion, I encountered a large body of ethnographic literature on magic and witchcraft. As a result, I was able to consider the evidence for ancient Mediterranean magical practices from a comparative and theoretical perspective, and not simply as an apologetic. The fact that Cyprus has produced a significant number of *defixiones* (curses and binding spells inscribed on lead tablets) added to the convergence of interests.

A third concern was that my first pastoral assignment was to a town where there was an active Wiccan group and at least one less benign pagan cult. Some teenagers and young adults who felt maginalized in the dominant Christian context had turned to these alternative forms of religious expression. The challenge faced by Paul in Acts 13, that of offering a viable alternative to a magical world view, paralleled what I now faced in rural Pennsylvania. The issues of center and periphery raised by the early Christian conflict with, and adaptation of, elements of magical belief remain with us today.

## WHAT HAPPENED IN PAPHOS?

When they had gone through the whole island as far as Paphos, they met a certain magician, a Jewish false prophet, named Bar-Jesus. He was with the proconsul, Sergius Paulus, an intelligent man, who summoned Barnabas and Saul and wanted to hear the word of God. But the magician Elymas (for that is the translation of his name) opposed them and tried to turn the proconsul away from the faith. But Saul, also known as Paul, filled with the Holy Spirit, looked intently at him and said, "You son of the devil, . . . the hand of the Lord is against you, and you will be blind for a while, unable to see the sun." Immediately mist and darkness came over him. (Acts 13:6-11)

Most first-century pagans, probably including the most excellent Theophilus, would undoubtedly have identified two magicians in this pericope, Bar-Jesus and Paul. Though Luke portrays Paul's actions as something other than magic,[1] Paul nonetheless curses his opponent using power granted him by the spirit of a person (Jesus) who died an early and violent death. As a result, Paul's words bound his rival's eyes and Bar-Jesus was temporarily blinded. Paul's actions contain elements of both necromancy, the "means of accomplishing magical goals through the instrumentality of spirits of the dead," and of cursing, an utterance or prayer designed to bring harm to another.[2]

Despite the unease arising from associations between Christianity and magic, both in the first century and in our postmodern context, it is clear that Luke and other early Christian authors utilized concepts drawn from Greco-Roman popular religious practices, including some associated with magic and witchcraft. This was part of a contextualized message, designed to demonstrate the superiority of the new faith in the religious marketplace of the first and second centuries. The Christianization of such concepts was also part of the church's efforts to occupy both the periphery, characterized by its attempts to draw distinctions between itself and the dominant culture, and the center, reflected by its goal of evangelizing the same dominant culture of its larger social world. Therefore, the relationship between faith and magic was part of a dance of marginality. Early Christian apologists could claim both to be part of the religious mainstream and, at the same time, distance their new faith from popular beliefs and practices as it suited their purpose.

## MAGIC IN THE GRECO-ROMAN WORLD

The study of Greco-Roman magic has enjoyed somewhat of a renaissance in the last two decades. The publication and translation of major bodies of magical texts and spells written on papyrus and curses inscribed on lead sheets have made these primary sources more accessible.[3] Several monographs and collections of essays on the subject have appeared during the same period. Simultaneously, the development of social-scientific criticism has introduced New

Testament scholars to the methods and insights of cultural anthropology. All of these factors have combined to make the study of magic in the early Christian experience a more acceptable academic pursuit.[4]

One of the most vexing questions is the problem of definition; the boundaries among religion, magic, and witchcraft have never been firmly established. The late nineteenth-century functionalist view that magic was either a primitive precursor to, or a degenerate form of religion has been abandoned. One person's religion is another's magic, when viewed from the outside.[5] For the Christian, the Eucharist may be a transcendent experience, a sharing in the body and blood of Christ. However, pagan observers often equated communion with magic, ritual murder, and cannibalism.[6] At the same time, when pagans consumed wine ritually identified as the body and blood of a pagan god as part of a love spell, Christians viewed these acts as the lowest form of magic.[7] The relationship between magic and witchcraft is also problematic. Almost all societies who believe in magic allow some forms but prohibit others. In Christina Larner's cross-cultural study of witchcraft beliefs, she asked, "Is all witchcraft really witchcraft?" She points out that curing, a form of ritual magic common to many cultures, was tolerated by both African tribal societies and in Christian premodern Europe. However, when similar rituals were undertaken with harmful intent, they became *maleficium* (witchcraft), legally and/or socially proscribed.[8]

For our purposes the following definitions will apply. Magic is considered a two-stage process. It includes both ritual activity (formal, repetitive, and required behavior) and performative utterance and/or gesture (words or gestures that accomplish desired ends).[9] The desired goal is the control of supernatural forces achieved through the ritual. Witchcraft is defined as magic that is both intended to do harm and that is socially and/or legally proscribed.[10] In other words, all witchcraft is magic, but not all magic is witchcraft. Admittedly, these definitions do not perfectly define the boundaries among religion, magic, and witchcraft. However, they were not precisely drawn in the ancient world either.

The Greeks noted three categories of magical practice: *theurgia, magia,* and *goetia,* listed here in their rough order of respectability. The first, *theurgia,* was commonly associated with holy men (shamans) and later on (second century C.E.) with religious and philosophical schools. It most closely corresponds with what today might be called white magic. Second, *magia* was a Persian loan word and referred primarily to astrology and divination. It had some respectability due to its supposed antiquity but was also suspect because of its barbarian origins. Third, *goetia* was the lowest form, the magic of spells, potions, and curses.[11] The legal status of magic in ancient Greece was problematic. Greek laws against magic varied from city to city, with Athens apparently among the most lenient.[12] Plato urged stricter legislation against magicians who

> despise their fellow human beings and seduce many of the living by pretending they could seduce the souls of the dead, and promise to persuade the gods through the magic of offerings, prayers, and incantations, thus proposing, in order to make money, to destroy individuals, families, and entire cities. (*Laws* 10.909)

Here magic is linked with impiety and atheism as well as with fraudulent behavior. Might certain televangelists who have committed fraud be charged with practicing magic under Plato's proposed laws?

Early Roman law had no direct prohibition against magic. The Twelve Tables did forbid the cursing of crops. However, it was the destruction of property rather than the means employed that was the issue.[13] This changed during the early principate, perhaps due to nervousness over the increasing influence of foreign cults. Augustus apparently crafted legislation outlawing both magic and witchcraft, the text of which has not survived. However, a third-century legal commentary tells us much about the law:

> Any who perform, or procure the performance of, impious or nocturnal sacrifices, to enchant, curse, or to bind anyone with a spell are either crucified or thrown to the beasts. Any who sacrifice a man, or make offerings of his blood, or pollute a shrine or temple are thrown to the beasts, or, if people of position, are beheaded. It is the prevailing legal opinion that participants in the magical art should be subject to the extreme punishment, either thrown to the beasts or crucified; but the magicians themselves should be burned alive. It is not permitted for anyone to have in his possession books of the magic art. If they are found in anyone's possession, when his property has been expropriated, and the books burned publicly, he is to be deported to an island, or, if he is a member of the lower class, beheaded. Not only the practice of this art, but even the knowledge of it, is prohibited.[14]

How accurately this later commentary reflects first-century attitudes is unclear. The wholesale prohibition of all magic and sanctions on practitioners is not certain. However, the first century saw a marked increase in the number of lawsuits where witchcraft was alleged. Hans G. Kippenburg's study of these legal records indicates that the defining feature of Roman witchcraft was that it was practiced in private.[15] Furthermore, by the time Luke-Acts was written during the last quarter of the first century, the traditional Roman boundary between *religio* and *superstitio* was increasingly drawn in geographical, ethnic, and social terms.[16] *Religio* was what Romans practiced; *superstitio* was what was done by foreigners. *Religio* honored traditional gods; *superstitio* was devoted to new and imported gods. Religious rites were practiced in the open; superstitious rites were done in secret. In Roman eyes, magic was the ultimate *superstitio*. To be accused of practicing it was to be maginalized on several fronts. Since defining characteristics of *supersitio* could be applied to Christianity, it was automatically marginalized as well.

It is impossible to offer more than a brief survey of magical beliefs as described in Greco-Roman literature. However, a measure of the fear and loathing generated by magic may be found in Book 5 of Horace's *Epodes* (The Incantations). Written during the reign of Augustus, Horace's description of Thessalian witches had a great impact on Roman attitudes toward magic and the occult. Unlike the beautiful witches such as Circe and Medea encountered in earlier Greek literature, Horace's witches are ugly, "like a stepmother or a wild beast." Canidia, the chief witch, has uncut fingernails, yellow teeth, and vipers braided in her hair. The witches are sexually suspect; one is known for her "masculine lust." The witches manufacture dreadful potions and invoke Diana (goddess of the moon and the hunt) and Hecate (the patron goddess of witches) in a ritual for drawing down power from the moon.[17]

The witches kidnapped a young boy to serve as a human sacrifice in their rituals. He accepts that he cannot change his fate but is promised that in death he will be empowered to revenge himself on his murderers. This episode introduces one of the most important principles of Greco-Roman magic. The spirits of humans who have died before their allotted time, who died unmarried or childless and/or died violently, were believed to be especially powerful beings.[18] Such a spirit, one of the special dead, was powerful in its own right and might also be a useful courier to evoke more powerful gods and demons. Such spirits were believed to be angry as well as powerful, truly useful tools for the magician.[19]

This belief facilitated one of the most common of all magical practices, the use of binding spells written on lead tablets. These spells were known as *defixiones* in Latin, from the practice of nailing or fixing them to the graves of persons who died untimely deaths. The purpose of the spell was to bind or restrain the object of the curse. The curse would then be activated through the agency of the malevolent spirit lingering near the grave. They might also be placed in wells or buried near temples dedicated to chthonic deities. The textual formulas might be simple, with only the name of the cursed written on the tablet, or complex, with lengthy invocations of gods and demons calling for the death of the person cursed. We have several tablets written in the same hand but cursing of different individuals, suggesting that some tablets were produced by professional magicians, the kind Paul encountered in Ephesus (Acts 19:19).[20]

Despite the contention that magic was primarily practiced among the lower classes, there is ample evidence that all levels of society feared the power of these binding spells.[21] According to Pliny, "There is no one who does not fear to be spellbound by curse tablets" (*Natural History* 24.4.19). Even the imperial family might be attacked by means of magic. The death of Julius Caesar Germanicus, adopted son of the emperor Tiberius, was attributed to black magic: "There were found hidden in the floor and in the walls disinterred remains of human bodies, incantations and spells, and the name of Germanicus inscribed on leaden tablets, half burnt cylinders spread with blood, and other horrors which by popular belief are devoted to the infernal deities" (Tacitus, *Ann.* 2.69). That Sergius Paulus, the procounsul of Cyprus, included a magician in his retinue is a further indication of the penetration of magical beliefs into the center of imperial society (Acts 13:7-8).

The most important other source for the study of ancient magic is the papyri from Egypt. These texts contain a wide variety of spells, incantations, prayers, liturgies, and hymns. Four basic types of magic are represented: apotropaic spells, curses, love magic, and prophetic magic.[22] Most of these texts seem to have belonged to a single library, written over time by a group of scribe-priest-magicians living in Thebes; some may have belonged to itinerant magicians.[23] The practices described in the papyri are closer to the religious end of the witch-craft-magic-religion continuum than are those found in the curse tablets.

Before closing this brief survey of pagan magical beliefs, it should be pointed out that in both Greek and Latin literature there is a strong and often negative association between magic and peoples outside the classical *koine*. The most famous magicians were foreigners, for example, Persian magi,[24] Egyptian priests, Medea from Cholchis, Dido from Carthage, and a number of Thessalian witches. Even an entire race might be viewed as having innate powers. Egypt, for instance, had a particular reputation for magical prowess. Thus Celsus claimed that Jesus' miracles were made possible only through the magic he had learned during his boyhood in Egypt (Origen, *Contra Celsum* 1.46). Also, Jewish people had a reputation as powerful magicians due to the antiquity and mysterious nature (in Roman perspective) of their religion.[25] The Jewish reputation for magical prowess was embellished by Josephus, who claimed that Jewish magicians inherited King Solomon's special powers over demons (*Ant. Jud.* 8.45-48). In Rome, foreign magicians enjoyed greater authority than the local practitioners: "But the Chaldean seers are apparently more to be trusted. What those astrologers say comes straight from the heart" (Juvenal, *Satires* 6.550). We shall see that this association between magic and those living on the margins affected the discussion of magic in both the canonical and apocryphal Acts.

## PAUL'S USE OF MAGICAL LANGUAGE

I have described above Paul's confrontation with Bar-Jesus as a "magical contest," a description that might seem odd if not inappropriate. Most commentators have agreed with A. D. Nock, who held the opposite opinion, that Paul's actions "represented Christianity in sharp contrast with *magia*."[26] My interpretation rests on demonstrating that Paul was conversant with the concepts and language of Greco-Roman magic.[27]

For example, in the magical papyri the use of repetitive prayers and nonsensical (to us) magical formulas was quite common. Instructions were given to repeat phrases three times, seven times, or with calendrical repetitions. The magician might "say [the formula] three times on an empty stomach, and you will know the power" and to repeat the phrase "BORKA BORKA PHRIX PHRIX" several times.[28] The Greek technical term for this repetitive praying, *battologēo,* has the sense of "to babble" or "to prattle."[29]

Galatians, particularly rich in passages with such magical associations, utilizes repetition in the famous verse from 3:28, "There is no longer Jew or Greek, there is no longer slave or free, there is no longer male or female; for all of you are one in Christ Jesus." The key here is the rhetorical device of definition through structural opposition, common to both classical literature and the curse tablets. An early example is found on a first-century B.C.E. tablet from Delos cursing an unknown thief or thieves who stole a necklace: "I register the genitals and private parts of the one who stole (it), and of those . . . whether male or female."[30] Among a large group of tablets found in a spring dedicated to Minerva in Bath, England, were two that contained close parallels to the Pauline formula. The first, dated to the second century, curses the person who stole a bronze vase:

> The person who stole my bronze vessel is utterly accursed. I give him to the temple of Sullis, whether man or woman, whether slave or free, whether boy or girl, and let him who has done this spill his blood into the vessel itself.[31]

The second, from the fourth century, is unique due to its mention of Christianity. It adds a religious element to the formula: "Whether pagan or Christian, whether man or woman, whether boy or girl, whether slave or free . . . "[32] It is also significant that both the Christian and pagan uses of these formulas occur in structurally similar ritual contexts, the exorcistic baptismal rite for forgiveness of sin and the punishment of wrongdoing in the curses. Both are ritual acts designed to alter a personal state of being.[33] The resemblance is striking, to say the least.

Furthermore, Paul employs a curse formula to condemn the Judaizers in Galatians 1:8-9: "Let that one be accursed!" (The same formula appears in 1 Corinthians 16:22.) While the word *anathema* may have the meaning of a consecrated offering to a god, its use here clearly represents "something delivered up to divine wrath, dedicated to destruction, and brought under a curse."[34] This powerful and magical language condemns the target to death. Hans Dieter Betz describes its use here as a "magical imperative" through which the entire letter assumes magical power. Therefore, obedience to Paul's commands is a matter of life and death for the Galatians.[35] In accusing his opponents of bewitching the Galatians in 3:1, he fights fire with fire.

The use of *anathema* as a word of power in pagan curse formulas is admittedly uncommon. However, it is interesting that it appears on a pagan curse tablet from a first- or second-century C.E. example from Megara, a city near Corinth. In this spell Hecate, the goddess of witchcraft, is invoked with the phrase, "we anathematize them."[36] The tablet's date, its recovery from a city close to Corinth, and the inclusion of "Hebrew oaths" in the invocation, all make a connection between this tablet and the Christian community at Corinth an intriguing possibility.

In Galatians 3:1 Paul asks the churches, "Who has bewitched you?," his only use of the term for "bewitched" in his letters. This term has three connotations, all connected with magic: "to bewitch," "to revile or curse," or "to cause harm through envy (the evil eye)."[37] Even so, Betz insists that its use here is "ironic or even sarcastic" and is not meant to be taken literally. Sam K. Williams holds a similar view, contending that the term is intended as a metaphor for the faults of his critics.[38] On the other hand, Jerome H. Neyrey and J. Louis Martyn contend that an actual charge of witchcraft was intended against his opponents.[39] I suggest that Neyrey's claim is suspect on methodological grounds, an issue too complicated to be addressed here. However, three points suggest that Paul's question was asked seriously and not as mere hyperbole. First, he twice accuses his opponents of frightening or troubling the Galatians (1:7; 5:10).[40] Fright seems to be an unlikely result if the charge of witchcraft was meant as a mere rhetorical device. Second, we have seen that Paul himself curses the Judaizers, a suitable response if his opponents have engaged in some sort of occult practice. Third, in 4:3 and 4:9 Paul claims that the Galatians have returned to the worship of the demonic astral spirits *(stoicheia)* who previously enslaved them.[41] One thing that pagans and Christians could agree on was that both groups believed that such spirits provided the power that enabled magic.

It may be that *baskainō* should be translated in this case as "overlooked" rather than as "bewitched." Paul seems to suggest that the evil eye, causing harm through envy, is at work in Galatia as opposed to actual ritual magic. Belief in the evil eye was common in both Judaism and paganism. More important, it was believed to be cast by insiders within a given community, the church in this particular case. The evil eye is associated with evil spirits who act upon a display of envy rather than as the result of their invocation through ritual magic. The motivation would seem to have been envy at Paul's successful mission to the Gentiles in Galatia. In any case, the magical associations found in this passage are strong.

Finally, in Romans 1:18 Paul declares that the wrath of God is revealed against those who "by their wickedness suppress the truth." Welborn has recently proposed another translation of the verb here that takes into account its magical connotations as the operative word in the binding spells discussed above. He suggests that Paul understood a more "demonic" origin of sin; it originates among those who "bind the truth of God under a spell."[42] Given Paul's use elsewhere of words and concepts associated with Greco-Roman magic, his familiarity with the language found in the *defixiones* is certainly plausible.

I suggest that Paul accomplishes one basic task in the passages cited above: The Christian message is contextualized through the use of language and concepts already familiar to his pagan audience. He employs a strategy of appropriation to demonstrate that whatever magic others can do, Christianity can do as well, if not better. We will see this same strategy employed in the descriptions of magical contests in both the canonical and apocryphal acts.

## PAUL CONFRONTS ELYMAS (BAR-JESUS)

The magical contest is an ancient literary motif. In Acts 13 the dispute between Paul and Elymas (Bar-Jesus) recalls the contests between Moses and Pharaoh's magicians (Exodus 7—8), as well as that between Elijah and the priests of Baal on Mount Carmel (1 Kgs 18:19-40). This literary device is also found in pagan magical literature. More recently it has found new life as a central feature of the widely popular Harry Potter books.[43] In any case, Susan R. Garrett's contention that Paul's actions seem as "'magic-like' as anything the magus himself might have done" is certainly accurate.[44]

While this story in Acts is widely regarded by many scholars as non-historical,[45] we can observe that the account does preserve genuine historical details. Cyprus was a senatorial province; therefore, Luke's use of proconsul as the governor's title is correct. The name Lucius Sergius Paulus belongs to a senator during the reign of Claudius. This man, or one of his family, could be the man named by Luke.[46] Furthermore, the evidence considered above establishes Paul's familiarity with magical terms and concepts. This knowledge supports the possibility that he had been in close contact with persons holding magical belief, either magicians themselves or their clients. As a result, Aune claims that the Paul who curses Elymas is "fully consonant" with the author of the letters.[47] A confrontation between Paul and Elymas is not necessarily improbable.

Does Paul's Spirit-filled blinding of Elymas constitute magic? Once again, while Luke draws a clear distinction between what Paul does and what Elymas does, the latter's power being demonic in nature, the distinction would have been lost to an outside observer. The malfunction of bodily organs was one of the most commonly desired effects of the curse tablets; Elymas's blinding is the result of a punitive magical prayer or *strafwunder*.[48]

For Luke's purpose the results of the events in Acts 13 are more important than the means by which they were obtained. Sergius Paulus, astounded at Paul's "teaching about the Lord," believes as the result of what he saw (13:12). Luke's audience would understand that Christianity had moved from the periphery of Roman society, the place reserved for followers of an executed enemy of Rome, with religious practices tinged with magic, to society's center. A Roman proconsul had seen and believed in both the power and teachings of Paul's gospel (2 Cor 11:4; Gal 1:8-9). At the same time, by blinding Elymas, Paul had bound one who was previously at the center, a Jewish magician in the governor's household, and exiled him to the margins as a powerless charlatan.

Perhaps even more important, Luke described Elymas as a "Jewish false prophet" (13:6) and later as a "son of the devil" (13:10). Here we see a further marginalization of magic. In order to distance the gospel from magic, the latter must be branded as a false teaching and the source of its power as demonic. Here we see an early connection between magic and Christian heresy. Not only is magic moved to the periphery of the Roman world, but Christianity marginalizes it as well.

The late second-century apocryphal book the Acts of Peter contains an interesting parallel to these events.[49] In this work even Christian infants are able to rebuke the renowned Simon Magus, the wonderworker who figures prominently in chapter 8 of the canonical Acts of the Apostles:

Now the child she suckled was seven months old, and it took the voice of a man and said to Simon: "You are an abomination of God and men, you destruction of the truth and most wicked seed of corruption. . . . Now I, an infant, am compelled by God to speak, and yet you do not blush for shame! . . . So now your evil nature shall be exposed and your evil nature destroyed. This last word I am telling you now: Jesus Christ says to you, 'Be struck dumb by the power of my name and depart from Rome until the coming Sabbath.'" And immediately he became dumb and could not resist, but left Rome until the Sabbath and lodged in a stable.[50]

The similarities between this account and Acts 13 should be clear. The invocation of Christ's name as a magical word of power *(vox magica)*, the binding of Simon's tongue, and his banishment, both literal and symbolic, to the margins (to live in a stable outside Rome) are all mirrored in Acts 13 and serve the same purpose. However, a full century later, the point can be made cynically, even a Christian baby can invoke powers stronger than those belonging to an adult magician.

In chapter 8 of the Acts of Peter, Peter and Simon Magus clash in the Roman forum. Again Christian prayers with magical overtones are invoked against demonic powers. Peter hurls an anathema against Simon, "A curse be on your words against Christ" (Acts of Peter 8:24). A few days later Simon promises the Roman mob that he can fly. When he does so, Peter shoots him down with a well-aimed prayer, and the crowd, by now tired of Simon's lies, stones him and he is converted to Christianity (Acts of Peter 8:30-32).

Once again, we see a magical contest help the new faith move from the margins to the center. In the Acts of Peter, this movement is not only symbolic and social but locational as well; these events take place in the Roman forum, the literal heart of the empire. As did Paul in his letters, and Luke did in the canonical Acts of the Apostles, the author of this apocryphal work appropriated magical themes, words, and concepts, and used them against the new faith's opponents. The dance of marginality continued.

## IMPLICATIONS FOR MISSION TODAY

While it is probably not wise for Christians to issue formal challenges of prayerful combat to Wiccans, Satanists, or others who hold a magical, contemporary world view, the same issues of contextualization and marginalization faced by the early missionaries remain. First, consider the postmodern context. For the first time since Emperor Theodosius forcibly closed all pagan shrines and temples in A.D. 392, Christianity is not the major defining feature of Western religious culture. Major non-Christian world religions, such as Islam, and non-orthodox Western religious movements, like the Latter Day Saints, are increasingly influential in the American religious scene. Additionally, a magical world view is proclaimed through Internet websites, any number of computer games, heavy metal rock music, popular books like the Harry Potter series, and even through some romance novels. The latter often present a type of Wiccan apologetics featuring female empowerment through magic.[51] An aggressive response to these cultural realities, such as burning Harry Potter books or demanding their removal from library shelves, is often counterproductive. The church sometimes seems intolerant and frightened. When we distance ourselves from our context, we make those who would join us travel farther to reach us. We should question whether this is an appropriate response to our culture. I suggest it might be more effective to do what the early church did with magical concepts two thousand years ago. Search for what is useful and adaptable and then "Christianize" it. For example, I have read and greatly enjoyed the first four Harry Potter books. To be sure, they are not explicitly Christian, but neither are they textbooks for future occultists. They are fantasies, not too far removed from the *Chronicles of Narnia* series by C. S. Lewis or the *Lord of the Rings* by J. R. R. Tolkien. Rather than ban and burn such works, we might recognize the many areas where their message is congruent with the Christian faith. The Harry Potter books teach that both good and evil exist and that one must choose between them. Harry and his friends learn that the choices they make matter and have consequences, both for themselves and for others. Hard work in school, loyalty to friends, the duty to respect and protect the weak, the principle that respect must be earned rather than be automatically bestowed by wealth and birth, all are among the positive lessons brought out in these remarkable flights of imagination. One Church of England congregation has even developed a Harry Potter liturgy. While that may be going a bit far, hosting family and church discussions of the books in which parents and pastors can guide the discussion might be an effective way of understanding the magical world view presented in the books.

What of marginalization? I began by referring to the occult groups I encountered in Pennsylvania. Much Christian literature on alternate spirituality spends a good deal of time on techniques for rescuing former Christians from these groups. It might be more productive to ask why people are leaving the church for these groups in the first place. Are there legitimate spiritual needs that are not being met by the church, even with the wide variety of programs available in contemporary Christianity?

While I do not claim to have a comprehensive answer, studies of modern paganism both in the United States and England may provide insights.[52] My highly tentative conclusions here are based on the books by Adler and Luhrman and an informal survey of websites maintained by neo-pagans. I have concluded that the authoritarian nature of both the High Church and Free Church traditions forces many young people out the door and into groups where a greater variety of religious opinion is tolerated. One of the frustrating aspects of studying neo-pagan groups is the difficulty of making generalized statements about their beliefs. It seems safe to say that there is no such thing as neo-pagan dogma.

Modern magic, like its Greco-Roman forbear, is highly ritualized. Many of those who leave the more liturgical and sacramental traditions (Roman Catholic, Orthodox, and Anglican) seem to be drawn to magical spiritualities because they are also highly ritualized. Pagan ritualism provides a certain continuity with their previous experience and may speak to a basic need for ritualization. Surprisingly, many who leave the non-liturgical and Low Church traditions (such as Baptist, Low Church Methodism, Pentecostal churches) are also attracted to the ritualized nature of the neo-pagan or magical experience. This speaks to a universal need for ritualized religious experience and may suggest that liturgical renewal across denominations might be helpful.[53] Finally, it is my impression that both men and women are drawn to the highly egalitarian nature of these alternate spiritualities. Many of the life stories published on Wiccan websites refer to the gender inequality in the church as the reason for leaving and the equality found in their new spiritualities as the reason for staying where they are. As long as the church continues to marginalize women by preaching submission to male authority, refusing to ordain women, and refusing to recognize the value of ministries undertaken by women, we have no one to blame but ourselves if the church loses women to more egalitarian alternate spiritualities.

In conclusion, Christianity has historically succeeded, perhaps too well, in moving from the margins to the center of dominant society. The magical world view, once occupying the center, is now marginalized. By living in the center, the church has forgotten its own journey and the techniques for the assimilation of popular religious culture that helped it succeed. Neither Paul in his letters, nor Luke in Acts, could be accused of sacrificing the truth of the gospel by irresponsible accommodation to pagan magical beliefs. Yet both incorporated what they discerned was appropriate, and the gospel was successfully proclaimed.

## REFERENCES

[1] For Luke, the distinction between magic and miracle is the source of the power utilized. Magic relies on demonic power; miracles are the result of power granted by Christ (see Susan R. Garrett, *The Demise of the Devil: Magic and the Demonic in Luke's Writings* [Minneapolis, Minn.: Fortress Press, 1989], 60, 79-80). However, this distinction would have been meaningless to those outside the church. To a pagan observer, the power granted in Christ's name would be just as magical as that granted through the invocation of any other spirit or god. This belief was the source of much early hostility toward the Christian faith (see Stephen Benko, "Early Christian Magical Practices," *SBL Seminar Papers* [1982]: 9).

[2] David E. Aune, "Magic in Early Christianity," *Aufstieg und Niedergang der römischen Welt* II.23.2 (Berlin and New York: Walter de Gruyter, 1980), 1545, 1552.

[3] Many of the most important Greek and Latin literary references to magic are collected in Georg Luck, *Arcana Mundi: Magic and the Occult in the Greek and Roman Worlds* (Baltimore: The Johns Hopkins University Press, 1985). For spells in Greek and Egyptian Demotic, see Hans Dieter Betz, ed., *The Greek Magical Papyri in Translation*, 2d ed. (Chicago: The University of Chicago Press, 1992), hereafter cited as PGM. For spells in Greek and Coptic (the language of Christian Egypt), with some overlap with Betz, see Marvin Meyer and Richard Smith, eds., *Ancient Christian Magic: Coptic Texts of Ritual Power* (San Francisco: HarperSanFrancisco, 1994). For a selection of curse tablets in Greek and Latin, see John G. Gager, *Curse Tablets and Binding Spells from the Ancient World* (Oxford and New York: Oxford University Press, 1992).

[4] For ancient magic in general, see Fritz Graf, *Magic in the Ancient World*, trans. Franklin Phillip (Cambridge and London: Harvard University Press, 1997); of major importance is the five-volume *Witchcraft and Magic in Europe*, ed. Bengt Ankarloo and Stuart Clark (Philadelphia: University of Pennsylvania Press, 1999), esp. vol. 1, *Ancient Greece and Rome*. On Christian magic, see David E. Aune, Susan R. Garrett, and John M. Hull, *Hellenistic Magic and the Synoptic Tradition* (Naperville, Ill.: Alec R. Allenson, 1974); Morton Smith, *Jesus the Magician* (San Francisco: Harper & Row). Of more limited use is Hans-Joseph Klauck, *Magic and Paganism in Early Christianity: The World of the Acts of the Apostles* (Edinburgh: T & T Clark, 2000). On the spiritual powers behind both pagan and Christian magic, see Valerie Flint, "The Demonisation of Sorcery in Late Antiquity: Christian Redefinitions of Pagan Religions,"

in Ankarloo and Clark, *Witchcraft and Magic in Europe,* 1:279-348. Magical terms and concepts used by Paul remain largely unstudied.

⁵ Aune, "Magic in Early Christianity," 1510-1515. The same problems of definition may arise even within a single religious tradition; for Judaism as an example, see Peter Schafer, "Magic and Religion in Ancient Judaism," in *Envisioning Magic: A Princeton Seminar and Symposium,* ed. Peter Schafer and Hans G. Kippenburg (Leiden: Brill, 1997), 19-44.

⁶ Stephen Benko, *Pagan Rome and the Early Christians* (Bloomington, Ind.: Indiana University Press, 1984), 60.

⁷ As in PGM 7:643: "Cup Spell . . . You are wine; you are not wine, but the head of Athena. You are wine; you are not wine, but the guts of Osiris" (PGM 136); Morton Smith, "Pauline Worship As Seen By Pagans," *Harvard Theological Review* 73 (1980): 247-248.

⁸ Christina Larner, *Witchcraft and Religion: The Politics of Popular Belief* (Oxford and London: Basil Blackwell, 1984), 80-81.

⁹ Meyer and Smith, *Ancient Christian Magic,* 4; Jonathon Smith, "Trading Places," in *Ancient Magic and Ritual Power,* ed. Marvin Smith and Paul Mirecki (Leiden: Brill, 1995), 15.

¹⁰ Aune's frequently cited definition of magic is "*all forms of religious deviance whereby individual or social goals are sought by means alternative to those normally sanctioned by the dominant religious institution. . . .* Religious activities which fit this first and primary criterion must also fit a second criterion: *goals sought within the context of religious deviance are magical when obtained through the management of supernatural powers in such a way that the results are virtually guaranteed*" (Aune, "Magic in Early Christianity," 1515). The problems with this definition are (1) that it makes virtually no distinction between magic and witchcraft, a distinction made by most societies, including Greece, where some forms of magic were not only legal but were considered necessary (see Julio Caro Baroja, *The World of the Witches,* trans. O. N. V. Glendinning [Chicago: The University of Chicago Press, 1964], 19). According to Aune's definition, Jesus could be considered not only a magician but possibly also a witch; (2) Aune fails to take into account the ritual nature of both magic and witchcraft in the ancient world (see Meyer and Smith, *Ancient Christian Magic,* 5); and (3) a magical ritual that does not work is still a magical ritual. It is the action's intent and content and not its efficacy that determines its nature.

¹¹ Luck, *Arcana Mundi,* 20-25.

¹² Fritz Graf, "Excluding the Charming: The Development of the Greek Concept of Magic," in Smith and Mirecki, *Ancient Magic and Ritual Power,* 29-42.

¹³ C. R. Phillips, "Nullum Crimen sine Lege: Socioreligious Sanctions Against Magic," in *Magica Heira: Ancient Greek Magic and Religion,* ed. Christofer A. Faraone and Dirk Obink (Oxford and New York: Oxford University Press, 1991), 262.

¹⁴ Cited in Morton Smith, *Jesus the Magician,* 75.

¹⁵ Hans G. Kippenberg, "Magic in Roman Civil Discourse: Why Rituals Could Be Illegal," in Schafer and Kippenburg, *Envisioning Magic,* 162.

¹⁶ *Religio* and *superstitio* are not well served by their English renderings, "religion" and "superstition." The dichotomy was not so much between truth and falsehood as between proper and improper or honorable and dishonorable religious practice. *Superstitio* might well be considered as "true," in that is was believed to be powerful. That is part of the reason it was feared and marginalized (see Mary Beard, John North, and Simon Price, *Religions of Rome* vol. 1, *A History* [Cambridge: Cambridge University Press, 1998], 214-219).

¹⁷ This account is found in Luck, *Arcana Mundi,* 73-75.

[18] In the relatively few cases where the age of death of the occupants of graves containing *defixiones* has been determined, they are usually sub-adults (see D. R. Jordan, "A Survey of Greek Defixiones Not Included in the Special Corpora," *Greek Roman and Byzantine Studies* 26:152).

[19] For a general discussion of the concept, see Robert Garland, *The Greek Way of Death* (Ithaca, N.Y.: Cornell University Press, 1985), 77-95; for the invocation of Jesus as a member of the special dead in early Christianity, see Aune, "Magic in Early Christianity," 1545-1549.

[20] Christopher Faraone, "The Agonistic Context of Early Greek Binding Spells," in *Magica Heira: Ancient Greek Magic and Religion*, ed. Christopher A. Faraone and Dirk Obink (New York: Oxford University Press, 1991), 4.

[21] Aune, "Magic in Early Christianity," 1521.

[22] Ibid., 1482.

[23] David Frankfurter, "Ritual Expertise in Roman Egypt and the Problem of the Category 'Magician'" in Schafer and Kippenburg, *Envisioning Magic*, 116; see also Betz, PGM, xlvi.

[24] The Magi in Matthew's gospel are representatives of a well-known larger group of magical practitioners.

[25] A. D. Nock, "Paul and the Magus," in *Essays on Religion and the Ancient World*, 2 vols., ed. Zeph Stewart (Oxford: The Clarendon Press, 1972), 325; see also Howard Clark Kee, *Medicine, Miracle, and Magic in New Testament Times* (Cambridge: Cambridge University Press, 1986), 116. For a description of Paul's actions as a "curse," see Garrett, *The Demise of the Devil*, 80-85. However, her interpretation is quite different from the one advanced here in that she downplays the magical associations of Paul's language and actions.

[26] Nock, "Paul and the Magus," 320.

[27] In this section reference is made only to letters generally agreed to be written by Paul.

[28] PGM 3:410-423.

[29] Gerhard Delling, "Battologeo," in *Theological Dictionary of the New Testament*, ed. Gerhard Kittel, trans. G. W. Bromley (Grand Rapids, Mich.: Eerdmans), 1:597. An oblique condemnation of the practice is found in Matthew 6:7 when Jesus warns against believing that a prayer's efficacy depends on repetition: "And in praying do not heap up empty phrases *(mē battalogēstēte hōsper)* as the Gentiles do; for they think they will be heard for their many words." Paul seems to have a higher opinion of repetitive prayer, reminding the Thessalonians that he is "praying earnestly day and night that we may see you face to face" and enjoining them to "pray constantly" (1 Thes 3:10; 5:17).

[30] Gager, *Curse Tablets and Binding Spells from the Ancient World,* 188.

[31] Ibid., 194.

[32] Ibid., 195.

[33] For the Galatians passage as a baptismal formula, see Sam K. Williams, *Galatians* (Nashville, Tenn.: Abingdon, 1997), 104.

[34] Delling, "Anathema," in *Theological Dictionary of the New Testament*, 1:354.

[35] Hans Dieter Betz, *Galatians: A Commentary on Paul's Letter to the Churches in Galatia* (Philadelphia: Fortress Press, 1979), 25, 50.

[36] Gager, *Curse Tablets and Binding Spells from the Ancient World,* 183 n. 14; see also Adolf Deissman, *Light from the Ancient East: The New Testament Illustrated by Recently Discovered Texts of the Graeco-Roman World,* trans. Lionel R. M. Strachan (New York: George H. Duran, 1927), 95.

[37] Delling, "Bewitched" *(baskainō),* in *Theological Dictionary of the New Testament,* 1:594-595.

[38] Betz, *Galatians,* 131; Williams, *Galatians,* 83; J. Louis Martyn, *Galatians: A New Translation with Introduction and Commentary* (New York: Doubleday, 1997).

[39] Jerome H. Neyrey, *Paul in Other Words: A Cultural Reading of His Letters* (Louisville, Ky.: Westminster/John Knox Press, 1990), 181-217; Martyn, *Galatians,* 282.

[40] The translation "frighten" rather than the more usual rendition "trouble" is suggested by Martyn, *Galatians,* 282.

[41] G. H. C. MacGregor, "Principalities and Powers: The Cosmic Background of Paul's Thought," in *New Testament Studies* 1:21-22.

[42] L. L. Welborn, "Sin in First-Century Rome," in *Receiving God's Righteousness: Grace and Glory in Romans,* ed. D. Lipe (Henderson, Tenn.: Free-Hardeman Press, 2000), 440-447.

[43] William H. Willimon, *Acts* (Atlanta, Ga.: John Knox Press, 1982), 123. For references on the magical contest, see H. J. Klauck, "With Paul in Paphos and Lystra: Magic and Paganism in the Acts of the Apostles," in *Neotestamentica* 28 (1994): 94. Klauck cites a parallel between Acts 13 and J. R. R. Tolkien's *Lord of the Rings.* For the Harry Potter series, see especially the fourth book, J. K. Rowling, *Harry Potter and the Goblet of Fire* (New York: Scholastic Press, 2000).

[44] Garrett, *The Demise of the Devil,* 79-80; see also Aune, "Magic in Early Christianity," 1553.

[45] See John Knox, *Chapters in a Life of Paul,* rev. ed. (Macon, Ga.: Mercer University Press, 1987), 44-45; see also, Hans Conzelmann, *Acts of the Apostles: A Commentary on the Acts of the Apostles* (Philadelphia: Fortress Press, 1987), 99-100; Bernard P. Robinson, "Paul and Barnabas in Cyprus," in *Scripture Bulletin* 26 (1996): 69.

[46] Colin J. Hemer, *The Book of Acts in the Setting of Hellenistic History* (Winona Lake, Ind.: Eiesbrauns, 1990), 166.

[47] Aune, "Magic in Early Christianity," 1553.

[48] Gager, *Curse Tablets and Binding Spells from the Ancient World,* 21. Since love magic played such an important role in binding spells, attacks on the sexual organs are very common, as in a second- or third-century C.E. tablet from Greece: "So too may Zolios be powerless to screw" (in Gager, *Curse Tablets and Binding Spells from the Ancient World,* 88, spell 20). However, cursing of other body parts is also known. Perhaps more germane here is the binding of the tongue belonging to a hostile witness in an Athenian court case: "I bind those . . . both him and the actions on Menon, his tongue and words and actions so that they might be useless to the authorities" (in Gager, *Curse Tablets and Binding Spells from the Ancient World,* 126, spell 39). For other New Testament accounts of *strafwunders,* see Aune, "Magic in Early Christianity," 1552-1553.

[49] Wilhelm Schneemelcher, *New Testament Apocrypha,* vol. 2, *Writing Related to the Apostles,* trans. R. McL. Wilson (Cambridge: James Clark and Co., 1991).

[50] Ibid., 299-300.

[51] Consider the *Silhouette Shadows* series of romances, all based on supernatural themes. They welcome readers to "the dark side of love." See the back inside cover of Jane Tombs, *Dark Enchantment* (New York: Silhouette Books, 1993). This particular book features a magical contest between a white witch and a black wizard. While this particular series has suspended publication, similar books are found in other popular romance series.

[52] Two of the best are, Margot Adler, *Drawing down the Moon: Witches, Druids, Goddess-Worshipers, and Other Pagans in America Today* (Boston: Beacon Press, 1986); and T. M. Luhrman, *Persuasions of the Witches Craft: Ritual Magic in Contemporary England* (Cambridge: Harvard University Press, 1989).

[53] According to the American Religious Identification Survey published in December 2001, the liturgically oriented mainstream Christian denominations all grew during the

1990s (Roman Catholics, 10.6%, Episcopalians/Anglicans, 13.4%, Lutherans 5.2%), while non-liturgical denomination such as Baptists (-.4%) and Methodists (-.2%) declined. During this same period the number of Americans willing to identify themselves as Wiccans grew by an astounding 1,575.0% (134,000 witches up from eight thousand in 1990) (see Anthony DeBarros and Cathy Lynn Grossman, "A Measure of Faith," in *USA Today* [December 24, 2001], D-4). This last figure may actually be underreported because of fear of reprisals from evangelical Christians directed against Wiccans who practice their religion openly. In any case, the concurrent growth of liturgical/sacramental denominations and the Wiccan movement support my comments about the efficacy of liturgical spiritualities in reaching new members. It may be simplistic to suggest that a "high church" liturgy is the only factor involved here, but it is the major element these denominations share. Certainly there are few similarities of ethnicity, class, or geographical location to account for their shared growth patterns.

# 16

## *Success in the City:*
## *Paul's Urban Mission Strategy*

### ACTS 14:1–28

### Roger S. Greenway

For many years I have identified personally with the passion shown by the apostles for planting churches in metropolitan centers. Therefore, it is understandable that I find Acts 14 to be an exciting chapter. It describes the apostles' urban mission strategy carried out in several cities, and it throbs with contemporary relevance for missions.

In 1965 the Lord placed on my heart a deep burden for reaching city people with the gospel and multiplying churches among them. My wife and I had already spent four years as missionaries in Colombo, Sri Lanka, where I learned how strong the opposition to the gospel can be. Forced out of Sri Lanka in 1963 by a change in the government's visa policy, we came to Mexico City, where a nominal form of Roman Catholicism dominated the religious scene.

My main assignment in Mexico City was to teach in a Presbyterian seminary located in the heart of this great city. Most of the students came from rural areas, and for several years I visited the students' village churches in my spare time. I worked closely with a Wycliffe Bible translator who was introducing the scriptures in the language of the Mazahua people in the State of Michoacán. It was exciting work, and the Lord used us to begin several new churches. I assumed that I would be continuing this ministry for years to come.

### A NEW VISION

To my surprise, the Lord gave me a new vision. It came about when Donald A. McGavran, founder of the Church Growth Movement, gave a seminar in Mexico City. McGavran asked me to take him to see the growing edge of the city, the areas where newcomers from the villages arrive and build their squalid homes. Standing in a dusty street in a densely populated neighborhood, McGavran said, "Roger, what you are doing out there in the villages is fine, but the missionary challenge of tomorrow is in the city. I want you to think about changing your focus to the city."

I resisted McGavran's challenge for a while. I loved getting away from the city, sleeping under the stars in mountain villages, seeing the marvelous response of many rural folk to the gospel, and best of all, planting new churches where no evangelical congregations had existed before. But I knew that in many villages, houses stood empty because younger families were moving to the city. The most familiar complaint I heard from village pastors was that their most energetic young people were leaving to find jobs in the city. I began to realize that McGavran was right. An enormous population shift was taking place, and if missions did not follow the migration to the city, it would mean an enormous loss to Christ's church. Cities had become the new frontiers of missions, and we had to adjust our strategy.

## WHERE AND HOW TO BEGIN?

Nobody had ever shown me how to start churches in a megacity. In rural areas I had followed certain anthropological guidelines that were helpful in identifying people groups and gaining access to them. But in big cities, where does one start? Mexico City at that time had a population of over six million, with inhabitants from every tribe and language group found in the nation. Was there any particular group that might be more receptive than others? I had no one to turn to for answers because at that time I knew of no other missionary dedicated to planting city churches. Today we have models of effective church planting to follow, but not then. Nor were most of the established churches reaching out to urban newcomers.

As wave after wave of immigrants arrived from the countryside, we kept asking where and with whom to begin. On Sunday afternoons students and I would place a map of Mexico City on our living-room table, kneel around it, and pray that God would lead us to the people whom God had prepared to hear the message of the Bible.

## SURPRISE DIRECTION

We were in for a surprise. At first we had tried to make contacts with the segment of population most like ourselves, the middle class, but we encountered stiff resistance. We tried to contact people in various apartment houses, from government-owned buildings with open stairways, to private complexes with guards, high walls, and surveillance systems. A few Bible studies were started, but nothing lasted. Reluctantly, we ventured into the squatter communities that surrounded the city, with their open sewers, "pirated" power lines, and thousands of small houses made of plywood, tar-paper, and corrugated sheet metal. To our surprise, it was there that we found open doors and hearts.

Over the next few years students and I started about fifty home Bible studies. Our method was simple: house-to-house visiting, prayer and Bible reading, interest in the households and their needs, and regular follow-up. Close to half of the home Bible study groups developed into house churches with weekly services. Many of these eventually became established congregations with their own pastors and buildings. The composition of the house churches was revealing. Approximately one-third of those who attended were former members of evangelical churches in the villages. Another third were new converts who came to faith through the evangelistic work of our teams and the home Bible studies.

A third group was composed of what I call "mass media" believers. They were people on the road to evangelical faith, people who had read parts of the Bible, tracts, and other Christian literature. Some of them had seen evangelical films and even completed Bible correspondence courses. But they had never made a public profession of faith in Christ as their Lord and Savior. Nor did they have any vital contact with a body of believers, and they probably would have stayed that way were it not for our coming to their door and inviting them to attend house church services. Back then, gospel radio broadcasts were not available for evangelicals in Mexico, but today that has changed, leading me to assume that the number of "mass media" inquirers has steadily increased.

## CONTACT POINTS IN THE CITY

The search for points of contact with people in the city is a matter of utmost concern for urban workers. Without meaningful personal contacts serving as bridges into the communities, church planting will not get off the ground. We found in Mexico City that the way to make contact with people was by wearing out our shoes. This meant going house to house, showing loving concern for people and their needs, and opening God's word to them. That experience is the background from which I interpret Acts 14, which tells how the apostles arrived in unfamiliar cities and made fruitful contacts where initially they themselves were strangers.

Acts 14:1 explains that at Iconium, Paul and Barnabas went as usual into the Jewish synagogue, where they spoke so effectively that "a great number of both Jews and Greeks became believers." What were Greeks doing in the Jewish synagogues? The answer to that question leads us back to the intertestamental period. Jews were dispersed throughout the Roman Empire and lived mostly in cities.[1] As people of trade and commerce, they were highly networked as far away as Persia, India, and China.[2] Wherever they went, they established synagogues.[3] Synagogues were centers of worship, religious instruction, and community identity. They were mainly composed of Jews but were open to Gentile inquirers and proselytes as well.

Scholars have estimated that at the time of Christ, one-tenth of the population of the Roman Empire consisted of Jews, only 2.5 million of whom were living in Palestine.[4] Biological growth alone cannot explain the numerical increase of the Jewish population. If the estimated Jewish population figures are correct, it must be assumed that a considerable number of Gentiles accepted Jewish monotheism, attended the synagogues, and in varying degrees adopted Jewish practices.[5] In time they became identified as Jews.

How ethnically protective Jews could accept Gentile inquirers and proselytes into their religion requires an explanation. It can best be attributed to the impact of the teachings of the Hebrew Bible itself. In the very first book the Lord promised Abraham that his descendants would be a blessing to all peoples (Gn 12:3). Psalmists prayed fervently that salvation would be enjoyed by all nations and that all peoples would worship the one true God (for example, Pss 66, 67, 100). Isaiah prophesied that the day was coming when saving light would shine forth from Israel, and it would reach to the ends of the earth (Is 49:6). Spiritually sensitive Jewish people understood that God's message was for all peoples and not exclusively for them.[6] As a result, Gentiles drawn to the Jewish God found a measure of welcome in the synagogues.

The message that the Jewish religion offered to the Gentile world consisted of the following:

1. There is only one true God who alone should be worshiped.
2. Idolatry and immorality are condemned by God's law, and this law applies to all peoples.
3. The Torah is a sacred book, the only authoritative divine revelation, and it should be read and obeyed by all.
4. Justice, truth, and mercy are to be practiced by all who worship God.
5. Circumcision and Sabbath-keeping are required of those who identify completely with the Jewish community.

Differences existed among the widespread groups concerning their adherence to other demands of the Mosaic Law.

## SPREAD OF THE JEWISH RELIGION

The first tool of spreading the Jewish faith was through the synagogues, which Jews of the dispersion established everywhere they went. About the synagogue, De Ridder says:

The Synagogue represented for Israel an entirely unprecedented form of religious activity: the popular worship of God, without sacrifice, and the instruction of the community in the implications of Scripture as applied to living according to Yahweh's will. The wonderful jewel Israel possessed might not be wrapped in a napkin, hidden and buried, but needed to be displayed, offered to all to see and share. The Synagogue provided the means to that end.[7]

When Jews of the dispersion began to share their faith with Gentile neighbors, the synagogues were the natural place for Jews and Gentiles to meet for instruction. Diaspora Judaism appealed to certain segments of the Gentile world because it represented a consistent monotheism, a moral code that promoted disciplined living, intellectual vigor, and the martyr tradition of a persecuted minority.[8]

Along with the synagogue, a second major means of instruction in the Greek-speaking world was through the Septuagint (LXX), the Greek translation of the Hebrew Bible. Designed primarily to instruct Jews whose language had become Greek, the LXX often utilizes the language "of the street" rather than the classical Greek of the scholars. This made the LXX a ready instrument for Jewish witness and later an instrument for Christian missions.[9]

Besides the LXX, there was a body of Jewish apologetic literature that Christian writers later adapted for their own use. In these writings Jews attacked polytheism, cruel practices, and sexual perversions. Predominant was the call to abandon idolatry, polytheistic worship and immoral practices.[10]

Jesus' words recorded in Matthew 23:15 provide an insight into the efforts of Jewish religious leaders, particularly the Pharisees, in proselytizing: "Woe to you, scribes and Pharisees, hypocrites! For you cross sea and land to make a single convert, and you make the new convert twice as much a child of hell as yourselves."

The passage only makes sense if indeed the scribes and Pharisees were known to be engaged in mission among the Gentiles. In actual fact, Jews in Jesus' day were apparently making serious efforts to make converts of their Gentile neighbors. Zealous religious leaders such as the Pharisees traveled to various places for the express purpose of making converts. Jesus' rebuke was not against their missionary zeal but against the legalism they imposed on their converts.[11] Jewish mission to Gentiles is probably the key to explaining another verse, John 7:35: "The Jews said to one another, 'Where does this man intend to go that we will not find him? Does he intend to go to the Dispersion among the Greeks and teach the Greeks?'"

We have explored at length the background of Acts 14:1 in order to interpret the passage. The apostles were well aware of the missionary endeavors of the Pharisees. Paul may even have participated in these endeavors before his conversion.[12] While Paul's primary mission was to the Gentiles, and the greatest receptivity to the gospel was with them, as a missionary looking for initial contacts and opportunities to preach Paul knew that the synagogues of the dispersion were strategically important. There he and his fellow missionaries would find, first of all, Jews who were accustomed to having Gentiles in their midst. Second, in the synagogues they would find Gentiles who believed in the God of Israel, regarded the Torah as God's revelation, knew of a messiah who was to come, and longed for a way to become fully acceptable to God, without circumcision if possible.[13]

That is precisely what Paul and Barnabas encountered at Iconium, as well as in other cities. Initially they found an open door at the synagogue, proclaimed the gospel to the Jews and Gentiles (God-seekers and proselytes) gathered there, and a "great number" believed. Then, as often happened, trouble broke out, with Gentiles and Jews both involved. The missionaries had to flee, but not before planting the seeds of the gospel firmly enough that when they returned afterward they found disciples whom they might encourage in the faith and could organize a church among them (vv. 21-23).

## ENOUGH TIME TO PLANT A CHURCH?

One wonders how the events recorded in Acts 14 allow for enough time to plant churches. The members of the new churches had been synagogue worshipers, which meant that many had an abundant religious background to support them. In these new churches there were Jews who had been schooled from childhood in the Torah, and there were Gentiles who had already made the giant step from paganism to the worship of the one true God. They knew the writings of Moses, the psalms, and the prophets. They were familiar with the organizational structure of the synagogues, with their religious communities ruled by elders. When they organized their new churches, with their forms of worship and standards for leadership, the apostles were building on familiar synagogue patterns. What was new in Paul's message was that in Jesus Christ all who believe and receive the gift of the Holy Spirit are equally children of God, without the need for circumcision or other Jewish rituals.

God loves Gentiles as well as Jews and saves them both through the blood of his Son. That was the spiritual flare that the apostles set off in city after city and that came to a climax in Acts 15. The dispersion of the Jews, with their synagogues and use of the Septuagint, made Paul's powerful church-planting strategy possible. God's providence had prepared the way long before the apostles arrived in Gentile territory.

## GOD AHEAD OF US

As I look back over forty-plus years of involvement in missions, I see a pattern in how God often works. Before breakthroughs occur there are events and circumstances, sometimes seemingly inconsequential at the time, which afterward prove to be God's way of preparing a harvest. At times it is a political change that causes a closed door to fly open. In other instances it is a war or a natural disaster that shakes the confidence of resistant people. In the twentieth century the dispersion of refugees led to more people turning to Christ than anyone can tabulate.[14] Fruit appeared from the labor of faithful workers who died thinking their efforts had been in vain. But in mysterious ways God used events and circumstances to prepare for a spiritual harvest in God's own time.

It is more than a pious observation to declare that God is always ahead of us. I would call it a working principle that missionaries and practitioners would do well to keep in mind, especially at times when they feel bewildered and wonder where to turn next. In general, wise strategy calls for looking for people whom God has prepared to listen and believe, like the Gentiles whom the apostles found in the synagogues of the dispersion. Missionaries should remember, too, that God will continue working long after they have gone. God will not neglect what was begun (Phil 1:6). Spiritual conversion or awakening may sometimes appear to occur in an instant, though invariably there are roots beneath it. But the transformation inherent in discipleship involves a process requiring patience, continual nurturing, and faith in the Holy Spirit. Acts 14 remains beyond our comprehension until we begin to understand these things.

## GOD'S HAND IN CONTEMPORARY MOVEMENTS

In summary, God used the dispersion of the Jews and their proselytizing efforts to prepare the ancient world for the spread of the gospel. This being the case, how do we interpret what is happening today? The four fastest-growing movements of the Christian faith—African independent churches, Chinese house churches, Pentecostals in South America, and secret believers in India (for instance, wives of devout Hindus)—do not conform to traditional standards of Christianity.[15] Yet they link millions to Christ. Is not God's hand visible in these movements? If so, is God calling us to break new ground, to explore beyond the boundaries of our mission strategy, as the apostles did when they approached the synagogues and brought Gentiles into Christ's fold?

## THE APOSTLES' STRATEGY

Acts 14 describes how Paul and Barnabas, fresh from planting a church in Antioch of Pisidia, went on to preach the gospel and start churches in the cities of Iconium, Lystra, and Derbe. We see here a pattern of concentrating on cities where the witness of the gospel would likely spread throughout the surrounding region.[16] Besides the strategic decision to concentrate on cities, the apostles' missionary strategy had the following components that are relevant to mission work today.

### They Aimed at Making Converts

At the heart of apostolic missionary strategy lay the presupposition that people everywhere needed to repent their sins and give allegiance to Christ. This conversion meant that they would be enrolled for a lifetime of active discipleship. They would be baptized and united with other believers in the church. Hardships, even severe persecution, could be expected, because that was the way into the kingdom of God (Acts 14:22).

This raises an issue of importance for mission work in our time, because in a postmodern culture *conversion* is an unpopular word. It is looked upon as an old idea that no longer fits reality in pluralist societies. Along with conversion, the biblical doctrines of human sin and depravity, the lostness of human beings outside of Christ, and the reprehensibleness of all forms of idolatry have been assigned to the dustbin of theological history. Stephen Neill, the late bishop of the Church of England, said this about the abandonment of conversion:

> For years I have been looking for a word which will take the place of the now very unpopular word "conversion," and have not found it. I am well aware of all the possible objections to the word. But I have an uneasy

feeling that those who hesitate to use the word are also rejecting the thing for which it stands. . . . Those of us who have come to Christ, even from a profoundly Christian background, have known what it means to be "without hope and without God in the world" (Eph 2:12). Are we prepared to use Paul's language, however unpopular it may be? We desire all men to say Yes to Christ. But there are countless ways to say Yes to Christ which fall short of the surrender that leads to salvation. Do we know what we are really talking about? . . . It seems to me that the time has come when we ought to be done with circumlocutions and not be ashamed to say exactly what we mean.[17]

Time has passed since Neill made those statements, but in the meantime negative attitudes regarding conversion have only hardened. The rise of religious inclusivism and pluralism challenges missions. Thus it is helpful to look afresh at how the apostles addressed the world of their day. Religious conversion was not a popular notion back then, any more than it is today.

Michael Green, in *Evangelism in the Early Church*, discussed the idea of conversion in Greco-Roman society. Contrary to certain writers he mentions, Green finds nothing in the religions of the ancient world that resembled Christian conversion. The apostles' preaching demanded a complete change of commitments and a radical moral change in the lives of its adherents. All this was utterly contrary to the customary attitude of Hellenistic people. Many Hellenists did not regard belief as necessary for worship or ethics as necessary for religion. They felt that people could adopt a new faith while still adhering to some degree to their former ones.[18]

### *They Maintained a* Compassionate Meta-narrative *in Their Presentation of the Gospel*

When they spoke to followers of other faiths, the apostles displayed a *compassionate meta-narrative*. They treated their non-Christian listeners with respect. They did not belittle them (17:22-23). They showed patience and compassion for those who were searching for a more satisfying faith. At the same time they made it clear that salvation was in none other than the Lord Jesus Christ. With the passion of firm belief that salvation came exclusively through Jesus Christ, the apostles became all things to all people and pleaded with their hearers to receive the message of the gospel seriously (1 Cor 9:19-23).

How do we regard other religions? There is hardly a more important question. At Lystra, the apostles addressed the question when they stood before the confused and irritated crowd. The people thought that Paul and Barnabas were incarnations of the Greek gods Zeus and Hermes. The apostles pleaded with the people to recognize their error and said, "Friends, why are you doing this? We are mortals just like you, and we bring you good news, that you should turn from these worthless things to the living God, who made the heaven and the earth and the sea and all that is in them" (14:15). They told the people that in the past God had let all nations go their own way, yet at the same time God manifested goodness to all nations by giving them rain, good crops, and food (14:16-17). Now it was time that the people of Lystra set aside their prior beliefs and accept the good news (14:15). There was no doubt that the apostles aimed to make converts, but they did so while declaring God's compassion for all people.

Although God is never left without a witness (14:17), the knowledge of God that people everywhere possess has been replaced by myths and unrighteousness. The missionary approach must take into account God's dealing with various nations before missionaries arrive, as well as with the myths and superstitions that have suppressed and superseded God's general revelation. This is a humbling thought. Ambassadors of the gospel must bear in mind that God's compassion has been revealed for centuries, and it is that divine compassion that has kept people from completely suppressing the truth.[19]

The late missiologist J. H. Bavinck sought the connection between God's universal witness and merciful provision. He felt that the way to test the intrinsic value of the Gentiles' religious songs and devotion to God is to reveal to them "the name of our Savior and King." If, upon hearing the story of the Incarnation and the work of salvation, they spontaneously begin to recognize God and believe in Jesus, "it may be taken for granted that it was really God whom their hearts were seeking."[20]

### Enduring Persecution

The ministry of Paul and Barnabas in the cities of Iconium, Lystra, and Derbe was characterized by the bold proclamation of the gospel and by accompanying signs and wonders (14:3, 9). Miracles were the Lord's way of confirming the truth of the apostles' words (14:3). The role of the miracles of confirmation cannot be overlooked because they played an important part in the spread of the gospel during the first century of the Christian era and in some parts of the world they continue to play a similar role. Even more than the signs and wonders, it was the persecution that Paul suffered and endured in these cities that persisted in his mind. Toward the close of his life Paul wrote to Timothy: "Now you have observed my teaching, my conduct, my aim in life, my faith, my patience, my love, my steadfastness, my persecutions and suffering the things that happened to me in Antioch, Iconium, and Lystra. What persecutions I endured! Yet the Lord rescued me from all of them" (2 Tm 3:10-11).

Those were not the only places where Paul experienced persecution, but the attacks in those cities remained in his mind. They were examples of the kind of opposition Christ's servants could expect in other times and places. After mentioning the persecution in these three cities, Paul tells Timothy that "all who want to live a godly life in Christ Jesus will be persecuted. But wicked people and imposters will go from bad to worse, deceiving others and being deceived" (2 Tm 3:12-13). In view of this Paul counseled Timothy to hold tightly to the faith as revealed in the sacred scriptures.

Acts 14:21-22 states that after preaching the gospel in Derbe and making many disciples, they returned to Lystra, Iconium, and Antioch. It required great courage to go back to the places where they had been persecuted. "There they strengthened the souls of the disciples and encouraged them to continue in the faith, saying, 'It is through many persecutions that we must enter the kingdom of God'" (Acts 14:22). Readers who live in a safe environment and enjoy religious liberty may easily pass over these words without feeling their impact. But persecution is a cruel reality for an increasing number of Christians throughout the world. These words are especially meaningful to them. The enemy does not relinquish one inch of territory without a fight, and those who live pure lives and witness to the gospel can expect to feel the enemy's wrath.

### *Starting and Organizing Churches*

In each of these cities the apostles evangelized and started churches. Later they revisited the churches and strengthened the souls of the disciples and encouraged them to continue in the faith (14:22). Besides this, they organized these groups of believers into churches, which were assemblies of Christ's disciples organized under local leaders, called elders. After prayer and fasting, the apostles entrusted these elders to the Lord's care and placed into their hands the supervision of the churches (14:23).

The apostolic strategy throughout the Book of Acts involved evangelizing and winning converts and forming believers into organized communities under spiritual leadership. That strategy remains valid in our own urbanized world. By New Testament standards what is suspect is missionary strategy that does not produce converts to Christ in a population that is receptive. By the same token, any strategy that lays little stress on starting and organizing churches, where circumstances permit, is equally questionable.[21]

In *A Biblical Church Planting Manual* Marlin Mull describes a missionary strategy of the Book of Acts. He refers to the apostles preaching the good news in the city of Derbe and winning a large number of converts (Acts 14:21). Then Mull states:

A new church cannot properly start without evangelism. Yet, it is possible to evangelize and not plant a new church. Many well-meaning leaders do evangelize, but omit planting new churches, the most effective evangelistic method, from their spiritual arsenal. . . . Various strategies compiled from many sources all come to the same conclusion. New churches do a better job of evangelism than older established churches.[22]

When churches are nourished by the teaching of God's Word and led by people with passion for souls and hearts toward the marginalized, they become dynamic agents of transformation in homes, neighborhoods, and society at large. Cities across the world need thousands of new churches of that kind to meet the spiritual and physical needs of their diverse populations.

## ACCOUNTABLE TO THE CHURCH

Acts 14 closes with the account of the apostles' return to Antioch, "where they had been commended to the grace of God for the work that they had completed" (14:26). They considered themselves accountable to the church that had commissioned them. The church members came together, and the apostles delivered their report. They "related all that God had done with them, and how he had opened a door of faith for the Gentiles" (14:27). The apostles gave God the credit for opening new doors of faith. They told stories of their missionary adventures from city to city, and they underscored that God had opened the door of faith to the Gentiles.

The simplicity of their report merits reflection. Humanly speaking, the apostles had not accomplished much. In their report nothing was said about precise numbers of people, money raised to support the mission, church buildings, or social programs inaugurated. They were faithful in telling the story of Christ, and people surrendered their lives to Christ. They focused on God's mighty acts—what God had done through them and how God had opened doors of faith. Then they stayed with the church at Antioch a long time.

With humble beginnings, through their first missionary journey, the apostles initiated the growth of the church in Gentile cities. Much more lay ahead. The young churches needed to be developed in faith, leadership, and ministry. Controversies would arise, and persecutions would come. There would be setbacks and times of renewal. But the apostles were confident that with God's blessing, the light and leaven of Christ's kingdom eventually would penetrate all levels of urban society. The good work of divine grace once started would be carried forward until the coming of Jesus Christ (Phil 1:6).

Some time ago I was invited back to Mexico City to preach at the dedication service of a new building constructed by one of the churches I had helped to start many years ago. Despite internal conflicts, relative poverty, and one serious schism, the church had grown steadily; this was its third or fourth new building. Hardly any of the current members knew or remembered me, but that did not matter. My co-workers and I had initiated a new church movement in an impoverished area of the city. Some of these communities had died out, as did many of the churches started by Paul. But others had grown strong and had become great centers of worship and ministry in the city. We take no credit for ourselves. With the apostles of old we declare that God gave growth to our small beginnings (1 Cor 3:7).

## REFERENCES

[1] In addition to the urban Jews there may have been Jews living in small agricultural villages, but information about them is lost. For an illuminating discussion of urban Jewish life, see Tessa Tajak, "Jews and Christians in a Pagan World," in *The Jewish Dialogue with Greece and Rome: Studies in Cultural and Social Interaction* (Leiden: Brill, 2001), 355-370.

[2] David Filbeck states that during the intertestamental period Jews were spread from Europe in the West to China in the East, from western Africa to India. Citing Salo Wittmayer Baron, *A Social and Religious History of the Jews,* vol. 1 (New York: Columbia University Press, 1952), Filbeck reckons that the worldwide population of Jews numbered some eight million people, or nearly 5 percent of the world's population (David Filbeck, *Yes, God of the Gentiles, Too: The Missionary Message of the Old Testament* [Wheaton, Ill.: Billy Graham Center, 1994]).

[3] Tajak, "Jews and Christians in a Pagan World," 463-478.

[4] Richard R. De Ridder, *Discipling the Nations* (Grand Rapids, Mich.: Baker Books, 1979), 9-10. De Ridder cites David Max Eichhorn, *Conversion to Judaism: History and Analysis* (New York: Ktav, 1966), 35-36; Solomon Grayzel, *A History of the Jews,* 2d ed. (Philadelphia: Jewish Publication Society of America, 1968), 138. Estimates of the Jewish population in the Roman Empire are affected by the definition used in defining a Jew. If sympathizers and proselytes to Jewish faith are included, the number naturally is greater.

[5] Filbeck explores the cause of the great population increase of the Jewish people in the four centuries before Christ. He feels that biological growth is a key factor, but not the only one: "Additional growth was due to Gentiles converting to the Jewish belief and way of life and becoming proselytes in the process." Among the reasons for converting to Judaism, Filbeck points to Esther 8:17, with its reference to many peoples of other nationalities becoming Jews (Filbeck, *Yes, God of the Gentiles, Too,* 120).

[6] De Ridder states that a large migration of Jews to India occurred after the destruction of the Second Temple by Titus. When some seventy Jewish families moved from Persia to the Malibar Coast in southern India, they acquired a treaty giving them permission to erect synagogues and to convert Hindus to Judaism. Note that the Jews were interested not only in practicing their religion but also in propagating it (*Discipling the Nations,* 64).

[7] Ibid., 77.

[8] Roger E. Hedlund, *The Mission of the Church in the World* (Grand Rapids, Mich.: Baker Books, 1991), 144.

[9] "In general the LXX vocabulary and accidence are those of Hellenistic or Koine Greek, but the syntax of most books is described as 'translation' or Hebraic Greek" (Sven K. Soderlund, "Septuagint," in *The International Standard Bible Encyclopedia,* 4 vols., ed. Geoffrey W. Bromiley [Grand Rapids, Mich.: Eerdmans, 1988], 4:407). The Pentateuch in particular is "distinguished by a uniformly high level of the vernacular style and by faithfulness to the Hebrew" (ibid.). Soderlund also points out that the Septuagint for many generations was the authoritative version for Greek-speaking Jews and Christians who were not fluent in Hebrew, thus influencing many cultures (ibid., 401).

[10] De Ridder, *Discipling the Nations,* 114.

[11] Ibid., 121. De Ridder points out that Roman law prohibited proselytizing, and the expulsion of the Jews from Rome in many instances may have been occasioned by Jewish proselytizing activities (cf. Acts 18:12) (ibid., 120).

[12] Before his conversion, Paul, a Pharisee, was probably what we would today call an overachiever. His fury against Christians took him to "foreign cities" to persecute them (Acts 26:11). Once he launched out as a Christian missionary, the accounts of his travels suggest that Paul was a very cosmopolitan person who was well acquainted with the cities of the Roman world and their Jewish communities. Given what Jesus said about the zeal of some Jewish people to spread Judaism, it is not inconceivable that Paul at an earlier stage of his life had sought to prove his own zeal for God by engaging in Jewish mission work.

¹³ In the heated debate among scholars as to whether a pre-Christian Jewish mission to Gentiles existed, Rainer Riesner vigorously rejects the position that there ever was such a mission, at least in the sense of an organized, intentional effort to convert Gentiles to Judaism (see "A Pre-Christian Jewish Mission?" in *The Mission of the Early Church to Jews and Gentiles*, ed. Jostein Adna and Hans Kvalbein [Tubingen: Mohr Siebeck, 2000], 224). While the evidence for intentional Jewish mission efforts is less plentiful than I might wish, there is enough to convince me that while the Jews probably did not have an organized mission enterprise as we know it today, conscious efforts were being made by Jews to attract Gentiles to the Jewish faith. Among pagans there was a longing for something better than what traditional religions offered. This was met by efforts on the part of zealous Jews to draw Gentiles toward Judaism, which Matthew 23:15 and John 7:35 imply. The Gentiles that are mentioned in connection with synagogues in Acts did not just "happen" to be there when the apostles arrived. Nor do we need to assume that Cornelius (in Acts 10) was an isolated case. As to early outside sources, I consider the witness of Philo and Josephus to the spread of Judaism among Gentiles to be especially compelling.

¹⁴ It is generally true that people pulled away from home and going through traumatic experiences, such as refugees, are less bound by old traditions and more open to new ideas, including religious beliefs. This is illustrated by Cambodian refugees, who converted to Christianity in large numbers during their time in refugee camps, though before the war Cambodians were known for their resistance to Christianity (Patrick Johnstone and Jason Mandryk, *Operation World: Twenty-first Century Edition* [Pasadena, Calif.: William Carey Library, 2001], 138-139).

¹⁵ While the first three are matters of general knowledge, the secret believers in India thrive underground; therefore, although I have tracked this for forty years, I cannot provide verification through standard resources.

¹⁶ Wayne Meeks points out that Paul was a city person and that the air of the city breathes through his language. Paul's metaphors were drawn mostly from the urban world. His Greek evoked the classroom more than the farm. Paul was most at home with the speech used in gymnasiums, stadiums, and workshops. The manual work with which Paul often supported himself was not that of a farmer but of an artisan, a "blue-collar" worker who belonged to the city. Not uncharacteristically, Paul boasted to the Roman officer arresting him that he was a "citizen of no ordinary city" (Acts 21:39) (Wayne A. Meeks, *The First Urban Christians: The Social World of the Apostle Paul* [New Haven, Conn.: Yale University Press, 1983], 8).

¹⁷ Stephen Neill, "Church of England Newspaper" (November 13, 1970), cited in *Church Growth Bulletin* (May 1971), 145.

¹⁸ Michael Green, *Evangelism in the Early Church* (Grand Rapids, Mich.: Eerdmans, 1958), 144-146.

¹⁹ Ibid.

²⁰ J. H. Bavinck, *The Impact of Christianity on the Non-Christian World* (Grand Rapids, Mich.: Eerdmans, 1949), 102-103.

²¹ See Roger S. Greenway, *Apostles to the City: Biblical Strategies for Urban Missions* (Grand Rapids, Mich.: Baker Books, 1978), 82-84.

²² Marlin Mull, *A Biblical Church Planting Manual* (Indianapolis, Ind.: The Wesleyan Church Corporation, Department of Evangelism and Church Growth, 2000), 35.

# 17

## *The Jerusalem Council:*
## *Some Implications for Contextualization*

### ACTS 15:1–35

### David K. Strong

"Can Christians eat *dinaguan*?" I asked. I was teaching a course on contextualization at the Alliance Biblical Seminary in Manila, where many Filipinos enjoyed the popular dish made from pork blood. A lively discussion ensued. Did not the Bible clearly prohibit eating blood, not just in the Old Testament but in the New? Were such regulations to be understood literally or culturally?

Questions about contextualization—the relationship of the Christian faith to its cultural context—have been central to my ministry for the past twenty years. Ten years prior to the question about *dinaguan*, I had served in Korea, where questions about ancestral rituals abounded. Now, ten years later, I serve on the faculty of a Christian college, where questions about worship styles and bodily adornment are the order of the day.

In seeking biblical guidance to the question of contextualization, I have been drawn irresistibly to Acts 15:1-35, for the story reflects the kinds of issues that arise repeatedly in cross-cultural settings. Using a narrative genre, it addresses complex questions such as, What must change in the lives of converts from another culture? Who decides what must change and on what basis? What values should control contextualization? In what sense are culturally divergent churches accountable to one another? The discussion that follows seeks answers to such questions using a combination of literary and exegetical methods.[1] At the same time, I endeavor to demonstrate the application of the passage to mission in the postmodern setting.

### THE IMPORTANCE OF ACTS 15

Acts 15:1-35 forms a self-contained, coherent narrative. It is marked off by the announcements that Paul and Barnabas "stayed" or "remained" in Antioch

196

(14:28; 15:35) and that "after some days" they embarked on another mission-ary journey (15:36). In addition, the passage begins with the plot conflict that is resolved in 15:35.

Structurally, the passage serves as the watershed of the overall narrative of Acts. It stands at the center of the book, and scholars have overwhelmingly acknowledged its importance for understanding Acts' overall message.[2] Acts 1:8 provides a convenient outline for Luke's work, narrating the expanding influence of the gospel from Jerusalem, through Judea and Samaria, to Rome, the center of the empire and the launching point to places beyond. Furthermore, just as Jerusalem and the apostle Peter dominate the action through chapter 15, Paul and the ends of the earth dominate the chapters that follow. The chapter also serves as the transition from the apostolic to the post-apostolic era as Peter sur-renders leadership to the elders (James) and the Pauline mission.

Acts 15 is central to Luke's story because it addresses the crucial question at the heart of the expansion of the church from Jerusalem to the ends of the earth: Will the Jerusalem church sanction unhindered outreach to the Gentiles? Paul and Barnabas had extended the frontiers of the church from Antioch to Cyprus and the province of Galatia (Acts 13—14). For continued growth, cul-tural questions had to be faced. Must new converts first become Jews, embrac-ing a foreign lifestyle, and thereby blunt the force of the gospel? Or could con-verts remain culturally Gentiles, in full and unfettered contact with family and friends? The fate of the expansion of the church and its character lay in the balance as the church debated the question.[3] The passage thus addresses whether the early impetus to the ends of the earth would be fulfilled or whether it would be checked. Luke's primary purpose is to underscore the fact that the Jerusa-lem church embraced the Gentile mission, a decision that enabled the church to continue growing to the ends of the earth. In the process Luke prioritizes mission over cultural constraints.

In contrast, many internal battles that the church fights today prioritize cul-tural constraints over mission. In the Philippines, for instance, a seminary stu-dent came to my office for counseling. A Korean missionary had employed him to serve in the church that the missionary was planting. He painstakingly in-structed the Filipino in Korean methods of ministry. "But, sir," wailed the stu-dent, "it won't work in our culture!" As a further example, when I returned to the United States on home assignment, I found churches embroiled in debate about the place of women in ministry. In many churches women were restricted from ministering in ways permitted to women missionaries, Filipino *pastoras*, and even Korean Bible women. While the churches were rightly concerned about biblical integrity, in the process of deciding they often curtailed legitimate ministries. Confronted with the advance of the gospel or cultural restrictions, Luke has, I believe, prioritized outreach.

## LESSONS FROM THE SETTING

While Luke's primary focus in Acts 15 is not contextualization per se, he cannot avoid questions that inevitably arise in the encounter between gospel and culture. As C. Peter Wagner observes, "The central missiological issue is contextualization,"[4] or as Lucien Legrand states, "ethnic compromise."[5] When the gospel expands across cultural boundaries, questions inevitably arise as to what must transfer and what need not. In answering these questions, I first turn to the cultural, geographical, and temporal settings of the narrative. Each contributes to a deeper understanding of the contextualization process.

### Cultural Setting

The cultural setting lies at the heart of the plot conflict. Two vastly disparate cultural complexes are arrayed against each other—Jew and Gentile. For centuries Jews had drawn their identity from their special relationship to Yahweh. They were God's special people (Gn 12:1-3; Ex 19:4-6). Israel demonstrated its relationship through obedience to the Torah (the Law). In particular, since the time of Abraham the rite of circumcision had been the sign of the covenant relationship (Gn 17:11). By the first century the Pharisaic community had emerged as models of piety for the Jewish people. In contrast to the "people of the land," they adhered rigorously to ritual laws and consequently considered themselves to be the true Israel.[6] Observance of sacred ritual thus lay at the core of Jewish identity. The Gentiles in Antioch, on the other hand, possessed an unenviable reputation for immorality. Residents participated in mystery religions and worshiped immoral Greek gods and even the Baals, replete with sacrifices, feasting, and sacred prostitution.[7] Jews found all of this repugnant.

The cultural setting introduces a specifically missionary dimension to the narrative. Missionaries constantly face the challenge of crossing cultural boundaries, whether in Korea, the Philippines, or postmodern America. In considering the cultural question, ritual observance proves crucial to identity formation in many societies. This is perhaps difficult for many American missionaries to grasp, because their religious identity seems separated from their cultural identity. In addition, their emphasis upon individual freedom in the midst of a pluralistic society hinders their understanding of a community bound together by common religious rituals. Just as the Pharisees created and maintained their cultural identity through observing the Torah, so Koreans create and reinforce their Confucian identity through ancestral rituals. From their earliest days parents teach children the deepest respect for their elders, living and dead. Participation in rituals of respect are tantamount to being Korean, because form is so closely related to meaning.[8] At the very least they will require functional substitutes, but given the intimate relationship between rituals and cultural identities, Acts 15 would also caution against simply trying to force another culture's religious rituals upon others, even if they were good rituals.

### Geographical Setting

Geographically the action moves from Antioch (15:1-2) to Jerusalem (15:4-29) and back to Antioch (15:30-35). Notably, the great majority of the action occurs in Jerusalem, reflecting the theological weight that Jerusalem held in Luke's thought. The early church did not simply rush to the ends of the earth. In Luke's understanding of salvation history, salvation came from the Jews, and they must be the first to hear the gospel. In time however, Jerusalem became the mother church of the church in Antioch, as Christians from Jerusalem preached to Jews and Gentiles in Antioch after they had been scattered (8:1; 11:19ff.). Due to its centrality in Jewish thought, the Jerusalem church had "authoritative oversight of the whole Christian mission."[9] Thus, even though the Gentiles expected freedom from the Jewish Law, "freedom from the Law can be declared only from Jerusalem."[10] There is an important message here: mother and daughter, older and younger churches are still integrally related.

Since contemporary missions are from every nation to every nation, the situation has become far more complex. In addition, postmodernism has tended to question all authority, advocating that every person's perspective is equally valid. Anthropology, too, with its advocacy of cultural relativism, has contributed to such thinking. It is small wonder, then, that advocates of contextualization might be tempted to believe that only the local church itself can decide what to incorporate and what to reject from the larger tradition.[11] In Acts, however, we find the Antioch church respecting the authority of a church from another culture. The pattern of contextualization is thus much closer to the critical contextualization advocated by Paul G. Hiebert, in which church and missionary collaborate, first to understand the culture deeply and then to bring scripture to bear appropriately on the culture.[12] In working with a mature national church in the Philippines, therefore, I found myself helping students think through the implications of scripture for cultural issues as wide-ranging as liberation theology and folk practices at sacred Mt. Banahaw. Through such a wide-ranging process local churches can be accountable to the larger church, and churches bent on paternalism are held in check. Missionaries thus become connecting agents between two cultural traditions, enabling the local church and the sending church to see themselves more accurately.

### Temporal Setting

Temporally, enormous debate surrounds the relationship of Paul's visits to Jerusalem in Acts and in Galatians. Acts ostensibly records three visits (9:26-29; 11:30; 15:3-29), while Galatians records only two (1:18-20; 2:1-10). Many scholars follow J. B. Lightfoot in identifying the two Galatian visits with the visits in Acts 9 and 15, which leaves the famine relief visit (11:30) unaccounted for in Galatians.[13] Others follow W. M. Ramsay in equating Galatians 2:1-10 with the famine relief visit, thereby placing the Jerusalem council subsequent to the dispute with Peter in Galatians 2:11-14.[14] The nuances of the debate cannot be addressed here, but certainly the circumstances of Galatians 2:1-10 and Acts 15 are similar. The locations and chronology, the participants with their dispute over circumcision, and the resulting freedom for Gentiles and recognition of the Gentile mission are all the same. The omission of the famine relief visit, furthermore, can be explained easily by the turbulence in Jerusalem at the time and by the fact that Acts does not report any contact with the apostles and elders.

More important for missiological purposes, however, is that in either case the contextualization question has not been settled once and for all. If Acts 15 is the visit of Galatians 2, then Peter subsequently departs from his declaration at the council by abstaining from table fellowship with Gentiles (Gal 2:11-14). If, on the other hand, Acts 15:1-2 occurs after Galatians 2:1-10, then the issue still has not been settled, for recalcitrant Jews from Judea refuse to submit to the decision recorded in Galatians and come to Antioch to plague the church with demands that Gentiles conform to the law. Even when we confine ourselves to Galatians, Peter departs from the earlier decision. Consequently, we observe that contextual issues once settled can be expected to resurface.

This should not be surprising; deep changes in foundational beliefs are among the most resistant to change. Korean churches, for example, are renowned for their prayer mountains. The practice, however, is based on a centuries-old practice of going to the mountains to be closer to the gods and to pray. The current practice has deep emotional and symbolic meaning based on their heritage, even though the fundamental theology has changed. Likewise, Koreans over the centuries have turned to shamans for healing. Is it any wonder, then, that many Korean Christians view their pastors as shamans and prefer their prayers and visits to those of elders? Although one Korean church leader fears that shamanism will infiltrate Christianity just as it did with Buddhism and Confucianism,[15] there are significant links with the past that must be deliberated in a new context. Contextualization thus must be viewed as a long process of addressing culture from scripture. Missionaries working toward change at the deepest level should therefore anticipate resistance and should develop both patience and perseverance.

## CONFLICT AND RESOLUTION

Against the background of the cultural, geographical, and temporal settings, Luke weaves a story of conflict between two Christian cultural factions. In light of the narrative structure the emphasis clearly lies upon the resolution. Vastly more space is devoted to the resolution (15:6-29) than to the development of the conflict (15:1-5), and the solution is virtually repeated in the form of a letter. It is the resolution of the conflict that transforms the church, inasmuch as the Gentile mission is not only affirmed but also equipped with a gospel free from the ritual law.

### *Plot Conflict*

The plot conflict bursts forth from the narrative's opening verse. Judean Christians contended that Gentiles could not be saved unless they were first circumcised. In classic understatement Luke records that "Paul and Barnabas had no small dissension and debate with them" (15:2). Verse 5 elucidates the conflict somewhat by adding the Pharisees' demand that Gentiles should be "ordered to keep the law of Moses."[16] The moral law was not the issue here, since Gentile Christians also were expected to live moral lives. At issue was the ritual law with its requirements for circumcision and abstinence from certain foods.[17] The question, therefore, was whether Gentile converts had to become Jewish proselytes prior to being saved.[18] Answering this question, however, created a second conflict that required further resolution. If Gentile Christians did not have to keep Jewish laws of purity, particularly those surrounding food, how could Jewish believers enjoy table fellowship with Gentiles? This conflict was resolved, as we will see, through the so-called apostolic decrees (15:20, 29).

### Plot Resolution

The resolution of the plot conflict proceeds in five stages: (1) a general discussion (15:6), (2) Peter's speech (15:7-11), (3) Barnabas and Paul's report (15:12), (4) James's speech (15:13-21), and (5) an official delegation and letter to the church in Antioch (15:22-29). The narrative ultimately concludes with peace restored, the church strengthened, and the word of the Lord advancing (15:30-35).

## GOSPEL OF GRACE

The conflict carried to Jerusalem ignites "much debate" among the apostles and elders of the Jerusalem church (15:6-7). The Jerusalem council is therefore not so much an ecumenical council (although representatives from Antioch and perhaps other churches attended) as it is a meeting of the Jerusalem leadership.[19]

After some time Peter, as the chief apostle, addresses the gathering. He reminds his listeners of his own experience in leading the Gentile Cornelius to faith some ten years earlier (Acts 10:1—11:18). Most significant, he views Cornelius's salvation as God's work. Evidence of this fact was provided by God's gift of the Holy Spirit, bestowed in the same manner that the apostles had experienced at Pentecost. Moreover, Peter asserts, Cornelius and his family had had their hearts purified. The Pharisees' questions of ritual purification are thereby rendered moot.[20] Furthermore, they were purified by faith in Jesus Christ. Hence, Peter concludes, there is no difference between Jew and Gentile in the matter of salvation. Given this conclusion, he asks, "Why are you putting God to the test by placing on the neck of the disciples a yoke that neither our ancestors nor we have been able to bear?" (15:10). Ernst Haenchen argues that this statement reflects Luke's Gentile perspective on the Law, since religious Jews did not consider the demands of the Law unbearable.[21] As Ben Witherington III observes, however, Jesus himself considered the yoke of the Law heavy (Mt 11:30), and there is also no plausible reason why a Galilean fisherman like Peter may not have found it burdensome as well.[22] In concluding that both Jewish and Gentile Christians are saved "through the grace of the Lord Jesus," rather than through ritual observance of the Law (15:11), Peter therefore promotes the same gospel that Paul preached (Acts 13:38-39). With his validation of Paul and Barnabas's Gentile mission, Peter disappears from the pages of Acts.

Peter's argument silences the assembly (15:12), and the council next hears from Barnabas and Paul. Like Peter, Barnabas and Paul argue from their experience. They emphasize that the work among the Gentiles is God's work. In addition, just as Peter had observed the evidence of the Holy Spirit's Pentecostal work, so also Barnabas and Paul had observed miraculous signs and wonders among the Gentiles.

Following Barnabas and Paul's report, James, the chief elder in Jerusalem, responds (15:13-21). He picks up Peter's argument and adds scriptural support to arrive at the same conclusion. For first-century Jewish Christians, James's argument proves most decisive, since the issue could only be resolved based on scripture.[23] James first acknowledges Peter's claim that God had taken from the Gentiles "a people for his name" (15:14), alluding to Zechariah 2:11 (LXX 2:15): "Many nations *(ethne)* shall join themselves to the LORD on that day and shall be my people *(laos)*." *Laos* is a term usually used of Israel in contrast to the Gentiles (cf. Dt 26:18-19; 32:8-9; Ps 135:4 [LXX 134:4]).[24] In the last days, however, the nations *(ethne)* will be incorporated with Israel into a single people *(laos)* of God.[25]

James continues the same thought in verses 16-17 with a quotation from Amos 9:11-12 (with further allusions to Hosea 3:5 and Jeremiah 12:15-16), ending in verse 18 with a brief quotation from Isaiah 45:21. He uses the Septuagint translation, which reflects a significant change from the Hebrew text. In the Masoretic text God promises Israel possession of "the remnant of Edom and all the nations who are called by my name." By reading "seek" *(yidreshu)* for "possess" *(yireshu)* and "peoples" *(adam)* for "Edom" *(edōm),* and by ignoring the object marker on "remnant," the translators have changed the verse to suggest that the remnant of the peoples and all the nations that bear his name seek the Lord. F. F. Bruce consequently observes, "Thus LXX depoliticizes and spiritualizes the text, making it refer to the turning of the Gentiles . . . to seek the God of Israel. This version lends itself admirably to James' argument."[26] Indeed, once again James has adduced biblical support for Peter's conclusion.[27] James concurs with Peter's conclusion that no undue burdens should be placed on Gentiles who turn to the Lord (v. 19).

There has been considerable consternation over the fact that James quotes the Septuagint, especially since it digresses from the Masoretic text. Haenchen, for example, observes, "Nearly every expositor concedes that the Jewish Christian James would not in Jerusalem have used a Septuagint text, differing from the Hebrew original, as scriptural proof."[28] Richard Bauckham, however, demonstrates decisively that James is skillfully conflating the text of Amos using contemporary Jewish exegetical methods.[29] There is no good reason, furthermore, why James could not have used Greek. He was probably bilingual, while those from Antioch were not. Moreover, even though the Septuagint diverges from the Hebrew text, both contain the thought that other peoples will be included among the people of God.[30]

The conclusion is clear: What must change first is not one's culture but one's faith in Christ. This is not to say that the converts' culture will not change under the impact of the gospel, but it affirms that the first order of the day is the convert's allegiance. This is foundational to any discussion of contextualization and means that, given the presence of the Holy Spirit in their lives, I must take seriously the faith commitment of those with whom I may disagree. As I labored alongside my Korean brothers and sisters, I was concerned about their hierarchical society with its exaltation of pastors and subservience of women. I was also concerned about their emphasis upon church buildings and furnishings and about the persistence of shamanistic thinking. At no time, however, did I question their deep commitment to Christ. Clearly, as in the case of the first-century Gentiles, God has done a remarkable work among them. The most fundamental question when entering into contextualization, therefore, is whether a people has placed its faith in Jesus Christ and whether there is evidence that it has done so.

## FELLOWSHIP AND TESTIMONY

Having resolved the fundamental question of salvation, James anticipates a problem that will arise from his decision. He does not expect Jewish Christians to renounce their Jewishness any more than he expects Gentiles to become Jews. Jewish believers will no doubt continue to observe the Law with its requirements of ritual purity (as in fact they do, cf. 21:20-24). But how then will they enjoy table fellowship, the closest kind of fellowship, with Gentile believers? According to their traditions they would be defiled by such contact. James, therefore, issues what have become known as the apostolic decrees (15:20), justified by an enigmatic statement in verse 21: "For in every city, for generations past, Moses has had those who proclaim him, for he has been read aloud every Sabbath in the synagogues."

In the decrees Gentiles are instructed "to abstain only from things polluted by idols *(eidōlothyta)* and from fornication and from whatever has been strangled and from blood." Many commentators understand the decrees as ritual requirements that will make fellowship possible. Wagner calls them a "diplomatic concession."[31] If it were not for the reference to fornication, the decrees could easily be related to food laws. Interpreting the "things polluted by idols" in verse 20 by "what has been sacrificed to idols" in verse 29, the Gentiles were simply being instructed to avoid meat sacrificed to idols, meat of strangled animals (since strangulation retains the blood), and blood itself. With the addition of abstinence from fornication, however, many view the decrees as encompassing the demands of Leviticus 17—18, which were specifically required of aliens living within the land. Here idolatry (Lv 17:8), partaking blood (Lv 17:10-14), and certain sexual relationships are explicitly forbidden (Lv 18:6-18),[32] although the extension of strangled to "what has been torn by animals" (Lv 17:15) seems less plausible. In this case the explanation that Moses had been proclaimed in every city for generations (Acts 15:21) would simply mean that the requirements should come as no surprise, since they were found in Leviticus and required of Gentiles in contact with Jews.[33] Understood in this way, the decrees call upon Gentiles to observe certain ritual requirements to avoid ritual defilement and prevent close fellowship. Although Gentiles were free from the demands of the ritual law, they should surrender that right for the sake of fellowship with their Jewish brothers and sisters. The decrees would thus prioritize the need for harmonious fellowship over individual freedom.

The issue can be illustrated from the inter-generational conflict that I have encountered while teaching at a Christian college in the United States. For several generations worship styles have divided the older and younger generations. Hymns and pianos have disappeared, to be replaced by bands and choruses. Worship styles have become less cognitive and more emotional. Older Christians miss the hymns, while many young people find them boring. In many ways the conflict reflects the challenge of contextualization. Inevitably when discussion arises in the classroom about such issues, an emphasis upon freedom predominates. Neither side seems willing to forgo its freedom for the sake of fellowship. Understood as a call for mutual submission, the apostolic decrees would call for a change on both sides. Young and old should be willing to forgo their preferred worship styles in order to worship in unity.

Two other understandings of the decrees are possible. First, in contrast to the view that the decrees represent certain ritual requirements for the sake of fellowship, the Western text gives a distinctly moral sense to the decrees. It has omitted "strangled" and added the negative Golden Rule ("do not do to others what you would not have them do to you"). The decrees therefore prohibit three cardinal sins—idolatry, sexual immorality, and murder—summarized by the Golden Rule. The moral view was particularly popular among the Western fathers.[34] Most scholars, however, view the Western text as a later understanding that arose after the original setting had been lost. In that case the reading provides a wonderful example of the inevitability of contextualization. People find it difficult, if not impossible, to interpret the scripture apart from their own frame of reference.

A third view probably lies closer to the original context. Witherington has argued convincingly that the setting for all of the commands was pagan worship.[35] "Things polluted by idols" is a general term for all associations with idolatry, which involved sacrificial meals (frequently with strangled sacrifices and tasting or drinking the blood) and sacred prostitution. While Kirsopp Lake objects that understanding *porneia* (fornication) in this way is unusual, Witherington contends correctly that prostitution is the basic meaning of the term.[36] According to this view Gentiles truly were not burdened with legal rules but were simply instructed to turn from idolatry and its accompanying immorality. They were to avoid every appearance of evil. Verse 21 thus expresses concern that Gentiles maintain a good testimony before the watching Jewish world, consisting of both believers and unbelievers. They should give no cause for complaint through any association with idolatrous practices.[37]

Read in this light, it is clear that proper contextualization cannot compromise a Christian's testimony. For example, one of my Filipino students sought advice regarding her father's funeral rites. As his favorite daughter, she was expected by the family to perform certain indigenous rituals. Together we examined the rituals, determining what was acceptable, what was not, and what could be modified. As a result she was able to participate in the funeral with a clear conscience, demonstrating proper respect for her father while distancing herself from clearly unacceptable practices. She was even able to give clear testimony to her faith! As another example, consider the question with which we began: Can Filipino Christians eat *dinaguan*? The apostolic decrees lead us to respond, "Yes and no." Since Filipino food habits exist in a completely different cultural milieu than first-century Judaism, they are probably free to partake with thanksgiving. When Filipino Christians live in contact with Muslims, however, the situation calls for a different response. Since Muslim cultures observe many of the same ritual requirements as early Judaism, the passage would suggest that Christians should abstain from *dinaguan* for the sake of their testimony to Muslims.

## CHARACTERIZATION

Luke's characterization offers important clues to his point of view. Through his presentation of the antagonists and protagonists we gain valuable insight into the stance he would have us adopt during periods of awkward contextual questioning.

### The Antagonists

The Judaizing elements are clearly the narrative's antagonists. The text is unclear whether the Judeans (15:1) and the Pharisaic believers (15:5) belong to the same group or whether they simply hold similar beliefs. The Pharisees, in particular, would have strongly embraced the traditions of the elders. Clearly, however, Luke perceives them negatively. They cause dissension and debate (15:2), as well as disturb and unsettle the Christians in Antioch (15:24). Luke consequently spends little time presenting their views.

The antagonists' answers to the questions of contextualization were simple. They would decide for the Gentiles what must change. Moreover, they had decided that Gentiles must not only embrace Christ but must first change cultures. How easy it is for evangelical missionaries to lapse into such Pharisaic particularism, the notion that the traditions of their elders are binding on the faith and practice of converts in other cultures. They too bring about disturbances and unsettle believers' minds. American missionaries, for instance, have done little to allay Filipino fears of the *aswang* (a vampire-like creature). Instead they have, for the most part, dismissed such fears as superstition. Given the opportunity to preach in a Filipino church on Ascension Sunday, I used the opportunity to assure the congregation that Jesus was now seated in the heavenly places, far above every other power, and they need not fear the *aswang*. As he left, a wizened grandfather warmly shook my hand and said, "Thank you, pastor, for telling me that I do not have to fear the *aswang*."

## *The Protagonists*

Just as clearly Paul and Barnabas are the protagonists. Representing the Gentiles in Antioch,[38] they appear at the beginning (15:2), middle (15:12), and end (15:35) of the narrative. The story builds around their experience, and it is ultimately their position and their mission that is vindicated. For protagonists, however, Barnabas and Paul are amazingly passive. Their sole action is to "report all that God had done with them" (15:4; cf. 15:12). Instead, Peter and James dominate the action of the narrative, granting approval to the Gentile mission. Although Paul and Barnabas say little, Luke's consistent portrayal is positive. They "brought great joy to all the believers" (15:3), and "they were welcomed by the church and the apostles" (15:4). The apostles and elders describe them as "beloved" (15:25) and as having "risked their lives for the sake of our Lord Jesus Christ" (15:26).

As protagonists, Paul and Barnabas offer examples for us to emulate. Whereas their opponents brought confusion and disunity, Paul and Barnabas brought joy. While their opponents spoke without authorization (15:24), they were fully submissive. Missionaries who identify with Paul and Barnabas will prioritize concern for unity and submission in their efforts at contextualization. Since by its very nature contextualization tends toward fragmentation as each group defines its own faith and practice, submission is often the vital first step toward achieving unity, diametrically opposing the postmodern demand to question authority. It also questions the American value of freedom. Faced with the choice of worship styles for the sake of others, many American students seem to have the attitude that others should "just get over it." It is small wonder that American missionaries find it hard to submit to those from other cultures, even though successful contextualization depends upon it.

## CONCLUSION

The circumstances surrounding the Jerusalem council amply illustrate the challenges of contextualization. Clearly, contextualization is necessary for the advancement of the gospel. Contextualization is particularly problematic, however, because it often involves the deepest levels of cultural identity. Small wonder, then, that it invariably raises concern and causes conflict. The foundational principle of all contextualization, it must be remembered, is the assurance that converts are truly saved by grace through faith in Jesus Christ and that God is working among them. While contextual questions are seldom settled once and for all, participants in the process who are conscious of the presence of God can adopt an attitude of mutual submission, prioritizing mutual accountability and fellowship over personal rights and freedoms. In addition, all efforts toward contextualization should seek to maintain an unblemished testimony before the watching world. Then, and only then, as in Luke's narrative, may the gospel advance meaningfully to the ends of the earth.

## REFERENCES

[1] I do not address source-critical approaches, preferring instead to view the text as a unified narrative. For discussions of sources in Acts see Ernst Haenchen, *The Acts of the Apostles: A Commentary,* trans. R. McL. Wilson (Philadelphia: Westminster, 1971), 81-90; Ben Witherington III, *The Acts of the Apostles: A Socio-Rhetorical Commentary* (Grand Rapids, Mich.: Eerdmans, 1998), 165-172. For discussions of Acts 15, see Witherington, *The Acts of the Apostles,* 449-450; Joseph A. Fitzmyer, *The Acts of the Apostles: A New Translation with Introduction and Commentary,* The Anchor Bible (New York: Doubleday, 1998), 540; Kirsopp Lake, "The Apostolic Council," in *The Beginnings of Christianity,* vol. 5, *The Acts of the Apostles,* ed. F. J. Foakes-Jackson and Kirsopp Lake (1932; reprint, Grand Rapids, Mich.: Baker, 1966), 203-204.

[2] See Hans Conzelmann, *Acts of the Apostles,* trans. James Limburg, et al. (Philadelphia: Fortress Press, 1987), 115, 121; Fitzmyer, *The Acts of the Apostles,* 538-539; Haenchen, *The Acts of the Apostles,* 461-462; Andreas J. Köstenberger and Peter T. O'Brien, *Salvation to the Ends of the Earth: A Biblical Theology of Mission,* New Studies in Biblical Theology 11 (Downers Grove, Ill.: InterVarsity Press, 2001), 151; Lucien Legrand, *Unity and Plurality,* trans. Robert R. Barr (Maryknoll, N.Y.: Orbis Books, 1990), 91-92.

[3] John B. Polhill, *Acts: New American Commentary* (Nashville, Tenn.: Broadman, 1992), 320-321.

[4] C. Peter Wagner, *Lighting the World* (Ventura, Calif.: Regal, 1995), 225.

[5] Legrand, *Unity and Plurality,* 125.

[6] Joachim Jeremias, *Jerusalem in the Time of Jesus,* trans. F. H. and C. H. Cave (Philadelphia: Fortress Press, 1969), 266-267.

[7] Michael Green, *Evangelism in the Early Church* (Grand Rapids, Mich.: Eerdmans, 1970), 113-114.

[8] For an excellent discussion of the relationship between cultural forms and meanings, see Paul G. Hiebert, "Form and Meaning in the Contextualization of the Gospel," in *The Word among Us,* ed. Dean S. Gilliland (Dallas, Tex.: Word, 1989), 101-120.

[9] Richard Bauckham, "James and the Jerusalem Church," in *The Book of Acts in Its First Century Setting,* vol. 4, *The Book of Acts in Its Palestinian Setting,* ed. Richard Bauckham (Grand Rapids, Mich.: Eerdmans, 1995), 426.

[10] Conzelmann, *Acts of the Apostles,* 121.

[11] Benigno P. Beltran, *The Christology of the Inarticulate* (Manila: Divine Word, 1987), 263; cf. Leonardo N. Mercado, *Inculturation and Filipino Theology* (Manila: Divine Word, 1992), 25-27, 62-63. Mercado was later silenced for his views. Robert J. Schreiter addresses the complexity inherent in the relationship between local church and the larger community (*Constructing Local Theologies* [Maryknoll, N.Y.: Orbis Books, 1985], 95-121).

[12] Paul G. Hiebert, "Critical Contextualization," in *Anthropological Reflections on Missiological Issues* (Grand Rapids, Mich.: Baker Books, 1994), 88-91.

[13] J. B. Lightfoot, *St. Paul's Epistle to the Galatians* (1865; reprint Lynn, Mass.: Hendrickson Publishers, 1981), 123-128; Fitzmyer, *The Acts of the Apostles,* 539-540; Haenchen, *The Acts of the Apostles,* 464ff.; Polhill, *Acts,* 321; David John Williams, *Acts,* New International Bible Commentary (Peabody, Mass.: Hendrickson, 1990), 257-261.

[14] W. M. Ramsay, *St. Paul the Traveller and the Roman Citizen* (New York: G. P. Putnam's Sons, 1901), 52ff.; and with variations, Witherington, *The Acts of the Apostles,*

440-449; F. F. Bruce, *The Acts of the Apostles: The Greek Text with Introduction and Commentary*, 3d rev. ed. (Grand Rapids, Mich.: Eerdmans, 1990), 330-331; I. Howard Marshall, *The Acts of the Apostles: An Introduction and Commentary*, Tyndale New Testament Commentaries (Grand Rapids, Mich.: Eerdmans, 1998 [1980]), 244-248; Bauckham, "James and the Jerusalem Church," 468-470.

[15] Son Bong-Ho, "Some Dangers of Rapid Growth," in *Korean Church Growth Explosion*, ed. Ro Bong-Rin and Marlin L. Nelson (Seoul: Word of Life Press, 1983), 337-339.

[16] The Western text adds this requirement to verse 1 as well, probably to bring it into conformity with verse 5.

[17] Polhill, *Acts*, 324.

[18] Witherington, *The Acts of the Apostles*, 453.

[19] Bruce, *Acts*, 320; for an opposing position, see Wagner, *Lighting the World*, 234.

[20] Haenchen, *The Acts of the Apostles*, 445-446.

[21] Ibid., 446; cf. Conzelmann, *Acts of the Apostles*, 117.

[22] Witherington, *The Acts of the Apostles*, 454; cf. Bruce, *Acts*, 337.

[23] Bauckham, "James and the Jerusalem Church," 452.

[24] Bruce, *Acts*, 339.

[25] Polhill, *Acts*, 329.

[26] Bruce, *Acts*, 341.

[27] Williams, *Acts*, 265; cf. Polhill, *Acts*, 329.

[28] Haenchen, *The Acts of the Apostles*, 448.

[29] Bauckham, "James and the Jerusalem Church," 453-456.

[30] Ibid., 457.

[31] Wagner, *Lighting the World*, 243; cf. Marshall, *Acts*, 243.

[32] Conzelmann, *Acts of the Apostles*, 118-119; cf. Bauckham, "James and the Jerusalem Church," 459-460; Bruce, *Acts*, 342-343; Williams, *Acts*, 266.

[33] Polhill, *Acts*, 332. Witherington counters that the laws only applied to Gentiles in the land (*The Acts of the Apostles*, 465).

[34] Lake, "The Apostolic Council," 207. Bauckham denies that the textual changes necessitate an ethical sense ("James and the Jerusalem Church," 466).

[35] Witherington, *The Acts of the Apostles*, 460-465; cf. H. Reisser, "Porneia," in *The New International Dictionary of New Testament Theology*, vol. 1, ed. Colin Brown (Grand Rapids, Mich.: Zondervan, 1975), 497-501.

[36] Lake, "The Apostolic Council," 206; Witherington, *The Acts of the Apostles*, 463.

[37] Witherington, *The Acts of the Apostles*, 463; cf. Polhill, *Acts*, 332.

[38] There is some debate whether the Antioch church or the Judeans appointed them as representatives (15:2).

# 18

## *Finding the Will of God:*
## *Historical and Modern Perspectives*

### ACTS 16:1–30

### Gene L. Green

"Would you like to come on as the assistant pastor of the church?" The question, though surprising, was not entirely unexpected. As a young Christian I was actively seeking to find the will of God for my life and had been considering whether or not to go into Christian service. My whole life plan, at least what there was of one at age twenty, had been thrown into confusion after my conversion to Christ. Many prayers were offered to God with the question of his will always burning and mostly unanswered. Pastor Wells's invitation put a new urgency in these petitions. Decision day was approaching fast. I needed to hear from God.

Even as a young Christian I was convinced that God was involved in our lives and had a plan for every created person. How to find that plan was something I was less certain about. Was God's will known by circumstances that guided us down a certain path or by the prompting of an inner voice? Since I was a member of a Pentecostal church, prophecy was another option. Not a few of my friends longed to have a "prophetic word" spoken over them to confirm God's will and calling. Should I hope for the same? And if there was prophetic direction, should it be accepted at face value without examination? Could God speak in a dream, or through someone's casual comment spoken at the appropriate moment, or through the Sunday night sermon, or in the lyrics of a chorus? Had not Augustine of Hippo been converted after hearing a child singing "Take up and read; take up and read"? He tells how he "rose up, interpreting it no other way than as a command to me from heaven to open the book, and to read the first chapter I should light upon" (*Confessions* 8.12.29). He obeyed and read Romans 13:13-14. On the other hand, maybe God would speak to me as I read his word. In our church, books dealing with the topic of the will of God were always on the recommended reading list, and we reveled in the tales of those spiritual giants, each with a "Macedonian call" (Acts 16:9). Being "led of the Spirit" appeared to be one of the greatest Christian virtues.

In the quest to discover God's will, both in our daily affairs and in the overall direction of our lives, the Book of Acts was the primary text as we read our questions back into Luke's narrative. How had Peter been directed by God? How did Paul find his calling? Could we expect that God would lead us in the same way they were led? The story that captured my imagination more than any other was Luke's account of Paul's trip through Asia Minor on his second missionary journey. In Acts 15:41 Luke recounts that after the Jerusalem council, Paul and Silas "went through Syria and Cilicia, strengthening the churches." This journey took the apostolic company through Paul's home of Tarsus (22:3) and then onward to visit those congregations founded on the first missionary journey (16:1). They delivered to these churches the decree of the council that exempted the Gentile believers from circumcision (16:4; cf. 15:22-29).

## DIVINE INTERRUPTION

After adding Timothy to their company (16:1-3), they journeyed "through the region of Phrygia and Galatia" (16:6) after having attempted to travel west along the main Roman military artery that traversed southern Asia Minor, the Via Sebaste. Their destination would have been the capital of the province of Asia, Ephesus, a thriving port city that would give them access to the Aegean region and beyond. Heavy commercial traffic plowed the seas between this city and isthmus just north of Corinth in Achaia. Goods and even ships were transported across the six-kilometer stretch of land over the portage road known as the *diolkos*. From the west side of the isthmus the sea journey would begin again through the Gulf of Corinth, across the Adriatic to Brundisium in Italy, and from there up the Via Appia to the imperial city of Rome. We cannot say that Paul had Rome in his sights this early in his ministry, though Romans indicates that the apostle "often intended" to come to them (Rom 1:13). Even if Rome was not part of Paul's agenda at this point, the prospects of evangelizing the urban hub of Ephesus drew him.

Paul's strategic westward journey was interrupted. Luke recounts that Paul and company were "forbidden by the Holy Spirit to speak the word in Asia" (16:6). How did the Holy Spirit prevent Paul and his associates from evangelizing the province of Asia? Was it simply by some inner prompting of the Spirit?[1] Possibly the Holy Spirit spoke through Paul's travel companion Silas, who was recognized in the church as a prophet (15:32). Certainly, Luke signals the association between the Spirit and prophecy early in the Acts narrative (for example, see the quotation from Joel 2 in 2:17-18).[2] Then in the following verse, Luke relates how they headed north by one of the interior roads and "when they had come opposite Mysia, they attempted to go into Bithynia, but the Spirit of Jesus did not allow them" (16:7). Once again, Silas could have been the agent God used to communicate the divine directive, which in this case forbade them to carry out their mission in the northern province of Bithynia.[3] Paul and his companions decided and acted according to a strategic plan but were somehow vetoed by the Spirit.

The apostolic company then turned westward and headed for the metropolis and port city of Troas (16:8). Once again, Paul made for a port that would have given him access to the Roman trade routes heading west. It was from Troas that ships traveled the Adriatic to the harbors of Neapolis (which served the city of Philippi), as well as Amphipolis and Thessalonica in the Roman province of Macedonia. Each of these cities lay along the Via Egnatia, the great military highway that covered Macedonia all the way to the Adriatic, where people could cross the sea and then travel northwest from Brundisium to Rome. Here God's divine direction took on another form, for "during the night Paul had a vision: there stood a man of Macedonia pleading with him and saying, 'Come over to Macedonia and help us'" (16:9). Paul communicated the content of his vision to his companions (Silas, Timothy, and the author of Acts),[4] whereupon they came to the conclusion "that God had called us to proclaim the good news to them" (16:10).

## DIVINE GUIDANCE IN THE FIRST CENTURY

This story has often been the starting point for discussions about knowing the will of God. The comment on the text usually runs like this: God opens doors, and God closes doors. God can tell us which way to go or can let us know if we are not pursuing the proper course. Even as we seek divine direction for our life and mission, we should be active and decisive because "it is much easier to steer a moving vehicle than a stationary one." However, is this the way that Luke and Theophilus (1:1) would have understood these journeys and the divine directive? In other words, how was the issue of divine guidance understood in the first century? Does the narrative in Acts 16 resonate with the thinking of that era about the way that God's will was disclosed? While Acts 16 appears to respond to our concerns about knowing the will of God, the mode of communication and understanding sounds strangely unfamiliar. While we may speak comfortably of the "inner prompting of the Spirit," the prospect of discovering God's direction through a dream is not the type of advice commonly found on the pages of the popular tomes on divine direction. However, I believe that this story resonated with ancient thinking on the topic of divine directive. Jews, Greeks, and Romans often discussed the issue of divine communication. How would they have understood this narrative?

Ancient Mediterranean societies held a common belief that the gods communicated and that their will could be known through various forms of divination. The Athenean Xenophon stated in the fifth century B.C.E. "That the gods know all things, that the present and the future lie before their eyes, are tenets held by Hellenes and barbarians alike. This is obvious; or else, why do states and nations, one and all, inquire of the gods by divination what they ought to do and what they ought not?" (*Symposium* 1.71).[5] Further, in the dialogue between the great Roman orator Marcus Tullius Cicero and his brother Quintus, Quintus affirms the widespread belief that one could know the divine will: "Even before the dawn of philosophy, which is a recent discovery, the average person had no doubt about divination, and, since its development, no philosopher of any sort of reputation has had any different view" (*De Divinatione* 1.39.86). In his defense of divination Quintus remarks that he is in very diverse, universal, and ancient company: "For I have on my side reason, facts, people, and races, both Greek and barbarian, our own ancestors, the unvarying belief of all ages, the greatest philosophers, the poets, the wisest men, the builders of cities, and the founders of republics." Inquiring the will of the gods was a universal practice and so the incident of Acts 16 would hardly sound strange to the ears of Luke's first readers.

Numerous forms of divination were known and practiced and could be classified as those that depended on "art" and those that were classified as "natural means." Those that depended on "art" were "the prophecies of soothsayers, or interpreters of prodigies and lightnings, or of augurs, or of astrologers, or of oracles" (1.6.12). On the other hand, those forms of divination by natural means were "the forewarnings of dreams, or of frenzy" (1.6.12).[6] While Christianity did not sanction pagan divination, many of the forms for knowing the will of the gods were also employed by the church, while others were not embraced. The early believers put great stock in ancient prophecies and understood that what was predicted by the prophets of Israel was now fulfilled (Acts 2:16, 30-31).

## DIVINE GUIDANCE IN THE EARLY CHURCH

The church itself was a community marked by prophetic speech (1 Cor 14:24-25), which was considered to be one of the primary signs of the presence of the Spirit within the community (Acts 2:17-18; 1 Cor 12:10 [though 1 Cor 12:29 indicates that not all had the prophetic gift]). Likewise, dreams of/for divine direction played a significant role in early Christian history (Mt 1:20; 2:12, 19-22; Acts 2:17; 18:9-10). Dying people, such as Stephen in Acts 7:54-60, were said to have the power to prophesy. Quintus Cicero, for example, lays out the "proof of the power of dying men to prophecy" (*De Divinatione* 1.30.64). Lightning as a divine sign is mentioned especially in New Testament apocalyptic passages (Mt 24:27; Lk 17:24; Rv 4:5; 8:5; 11:19; 16:18), and the prophetic value of such signs was accepted. Quintus asked, "Is it possible for us to doubt the prophetic value of lightning?" (*De Divinatione* 1.10.16).

Earthquakes were understood almost universally as a form of divine warning (Mt 27:54; Rv 6:12; 8:5; 11:13, 19; 16:18). As Quintus Cicero observed, "For many a time the rumblings and roarings and quakings of the earth have given to our republic and to other states certain forewarnings of subsequent disaster" (*De Diviniatione* 1.18.35). While ancient augurs would observe the flights of birds to discern the divine will, nothing of this practice is found in the New Testament.[7] However, Marcus Cicero makes note of the belief that "the gods conveyed prophecies to men by the crowing of cocks" (2.26.57), though he does not abide by such practice. Yet the crowing of a cock is understood as a divine communication as Peter denied the Lord (Mt 26:34, 74-75; see also parallels). Inductive divination through the casting of lots was another form of divination that, while known, was not universally accepted.[8] However, Quintus Cicero stated, "Divination by lot is not in itself to be despised" (*De Divinatione* 1.18.34), and the early church embraced this practice before Pentecost as a valid means of choosing Judas's replacement, Matthias (Acts 1:23-26). After the coming of the Spirit this means of discerning the divine will is conspicuous in its absence in the record of the early church.

While these commonly accepted forms of knowing the divine will were employed in the church, consulting oracles, frenzied inspired speech, augury, and astrological predictions were not embraced by the church. The flight of birds, the examination of animals' organs, and predictions based on the zodiac are also not found among the Christians. (Among the first believers the source of revelation always was indicated.) When Paul had his dream in Troas, he recounted the same to his companions and all came to the conclusion "God had called us to proclaim the good news" to the Macedonians (Acts 16:10). Peter's Pentecost sermon begins with an apologetic from Joel 2 in which the Holy Spirit was signaled as the source of the prophetic inspiration:

> "I will pour out my Spirit upon all flesh,
>   and your sons and your daughters shall
>     prophesy. . . .
> Even upon my slaves, both men and women,
>   in those days I will pour out my Spirit;
>     and they shall prophesy." (Acts 2:17-18)[9]

Not "the gods" (Acts 14:11) but "the living God" (14:15) is the source of divine revelation and the true object of worship.

The superiority of Christian revelation over pagan divination is also underscored in Paul's encounter with the slave girl in Philippi who, according to Luke, "had a spirit of divination and brought her owners a great deal of money by fortunetelling" (16:16). The spirit that possessed this girl is called Python,[10] which was the venerable name of the spirit behind the most famous Greek oracle at Delphi. Plutarch, the priest of Delphi at the end of the first century C.E., comments, "The god himself after the manner of ventriloquists, . . . called . . . now Pythoness, enters the bodies of his prophets and prompts their utterances" (*Obsolescence of Oracles* 414E). The Python was the serpent that Apollo killed (Ovid, *Metamorphasis* 1.438-447) and the prophetesses at the oracular site of Delphi took their name from this creature (Plutarch, *Obsolescence of Oracles* 414E, 432C-433C, 404B-405A). This was the most respected and revered of the ancient oracles, though by the end of the first century C.E. we find Plutarch defending its validity against the Epicureans. This was no common example of divination; the highest status of oracular power is possessed of this young slave girl. Could it be that her owners had also paid a great price for this woman who had such supernatural talent? According to Lucian's *Alexander the False Prophet*, Alexander was able to charge one drachma and two obols per question, which totaled something like seventy thousand to eighty thousand drachmas a year.[11] This practice was condemned in Judaism[12] and clearly was not countenanced in the church either. The superiority of Christianity to such practices is highlighted in this narrative.

While Luke presented a polemic against pagan divination by showing the superiority of divine guidance (Acts 16:6-10) and the power of the name of Christ over the spirits that controlled divination (16:16-18), he never called into question the possibility of divine speech in its multiple forms. His position counters the trend in some quarters during that era to discount the reality of any form of divine communication. In spite of the general acceptance of divination, skepticism about such practices can be traced back all the way to the sixth century B.C.E.[13] Euripides in the fifth century likewise quipped, "Now indeed I see how worthless the seers' doings are, and how full of falsehood" (*Helen* 744-745). The best course of action is not found by divination, "But sound judgement and discernment are the best of seers" (*Helen* 757). Marcus Cicero takes up the cause of skepticism and affirms the ancient opinion of Carneades and that of his contemporaries, the Epicureans: "Therefore I am inclined to think that there is no such thing as divination." He supported his case from Euripides, "The best diviner I maintain to be, the man who guesses or conjectures best" (*De Divinatione* 2.5.12).[14] During the first century C.E. and even before, there were clear signs that divination was on the decline. Commenting on the oracle of Delphi, Quintus Cicero remarked, "At present its glory has waned because it is no longer noted for the truth of its prophecies." He conjectured that "the subterraneous exhalations which used to kindle the soul of the Pythian priestess with divine inspiration have gradually vanished in the long lapse of time" (1.19.38). Marcus Cicero would not accept that explanation of the decline and came to the conclusion that divination was a blend "of a little error, a little superstition, and a good deal of fraud" (2.39.82).

Marcus Cicero followed the opinion of the Epicureans (2.17.40-41), the very same philosophical school Plutarch squared off against in his defense of the oracle at Delphi. This priest of Apollo and philosopher wrote at the end of the first century C.E. that the Epicureans "have an arrogant contempt . . . for all such things as oracles" (*De Defectu Oraculorum* 434D). Over a century earlier Cicero echoed the opinion, "Why are Delphic oracles . . . not uttered at the present time and have not been for a long time? And why are they regarded with the utmost contempt?" (*De Divinatione* 2.57.117). The Roman satirist Juvenal likewise quipped, "For now that the Delphian oracles are dumb, man is condemned to darkness as to the future" (*Satura* 6.555-556). Strabo the geographer similarly observed, "Among the ancients both divination in general and oracles were held in greater honour, but now great neglect of them prevails" (*Geography* 17.1.43). In his *De Defectu Oraculorum* Plutarch presented a dialogue in which one of the characters, Demetrius, observed that the oracles are not only in decline but also reported "the total disappearance of all [the oracles] but one or two" (411E). "As for the rest, silence has come upon some and utter desolation upon others" (411F).

While it would be overmuch to say that Luke is directly attempting to enter this debate about the decline of oracular speech, he spoke into an environment where this issue was well known. He affirms that Christianity is a true prophetic movement inspired by the divine Spirit. Pagan forms of divine knowledge, on the other hand, are weak and false and are attributed to spirits. God does speak and directs people. Luke will not entertain the cynicism that not a few had embraced.[15]

Luke's presentation of divine directive is also distinct from the pagan practices in the clarity of the revelations. While Paul at times did not know what the divine direction was, when it was given there was no doubt regarding the nature of God's will (Acts 16:6, 7, 10). Such clarity of revelation was not characteristic of the oracles in the classic era. Plutarch noted that in the past the gods "put a cloak of intimations and ambiguities which concealed the communications," principally to protect those mortals who declared the divine will from wicked people (*De Pythiae Oraculis* 407E). Now, however, Plutarch praises the oracle for clarity of communication rather than speaking through the medium of poetry (406E-407B). Christian revelation was marked by clarity and directness, and Paul even calls for such clarity when tongues are employed in the Corinthian congregation so that the church will be edified (1 Cor 14:6-12) and unbelievers will be convicted through divine revelation (1 Cor 14:23-25). The expression of the divine will in the church is not marked by ambiguity. Clarity and directness characterize God's revelation.

From both the Greek and the Roman perspective, the picture of divine guidance presented in Acts would have been recognizable and compelling. The church was a community whose mission was carried forward under divine direction, which itself marked the movement as bearing the seal of God's approval. The fact that the church encountered suffering over and over again does not mean that the apostolic company was somehow outside the will of God. This point, emphasized in Acts, became one of the points underlined in Acts 16. After receiving the night vision of the Macedonian man, Paul and his company obeyed and sailed to the Macedonian port of Neapolis and from there they traveled up to Philippi. After the exorcism of the Python spirit from the slave girl, Paul and Silas were arrested and thrown into jail (Acts 16:19-24). Paul had commanded the demon to "come out" of the woman and the spirit "came out that very hour." But the demon was not the only thing that "came out"! Acts 16:19 says that "her owners saw that their hope of making money was gone" (literally "came out"). Their "legitimate business interests" were prejudiced by the gospel, and they could not hope for compensation but only revenge. The law courts in the Roman Empire were forums in which personal enmity and revenge were played out. The slave girl's masters not only faced financial loss but their honor was affronted. They were humiliated by these traveling preachers, and if a Roman "showed himself reluctant to respond and retaliate for hostile acts," he would suffer further humiliation and loss of prestige. "A Roman, governed by a harsh ethos, simply could not afford to 'turn the other cheek' and expect to maintain his position in society."[16] Cornelia, a Roman mother, said, "You will say that it is beautiful to take revenge on your enemies. I consider revenge as important and glorious as anyone, but only if it can be attained without harm to the Republic."[17] The owners were under a social obligation to obtain revenge, and the courts were an appropriate forum. The way the accusation is couched in patriotic terms further legitimizes the action taken against the apostles in the public eye (16:20-21).[18] Cicero, for example, said, "Know that they will find me a great deal more persistent and more forcible against those men with whom I shall take up enmity in the interest of the welfare of the Roman people."[19]

## DIVINE RESPONSE TO THE JAILING OF PAUL AND SILAS

After being thrown into jail, Luke recorded that Paul and Silas "were praying and singing hymns to God" about midnight (16:25). The divine response was an earthquake that released Paul, Silas, and the other captives (16:26). This would have been viewed as a divine omen by a Roman and not simply a natural event (Cicero, *De Divinatione* 1.18-36), and this very knowledge could have been one of the factors that moved the Philippian jailer to come to Paul and Silas trembling and asking, "Sirs, what must I do to be saved?" (Acts 16:30). He had heard their hymns (16: 25) and had witnessed the divine omen![20] Luke showed his reader, Theolphilus, that though suffering may be the outcome of Christian mission, such adversity does not signal that the missioners are somehow outside the will of God. God had guided Paul and Silas to Macedonia, had overcome the spirit that possessed the slave girl, and now liberated them from prison.

Luke's perspective on divine guidance in Acts 16 may also be examined in contrast to Jewish thoughts on this question. Leading up to the first century C.E. some Jewish opinion upheld the idea that the prophetic tradition within Israel had ceased with the last of the writing prophets. So, for example, 1 Maccabees tells the story of the quandary over what to do with the defiled stones of the altar of burnt offering: "So they tore down the altar, and stored the stones in a convenient place on the temple hill until a prophet should come to tell what to do with them" (1 Mc 4:45-46). Some chapters later the author declared, "So there was great distress in Israel, such as had not been since the time that prophets ceased to appear among them" (9:27). Simon was declared leader and high priest "until a trustworthy prophet should arise" (14:41). Similarly, the first-century Jewish historian Josephus declares that a complete history of the Jews had not been written since the time of Artaxerxes "because of the failure of the exact succession of the prophets" (*Contra Apionem* 1.41). Yet at the same time Josephus tells how Vespacian found that Josephus "proved a veracious prophet in other matters" (*Bellum Judaicum* 3.399-408). The very fact that the "Egyptian false prophet" could gain "for himself the reputation of a prophet" (2.261; cf. Acts 21:38) in the first century C.E. underscores that not everyone accepted the notion that prophecy had altogether gone out of Israel. As Craig S. Keener comments, "Particularly outside the rabbinic literature, prophecy was *generally* not believed to have ceased."[21] Christianity stood in the line of the prophetic movement in Israel and promised that the prophetic voice would be a hallmark of this community (Acts 2:17-18). Here in Acts 16, divine guidance is carried out in the church through the prophetic voice (16:6-7).

The type of appearance in a dream which Paul witnessed (16:9) was known within Judaism as well. Dreams as a medium of divine communication are well attested in the Old Testament and are also acknowledged in Jewish literature.[22] Also known within Judaism was the *bat kol*, the "daughter of the voice," which was a voice directly from the heavens that revealed God's will.[23] This voice arrested Paul on his way to Damascus and was the agency through which God brought this persecutor of the church to proclaim Jesus as the Christ and Lord (Acts 9:4-7; 22:7-10; 26:14-18).

When set against its historical background, the narrative in Acts portrays the apostolic mission as an endeavor guided by God from the very outset (Acts 13:1-3) and given divine direction at significant junctures (16:6-10). The way that the church was led was in certain ways similar to the ancient belief about divine guidance, both within pagan and Jewish circles. On the other hand, numerous forms of pagan divination are not attested, and we can well assume that they were rejected, as they had been within Judaism.

The composite picture is surprisingly different than our current endeavors to "find the will of God for our lives" or "seek direction from the Lord" in his work. Most of us would be highly skeptical if someone declared that God had told him or her in a dream to embark on a certain mission. Likewise, few churches or individuals would be prone to accept prophecy as a legitimate means of guiding mission outreach. Could we imagine a mission committee moved to act by a prophecy spoken in their midst? Further, we consider earthquakes to be tectonic plate movement, not divine portents.

On the other hand, the Acts narrative is conspicuously silent about what we consider to be the primary form of God's leading. While we commonly speak about the inner prompting of the Spirit, Acts seems strangely silent on this issue. Paul spoke to the Ephesian elders in Miletus about the way "that the Holy Spirit testifies to me in every city that imprisonment and persecutions are waiting for me" (Acts 20:23), but such revelations probably came from external sources rather than inner promptings. So in Acts 21:10-11 Luke tells that Agabus the prophet "took Paul's belt, bound his own feet and hands with it, and said, 'Thus says the Holy Spirit, "This is the way the Jews in Jerusalem will bind the man who owns this belt and will hand him over to the Gentiles."'" While we would speak about being led through circumstances, the picture in Acts 16 seems to run contrary to that opinion. The circumstances of Paul and Silas were entirely contrary, and had Paul not received prophetic direction, a night vision, and divine intervention through the earthquake, the reader of Acts could easily come to the conclusion that these men were decidedly not guided by God. We should therefore be cautious about using Acts 16 to support some of our more cherished notions about the nature of divine guidance. The picture presented there should be read within its historical context and not morphed to agree with our notions of finding the divine will.

## CONCLUSION

What positive orientation can we glean from Acts that will help us in our endeavor to discover the divine will? First, we understand, as they did, that God is active in the life and mission of his church. Our God knows the future and has a plan that includes his people. Second, Acts tells us that God is effective in guiding the mission of the church. God is able to give both positive direction and prohibit the progress of the mission in certain directions. Third, the divine will is not easily known from adverse circumstances. The very fact that the mission meets with opposition does not imply that actions taken were somehow outside the will of God. Fourth, the will of God is not always revealed and known, yet this fact should not detain the mission. While Paul at times had very clear guidance about what to do and where to go, most of the narrative shows an apostle who planned and acted according to a strategic plan. For example, the gospel was "to the Jew first and also to the Greek" (Rom 1:16; see also Acts 13:46). This understanding led Paul to go primarily to those cities where there was a Jewish presence, and he addressed those in the synagogue before turning to the Gentiles. Fifth, knowledge of the divine will was more community oriented than individualistic. The community was involved both in prophetic leading and the interpretation of the vision, which Paul received (Acts 16:6-10). This community-based understanding of divine leading is one of the most notably absent elements in current discussions about divine leading. Due to our Western individualistic orientation, the declaration that "God showed me" is calculated to end all discussion about what God's will is in a certain circumstance. Yet Paul and his associates were together "convinced that God had called us" (16:10). Sixth, the church should rediscover its roots as a true charismatic community in which the gifts of the Spirit operate and where one can come and witness that "God is really among you" (1 Cor 14:25). Paul's approach to excess and abuse of the divine gifts given by the Spirit (1 Cor 12:7, 11) is to place community control upon their use (1 Cor 14). Both worship and mission should be filled with the powerful outworking of the Spirit of the living and active God. In this context of control we may discover anew the power of the prophetic voice (1 Cor 14:29; 1 Thes 5:19-22; cf. 1 Jn 4:1-3).

When my pastor asked me to continue as the assistant pastor of the church, I never really did "hear" from God whether or not I was to go into the ministry. The pastor had recognized the gifts that God had given me and, in time, others recognized them as well. During those seasons of prayer about God's will for my life, I also began to think about teaching in Latin America, something I did for thirteen years. There was no vision, no prophecy, no *bat kol*, no other sign that led me in that direction. Yet the interest and the passion were there and became integrated into my life. I would not call that my "Macedonian call" but simply the outworking of a clear sense that God had called me for his service. Perhaps it would be wrong to limit God by saying that he does not speak to our innermost being about the direction we are to take. But it would be incorrect to read that experience back into the dramatic events that led to the great Macedonian ministry.

## REFERENCES

[1] The participle used *(kōluthentes)* signifies that they were prevented from preaching in Asia (*BAGD*, 461).

[2] Roger Stronstad, *The Prophethood of All Believers: A Study in Luke's Charismatic Theology* (Sheffield, UK: Sheffield Academic Press, 1999), 141; Robert P. Menzies, "The Spirit of Prophecy, Luke-Acts and Pentecostal Theology: A Response to Max Turner," *Journal of Pentecostal Theology* 15 (October 1999): 49-74.

[3] Similarly, 1 Peter 1:11 speaks of the "Spirit of Christ" as the inspiration for ancient prophetic activity. 1 Peter was addressed to churches in Asia Minor, including those in the joint province of Bithynia and Pontus (1 Pt 1:1). We do not know how these churches came into existence. Pliny the Younger, in his correspondence with the emperor Trajan (112 C.E.) notes that churches in Bithynia had been established for some time and that the Christian religion moved from the cities and towns to the rural regions (*Epistles* 10.96).

[4] The narrative changed from the third person to the first person plural at this point.

[5] All translations from classical literature in this chapter are from the *Loeb Classical Library* (Cambridge, Mass.: Harvard University Press).

[6] "Frenzy" *(vaticinatio)* is a reference to prophetic speech uttered in a frenzied or ecstatic state.

[7] The Jewish scorn for discerning the divine will through such augury is underscored by Josephus, who noted how a Jew in Alexander the Great's army took his bow and arrow and shot dead a bird that a seer (diviner) looked to for a sign whether the army should halt or advance. The Jew Mosollamus quipped, "Pray, how could any sound information about our march be given by this creature, which could not provide for its own safety? Had it been gifted with divination, it would not have come to this spot, for fear of being killed by an arrow of Mosollamus the Jew" (*Contra Apionem* 1.201-204).

[8] See Aristotle, *Politicus* 1300a, 19; Ps. Xenophon, *Constitution of the Athenians* 1.2. This practice was not respected by the Alexandrian Jew Philo (*Quis Rerum Divinarum Heres* 179).

[9] The recorded quotation is taken from the Septuagint translation of Joel 2:28-32 (LXX 3:1-5) with the addition of the words in Acts 2:18, "and they shall prophesy."

[10] "Apollo learned the art of prophecy from Pan, the son of Zeus and Hybris, and came to Delphi, where Themis at that time used to deliver oracles; and when the snake Python, which guarded the oracle, would have hindered him from approaching the chasm, he killed it and took over the oracle" (Apollodorus, *Library and Epitome* 1.4.1).

[11] A Greek drachma was equal to a Roman denarius, the daily wage of a laborer.

[12] Mishna Sanhedrin 7.7 says, "'He that has a familiar spirit' (such is the Python which speaks from his armpits), 'and the soothsayer' (such is he that speaks with his mouth) these are [to be put to death] by stoning, and he that inquires of them transgresses against a warning"; see also Strabo, *Geog.* 9.3.5.

[13] Marcus Cicero notes, for example, "Xenophanes of Colophon, while asserting the existence of gods, was the only one [of the ancients] who repudiated divination in its entirety" (*De Divinatione* 1.3.5).

[14] Euripides is likewise quoted by Plutarch in his defense of the Delphic oracle (*De Defectu Oraculorum* 432C; see also 399A).

[15] Paul's statement about the cessation of the charismata in 1 Corinthians 13:8—"But as for prophecies, they will come to an end; as for tongues, they will cease"—should

be read against the backdrop of this ancient debate about the cessation of oracles and other forms of divination. Since the publication of B. B. Warfield's *Counterfeit Miracles*, in which he levels an attack against the charismatic Irvingites, this text has been read in light of the question of whether or not the gifts of the Spirit continued beyond the apostolic age. For a summary of that debate, see Jon Ruthven, *On the Cessation of the Charismata: The Protestant Polemic on Postbiblical Miracles* (Sheffield: Sheffield Academic Press, 1993).

[16] David F. Epstein, *Personal Enmity in Roman Politics 218-43 B.C.E.* (London: Croom Helm, 1987), 2.

[17] Ibid., 20.

[18] Epstein comments, "Romans often sought and found glory in the claim that their publicmindedness forced *inimicitiae* upon them as a cross to bear in the national interest."

[19] Ibid., 22-23.

[20] Another possibility for the jailer's fear and attempted suicide may be related to the likelihood of his execution if the prisoners escaped (see Acts 12:19).

[21] Craig S. Keener, *The Spirit in the Gospels and Acts: Divine Purity and Power* (Peabody, Mass.: Hendrickson, 1997), 16. See also David E. Aune, *Prophecy in Early Christianity and the Ancient Mediterranean World* (Grand Rapids, Mich.: Eerdmans, 1983), 103-106; Richard A. Horsley and John S. Hanson, *Bandits, Prophets, and Messiahs: Popular Movements at the Time of Jesus* (Minneapolis, Minn.: Winston Press, 1985), chap. 4.

[22] E.g., Gn 31:11; 1 Kgs 3:5; Jer 23:28; 29:8; Dn 2:1-49; Jl 2:28 (Acts 2:17); and 4 Esdras 10:59; 11:1; 12:35; 13:1, 15, 53; Eccles. Rabbah 9.10.1; Ta'anit 21b.

[23] See George Foot Moore, *Judaism in the First Centuries of the Christian Era*, 2 vols. (New York: Shocken Books, 1971), 1:422; Aune, *Prophecy in Early Christianity and the Ancient Mediterranean World*, 104; Heinrich Graetz, *History of the Jews*, 6 vols. (Philadelphia: Jewish Publication Society of America, 1967), 2:337.

# 19

## *Paul's Speech on the Areopagus:*
## *A Model of Cross-cultural Evangelism*

### Acts 17:16–34

### Lynn Allan Losie

As an American of Anglo-European ethnicity, I have become used to hearing the question, "What sort of name is that?" when introducing myself to someone for the first time. America has been populated, to a large extent, by immigrants, and the surnames carried by Americans are a vestige of this fact. But beyond this initial curiosity over ancestral origins, my experience has been that Americans like me are not much concerned about genealogies, except as a possible hobby or a pastime. We have inherited a national ethos that places a high value on individual achievement, and we aim to make our own way in the world without much care for passing on traditions established by our family or more distant relatives. On the other hand, those of us of Anglo-European origin also take for granted that we are part of a Western tradition that has roots deep in antiquity, and in this we feel secure, despite our desire to maintain the freedom to make our own mark as individuals. And if we have come to Christian faith, as an individual decision, we can assume that our ancestors, if we should think of them, have had that same opportunity to respond to the message of the gospel of Jesus Christ, the fulfillment of God's promises to the patriarch Abraham, who was the heir of God's saving work in the world from the time of its creation (Lk 3:23-38; Gal 3:6-9, 16, 27-29).

Such, however, is not the ethos or heritage of people of East Asia. I have had to consider the implications of this difference for the proclamation of the gospel as I have taught in a graduate theological program for Korean pastors and teachers in the cosmopolitan city of Los Angeles, California. In contrast to the American emphasis on the individual, Korean culture places a high value on group identity and the Confucian virtue of filial piety, which includes the honoring of ancestors into the distant past.[1] This respect for one's ancestral heritage is aptly captured in the Confucian saying, "A person who for three years refrains from reforming the ways of his late father can be called a filial son."[2] It is not

221

unusual for Koreans to have family genealogies that go back five hundred years to the time of the Yi dynasty. These genealogies need to be consulted when marriages are arranged in order to maintain the intricate incest taboos of the culture.[3] Christianity, however, is a rather recent arrival in the land of Korea, where ancestral traditions are so venerated. The history of the church in Korea can only claim a history of a little over two centuries, back to contacts with Jesuit missionaries in 1783 and Protestant missionaries in 1866.[4] Thus a perennial question raised by Korean students in my classes concerns the relationship between the beliefs of their ancestors, both near and distant, whom they honor, and their Christian faith. Can they take any comfort in the fact that some Confucian sayings parallel and support their Christian beliefs, as, for example, in the following saying that promotes the Golden Rule?

> Zigong asked, "Is there one expression that can be acted upon until the end of one's days?" The Master replied, "There is *shu* [putting oneself in the other's place]: do not impose on others what you yourself do not want."[5]

Or, to use the terminology of theologians, can an appeal be made to general revelation when proclaiming the gospel to a culture that is not in direct continuity with the special revelation of the Christian scriptures?

These questions raise the specter of natural theology, which has been a contentious issue in the history of the church. As defined recently by James Barr, natural theology holds "that 'by nature,' that is, just by being human beings, men and women have a certain degree of knowledge of God and awareness of him, or at least a capacity for such an awareness; and this knowledge or awareness exists anterior to the special revelation of God made through Jesus Christ, through the Church, through the Bible."[6] Protestant theologians have tended to abandon natural theology as a Roman Catholic concern and reject the Scholastic attempts to prove the existence of God through unaided human reason. Evangelical theologians have harbored an additional fear that natural theology might lead to a liberalism of the type introduced by Friedrich Schleiermacher, who based his theology on religious feeling that can be found in various forms in all religions, rather than on the special revelation in the Christian scriptures.[7] Early in the twentieth century the lines were drawn sharply in a debate between neo-orthodox theologians Emil Brunner and Karl Barth.[8] In response to Brunner's call for a new attempt, in distinction from Schleiermacher, to articulate a "point of contact" through which special revelation could be received by human beings, Barth declared "Nein" and repudiated all natural theology. His position captured the minds of the proponents of the growing Biblical Theology Movement, which looked for distinctiveness in the Bible in contrast to its religious environment, and natural theology became a neglected topic in biblical studies.[9]

A hidden irony in this, however, has been explored by Barr in his Gifford Lectures, delivered at the University of Edinburgh in 1991.[10] After reviewing the abandonment of natural theology in the past century, which he attributes to the influence of Barth's emphasis on the priority of biblical revelation, Barr asks, "What if scripture itself sanctions, permits, evidences, or in some other way depends upon natural theology or something like it?"[11] He broadens the definition of natural theology to include "interreligiosity or interculturality," that is, "anything in the Bible that shares conceptuality or attitudes with religions or philosophies outside the accepted circle of revelation,"[12] and then proceeds to find evidence for this phenomenon in the Hebrew Bible, early Jewish tradition outside the Jewish canon of scripture, and the New Testament. His purpose is not to rehabilitate natural theology as a theological method that can operate from reason alone, and in fact on this point he confesses sympathy with Barth's critique, but he wants to show that the Bible incorporates and validates religious ideas from many sources, including some that come from outside the covenant community of Israel and its heir, the early Christian church. Barr begins his study of the biblical evidence with an analysis of Paul's speech on the Areopagus in Acts 17:16-34, and it is to this passage that we now turn, drawing on insights from many sources, to see if it indeed provides an example of the use of general revelation in the proclamation of the gospel in a cross-cultural situation.[13]

## THE SETTING OF THE SPEECH

Athens is the only city where the Acts of the Apostles portrays the apostle Paul preaching in the marketplace (Acts 17:16-17). In general, a marketplace, filled as it might be with all kinds of people—sophists and their disciples, writers, poets, jugglers, fortunetellers, lawyers, peddlers, and so on[14]—would not be a setting for the dissemination of serious ideas. But in Athens the marketplace was the location of the famous Painted Colonnade *(Poikilê Stoa)*, where Zeno, the founder of the Stoics (people of the *Stoa*), had propounded his teaching;[15] it was also remembered as the site where Socrates had carried on dialogues with his students.[16] Down the road was the Garden, where Epicurus, the founder of the Epicureans, had established his community of friends and where his philosophical school still flourished.[17] The marketplace in Athens was thus a scene of philosophical debate, and it is not surprising that the reader soon finds Paul encountering "some Epicurean and Stoic philosophers" there (Acts 17:18).[18]

The reaction of the philosophers to Paul's preaching, or as Luke characterizes it in philosophical language, "disputation," is varied.[19] Some respond, "What does this babbler [*spermologos*] want to say?" (Acts 17:18). This calls to mind a term used by the Stoic philosopher Dio Chrysostom (c. 40-112 C.E.) to dismiss the teaching of the Cynics, who "post themselves at street-corners, in alleyways, and at temple-gates, pass around the hat, and play upon the credulity of lads and sailors and crowds of that sort, stringing together rough jokes and much babbling [*spermologian*] and that rubbish of the marketplace."[20]

Presumably, however, this reaction to Paul is that of the Epicureans, who are mentioned first by Luke and who had little use for religion, regarding most popular belief about the gods to be superstition.[21] Dio Chrysostom, from a Stoic point of view, complained about the lack of religious concern among these philosophers:

Why, certain men . . . despise all things divine, and having set up the image of one single female divinity, . . . to which they give the name of Pleasure, . . . her they prefer in honor and worship . . . and all this universe above us they assert is without purpose or intelligence or master, has no ruler or even steward or overseer, but wanders at random and is swept aimlessly along, no master being there to take thought for it now, and no creator having made it in the first place, or even doing as the boys do with their hoops, which they set in motion of their own accord, and then let them roll along of themselves.[22]

The Epicurean philosopher Lucretius (c. 94-55 B.C.E.), however, took pride in having relieved humanity from the burden of religious superstition:

When human life lay grovelling in all men's sight, crushed to the earth under the dead weight of superstition whose grim features loured menacingly upon mortals from the four quarters of the sky, a man of Greece was first to raise mortal eyes in defiance, first to stand erect and brave the challenge. Fables of the gods did not crush him, nor the lightning flash and the growling menace of the sky. . . . The vital vigour of his mind prevailed. . . . Therefore superstition in its turn lies crushed beneath his feet, and we by his triumph are lifted level with the skies.[23]

But not all the philosophers who encounter Paul are so dismissive of his preaching. Luke informs us that some take an interest in engaging him further in discussion: "He seems to be a proclaimer of foreign divinities. . . . May we know what this new teaching is that you are presenting? It sounds rather strange to us, so we would like to know what it means" (Acts 17:18-19). The Stoics, the second of Luke's philosophical groups, are probably the ones speaking here, since they had a more positive attitude toward religion and piety, as will be developed in more detail below.[24] Luke explains their interpretation that Paul is preaching about "foreign divinities" with the parenthetical remark, "This was because he was telling the good news about Jesus and the resurrection" (Acts 17:18); John Chrysostom (c. 347-407 C.E.) amplifies the foreign concept of the resurrection with the comment, "for in fact they supposed 'Anastasis' [the resurrection] to be some deity, being accustomed to worship female divinities also."[25]

It is these Stoics who, Luke tells us, "took him and brought him to the Areopagus" (Acts 17:19). Here, however, interpreters differ concerning the intention of this action and the identity of the venue where the further encounter would take place. Are we to understand that Paul is arrested and brought to a law court for a judicial proceeding (by the Council of the Areopagus), or that he is simply invited to join the philosophers at a location more conducive to serious discussion (on the Hill [*Pagos*] of Ares)?[26] The former interpretation is suggested by the Stoic reaction (or charge?) that Paul is "a proclaimer of foreign divinities" (Acts 17:18), which seems to echo the famous indictment against the philosopher Socrates centuries earlier, as recorded by Xenophon:

"Socrates is guilty of rejecting the gods acknowledged by the state and of bringing in new divinities; he is also guilty of corrupting the youth."[27] For his preliminary hearing Socrates appeared before the king's magistrate, who presided at the King's Colonnade in the marketplace of Athens.[28] The Council of the Areopagus, the highest administrative and judicial body in Athens, also met there, though Socrates was not tried before this court.[29] If this parallel with Socrates is given weight for interpreting Luke's description of the Stoic reaction to Paul, the Stoics may be understood to "seize" Paul and bring him to the Council of the Areopagus for some sort of trial.[30] But this appears to be reading too much hostility into Luke's portrayal of the philosophers' reaction. Luke's interpretation of their intention seems to be much more benign, especially in light of his comment in Acts 17:21: "Now all the Athenians and the foreigners living there would spend their time in nothing but telling or hearing something new."[31] Trial scenes in Acts are not difficult to identify,[32] and Luke's description of the action of the philosophers in Acts 17:19 is closer to his account of what Barnabas did when he brought the recently converted Paul to meet with the apostles in Jerusalem: "Barnabas took him, brought him to the apostles, and described for them how on the road he had seen the Lord . . . and how in Damascus he had spoken boldly in the name of Jesus" (Acts 9:27).[33] The Stoics therefore are simply pictured as transferring Paul to a quieter yet prominent venue, the Hill of Ares. Luke is thus setting the scene for a discourse by Paul that can engage the philosophical thinkers of the Greco-Roman world.[34]

If Luke has chosen this story as an example of how evangelistic preaching might be undertaken in an environment that is not Judeo-Christian, his emphasis on the philosophical setting of Paul's proclamation would be important for his purpose. It was in the philosophical traditions of the Greco-Roman world, rather than in its religions, that Christian preachers could find a point of contact for the proclamation of the gospel. The myths of the traditional gods were full of tales of corruption and intrigue, and serious scholars among the Greeks and Romans recognized that their religious traditions could not form a basis for morality. Xenophanes of Colophon (sixth century B.C.E.) summed up the situation when he said, "Homer and Hesiod have attributed to the gods all things which are shameful and a reproach among humans: stealing and committing adultery and deceiving one another."[35] Likewise, Luke begins his story of Paul in Athens by noting that "he was deeply distressed to see that the city was full of idols" (Acts 17:16).[36] On the other hand, the philosophers thought profoundly about nature and the gods (or God). The purpose of their inquiries was not to gain access to or find ways to manipulate divine power through religious ritual, but to give guidance to people on how to live an ethical life that would be a benefit to society. The essay entitled *The Education of Children,* which is attributed to Plutarch (c. C.E. 50-120) and introduces the collection of his *Moralia,* promotes philosophy as "the head and front of all education":

For through philosophy and in company with philosophy it is possible to attain knowledge of what is honourable and what is shameful, what is just and what is unjust, what, in brief, is to be chosen and what is to be avoided, how a man must bear himself in his relations with the gods, with his parents, with his elders, with the laws, with strangers, with those in authority, with friends, with women, with children, with servants; that one ought to reverence the gods, to honour one's parents, to respect one's elders, to be obedient to the laws, to yield to those in authority, to love one's friends, to be chaste with women, to be affectionate with children, and not to be overbearing with slaves; and, most important of all, not to be over joyful at success or overmuch distressed at misfortune, nor to be dissolute in pleasures, nor impulsive and brutish in temper. These things I regard as pre-eminent among all the advantages that accrue from philosophy.[37]

If there was general revelation in the Greco-Roman world on which evangelistic preaching could draw, Christian missionaries like Paul would have their best chance of finding it in the considered work of the philosophers.

## THE FORM OF THE SPEECH

The setting established for Paul's encounter with the philosophers in Athens calls for a deliberative *(symbouleutikos)* speech, according to the conventional genres of Greco-Roman rhetoric, in which the speaker attempts to exhort the audience to come to a decision on an important private or public concern.[38] Paul has been given a forum to proclaim the gospel in order to convince the philosophers to repent and turn to Jesus, whom God has appointed as the judge of the world (Acts 17:30-31). Religion was an accepted topic for a deliberative speech in Paul's day, so his audience would be disposed to listen to him.[39] His audience would expect his presentation to follow an established format: (1) introduction, (2) thesis, (3) narrative of facts on which the argument is built (although this was not always part of a deliberative speech), (4) argument, and (5) conclusion.[40] To be effective in his effort, Paul needed to use the accepted techniques of persuasive rhetoric, especially the attempt to evoke the good will of his audience.

In order to understand how the design of Paul's speech on the Areopagus relates to its intended purpose, we may compare it with his speech in the synagogue of Antioch in Pisidia (Acts 13:13-41), the first of the two evangelistic speeches by Paul presented in Acts. The speech is delivered before an audience of Jews and devout Gentile proselytes (Acts 13:42-43). Luke's order of these two speeches in Acts portrays Paul's missionary strategy, in which Paul continually proclaims the gospel first to a Jewish audience and then to Gentiles, even in Athens (Acts 17:16-17).[41] The main divisions of the speech in Antioch are signaled by introductory formulas,[42] and its structure and content, similar to the speech delivered by Peter on the day of Pentecost (Acts 2:14-36),[43] may be outlined as follows:

1. *Introduction* (Acts 13:16b-22): Paul recounts God's election of Israel and the history of its leadership, culminating in King David, of whom God

testifies, "I have found David, son of Jesse, to be a man after my heart, who will carry out all my wishes" (Ps 89:20; 1 Sm 13:14; Is 44:28).

2. *Thesis* (Acts 13:23-25): Paul asserts that Jesus, a descendant of David, is the savior of Israel, whose coming has been prepared for by John and his baptism of repentance.

3. *Narrative of Facts* (Acts 13:26-31): Paul declares that the message of salvation, foretold in prophecy, concerns the resurrection of Jesus, who was condemned by Jewish residents of Jerusalem and killed by the Roman governor Pilate, but after his resurrection appeared to his apostles, who now are his witnesses to the people.

4. *Argument* (Acts 13:32-37): Paul argues that Jesus is the promised savior from the line of David, because his resurrection fulfills the prophecies in Psalm 2:7, Isaiah 55:3, and Psalm 16:10.

5. *Conclusion* (Acts 13:38-41): Paul appeals to his audience to accept the forgiveness that comes through belief in Jesus and issues a warning from the prophet Habakkuk (1:5) that they not suffer the fate of their ancestors.

Christians today of Western European heritage, reviewing this speech, may take for granted its seamless flow of redemptive history from the hopes of Israel to their fulfillment in Jesus as the Davidic Messiah. After all, "The Messiah" of George Frederick Handel has been the centerpiece of the festal celebrations of Christmas and Easter in Western churches for over two centuries, and the Redeemer of Israel has become the Savior of the West. But this familiarity and identification with the subject matter should not blind Western interpreters to the careful way in which the rhetoric of the speech is designed to persuade its original audience, which consisted of Jews and Gentile proselytes. The introduction appeals to the good will of the listeners by reminding them of their heritage as the elect people of God and their hope that God would deliver them in the future from their bondage to foreign powers through a messiah from the line of David. The narrative of facts establishes recent events in their ancestral homeland, about which they may have heard, and then the argument supports the thesis by an appeal to prophecies in the Hebrew scriptures. The conclusion also makes use of the Hebrew scriptures to call the audience to a decision. The speech is thus about Jews and for Jews, presenting Jesus as he relates to Jewish national aspirations.

An outline of the structure and content of Paul's speech on the Areopagus (17:22-31) demonstrates how it is similar to the speech in Antioch in Pisidia in its appeal to the audience. The various divisions of the speech are not as clearly indicated by introductory formulas,[44] but a bracketing term identifies and frames the middle section (Acts 17:23: "What therefore you worship without knowing [*agnoountes*]"; 17:30: "So then God, having overlooked the times of ignorance [*agnoias*]"). Some recent analyses of the speech with respect to Greco-Roman rhetoric, while agreeing in general with the delimitation of the sections listed below, differ in the labeling of their content, preferring to identify Acts 17:24-29 as the argument and 17:30-31 as the conclusion, and omitting a section giving a narrative of facts.[45] As precedent for this, they cite statements in the ancient studies of rhetoric that a narrative of facts is not necessary in a deliberative speech.[46] Yet Quintilian (born c. 30-35 C.E.), the famous Roman rhetorician, does not rule out the use of a narrative of facts in a deliberative speech before a public assembly, as opposed to a private gathering, where it may "be necessary to set forth the order of the points which have to be treated."[47] This is especially needed in speeches where the authority of the speaker may be in question, "For he, who would have all men trust his judgment as to what is expedient and honorable, should both possess and be regarded as possessing genuine wisdom and excellence of character."[48] Paul certainly would have been in this position before the Stoic philosophers on the Areopagus. If, as will be shown below, the narrative of facts in Paul's speech demonstrates his homage to, rather than critique of, the "unknown god" of the Stoics, it would serve to establish his credentials before this august group. Moreover, there are some indications within the text of the speech itself that 17:30-31 begins the argument rather than the conclusion: it picks up a significant catchword from the thesis (17:23b: "without knowing [*agnoountes*]; 17:30: "the times of ignorance [*agnoias*]), which does not appear in 17:24-29, and uses the Greek word *pistis* in its technical rhetorical sense of a "proof" of an argument, rather than in its usual New Testament sense of "faith" (17:31: "supplying proof to all by raising him from the dead").[49] With these considerations in mind, we may outline the speech on the Areopagus as follows:

1. *Introduction* (Acts 17:22b-23a): Paul observes that the Athenians are extremely religious and focuses on one particular object of their worship, represented by an altar "To an Unknown [*agnôstô*] God."
2. *Thesis* (Acts 17:23b): Paul asserts that he will proclaim this object, which the Athenians reverence without knowing *(agnoountes)*.
3. *Narrative of Facts* (Acts 17:24-29): Paul lists what has been said by Greek philosophers about the "unknown god," whom Paul characterizes as God: (a) he is the creator of the cosmos, who does not live in shrines nor need anything from human beings; (b) he created from one stock all the nations of the human race, establishing seasons of the year and habitable zones, in order that they might seek for and perhaps apprehend him;[50] (c) he is close to us as human beings because "in him we live and move and have our being" (Epimenides?) and "we too are his offspring" (Aratus). He should not be compared to the images created by humans.
4. *Argument* (Acts 17:30-31): Paul argues that God is now commanding all people to repent because "the times of ignorance [*agnoias*]" have come to an end, that is, the time in which God has remained "unknown." God has set a time for the judgment of the world, and this will be accomplished through a man whom God has appointed, supplying proof *(pistis)* of this by raising him from the dead.
5. *Conclusion*: The speech is interrupted before the conclusion is reached (Acts 17:32-34).[51]

The first impression of this speech is that it appears to be designed to criticize the audience. In the introduction, when Paul refers to the Athenians being "extremely religious [*deisidaimonesterous*]" (Acts 17:22), he uses a term that could be translated "extremely superstitious." This is reminiscent of the famous character sketch of "The Superstitious Man [*deisidaimôn*]" by Theophrastus (c. 370-285 B.C.E.), which was a satire of popular Greek religion.[52] But this impression does not take into account the rhetorical strategy of a deliberative speech, in which it would not be in the best interest of the speaker to offend his audience. We have seen above that the Epicurean philosophers, if they were part of Paul's audience, would not be insulted by a characterization of Greek religion as superstition, and thus Paul might be using this apparently critical observation as means of establishing the good will of his audience, as he does in the introduction to his speech in the synagogue of Antioch in Pisidia. But since Paul's audience is likely to have included Stoics, who did have a respect for religious piety, he is probably capturing their attention in a less sarcastic way by introducing a topic, with which they would be familiar, on the misguided religiosity of the common people. In the latter part of the first century C.E., the Platonic philosopher Plutarch, in a similar fashion, attempted to reveal the dangers of popular superstition while at the same time avoiding the opposite extreme of Epicurean atheism. He begins his discourse, as does Paul, with a reference to ignorance: "Ignorance and blindness [*agnoias*] in regard to the gods divides itself at the very beginning into two streams, of which the one produces in hardened characters, as it were in stubborn soils, atheism, and the other in tender characters, as in moist soils, produces superstition [*deisidaimonian*]."[53] His concluding advice, following the Golden Mean of Aristotle, is that people should not plunge from one extreme to the other: "For thus it is that some persons, in trying to escape superstition, rush into a rough and hardened atheism, thus overleaping true religion which lies between."[54]

Paul's point of departure for his speech, using the altar "To an Unknown [*agnôstô*] God" to which he claims the Athenians show reverence "without knowing [*agnoountes*]" (Acts 17:23), also picks up a theme in Stoic philosophy.[55] On the occasion of the dedication of a famous statue of Zeus created by Pheidias at the Olympic Games in 97 C.E., the Stoic Dio Chrysostom gave an oration in which he used the image of the god as a springboard for a discourse on "the nature of the gods in general, and especially that of the ruler of the universe."[56] The knowledge of this supreme god, according to Dio Chrysostom, is "inevitable and innate in every creature endowed with reason, arising in the course of nature without the aid of human teacher and free from the deceit of any expounding priest." Thus he asks, "How, then, could they have remained ignorant [*agnôtes*] and conceived no inkling of him who had sowed and planted and was now preserving and nourishing them, when on every side they were filled with the divine nature through both sight and hearing, and in fact through every sense?"[57] The Stoic philosopher Epictetus (c. 55-135 C.E.) echoes the same sentiment: "You are a fragment of God; you have within you a part of Him. Why, then, are you ignorant [*agnoeis*] of your own kinship? . . . You are bearing God about with you, you poor wretch, and know it not!"[58] In the introduction to his speech on the Areopagus, Paul thus builds a bridge to his audience, even in what may seem to be critical remarks. In fact, the whole speech, with the exception of the argument, makes use of concepts of the supreme god familiar to Paul's Stoic listeners. Paul presents this god as the Christian God. This speech is therefore as much in tune with its intended audience as is the speech delivered to the synagogue in Antioch in Pisidia.

## THE CONTENT OF THE SPEECH

Concepts of God and God's relation to creation that appear in Paul's speech on the Areopagus can be found in the Hebrew Bible (e.g., Is 42:5, 8) and the traditions of hellenistic Judaism, as has been shown by many interpreters.[59] These sources of tradition would certainly have been formative for Paul's thinking and also for Luke's.[60] But as Martin Dibelius has forcefully argued, the way these concepts are phrased in the speech draws on the language of the Greco-Roman philosophical world, particularly the world of Stoicism, so that "what we have before us is a *hellenistic* speech about the true knowledge of God."[61] The parallels with Stoicism are not surprising, since, in the judgment of W. W. Tarn, "the philosophy of the Hellenistic world was the Stoa; all else was secondary."[62]

We have already observed how the introduction to the speech would capture the attention of Stoic philosophers, establishing good will by appealing to common concerns. We now consider how the rest of the speech reflects Stoic thinking not through a detailed comparison of the speech with Stoic terminology and thought,[63] but through the citation of a few important Stoic texts where the echoes of ideas in the speech can be seen to be transparent. Stoic theology was a form of pantheism, in which the supreme god was equated with the cosmos and could be referred to as "Nature [*physis*]."[64] But since the Stoics also held that the ruling force of the cosmos was reason *(logos)*, a distinctively human trait, they could personify this force with many divine names (for example, Zeus, as the supreme god), and thus expressed their belief in terms that often sounded similar to Jewish and Christian monotheism.[65] Stoic statements about the supreme god would thus have been a point of contact that Paul could use for a speech that would lead to the proclamation of Jesus as God's agent, appointed to judge the world.

In our brief survey of Stoic texts we call attention, first of all, to a deliberative speech by the Roman orator and philosopher Cicero (106-43 B.C.E.) that offers evidence that the statement of facts in Paul's speech (Acts 17:24-29) addresses the major points of Stoic belief about the gods. This speech by Cicero begins with a thesis that outlines the Stoic view of the gods under the following headings: "First they prove that gods exist; next they explain their nature; then they show that the world is governed by them; and lastly that they care for the fortunes of mankind."[66] The correspondence of these themes with what Paul has to say about God shows that he approaches this topic in the standard way that would have been expected by his audience. He thus establishes his credibility as one who should claim their attention.

Next we turn to the two philosophers who are actually quoted in the speech. We may pass over the first citation, "In him we live and move and have our being" (Acts 17:28), since it is not certain whether it comes from Epimenides (c. seventh or sixth century B.C.E.) or some other source, and its sentiment is expressed by a number of Stoic philosophers, as will be seen below.[67] But the second citation, "for we too are his offspring" (Acts 17:28), comes from a poem about celestial phenomena by the Stoic poet Aratus (c. 315-239 B.C.E.), which was widely known in the ancient world and deserves to be seen in its context. The poem personifies the supreme god of the Stoics with the name of Zeus, but Aristobulus of Alexandria, a hellenistic Jewish scholar of the second century B.C.E., saw this as a clear reference to God, the Lord of Israel, and thus felt free to change the name when he quoted the poem.[68] The introduction to the poem places the line cited by Paul in a context that includes the work of the supreme god in establishing the seasons:

> From Zeus let us begin; him do we mortals never
> leave unnamed;
> Full of Zeus are all the streets and all the
> marketplaces of men.
> And full is the sea and the havens thereof; always we
> all have need of Zeus.
> For we are also his offspring; and he in his kindness
> unto men giveth favourable signs
> And wakeneth the people to work, reminding them of
> livelihood.
> . . . . . . . . . . . . . . .
> For himself it was who set the signs in heaven
> And marked out the constellations, and for the year
> devised
> What stars chiefly should give to people right signs of
> the seasons,
> To the end that all things might grow unfailingly.
> Wherefore him do men ever worship first and last.
> Hail, O Father, mighty marvel, mighty blessing unto
> men,
> Hail to thee and to the Elder Race![69]

Another famous poem from the ancient world, which contains the phrase "we are your offspring," is the "Hymn to Zeus" by the Stoic philosopher Cleanthes (331-232 B.C.E.). In the lines of the poem selected here, the supreme god of the Stoics is again personified as Zeus, but he becomes an object of praise because of his providential ordering and unifying of the world, a theme also found in Paul's speech:

> Most majestic of immortals, many-titled, ever
> omnipotent Zeus,
> Prime mover of nature, who with your law steer all
> things,

> Hail to you. For it is proper for any mortal to address
>      you:
> We are your offspring, and alone of all mortal
>      creatures
> Which are alive and tread the earth we bear a likeness
>      to god.
> Therefore I shall hymn you and sing forever of your
>      might.
> All this cosmos, as it spins around the earth,
> Obeys you, whichever way you lead, and willingly
>      submits to your sway.[70]

Finally, we may cite the Stoic philosopher Epictetus, born at the height of Paul's missionary activity, who makes an impassioned appeal to his followers to look for God within their own being, rather than to an image made of silver or gold:

> You are a fragment of God; you have within you a part of Him. . . . Do you suppose that I am speaking of some external God, made of silver or gold? It is within yourself that you bear Him, and do not perceive that you are defiling him with impure thoughts and filthy actions. Yet in the presence of even an image of God you would not dare to do anything of the things you are now doing. But when God Himself is present within you, seeing and hearing everything, are you not ashamed to be thinking and doing such things as these, O insensible of your own nature and object of God's wrath?[71]

From these few examples, we can see how clearly Paul's speech on the Areopagus reflects the theological thinking of the Stoic philosophers. For the Stoics, the idea of the supreme god was innate in human beings and could be deduced, as argued by Dio Chrysostom, with the aid of "the poets, the lawgivers, . . . the creative artists [e.g., sculptors], . . . [and] the philosopher, the one who by means of reason interprets and proclaims the divine nature, most truly, perhaps, and most perfectly."[72] The speech on the Areopagus acknowledges the existence of general revelation and uses it as the basis for an evangelistic appeal.[73] Ironically, the "unknown god" is, in fact, the God who is known.

## THE REACTION TO THE SPEECH

In the opinion of W. R. Ramsey, "It would appear that Paul was disappointed and perhaps disillusioned by his experience in Athens. He felt that he had gone at least as far as was right in the way of presenting his doctrine in a form suited to the current philosophy; and the result had been little more than naught. When he went on from Athens to Corinth, he no longer spoke in the philosophic style."[74] But is this really the impression that Luke intends his readers to have at the conclusion of the story? Luke describes the reaction to Paul's speech as mixed, and then, significantly, names two of those who believed (Acts 17:32-34). This response, in fact, is much the same as the response to Paul's speech to the Jewish and Jewish-sympathizing audience in Antioch in Pisidia (Acts 13:42-52; cf. Acts 14:1-2, 4; 17:4-9; 28:24). Thus, Paul's effort should be judged a success.[75] The meeting is divided because that, as Luke wishes to show, is the result of the proclamation of the gospel, not only among Jews but also among Gentiles (Lk 2:25-35).[76]

## CONCLUSION

Since Luke offers only two evangelistic speeches by Paul in Acts, it is likely that he intends these as paradigms of how the evangelistic enterprise is to be carried out in different situations.[77] Paul's speech on the Areopagus is thus a model of how the gospel may be proclaimed in a cross-cultural situation where the traditions of Judaism (and in our day, Christianity) are foreign. It validates the theological concept of general revelation and shows how it may be pressed into the service of the missionary task.

When I present this reading of Paul's speech to my Korean students, I find that it comforts them. They are part of a culture that values antiquity, and they are relieved to find in this speech a precedent for honoring the traditions of their ancestors while at the same time being faithful in the proclamation of the gospel. Paul's speech provides courage for them to move forward with this task, as they follow the lead of Asian theologians like Khiok-Khng Yeo, who uses the speech as a springboard for a creative dialogue between Christianity and Chinese Taoism.[78]

The further issue raised by Paul's speech—how theologians can use the traditions of cultures foreign to Judaism and Christianity to provide insights for further development of Christian theology—is too large to be considered here, but it is nonetheless important. As James Barr suggests, "Since the Bible itself built its account of revelation, at least in part, upon beliefs and principles of its own people and those of their ancestors and neighbors, it should not be surprising if modern theology has to do the same in relation to the beliefs and principles of our own time."[79] The early church of the post-apostolic age entered quickly into dialogue with Greco-Roman philosophy, although this was a controversial move not without its dangers, as witnessed by Tertullian's famous cry, "What indeed has Athens to do with Jerusalem?"[80] No less controversial was the engagement of the early Nestorian missionaries in China with the religions there.[81] In our postmodern world, however, as Western theologians are becoming more aware of the influence of Western traditions on their theological formulations, Asian theologians need to be liberated from overly Westernized forms of theology, especially when their own cultural traditions are in many ways more in tune with the ancient values of biblical cultures and thus can provide insights for the development of theology.[82] Creative efforts to move forward in this dialogue, which are now going on, are thus a great service to the church and its mission to the world.[83]

## REFERENCES

[1] S. V. Hur and B. S. Hur, *Culture Shock! Korea,* rev. ed. (Portland, Oreg.: Graphic Arts Center, 1993), 23-29, 39-43, 88-92; J. Y. Lee, *Korean Preaching: An Interpretation* (Nashville, Tenn.: Abingdon, 1997), 34-40.

[2] R. T. Ames and H. Rosemont Jr., trans., *The Analects of Confucius: A Philosophical Translation* (New York: Ballentine, 1998), 74, 93 (Sayings 1.11; 4.20).

[3] Hur and Hur, *Culture Shock! Korea,* 29.

[4] G. T. Brown and S. Rhee, "Korea," in *A Dictionary of Asian Christianity,* ed. S. W. Sunquist (Grand Rapids, Mich.: Eerdmans, 2001), 446-449.

[5] Ames and Rosemont, *Analects,* 189 (Saying 15.24); cf. Confucian Sayings 4.15; 5.12; 6.30; 12.2; Tb 4:15; Mt 7:12; Babylonian Talmud, *Shabbat* 31a (Rabbi Hillel); Targum Yerushalmi I on Leviticus 19:18.

[6] James Barr, *Biblical Faith and Natural Theology* (Oxford: Clarendon, 1993), 1.

[7] Friedrich Schleiermacher, however, did not characterize his program as natural theology (*The Christian Faith* [Edinburgh: T. & T. Clark, 1928], 44-52 [§10]; cf. Barr, *Biblical Faith and Natural Theology,* 106).

[8] The English translation of the debate was published as E. Brunner and K. Barth, *Natural Theology,* ed. J. Baillie (London: Bles, 1946).

[9] Barr, *Biblical Faith and Natural Theology,* 2-20.

[10] Ibid., 1.

[11] Ibid., 19.

[12] Ibid., 5.

[13] Influential studies of the speech that have appeared in English are M. Dibelius, "Paul on the Areopagus," in *Studies in the Acts of the Apostles,* ed. H. Greeven (London: SCM Press, 1956), 26-77, who compares it to Stoic ideas; N. B. Stonehouse, *The Areopagus Address* (London: Tyndale, 1949; reprinted as *Paul before the Areopagus and Other New Testament Studies,* Grand Rapids, Mich.: Eerdmans, 1957, 1-40), who finds the background in the Old Testament; and B. Gärtner, *The Areopagus Speech and Natural Religion* (Lund: Gleerup, 1955), who relates it to Hellenistic-Jewish traditions. K. Barth's exegetical analysis, which denies the presence of any natural theology, is in *Church Dogmatics,* vol. 2.1 (Edinburgh: T. & T. Clark, 1957), 117-123.

[14] Dio Chrysostom, *Discourses* 8.9, describing Corinth. Unless otherwise noted, the translations of ancient sources are from the Loeb Classical Library (Cambridge, Mass.: Harvard University Press).

[15] Diogenes Laertius, *Lives of Eminent Philosophers* 7.5; Pausanius, *Description of Greece* 1.15.

[16] Plato, *Apology* §17c; Xenophon, *Memorabilia* 1.1.10; Diogenes Laertius, *Lives of Eminent Philosophers* 2.21. Cf. Ernst Haenchen, *The Acts of the Apostles: A Commentary* (Philadelphia: Westminster, 1971), 517; K. O. Sandnes, "Paul and Socrates: The Aim of Paul's Areopagus Speech," *Journal for the Study of the New Testament* 50 (1993), 21.

[17] Diogenes Laertius, *Lives of Eminent Philosophers* 10.10, 16-17.

[18] Translation from the Bible in this chapter generally follows the NRSV, but when it does not, it is the author's own.

[19] The Greek term *dialegomai,* "argue" (Acts 17:17), is used to refer to the teaching methods of philosophers (Plutarch, *Cicero* 24.5; Diogenes Laertius, *Lives of Eminent Philosophers* 2.20, 45, 122), and *symballô,* "debate" (Acts 17:18), can mean "dispute" (cf. Haenchen, *The Acts of the Apostles,* 517; Sandnes, "Paul and Socrates," 21). The

traditional name, Luke, will be used for the author of the two-volume work, the Gospel according to Luke and the Acts of the Apostles.

[20] *Discourses* 32.9, trans. A. J. Malherbe, *Paul and the Popular Philosophers* (Minneapolis, Minn.: Fortress Press, 1989), 151.

[21] Haenchen, *The Acts of the Apostles*, 517. See examples in A. A. Long and D. N. Sedley, *The Hellenistic Philosophers*, vol. 1, *Translations of the Principal Sources, with Philosophical Commentary* (Cambridge: Cambridge University Press, 1987), 139-149 (§23).

[22] *Discourses* 12.36-37.

[23] *On the Nature of the Universe* 1.63-80, trans. R. E. Latham, *Lucretius: On the Nature of the Universe*, Penguin Classics (Harmondsworth: Penguin, 1951), 29; cf. 5.146-155, 1161-1225; 6.68-79. Cf. also C. K. Barrett, "Paul's Speech on the Areopagus," in *New Testament Christianity for Africa and the World*, Festschrift for H. Sawyerr, ed. M. E. Glasswell and E. W. Fasholé-Luke (London: S.P.C.K., 1974), 74-75, 77, who also cites Epicurus, *Letter to Menoeceus* 123-124, and Plutarch, *Superstition*, which appears to be a critique of Epicurus.

[24] Haenchen, *The Acts of the Apostles*, 517-518. See examples in Long and Sedley, *The Hellenistic Philosophers*, 274-279 (§46).

[25] *Homilies on the Acts of the Apostles* 38.1, trans. in *Nicene and Post-Nicene Fathers*, ed. P. Schaff, series 1, vol. 11 (Buffalo, N.Y.: Christian Literature Publishing Company, 1886-1889).

[26] Haenchen, *The Acts of the Apostles*, 518.

[27] *Memorabilia* 1.1.1; cf. Plato, *Apology* §24b; idem, *Euthyphro* §3b; Diogenes Laertius, *Lives of Eminent Philosophers* 2.40. Further echoes are found in Acts 17:20, where the Stoics say, "For you bring [*eisphereis*] strange things to our ears," and 17:21, where the Athenians "spend their time in nothing but telling or hearing something new [*kainoteron*]." Josephus relates that the indictment by which the Athenians put a priestess to death concerned "foreign gods [*xenous . . . theous*]" (*Against Apion* 2.37 §§262-8). Cf. Haenchen, *The Acts of the Apostles*, 518; Sandnes, "Paul and Socrates," 21-22.

[28] Plato, *Euthyphro* §2a; cf. Pausanius, *Description of Greece* 1.3.1. Cf. C. J. Hemer, "Paul at Athens: A Topographical Note," *New Testament Studies* 20 (1974), 345.

[29] Demosthenes, *Against Aristogeiton* 25.22-3. T. D. Barnes argues, on the basis of statements by second-century C.E. writers Aelius Aristides, Pausanias, and Lucian, that the Council of the Areopagus still met on the Hill of Ares in Paul's day ("An Apostle on Trial," *Journal of Theological Studies* n.s. 20 [1969], 407-419), but Hemer suggests that both venues were used, citing the recent archaeological discovery of the King's Colonnade in Athens ("Paul at Athens," 341-350).

[30] K. Lake and H. J. Cadbury, *The Beginnings of Christianity*, ed. F. J. Foakes Jackson (New York: Macmillan, 1933), 4:212-213. The Greek participle *epilabomenoi*, translated "took" above, can also mean "seized" (Acts 16:19; 18:17; 21:30, 33; cf. Lk 20:20, 26; 23:26). W. R. Ramsey envisaged an address before the council, rather than a formal trial, which could have been observed by onlookers in the marketplace (*St. Paul the Traveller and the Roman Citizen*, 3d ed. [New York: Putnam's Sons, 1898], 243-247).

[31] Cf. Demosthenes, *Philippics* 1.10; Thucydides, *The Peloponnesian War* 3.38.5.

[32] See Acts 4:1-22; 5:17-42; 6:8-7:60; 16:16-39; 17:5-9; 18:12-17; 21:27-22:29; 22:30-23:10; 24:1-23; 25:6-12; 25:23-26:32.

[33] For other instances of *epilambanomai* meaning "take" rather than "seize," see Lk 9:47; 14:4; 23:19.

[34] Pausanius, *Description of Greece* 1.28.5; cf. Dibelius, "Paul on the Areopagus," 67-69.

[35] Fragment 11, trans. D. G. Rice and J. E. Stambaugh, *Sources for the Study of Greek Religion* (Missoula, Mont.: Scholars Press, 1979), 31.

[36] Cf. Pausanius, *Description of Greece* 1.17-19.

[37] *The Education of Children* 10 (*Moralia* §7d-f).

[38] Aristotle, *Rhetoric* 1.3 §§1358a-1359a; 1.4-8 §§1359a-1366a; Anaximenes of Lampsacus, *Rhetoric to Alexander* 1 §§1421b-1423a; 29-35 §§1436a-1440b; Quintilian, *On the Education of the Orator* 3.4, 8. Cf. D. Zweck, "The *Exordium* of the Areopagus Speech, Acts 17.3, 23," *New Testament Studies* 35 (1989), 94-103; K.-K. Yeo, "A Rhetorical Study of Acts 17.22-31: What Has Jerusalem to Do with Athens and Beijing?" *Jian Dao* 1 (1994), 77-78. G. A. Kennedy, who argues that the situation calls for a judicial (*dikanikos*) speech, admits that the goal of the speech is deliberative (*New Testament Interpretation through Rhetorical Criticism* [Chapel Hill, N.C.: University of North Carolina Press, 1984], 129).

[39] Anaximenes of Lampsacus, *Rhetoric to Alexander* 2 §1423a; Quintilian, *On the Education of the Orator* 3.8.15, 29. Cf. Zweck, "The *Exordium* of the Areopagus Speech, Acts 17.3, 23," 98.

[40] Aristotle, *Rhetoric* 3.13 §§1414a-b; Quintilian, *On the Education of the Orator* 3.8.6-13, 59-60. Cf. Kennedy, *New Testament Interpretation through Rhetorical Criticism*, 24.

[41] J. Jervell, *Luke and the People of God: A New Look at Luke-Acts* (Minneapolis, Minn.: Augsburg, 1972), 41-74.

[42] Acts 13:16: "Men, Israelites and you who fear God, listen"; 13:26: "Men, brothers, sons of the family of Abraham and those among you who fear God"; 13:32: "And we proclaim good news to you concerning the promise that came to the fathers that . . . "; 13:38: "Let it be known to you, therefore, men, brothers, that. . . . " Acts 13:23 is not introduced by a formula, but it begins a new sentence and is clearly the thesis of the speech.

[43] M. D. Goulder, *Type and History in Acts* (London: S.P.C.K., 1964) 83; C. H. Talbert, *Literary Patterns, Theological Themes and the Genre of Luke-Acts* (Missoula, Mont.: Scholars Press, 1974), 23-26; Gerhard A. Krodel, *Acts* (Philadelphia: Fortress Press, 1981), 47-55.

[44] Acts 17:22: "Men, Athenians"; 17:30: "So then . . . "; cf. Haenchen, *The Acts of the Apostles*, 525.

[45] Zweck, "The *Exordium* of the Areopagus Speech, Acts 17.3, 23," 96-101; Yeo, however, finds a narrative of facts in verse 23a ("A Rhetorical Study of Acts 17.22-31, 77-80").

[46] Aristotle, *Rhetoric* 3.13.3 §1414a; 3.16.11 §1417b; Quintilian, *On the Education of the Orator* 3.8.10. Cf. Zweck, "The *Exordium* of the Areopagus Speech, Acts 17.3, 23," 95.

[47] Quintilian, *On the Education of the Orator* 3.8.11; cf. 3.8.59-60; Anaximenes of Lampsacus, *Rhetoric to Alexander* 30 §§1438-b.

[48] Quintilian, *On the Education of the Orator* 3.8.13.

[49] Cf. Aristotle, *Rhetoric* 3.13.4 §1414b; Anaximenes of Lampsacus, *Rhetoric to Alexander* 32 §§1438b-1439b.

[50] This reading, which highlights the parallels with Greco-Roman thought, follows Dibelius, "Paul on the Areopagus," 27-37. For a contrasting interpretation, which understands the text to speak, in more Jewish terms, of "historical epochs" and a "boundary-

line drawn between two inhabited areas [i.e., nations]," see Gärtner, *The Areopagus Speech and Natural Religion,* 145-161.

⁵¹ Dibelius, "Paul on the Areopagus," 57.

⁵² *Characters* 16.

⁵³ *Superstition* 1 (*Moralia* §164e).

⁵⁴ Ibid., 14 (*Moralia* §171f).

⁵⁵ Altars to unknown gods in Athens are mentioned by Pausanius, *Description of Greece* 1.1.4; Philostratus, *Life of Apollonius of Tyana* 6.3.5.

⁵⁶ *Discourses* 12.27; cf. 12.12, 16, 21.

⁵⁷ Ibid., 12.27, 29; cf. 12:36.

⁵⁸ *Discourses* 2.8.11-12.

⁵⁹ E.g., Stonehouse, *Paul before the Areopagus and Other New Testament Studies,* 25-31; Gärtner, *The Areopagus Speech and Natural Religion,* 144-202; S. G. Wilson, *The Gentiles and the Gentile Mission in Luke-Acts* (Cambridge: Cambridge University Press, 1973), 198-210.

⁶⁰ Cf. J. D. G. Dunn, *The Theology of the Paul the Apostle* (Grand Rapids, Mich.: Eerdmans, 1998), 27-50 (§2); J. Jervell, *The Theology of the Acts of the Apostles* (Cambridge: Cambridge University Press, 1996), 1-25; Barr, *Biblical Faith and Natural Theology,* 21-57.

⁶¹ "Paul on the Areopagus," 57.

⁶² W. W. Tarn, *Hellenistic Civilization,* 3d ed. rev. W. W. Tarn and G. T. Griffith (New York: New American Library, 1952), 325, cited in Barrett, "Paul's Speech on the Areopagus," 76 n. 13.

⁶³ For this, see Dibelius, "Paul on the Areopagus," 27-57.

⁶⁴ Diogenes Laertius, *Lives of Eminent Philosophers* 7.148-149.

⁶⁵ Ibid., 7.135-136, 147; cf. A. A. Long, *Hellenistic Philosophy: Stoics, Epicureans, Sceptics,* 2d ed. (Berkeley and Los Angeles: University of California Press, 1986), 147-150.

⁶⁶ *On the Nature of the Gods* 2.4, cited in Zweck, "The *Exordium* of the Areopagus Speech, Acts 17.3, 23," 99.

⁶⁷ The statement is only indirectly attributed to Epimenides by the ninth-century C.E. Nestorian bishop Isho'dad in a commentary on Acts (Dibelius, "Paul on the Areopagus," 48-50).

⁶⁸ Fragment 4 (from Eusebius, *Preparation for the Gospel* 13.13.7), in *The Old Testament Pseudepigrapha,* vol. 2, ed. J. H. Charlesworth (Garden City, N.Y.: Doubleday, 1985), 841.

⁶⁹ *Phaenomena,* lines 1-16 (translation versified by the present author).

⁷⁰ Long and Sedley, *The Hellenistic Philosophers,* 326-327 (translations versified by the present author).

⁷¹ *Discourses* 2.8.11-14. Cf. Dio Chrysostom, *Discourses* 12.52, 59, 80, 83, although he is honoring a statue of Zeus. D. L. Balch cites traditions in Plutarch, *Superstition* 6 (*Moralia* §167d-e), and Strabo, *Geography* 16.2.35-9, which may be attributed to the influential Stoic Posidonius (c. 135-50 B.C.E.), that oppose images of God ("The Areopagus Speech: An Appeal to the Stoic Historian Posidonius against Later Stoics and the Epicureans," in *Greeks, Romans, and Christians,* Festschrift for A. J. Malherbe, ed. D. L. Balch [Minneapolis, Minn.: Fortress Press, 1990], 67-72).

⁷² *Discourses* 12.47.

⁷³ Balch also cites traditions from Posidonius that may indicate that Paul's warning of divine judgment had parallels in Stoic thought ("The Areopagus Speech," 58-67).

[74] *St. Paul the Traveller,* 252.

[75] Haenchen, *The Acts of the Apostles,* 526.

[76] Cf. Jervell, *Luke and the People of God,* 41-74.

[77] Dibelius, "Paul on the Areopagus," 72-77.

[78] Yeo, "A Rhetorical Study of Acts 17.22-31," 100-106.

[79] *Biblical Faith and Natural Theology,* 221. Barr makes a further appeal for a biblical theology built upon a broader base in *The Concept of Biblical Theology: An Old Testament Perspective* (Minneapolis, Minn.: Fortress Press, 1999).

[80] *Prescription against Heretics* 7.

[81] S. H. Moffett, *A History of Christianity in Asia,* vol. 1, *Beginnings to 1500* (Maryknoll, N.Y.: Orbis Books, 1998), 302-314.

[82] A corrective to overly Western readings of the Bible is found in B. J. Malina, *The New Testament World: Insights from Cultural Anthropology,* 3d ed. (Louisville, Ky.: Westminster/John Knox Press, 2001).

[83] An example is Andrew Sung Park's use of the Korean concept of *han* for understanding the Christian doctrine of atonement and reconciliation (*The Wounded Heart of God: The Asian Concept of Han and the Christian Doctrine of Sin* [Nashville, Tenn.: Abingdon, 1993]; see also idem, *Racial Conflict and Healing: An Asian-American Theological Perspective* [Maryknoll, N.Y.: Orbis Books, 1996]).

# 20

## *The Art of Finishing Well: Paul as Servant Leader*

ACTS 18:1–28 AND 20:17–38

### Grace Preedy Barnes

My father, Clarence Preedy, was a British pioneer-style missionary with the China Inland Mission back in the 1930s. He and my mother were both raised as missionary kids in China. They met in China, my father from England and my mother from the United States. Their children, the four of us, were also raised as MKs (missionary kids), three of us born in China, one in the Philippines during World War II, where we were captured and held for over three years. Following the war and some rest time in the United States and England, we eventually returned to China until the communists took over. Our father, held for three years until he was finally released, joined us in the United States during the 1950s. My parents finally settled in the United States, working with a couple of other mission organizations, teaching and working in their training schools. My dad eventually died at the age of 86. I was privileged to be with him during the last week of his life. During a conversation about our family, I was able to tell him the impact he had had on my life. Because of our many separations, his war experiences, and his own tendency to be a private person, he often felt he was not a good father. In many ways he was not ideal, but the way he lived his life, his principles, and his commitments to God and to China were exemplary. He taught many young people with his life, preaching and teaching both in Bible school courses and missionary boot-camp training. After his death we found that he had been corresponding with about three hundred people, many who were former students and whom he had discipled and mentored both in person and through letters. He continued to be about God's work to the end of his life.

The passages of Acts 18—20 about Paul remind me of my dad. Both were strong leaders, plunged daringly into new contexts, faced many trials and sufferings, made mistakes along the way, but were faithful to God's mission until the end. One ought to be able, like Paul, to come to the end of one's life and ministry and be able to rehearse their integrity.

Studies on leadership in recent decades, however, have shown that biblical, historical, and contemporary leaders do not tend to finish well for a variety of reasons: unexpected difficulties, trials, death of loved ones, moral or discipline problems, disillusionment, learning or growth plateaus, and lack of mentoring. In contrast, Paul's farewell address to the elders at Ephesus demonstrates how a leader finishes well (20:17ff.). Even though Paul had sinned boldly as a young man and made mistakes along the way, he demonstrated how he had lived and worked with them. In humility, tears, and empathy, he continually warned them of possible dangers (20:19). He tried to serve them by being helpful and teaching them publicly; traveling house to house he built relationships in various contexts (20:20). He believed he was called to both Jews and Gentiles and was faithful to the gospel of faith in Jesus Christ through repentance (20:21). He was a discipler, a mentor, and a friend. Not only willing to serve but to commit to the unknown, Paul exhorted leaders to watch over the flock as well as themselves. Personal leadership development is as important as leading others and necessary for effective servant leadership (20:25-31). As we will explore later, he provided for his own needs and worked with people incarnationally rather than expecting them to take care of his needs. Paul was not a burden to his followers. One of the paradoxes of scripture is the principle that says "in giving we receive" (20:32-35). Paul's leadership model affirms the principles that I gained in my work with Young Life. It is important to explore people beneath the surface in the following ways:

1. Go where people are.
2. Win the right to be heard.
3. Learn their language (what communicates to them).
4. Share the gospel in life and words.

Paul's life profoundly influenced the church at Ephesus and its elders. They shared an emotional goodbye, praying and weeping together. He and they knew that danger lay ahead for Paul and that they would not see him again (20:36-38). But Paul knew that he could leave the work in their hands. He knew he could trust them to continue and develop future leaders, as he had done for them. Struggles and persecutions would be a continual part of Paul's life and work. This was promised by the Holy Spirit (20:22-23). Servant leadership is costly, and Paul's followers had seen him handle the difficult situations that came into his life. What a marvelous example for them to follow.

My personal interest in the subject of servant leadership began twenty years ago when I was asked to teach a course entitled "Exploration into Servant Leadership" as part of Azusa Pacific University's overseas master's degree in leadership studies, called Operation Impact, which is offered worldwide primarily to missionaries and other Christian workers. In researching this topic I placed myself on the mailing list for such groups as The Robert K. Greenleaf Center, the Servant Society, and the Servant Leadership School at the Church of the

Saviour in Washington, D.C. I began to discover a network of people not only interested in living out these ideas but also in applying them to organizational settings.

Even though the concepts of servanthood and leadership were familiar to me and had biblical roots, I was surprised to find that the term *servant leadership* was initiated through the vision and works of Robert K. Greenleaf, who was employed by AT&T for many years. In his later years he became an organizational consultant to educational, business, and religious institutions. Greenleaf once read a story that profoundly affected what he saw as a crisis in leadership. The story that he read was in Herman Hesse's *Journey to the East*, a book often read by university students during the turbulent times of the late 1960s.

> In this story we see a band of men on a mythical journey probably also Hesse's own journey. The central figure of the story is Leo who accompanies the party as the *servant* who does their menial chores, but also sustains them with his spirit and his song. He is a person of extraordinary presence. All goes well until Leo disappears. Then the group falls into disarray and the journey is abandoned. They cannot make it without the *servant* Leo. The narrator, one of the party, after some years of wandering finds Leo and is taken into the Order that had sponsored the journey. There he discovers that Leo, whom he had known first as *servant*, was in fact the titular head of the Order, its guiding spirit, a great and noble *leader*.[1]

Greenleaf responded with a desire to serve and began promoting a leadership style in which one leads by serving. Even after his death Greenleaf's books and essays are still being read, and many "followers" are writing about the paradoxical nature of servant leadership.

Greenleaf observed that the idea of the servant is deep in Judeo-Christian heritage. The Bible lists over thirteen hundred references to "servant," "serve," and "service." There are numerous illustrations of servant leadership in the Old and New Testaments. Two types of servant leadership emerge. One seems to represent those on the lower rung or who are the weak in society and are later lifted up like Esther, Rahab, David, Ruth, and Timothy. The more common are those who started out on the higher levels of society and were "forced into servant-learning school" by God, either through being sent to the wilderness, being thrown into prison, or being blinded, such as Moses, Joseph, and Paul. Some, like the disciples, had to change course and experience what it meant to serve before they could lead in God's kingdom. Even Jesus spent time in the desert. The scriptural pattern seems to start with servant learning and then is followed by the influence of leadership that comes through experience, maturity, and a desire to serve.

The focus for this chapter is on Paul as servant leader and his philosophy of leadership development that led him to finish his life well. Paul had a great deal of motivation to imitate his primary leadership model, that of Jesus Christ, but he also had freedom to build the church of Christ throughout the world without any previous models outside of Judaism.

## PAUL SERVED ALONGSIDE ORDINARY PEOPLE (ACTS 18:1-23)

In Acts 18:1-3 Paul met and stayed with Aquila and Priscilla, fellow Jews and fellow tentmakers. Paul is depicted working in a secular trade alongside fellow Jewish believers in Christ, providing for his own needs rather than expecting others to support his ministry. He was called to be a partner in God's work; his ability to work at a skill allowed him to live with and identify with common people.[2] Paul served as a steward of God's message. This indicated a life principle from his rabbinic days, when students adopted a trade so that they did not need to depend on their teaching for financial support.[3] In fact, James D. G. Dunn observes: "'Working with one's hands' was quite acceptable in rabbinic circles, but would generally be regarded as beneath the dignity of the well-to-do."[4] Thus, as a servant, Paul counter-culturally placed himself alongside ordinary people. While the reader might assume that Paul roved about looking for people to argue with (18:4), archeology reveals that tentmaking stalls tended to be in or near markets in Corinth, allowing ample opportunity for Paul to engage with those who passed by or sought to do business. Thus Paul probably shared his faith naturally while at work.[5] This suggests another emerging principle: All work is sacred if done unto the Lord and for God's purposes in this world.

In the religiously pluralistic context of Corinth, Paul entered the synagogues and sought to "convince" Jews and Greeks, but in particular testified to Jews that Jesus was the Messiah (18:4-5). Unfortunately, he received an abusive response and "shook the dust from his clothes," declaring, "Your blood on your own heads!" Then he moved on to the Gentiles (18:6). On the surface one might conclude that Paul did not "finish well" in the Corinthian synagogue. However, Paul maintained in 18:4 what had become an established pattern of going first to the synagogues to provide opportunities for Jews to respond to Christ (18:5; cf. 13:14; 14:1; 17:1-2). Furthermore, after a hostile response, in spite of his harsh rebuke, he began a congregation next door to the synagogue in the house of Titius Justus, likely a Gentile, as indicated by his Roman name (18:7). Moving in next door to the synagogue may not seem the way to make good relations, but the narrative continues in recapping Paul's bold move by stating that the synagogue official, Crispus, "became a believer in the Lord, together with all his household" and that "many of the Corinthians who heard Paul became believers and were baptized" (18:8). Clearly, Paul continued to be a servant of all—Jews and Gentiles.

The text indicates Paul's eagerness to contexualize by entering into the home of a Gentile coupled with Paul's eagerness to continue to minister to Jews of the synagogue. Furthermore, Paul did not cease his pattern of entering into the synagogue in the subsequent cities he would visit (see 18:19). William Neil concludes that Paul's new headquarters in the home of a Gentile beside a hostile synagogue "was not an act of provocation on the part of Paul, but a suitable venue for easy contact with the Gentiles who frequented the synagogue as 'God-fearers.'"[6]

## PAUL REPRODUCED SERVANT DISCIPLES

The city of Corinth, one of the largest, most prosperous, and cosmopolitan cities in Greece in the 50s c.e., contained people who were transient or new, providing Paul with an excellent opportunity to evangelize people from a variety of contexts.[7] Evangelism was not the final word for Paul, however, but the beginning stage of discipleship. After spending a year and a half in Corinth (18:11), Paul made his way back to Antioch, his home base. After spending some time there, "he departed and went from place to place through the region of Galatia and Phrygia, strengthening all the disciples" (Acts 18:23). In "strengthening all the disciples," Paul modeled the Christian lifestyle and encouraged others by revisiting and reinforcing the believers who had become part of the churches during his earlier mission journey. This produced a reproduction and multiplication of disciples. Paul's disciples also modeled and reproduced, becoming "an example to all the believers in Macedonia and in Achaia," as indicated in 1 Thessalonians 1:7-8, so that "the word of the Lord has sounded forth from you not only in Macedonia and Achaia, but in every place your faith in God has become known."

In several introductions to his epistles Paul refers to himself as an apostle or as a servant of Christ Jesus and refers at times to Timothy and himself as servants. It thus appears that in Paul's mind an apostle was also a servant. This brings the aspects of servant and leader together. He named his disciples as co-authors and co-servants with him in his letters. There does not seem to be a sense of hierarchy in Paul's writings. Rather, he assumes that an apostle or leader is also a servant of Jesus Christ. His high sense of calling to serve was what seemed to propel him to endure a multitude of afflictions and misunderstandings. He drew people alongside him in this calling. We know from his letters that Paul and his multiplying network of disciples specifically encouraged others to serve the Lord, each other, and strangers:

> Let love be genuine; hate what is evil, hold fast to what is good; love one another with mutual affection; outdo one another in showing honor. Do not lag in zeal, be ardent in spirit, *serve* the Lord. Rejoice in hope, be patient in suffering, persevere in prayer. Contribute to the needs of the saints, extend hospitality to strangers. (Rom 12:9-13)

## PAUL EMPOWERED MALE AND FEMALE DISCIPLES AS SERVANT LEADERS (ACTS 18:24-26)

Two of Paul's Corinthian disciples, Priscilla and Aquila, while faithfully attending the synagogue, heard Apollos speak eloquently on the scriptures and on Jesus with burning enthusiasm, but Apollos "knew only the baptism of John" (Acts 18:25). So Priscilla and Aquila "took him aside and explained the Way of God to him more accurately" (18:26). Priscilla's name occurs before Aquila's in the context of teaching a prominent man. The translators of the King James

Version, unable to cope with a woman's leadership role in explaining God's truth more accurately to a man, reversed the order and put Aquila's name first. However, in the Greek, and reflected in modern translations, Priscilla's name appears first. This demonstrates that Paul not only was a servant to all but allowed women and men to serve together, to teach and even prophesy to one another in the context of community, whether male or female (cf. 1 Cor 11:5; Gal 3:26-29; Acts 21:8-9). Just as Paul empowered men for ministry, so he empowered women. The empowerment came through the work of the Holy Spirit and the practice of spiritual gifts (see Rom 12; Eph 4:11-16; 1 Cor 12; 1 Tm 4:14). His emphasis on the Holy Spirit is evident in the next chapter of Acts, when Paul passed through Ephesus and discovered disciples who had not received the Holy Spirit when they became believers. Then he laid hands on them, and they began to practice the spiritual gifts, in this case tongues and prophecy (19:1-6). Paul emphasized striving for and excelling in spiritual gifts that build up the church (1 Cor 14:12). The use of spiritual gifts to build up and empower others is consistent with Paul's emphasis on service to the body of Christ. Paul selected leaders according to giftedness rather than position and title.

Paul's evident focus on being a servant apostle (leader) of God on behalf of others is supported and endorsed by some of the more current writings about Paul. For example, in 1993 the Evangelical Covenant Church in the United States published a two-volume series entitled *Servant Leadership* as a review on the subject of authority and governance referencing Paul's writings as part of the foundational basis for discussing leadership today. It expresses that "the New Testament emphasis on servanthood is one of the most consistent and overarching components of the Christian message" and observes that "servant texts that were understood as referring to Jesus are elsewhere in the New Testament applied to Paul and other Christians." It further states that

> such servant living is not limited to the laity; it is required first of leaders, not as some special feat or task, but only as one example of what is required of every believer. Servant-Leadership is merely the application of the dynamic of the gospel to the task of leadership.[8]

We have observed that authentic ministry occurs in the service of the gospel by the entire body of Christ through the gifts of the church that edify the church within particular contexts. Authority and leadership, as demonstrated and delegated by Paul, are not based on fixed structures or lofty titles but on an incarnational presence in relational contexts of ministry.[9]

Paul's ability to teach, equip, and turn over was evident throughout his church-planting days. His model is a catalyst for the servant-leadership focus on the group and its ownership. Roland Allen eloquently expresses Paul's ability to lead in this way by example:

> He [Paul] did not establish a constitution, he inculcated principles. He did not introduce any practice to be received on his own or any human authority, he strove to make his converts realize and understand its relation to

Christ. He always aimed at convincing their minds and stirring their consciences. He never sought to enforce their obedience by decree; he always strove to win their heartfelt approval and their intelligent cooperation. He never proceeded by command, but always by persuasion. He never did things for them, he always left them to do things for themselves. He set them an example according to the mind of Christ, and he was persuaded that the Spirit of Christ in them would teach them to approve that example and inspire them to follow it.[10]

Discipleship means to serve one another in love. Every member was responsible for each other. This was revolutionary. Greatness was achieved through service. Paul built on the concepts of Jesus and further developed the idea of service:

> His [Paul's] aim was to confirm, encourage, and strengthen the fellowship. . . . It was not to rebuke or to show his authority or to have his personal way. It is unfair to Paul to picture him as a stern man who had no feeling for the deep needs of people. The Corinthians admitted that he was humble when he was with them. . . . He was careful not to give "commands."[11]

## SERVANT LEADERSHIP GIVES CREDIBILITY

In *The Servant as Leader* Greenleaf identified servant leaders as those who are seekers, listeners, able to withdraw and reorient themselves, accepting, tolerant of imperfection, having a sense of the unknowable, intuitive, live by faith, have foresight; they are disturbers and awakeners, healers; they create dangerously and are fully human. "The servant-leader is functionally superior" because the servant leader "is closer to the ground," and "hears things, sees things, knows things" with intuitive and exceptional insight that makes the servant leader "dependable and trusted."[12] Paul, I believe, exemplified these characteristics in his life and in the way he developed his ministry with people.

In 1987 Mark V. Attard, Procurator General, gave an inspirational address in which he identified the great leader as a "servant" foremost:

> In their own silent, hidden and unobtrusive way, *servant-leaders* get things done while making the followers feel that they accomplished it all by themselves. . . . *Servant-leaders* influence through example and convince by their presence . . . characterized by interdependence, mutual responsibility, collegiality and creativity. It is plural in such a way that interdependent group decision-making becomes a normal process, where communal consensus transcends the individual's opinion and *leadership* is always exercised with others in a corporate way. It is such *leadership* that sustains trust and guarantees credibility.[13]

I believe that Paul demonstrated this style of leadership when he established churches, selected and trained leaders, and left them to govern themselves.

Paul's impressive servant-leadership-style farewell to the Ephesian elders in Acts 20:17-38 was given at a ripe time in his ministry. He, like all leaders, had to attend "servant-learning school," first, making mistakes and learning from them, then going on to make his ultimate contribution. He finished his life well and gave us a full example of what it meant to be a servant leader. Acts concludes with a powerful statement of Paul's relentless servant-leadership approach. It states that Paul lived in Rome two years "at his own expense and welcomed all who came to him, proclaiming the kingdom of God and teaching about the Lord Jesus Christ with all boldness and without hindrance" (28:30-31). Paul's desire to use his own resources and minister among the people whom he evangelized and discipled never waned. Paul inclusively ministered as a servant to all who would come to see him. "Finishing well" was not merely an ending but a new beginning. True, Paul had prevailed in the face of the most feared powers of Rome, antagonistic religious leaders, and the realm of the demonic. But Acts does not conclude in idealistic triumph. It concludes with Paul finishing well, but with an unfinished task. Acts concludes with anticipation of the next phase of mission in which Paul's multiplying disciples throughout large regions of the world would continue to carry out the same mission after his death.

Today's worldwide, unprecedented growth of the church challenges us to "welcome all" who come to us in our global villages and to proclaim boldly "the kingdom of God and teaching about the Lord Jesus." If we do this well, in the spirit of servanthood, then what we finish on this earth becomes a new beginning for a new generation. In summary, Paul's servant leadership included the following:

1. a focus on serving Jesus Christ;
2. a focus on empowering others to serve Jesus Christ and others;
3. being mentored and mentoring others;
4. dealing with very tough issues in a personal way;
5. a focus on responsibilities of the body of Christ;
6. participative leadership by persuasion and modeling;
7. the reproductive process of leadership training;
8. a patient process rather than product orientation;
9. contextualizing within a multi-cultural environment; and
10. finishing well.

## CONCLUSION

Some complex contemporary issues are not addressed in Paul's writings, such as how to apply Paul's principles to groups when they become institutionalized, have established educational and training programs, and have second-generation Christians. In many ways church-planting and para-church groups can apply Paul's style of mission and church planting more easily because they do not have the bureaucratic barriers and traditions of individuals and institutions that might inhibit growth and development.

While in Brazil with Young Life we were able to establish a youth ministry with national ownership and leave within a few years. Today only a sister and at times advisory relationship remains. This model has now been duplicated even more speedily in several other Latin American countries. It appears that the reproductive process becomes more complicated with established mission and denominational organizations. "Don't trust the local people to keep the organization going," we were warned. Paul certainly trusted people and empowered them to develop and grow but also to be responsible for the consequences of their ownership. Paul's revolutionary style of servant leadership is desperately needed in today's complex, multicultural, urbanized, and changing world. The message that motivated Paul's mission and gave impetus to his strong beliefs in serving Christ and people can be summed up in his own words during his farewell to the Ephesian church: "But I do not count my life of any value to myself, if only I may finish my course and the ministry that I received from the Lord Jesus, to testify to the good news of God's grace" (Acts: 20:24). I am challenged to finish my life well by continuing to seek to be a servant leader and partner with God in the work of God's kingdom throughout the world.

## REFERENCES

[1] Robert K Greenleaf, *The Servant as Leader* (Indianapolis, Ind.: Robert K. Greenleaf Center, 1970), 1.

[2] Other passages (such as 1 Cor 4:12; 1 Thes 2:9; 2 Cor 11:7) indicate Paul's pride in his self-support.

[3] Kenneth O. Gangel and Max Anders, eds., *Holman New Testament Commentary: Acts* (Nashville, Tenn.: Broadman and Holman, 1998), 303.

[4] James D. G. Dunn, *The Acts of the Apostles* (Valley Forge, Pa.: Trinity Press International, 1996), 241.

[5] Ibid.

[6] William Neil, *The New Century Bible Commentary: The Acts of the Apostles*, ed. Ronald E. Clements and Matthew Black (1973; reprinted, Grand Rapids, Mich.: Eerdmans, 1987), 196.

[7] Ben Witherington III, *New Testament History: A Narrative Account* (Grand Rapids, Mich.: Baker Books, 2001), 271.

[8] Klyne R. Snodgrass, "Your Slaves—on Account of Jesus," in *Servant Leadership*, vol. 1, ed. James R. Hawkinson and Robert K. Johnston, 9-16 (Chicago: Covenant Publications, 1993), 10.

[9] For more details on this approach see David M. Scholer, "Patterns of Authority in the Early Church," in Hawkinson and Johnston, *Servant Leadership*, 1:45-65.

[10] Roland Allen, *Missionary Methods: St Paul's or Ours?* (Grand Rapids, Mich.: Eerdmans, 1962), 149.

[11] Dean S. Gilliland, *Pauline Theology and Mission Practice* (Grand Rapids, Mich.: Baker Books, 1983), 285.

[12] Greenleaf, *The Servant as Leader*, 32.

[13] Mark V. Attard, "Inspirational Leadership Keynote Address," paper distributed at a Servant Leadership Conference sponsored by the Greenleaf Center, Atlanta, Georgia (June 11, 1987), 6.

# 21

## The Fourth Pentecost:
## Paul and the Power of the Holy Spirit

ACTS 19:1–22

## Stephen J. Pettis

So the word of the Lord grew mightily and prevailed.

—ACTS 19:20

Having been born and raised in a family deeply influenced by the Wesleyan-Arminian tradition, exposure to issues relating to the Holy Spirit occurred often. Very seldom did a month go by that we did not hear from the pulpit or in a Sunday School class of the need to be filled with the Spirit. Annual "revivals" focused on renewing our dependence upon the Spirit for our spiritual lives. Each year I made my way to the altar to find that experience.

In joining the church at the age of twelve I publicly testified to an acceptance of the Spirit as the Third Person of the Trinity. I acknowledged that the Spirit had been sent by the Father and the Son to cleanse me from sin and empower me to live the Christian life. As the years passed I continued to learn the terminology, to say the right things, and to go to the right places that fit the evangelical image. I also continued to make those trips to the altar. Yet, after four years of college, three years of seminary, and six years in the pastorate I was still asking the same questions: Where is the power? Why haven't I experienced the power? What am I doing wrong? Even after several years as a missionary in Portugal, where I had seen God work in the people's lives, something was still missing in my life. There was no question in my mind that I had received forgiveness from sin through the gift of God's grace in Christ. But my struggles with the issues of the world would not go away. The power to be victorious in the face of the enemy was very rare indeed.

As the circumstances of my life changed, and my career as a missionary concluded, I found myself back in graduate school. Once again I heard stories of how the Holy Spirit was working miracles. People, locked in spiritual bond-

248

age, were being set free. But signs and wonders were not for me. They were just a little too "Pentecostal," and I had come to accept the fact that we all have our addictions and sometimes we just have to learn to live with them.

Even though I knew the Holy Spirit intellectually, I found myself in the same position as the disciples in Ephesus, Acts 19:2; they acknowledged that they had not heard that there was a Holy Spirit. What was even more disconcerting was that this same pattern was being reproduced in my children. They had grown up in the church and heard their dad preach on the power of the Spirit but had not experienced that power in their own lives.

## THE CITY OF EPHESUS

Ephesus was a prominent city in Asia known by some as the light and market of Asia.[1] Roads from the Euphrates and Mesopotamia, Galatia and the Meander Valley converge at Ephesus and from there go on to Rome. As a result it became a key ancient financial center. A self-governing city, Ephesus served as the site for a provincial court under a Roman governor. This cosmopolitan city had a population of over 250,000 drawn from around the Mediterranean world. Ephesus became a meeting place for old and new ideas, superstitions and philosophies from the East and West. Different ethnic groups brought their languages, commerce, and arts, and also their religions. In Ephesus there were temples to Claudius, Nero, Hadrian, and Severus. It was a city of astrology, magic spells, sorcery, divination, and the demonstration of power from a variety of sources.[2]

At the heart of all of this was the Temple of Artemis, one of the seven wonders of the ancient world. It served as a center for sacred prostitution. Artemis was originally an Anatolian fertility goddess who became the focus of a cultic worship at Ephesus. Its accompanying tourism sales of talismans and souvenirs flourished, and it had a prosperous silversmith guild that made idols.[3]

## THE CHURCH AT EPHESUS

It would seem in an environment steeped in this kind of evil and experimental activity that any church would need to focus on unity and power. Apparently Paul believed this to be true for the church in Ephesus. Writing to the Ephesian Christians he uses unity and power as his thesis. Regarding unity in Ephesians 2:1-10 he reminds them that all have sinned and all are made alive in Christ. In Ephesians 2:11-22 Paul states that all are made one in Christ. Turning to Ephesians 3:1-13, we see that the mystery of salvation has been made known to all. And in Ephesians 4:1-6 the unity of the Godhead brings unity to the body.

Paul continues this discussion on Christian unity with reference to power: there is power for those who believe (Eph 1:19); the power of Christ is over all (Eph 1:20-23); God's power gives grace (Eph 3:7); power comes through the Holy Spirit establishing Christ in us (Eph 3:16); the purpose of power is to bring full knowledge (Eph 3:18); God's power extends beyond our imagination (Eph

3:20); our strength comes through the power of the Lord (Eph 6:10), and our struggle is against the power of evil (Eph 6:12).

Further, in the gospel of John we discover these concepts rooted in a continuing sense of unity created between believers and the Father through the presence of the Counselor. This Counselor, exactly like Christ, teaches, reminds, convicts and guides the disciples in relation to all that Christ has done. This is in fact Christ himself, who comes to the believer through the Holy Spirit, thus joining us to the Father (Jn 14:15-26).[4] Some years later this is applied to the church in Ephesus, which had been faithful in the midst of persecution. It was a church committed to preserving its unity as it examined those who would bring division (Rv 2:1-3). Unfortunately, it was also a church that had lost its first love for Christ, perhaps because its desire for solid teaching and hatred of heresy had lead to a rigid orthodoxy (Rv 2:4-7).[5]

From the above discussion we see that if the church is going to mature it must find a way to maintain unity in Christ. A significant key to this development is the power of Christ in the Christian community through the indwelling presence of the Holy Spirit. At the same time we must ensure that our attention remains on Christ and not on unity or power in themselves. As we approach Acts 19, we find this to be at the heart of Paul's missionary work.

## THE CONTEXT OF PAUL'S VISIT TO EPHESUS

Paul's first visit to Ephesus came at the end of his second missionary journey. He had left Corinth with Priscilla and Aquila, but when they came to Ephesus the couple stayed behind while Paul continued on to Caesarea and eventually Syrian Antioch. About this time Apollos, a gifted speaker and evangelist, came to Ephesus speaking boldly in the synagogue about the Lord Jesus (Acts 18:18-26).

Paul then returns to the city of Ephesus to encourage the Christians (Acts 18:19). Apparently he had given the church's leadership to Priscilla and Aquila during his earlier visit. Upon his return he discovers a group of twelve believers who have experienced only a part of the gospel message (19:1-7). What follows must be a significant concern for those involved in the cross-cultural communication of the gospel. It would seem that these disciples were believers in Christ (8:14-17). Since they are called disciples and have been baptized, it seems difficult to believe that they had heard nothing of the Holy Spirit. So it is likely that what Paul is dealing with is not a lack of knowledge of the existence of the Spirit but the absence of an awareness of the Spirit's active presence, that his baptism had come and that his power was available to all who believe.[6]

We have already observed three Pentecosts: (1) In Jerusalem the initial pouring out of the Spirit occurs (2:1-13). (2) In Samaria Peter and John come from Jerusalem to lay hands on Samaritan believers who receive the Spirit (8:14-17). (3) In Caesarea the Spirit falls on all who heard while Peter is in the home of a Gentile, Cornelius (10:44-48).

Each Pentecost indicates a progression of mission (according to the Acts 1:8 outline) from Jerusalem, to Samaria (the fringes of Judea), to Caesarea (the Gentiles along the Palestinian [Mediterranean] coast). This fourth Pentecost in Ephesus leads to a further spread of the gospel in which "all the residents of Asia, both Jews and Greeks, heard the word of the Lord" (19:10). Thus each Pentecost serves as a catalyst that enhances the spread of the gospel. In the first three Pentecosts at least one apostle from Jerusalem is present to affirm the work of the Spirit and/or to lay hands on for the giving of the Spirit. The second and third Pentecosts authenticate the work of the Spirit in other lands and unite believers across cultural barriers. In this fourth Pentecost, however, a Jerusalem apostle no longer needs to be present. Now that the gospel has spread far and wide, Paul, the apostle to the Gentiles, initiates the work of the Spirit in new lands.

This incident is a reminder of the wholeness of the gospel. A partial understanding of the gospel is likely to lead to shallow Christianity. Is it possible that this was the issue the Ephesians were facing with the emergence of the teaching of the Nicolaitans (Rv 2:6,15)? Were there some in this church who began to build their lives on a partial understanding of Christian liberty through grace and ended up in a life of self-indulgence, a Christianity willing to compromise with pagan society?[7] Contextualization cannot be mere compromise.[8] Undoubtedly Priscilla and Aquila did not intend to plant a self-indulgent church, but leaders need to be careful.

We faced this situation several times on the mission field. Unfortunately, the results were never positive. In one case the church testified to salvation in Christ but saw very little necessity of releasing its hold on the things of this world. What resulted was a self-absorbed body of believers ineffective in influencing their community with the gospel. In another case we lost what could have been a very effective pastor due to a combination of the desire to protect the church's image and legalism in the absence of grace and compassion.

## THE FULL GOSPEL: FROM REPENTANCE TO POWER

In Acts 19:4 Paul turns to bringing balance to the new believers in Ephesus as he addresses the need to move from repentance to power. He explains that John's baptism was one of repentance and belief. It was a first step in the process that was intended to transform all of life. John confronted people with their sin, calling them to flee from the judgment to come (Lk 3:2-14). F. F. Bruce calls this a "pre-Pentecostal baptism" that anticipated the fullness of the Messiah to come.[9]

John the Baptist proclaimed the salvation that would be found in Christ but also indicated that Christ would usher in something more: a baptism in the Holy Spirit and fire (Lk 3:16). Now, rather than trying to follow all the instructions of the Law, Christ would bring a life full of grace and hope that comes with surrender to God, who alone has the authority to empower. Could it be that this "something more" began with what Jesus did to the early disciples in John

20:21-23? They believed that Jesus was the Messiah but had been baptized only into John's baptism. So the resurrected Lord came to breathe on them, imparting the authority of the Spirit for them to proclaim his teaching. The believers, having received the authority to be Jesus' witnesses, are commanded by him to stay in the city of Jerusalem until they are clothed with the power of the Spirit (Lk 24:49). The Ephesian disciples discovered this authority and power of the Spirit in Acts 19:5-6. As in 2:1-4 and 10:44-47, they spoke with ability they did not have before, both in form and content. Because of the experience of the apostles at Pentecost there was no denying the authenticity of this experience. The key element here is that the knowledge of Christ was transformed into a dynamic relationship. The personal struggle for growth and accomplishment was replaced by a total surrender to God.

My struggle to achieve "spirituality" and discover power had resulted in failure. Saying all the right things and going to all the right places, both as a pastor and missionary, did not prove fruitful. I could not find the experience of the early Ephesian believers. Then one weekend I gave up. In the middle of a retreat focusing on cleansing, the Spirit provided what I could not. While I did not speak in new languages or prophesy, God met me where I was and provided what I needed beyond the intellectual experience. Bondage to addictions were broken and I found peace. I also began to discover that the power of the Spirit and the miraculous was not only displayed in exciting ways but also in the mundane events of life.

What follows is a brief picture of what the Spirit was able to accomplish through Paul and the Ephesian congregation that developed around him. As was his custom, Paul began with the Jews in the synagogue, where the proclamation of the word was in boldness and power. The hope was that those close to the kingdom would respond to Christ in faith and obedience. However, as Jewish opposition grew and many chose to reject Paul's message, he moved on to the Gentiles, where God began to move in mighty ways to vindicate his name and accomplish his task. Through his servant, God's power was demonstrated in healing and exorcism (19:8-12; see also Eph 1:19-23; 3:20).

God still desires to demonstrate healing power today. On a bright spring afternoon a group of Romanian and American college students gathered on a hillside overlooking a village in north-central Romania. In this village poverty was extreme, alcoholism rampant, and physical and emotional abuse prolific. For some time attempts had been made to enter the village with health care, education, housing, and the gospel. There were moments of breakthrough, especially with the children, but confrontation and opposition from particular men invariably followed. That afternoon some of the students sat on the grass, while others stood or paced back and forth. Led by an unassuming, volunteer British missionary, they began to pray for the village. After some time a group of the village men approached the believers and the atmosphere grew tense. From their behavior it appeared that they had been drinking, and they were clearly not pleased. As the men moved to encircle the students, the missionary stepped forward to speak to them and the students moved down the hill. From a distance we watched a very heated discussion. After a while tensions eased and amazingly the missionary began leading the men in prayer. When he rejoined the group, permission had been given to work within the village. The next Sunday morning five of the men were in the worship service. God performs miracles through his praying people.

Let me give another example of God's praying people. Because of past circumstances one of the major areas of concern in Romania has been the plight of children, especially those in orphanages. The church has sought to respond to these needs in a variety of ways. At the beginning of 2000 the situation was especially critical in one of the orphanages where my wife and I had worked for a number of years. Because of a lack of human and medical resources the nursing staff was overwhelmed with the needs of the children: feeding, changing diapers, the deep need for human contact. More and more of the children were being neglected. Both Romanian and expatriate volunteers were on hand and ready to step in. Fresh supplies were available. But the government would not allow it. The local church leaders had tried everything politically, but nothing had happened. In fact, the situation grew worse. The volunteers were told they could not come back. So finally the church turned to God in prayer for the power to do what only the Lord could accomplish. Within just a few days the workers were back in the orphanage. The overall needs continued to exist, but access has been restored and there is hope. God did extraordinary miracles through ordinary people. In both of these cases the focus was and is not on people but on the Spirit of God working in the face of opposition to prove that God is greater than the prince of the power of darkness. We are vessels of God's work (see Eph 6:10-18).

This was also the situation in Ephesus, in which the circumstances allowed for the possibility of counterfeiting the authentic nature of God with an attempt to misuse the name of the Lord Jesus (19:13; see also Acts 8:9-23). As discussed above, true power resides not in the individual but in a dynamic relationship with God. Authentic power seeks not to bring attention to itself, but to its source. Power is not found in a magical recitation for personal aggrandizement but in surrender to the ultimate source of all power.[10] What tends to result from the misuse of power is humiliation and shame (19:13-16).

In Acts 19 the thin line that exists between magic and Christian miracles emerges. On the one hand, we have magic as the human attempt to control the supernatural and manipulate the power of God. Miracles, on the other hand, may be understood as the in-breaking of the supernatural into human history in order to demonstrate divine power in an attempt to call humanity into a relationship.[11] The problem with the seven sons of Sceva was that they did not share the life of Christ, so they could not share the power of that life. The sons of Sceva interpreted Paul's miracles as feats of magic, assuming that they could tap into that power by iterating words that had magical connotations, "I adjure you," and utilizing a formula, "by the Jesus whom Paul proclaims" (19:13). What really matters to the demons, however, is whether the demons recognize that the exorcists are endowed with the authority to call upon the holy name of Jesus.[12]

This is not an unusual experience when bringing the gospel to those who have learned to depend on the quasi-magical use of ritual to meet their physical, emotional, and spiritual needs. It is much too easy to develop a "cargo cult" mentality and expect both the benefits and the power to be available with no regard to the source. Having encountered this both in the Azores of Portugal and in Romania, I am learning to be careful in distinguishing the difference between the message of Christ and the anticipated "goods" to be received from that relationship. The gospel will bring transformation, but not always in the way we anticipate it.

## THE RESULTS

What difference does Acts 19:17-20 make in our life, our relationship with Christ, and the lives of those around us? This text demonstrates God's power will produce changed lives. True repentance and faith must always be demonstrated in obedience. In this case those who believed openly confessed the error of their past.

As previously discussed, Ephesus had a reputation as a center for the practice of magic and sorcery. In various cultures those people who hold power in the spiritual realm are those who know the words, rituals, and secrets that allow them to control the power of the supernatural. Magicians, even today, are extremely reluctant to reveal their secrets because much of the power of an incantation is linked to its secrecy. This is one reason why initiation is crucial; individuals are carefully selected to learn and carry out the responsibilities of dealing with the gods. In this process particular people are empowered, while the masses are excluded from the secret.

As presented in Acts 19, one of the best ways of breaking the power of evil is through Spirit-filled confrontation. This continues to be true in our dealings with evil today, in whatever form it takes. As we expose evil by naming and renouncing it, its power over us is broken. I mentioned earlier the weekend in which I experienced cleansing, freedom, and empowerment. Initially there was confession, repentance, and a renewed commitment to Christ (1 Jn 1:9). Second was a recognition and renunciation of the specific problem that I faced (Rom 13:12; 2 Cor 4:2). The next step was to seek the fullness of the Holy Spirit in place of the evil (Mt 12:43-45; Jn 14:15-16; 16:5-14).[13] The final step in the process was separation from that which held me in bondage. In the Ephesian situation the scrolls containing the spells and incantations that were destroyed symbolized the separation of the community from the demonic practices (Acts 19:19).

I have already shared that my children were following the same path as their father with reference to the absence of the power of the Spirit in their daily lives. Six months after my transforming experience, my wife and I returned to the same seminar, this time taking our son and daughter. What follows is a description of my daughter's experience:

> I had always thought I knew what kind of a Christian I was and felt strongly about my convictions. I would never drink, do drugs, or have sex before marriage. I was a strong Christian and that would never change.

It started out slow, as I began hanging out with people who did not hold the same values. I went to places where no one ever thought they would have found me. Gradually, I let go more and more, lying to myself that I was still a strong Christian. I became everything I had said I would never become.

After about three and a half years I heard about Cleansing Stream Ministries. I remember thinking to myself, "I have to break free. My life needs to change, but I cannot do it by myself." Something was choking me, and it would not let go.

I was a little scared. I did not want to air my dirty laundry, especially in front of my family. I did, though, and it felt good to get it out. I shared with my mom and my aunt what I had been going through, and they shared their stories with me. I was amazed to find that I was not the only one to struggle.

As we prayed together I was able to start letting go of past hurts and mistakes. I was finally free because I admitted my past to God and allowed him to take it and crush it, breaking the power it had over me.

When I got home, I began getting rid of the things that linked me to my past, old pictures, stuffed animals, anything that took me back. I even quit my job. I did not have another job and did not know how I would pay my bills, but I could feel the difference God had made in my life and I was at peace. I belonged to Jesus Christ, and he was all I needed.

The story for our son was very much the same. He went home at the end of the seminar and got rid of hundreds of dollars worth of comics and music that he had been saving for years. Four years later he was still sharing with us that the Spirit was still guiding and correcting him when he faced challenges to return to his past life. Confession, repentance, renouncing, and a continuing openness to the filling of the Spirit were keeping his experience alive and fresh.

## CONCLUSION

The summation of this study is found in Acts 19:20. "So the word of the Lord grew mightily and prevailed." As God through the Spirit works in mission and people respond in obedience, the word goes forward to produce transformation in lives and God is glorified. This in turn leads to a display of God's power. The key to the manifestations of this power is a relationship with God. As we are led in mission we are reminded to stay in relationship, proclaim relationship, and disciple toward relationship.

## REFERENCES

[1] William Barclay, *The Revelation of John* (Philadelphia: The Westminster Press, 1977), 1:58.

[2] Simon in Samaria, Acts 8:9-24; Elymas in Paphos, Acts 13:6-12; a slave in Philippi, Acts 16:16-24.

[3] E. M. Blaiklock, *The Acts of the Apostles,* Tyndale New Testament Commentaries (Grand Rapids, Mich.: Eerdmans, 1977), 154.

[4] See the following references for the relationship between the Spirit of Christ and power: Mt 12:28; Mk 3:15; 5:27ff.; 6:56; Lk 2:27; 4:1, 36; 5:17, 24; 10:19; Jn 7:37-39; Rom 8:2, 4-6, 9-11, 13-17; 15:18-19; 1 Cor 2:4-5; 6:11; 2 Cor 3:17-18; Gal 5:16-26; 2 Thes 2:13.

[5] Robert H. Mounce, *The Book of Revelation: The New International Commentary on the New Testament* (Grand Rapids, Mich.: Eerdmans, 1977), 88-89.

[6] See F. F. Bruce, *The Book of Acts: The New International Commentary on the New Testament* (Grand Rapids, Mich.: Eerdmans, 1977), 385; Blaiklock, *The Acts of the Apostles,* 154.

[7] William Bucklay, *The Revelation of John,* The Daily Study Bible Series (Philadelphia: The Westminster Press, 1977), 1:67; Mounce, *The Book of Revelation: The New International Commentary on the New Testament,* 89.

[8] Paul G. Hiebert, *Anthropological Insights for Missionaries* (Grand Rapids, Mich.: Baker, 1985), 171-192.

[9] Bruce, *The Book of Acts: The New International Commentary on the New Testament,* 386.

[10] I believe that what we do in relation to the Spirit is in direct correlation with what the Spirit does in relation to the Father and the Son. For a discussion of this against the backdrop of a Portuguese context, see Stephen J. Pettis, *A Festa Do Divino Espirito Santo: The Expression of Meaning in an Azorean-American Context* (Pasadena, Calif.: Fuller Theological Seminary, 1996), 236-290.

[11] Theodore P. Ferris, *The Acts of the Apostles: The Interpreter's Bible* (New York, Abingdon, 1954), 252-257. For an anthropological discussion of the relationship between magic and religion/miracle, see Bronislaw Malinowski, *Magic, Science, and Religion* (Prospect Heights, Ill.: Waveland Press, 1992), 69-90.

[12] Susan R. Garrett, *The Demise of the Devil: Magic and the Demonic in Luke's Writings* (Minneapolis, Minn.: Fortress Press, 1989), 92-93.

[13] Don Basham, *Deliver Us from Evil* (Grand Rapids, Mich.: Chosen Books, 1996), 202-208; see also Timothy Davis, *Session Four: Cleansing, Cleansing Seminar Workbook* (Northridge, Calif.: Glory Communications International, 1995).

# 22

## For Missionaries and Leaders: Paul's Farewell to the Ephesian Elders

ACTS 20:17–38

### Dean S. Gilliland

Paul's experiences at Ephesus (in Acts 19) were a concentration of every-thing that could be hoped for in a case study for missions.[1] There was eager receptivity of the word along with teaching over many months, accompanied by dynamic and effective witnessing beyond the city itself.[2] Nowhere did the gospel result in such a phenomenal demonstration of miracles and evangelis-tic activity. It took place in a city that had a long reputation for supernatural-ism and occult power. It was this pagan fame of Ephesus that accounted for the remarkable phenomena of this mission story. Unquestionably, the apostolic witness created widespread emotion and hysteria. Jewish sorcerers attempted exorcism in a new and powerful name—the name of Jesus—which brought disastrous results. Practitioners of the greatest of Asian divinities, Artemis (Diana), were so threatened by the new religion that they reacted to the point of frenzy (19:28). Luke memorably records this clash between power sources and power figures. The record shows a chaotic situation that touched every aspect of life—religion, culture, nationalism, economics, and politics. Paul with his disciples and, most of all, the Holy Spirit, radically invaded this animistic urban shrine. The result was something everyone could witness because "the word of the Lord grew mightily and prevailed" (19:20).

The prolonged stay in Ephesus took place during Paul's third missionary journey. Prior to this he did have a brief encounter with the people of Ephesus as he was returning to Jerusalem. During that visit the Jews showed immense interest in the way Paul discussed[3] his case in the synagogue (18:19). They wanted him to stay longer. He resisted their invitation, but upon taking his leave he did promise to return (18:21). It was after he had an important but rather brief ministry in Corinth that he reconnoitered along the northerly route around the Aegean Sea and finally came again to Ephesus (19:1) for his extensive mission.

The aim of this chapter is to look at the words of farewell that Paul left with the elders of the church at Ephesus (chapter 20). As he speaks to them, he reviews principles that model what is expected of those who will plant and lead churches in the name of Jesus Christ.

## PAUL'S FAREWELL: MODELING THE SPIRIT OF MISSION (ACTS 20:17-38)

The reunion Paul had with the elders at Miletus was a poignant and highly emotional experience. This is all the more obvious to missionaries, such as myself, who have had time to gather memories and become close to the people where they lived. The farewell event carries the kind of immediacy and power I can instantly recall when I think of our own years as missionaries. After an extremely difficult term as superintendent of the Nigeria mission, I recall when I and my wife, Lois, and our five children were leaving Nigeria for a one-year furlough in 1963. This African church has always had to deal with the painful problem of tribalism. Over six major language groups make up the total membership. Each ethnic group struggled to keep its own people in leadership positions and to gain attention for its own particular causes. I, along with three other church leaders, had recently negotiated that the headquarters of the church be moved from its traditional site to a more promising place, a location more central to the whole church. This meant that the people in the historic location had lost the prestige that comes with residing at the official center of power. The church leaders came to the airfield to celebrate our farewell. They had actually arranged a service that included speeches, songs, and prayers. Africans are very careful about saying good-bye so that their guests will carry a special kind of memory as they depart. The purpose of the farewell was to review our progress and to attempt to quiet down the controversy that had ensued with the moving of the headquarters. The farewell was meant to show honor and to ensure that, during our absence, we would not forget events or promised intentions.

However, the African leaders were not aware of the stress this farewell would have on the pilot's schedule or on the other passengers who were en route. Even though little patience was being shown for the farewell, the African leaders were not moved. They eloquently summed up what they had to say, presented my wife and me with new African clothes, sang an African hymn, and closed with prayer. The meaning of the entire event was meant to say, "Missionaries, you have been with us and have led us. Now, as you leave, promise that you will not forget the work we have already done together and that you will keep your commitment to finishing what we have started."

Unlike a lot of missionary work, Paul's three-year stay in Ephesus was productive right from the start. Frankly speaking, he was able to do far more during three years in Ephesus than most missionaries today, who work in situations that are culturally different from their own. By the time he came to Ephesus, Paul was experienced in mission travel, cultural diversity, and changing local situations. Upon entry into any city he had the advantage of knowing both the Roman and Greek world and could claim the rights of his Roman citizenship.

He would have had no difficulties with the popular language, and he almost always contacted first his familiar people—the Jewish community. His three years at Ephesus were intense and controversial. Intimate personal relationships would have developed out of a situation like this. But for space, I might describe the deep attachments that missionaries and local people can make as they live and work together.

Some scholars have negative criticisms of this farewell passage. I am sure that those who have reservations about textual and historical issues cannot easily identify with the missionary dimension of this passage.[4] They do not know what it is like to be reunited with those who have been at the missionary's side during the joys and sorrows of planting a church in the environment of unbelief. Additionally, this farewell meeting came very soon, comparatively speaking, after the three-year mission. Memories were fresh and relationships fully intact, so a sense of fraternity in the bonds of the gospel is almost palpable. This is a highly personal account. Luke is actually with Paul and writes from firsthand recollection. There are not many "we" passages in Acts (16:10-17; 20:5—21:18; 27:1—28:16). This narrative, being one of them, has the authority of an eyewitness account. It means that we are, in a sense, standing very close to Paul himself. We are hearing Paul's own words and are involved in nuances of communication with his closest colleagues. The fact that the references are almost completely personal without digression into doctrine or preaching makes this a very special passage.[5]

As we turn to the instruction that is available to us in the address, I want to emphasize again the contextual method. Of course, the principles of hermeneutics always apply, including the etymological task of deriving meanings from the text. But when we do a contextual search for meaning, we should keep in mind that the words of Paul to the elders are not taken out of the air in some kind of a supernatural way that is disconnected from experience or memory. These powerful words are grounded in the dynamic, unforgettable events that occurred. They touch immediately on what actually happened, drawing from the crucible of experiences that bonded Paul with the elders and the elders with one another. The way Paul speaks to the elders, the very words he chooses and the relational dynamics that are revealed between the elders and Paul, can be fully understood only if we know the context.[6]

The farewell address falls into two sections, and we shall look at each section in turn. First, Paul appeals to his own ministry as a model for caretakers of the church. Second, Paul exhorts the elders directly, touching on the qualities expected of them when shepherding the flock as well as personal qualities required of the shepherd.

## PAUL'S PERSONAL EXAMPLE (ACTS 20:18-27)

Paul does not hesitate to remind his friends how he lived among them. The first-generation church had no precedent, no history of saints or fathers of the faith. Paul had confidence in the way he represented Jesus Christ to the first Christians. In another familiar context he commended the believers at Corinth because they remembered him in everything and because they maintained faithfully the traditions he showed them and taught them (1 Cor 11:2). There is a very fine line to observe in setting oneself up as an example (Phil 4:9) and in doing so with humility (1 Cor 2:3; 2 Cor 10:1). One thing is certain: There is no point in our talking about truth if daily life with people does not support what we say. Paul had no problem in this area.

### The Missionary's Integrity Is Based on Personal Relationships

> "You yourselves know how I lived among you the entire time from the first day that I set foot in Asia." (20:18)

Immediately Paul turns to relational proof to verify his words. Words must be backed up by relationships that are consistent with what the missionary says, or they mean nothing. The people we live with through the good times and the bad remember what took place. The example of life is, as it were, an open book (2 Cor 3:2-3). In saying, "You *know*," Paul uses the emphatic form *(umeis)*, so that, as R. C. H. Lenski remarks, what Paul speaks about here are "things not open to question."[7] It was obvious to any and all from the "first day" and continuing for three years that what Paul said was supported by his actions.

### The Missionary's Ministry Requires Personal Qualities That Do Not Come Easily

> "[I was] serving the Lord with all humility and with tears, enduring the trials that came to me through the plots of the Jews. I did not shrink from doing anything helpful, proclaiming the message to you and teaching you publicly from house to house." (20:19-20)

*Serving the Lord with all humility . . . :* This is the first word from Paul, and the account of his mission in Ephesus bears out his right to say this. However, humility is not something one can work to achieve or self-consciously develop. This is especially true on the mission field, where the missionary's role of initiative, creativity, and courage can deceptively result in an overbearing attitude. Paul's eloquent *kenosis* passage (Phil 2:5-11) is the sublime standard for all who work in spreading the gospel. Yet it would be honest to say that even Paul had his periods of subjective melancholy. The most obvious case was brought on by his broken fellowship with the church at Corinth. This led him to say things that seem arrogant rather than humble. Some of what he writes in the "stern letter" (2 Cor 10:1—13:10) shows how difficult it is to maintain humility when one has to engage in self-defense.

. . . *with tears:* As Luke writes he remembers a phrase that was common to Paul's speech and writing. Paul mentions his tears three times in his letters (2 Cor 2:4; Phil 3:18; Rom 9:2). Luke knew Paul very well. From his close association with Paul he had no reservation about showing him to be highly emotional, revealing his confrontational style when called for as well as his sensitivity. When some people cry, they do not want anyone to see or know. Paul could weep, then write and speak openly about it. There was reason for tears at Ephesus. I. Howard Marshall associates Paul's tears with the personal concern Paul has for the plight of his converts.[8] F. F. Bruce believes the weeping comes from the plots made against him by the Jews referred to in this same verse,[9] while John Calvin thinks the tears come from trials caused by Satan, the ungodly, and disorders in the church.[10] These were not maudlin or sentimental tears. They were connected to the anguish that comes from "enduring the trials." Ironically, often the trials that missionaries must endure are caused by those who are, or who should be, closest to them. What was behind the scenes at Ephesus can only be imagined, but we do remember that the Jews stubbornly refused his word in the synagogue; the sons of Sceva, the Jewish high priest, brought open shame to Paul; and Alexander, a Jew, was cause for chaos in the theater.[11]

*I did not shrink from doing anything helpful . . . :* Other translations expressed this as, "I suppressed nothing." The phrase gives no reason to say, as some scholars do, that perhaps Paul had been accused by some of holding back the whole truth because of pressures from both Greeks and Jews.[12] Paul wants these church leaders to know that they, like him, must have a broad sense of what it is to be a servant of the Lord Jesus. It can be inferred that beyond what we might call verbal evangelism, Paul built up the whole life of the church and met the needs of both believers and unbelievers in a variety of ways. It is clear from what he adds that the proclamation of the gospel is carried out not only in public gatherings, but also through meeting people in personal ways, contacting them in the course of their daily lives, and spending time with them in their homes.

At Ephesus we know about the synagogue period and the daily teaching in the hall of Tyrannus. Beyond this, we can gather from this statement that Paul also made use of every opportunity, whether in public or in private, to declare the message through a variety of encounters. At this point we recall that his message was met with opposition from Jews in the synagogue and eventually caused an uproar over conflict with Artemis, the city goddess. He did not shrink from helping by healing the sick, nor did he pull back from the power struggle with the city's magicians and cultic priests. This whole scene is passing before the minds and memories of the elders as Paul refers to himself as a model for ministry.

In these verses we are looking at qualities of the missionary in ministry that do not come easily. The comprehensive way in which Paul carried out his daily work and the total commitment he showed by methods that touched the whole of life were full of difficulties. Preaching the cross is a message that will offend. Faithfulness in declaring the whole gospel will cause some to stumble (Gal 5:11). There is no question in Paul's mind about this. The preaching and teaching of the total gospel are required of all who are leaders. While the methods need to be carefully thought out from place to place, Paul insists that there can be no suppression of the cost of believing and following the Lord; neither can there be a watering down of the message for the sake of comfort to the messenger.

## The Mission Message Is about Repentance and Faith

"I testified to both Jews and Greeks about repentance toward God and faith toward our Lord Jesus." (20:21)

The whole gospel embraces more than the truth contained in these two terms, but there is no gospel without repentance and faith. It is interesting how scholars treat this verse, especially these terms. On one hand, giving little notice of the phrase, Kirsopp Lake and Henry J. Cadbury say using faith and repentance together is an example of Luke's tendency to use pairs of words.[13] Objecting to this, we have shown that Luke is bringing us very close to Paul himself. To say that Luke uses his own editorial habits undermines the meanings we are looking for. On the other hand, Calvin claims that the gospel "consists of these two elements alone."[14] Anyone who has evangelized in various cultural situations knows by experience that Calvin does not overstate the truth. Understanding the force of faith and repentance is where the Christian life begins. Luke uses a single article to cover both terms, as though this is an integrated way of speaking about the way a person experiences salvation.

*Repentance* in Paul's theology of salvation has both human and divine dimensions. The human side is that a person must think and act differently as an expression of conversion. Not having a precise word in the New Testament for "conversion," as we use it today, Paul expressed conversion as *epistrepho* and *metanoia*. Where *epistrepho* is used, as it is most frequently, the meaning is to "change direction." This colorful word applies not only to a change in direction of objects and things (like ships at sea or birds in flight) but is also used to show a change in mental attitude, a "turning of the mind," as it were.[15]

The second term is the one Luke uses here. It is *metanoia*, which literally means "afterthought." The popular way it is used in *koine* Greek actually falls short of what is expected as an expression for the deep issues of repentance. However, *metanoia* is used with such force in the New Testament that it expresses much more than the etymology of the word implies. This "change of mind," as William Barclay says, "comes to involve not only a new judgement on some previous action, but also regret and sorrow for it. Here then is the meaning of repentance. Repentance is the awakened awareness and regret of past sins."[16] Obviously then, "turning" and "change of mind" are joined in the term we speak of as "conversion," and both are needed to express what actually takes place when one is converted. It does not take much imagination, once we understand the Ephesian context, to see how this is directly related to the mission at Ephesus and what both Paul and the elders remember.

*Faith* is the divine side of the message. To have faith in the person Jesus Christ, especially for these who have never known him or seen him, requires a gift from God. What leads Paul later to write this to the Ephesians had become almost a centerpiece of Christian faith. "For by grace you have been saved *through faith,* and this [faith] is not your own doing; it is the gift of God" (Eph 2:8, emphasis added). Faith, in the case of the Jew, was not loyalty to tradition or philosophizing about dogma. To the non-Jew it was not slavery to manufactured gods or talismans, or in the repetition of myths, as was true everywhere in Ephesus. In the "turning" Paul did not require a statement of faith or confession of creed. Faith is the reaching out, as this verse says, toward the Lord Jesus. Jesus rewards the person who accepts him by faith, even when that person has little or no knowledge of what is taking place. Faith is inseparable from Christ. The memory of the preaching and teaching of Paul about Jesus and the miracles he did in the name of Jesus at Ephesus is all here as reality when he uses this language.

### The Missionary and the Mission Are Ruled by the Holy Spirit

> "And now, as a captive to the Spirit I am on my way to Jerusalem, not knowing what will happen to me there, except that the Holy Spirit testifies to me in every city that imprisonment and persecution are waiting for me. But I do not count my life of any value to myself, if only I may finish my course and the ministry that I received from the Lord Jesus, to testify to the good news of God's grace." (20:22-23)

Whatever happens, those who have charge over the church must remember that everything is under the control of the Holy Spirit. Paul refers to the Holy Spirit here in a natural, almost casual way. It is obvious that this was his manner of living and teaching at Ephesus. Paul could not think or move without an intimate, practical connection with the Spirit. The fact that here are two references to the Holy Spirit in quick sequence is neither accidental nor a device of the writer. Paul would have spoken about this over and over again during those years at Ephesus. The Holy Spirit is driving Paul to Jerusalem (20:22), and it is this same Spirit that warns him to be prepared for any and all eventualities once he is there (20:23). Paul declares here that he is literally "captive" to the Holy Spirit, as now the elders must be.

If only the missionary could be in constant communication with this gift to believers and the church! It is a principle that Paul insisted on from the very beginning. There is no more accurate way to describe Christians than to say that they are believers who have the Spirit of Jesus living within (Rom 8:9, 16; 1 Cor 2:12). I have written quite extensively in *Pauline Theology and Mission Practice* on this point because I, myself, knew so little about this "captivity" to the Spirit in the early days of my missionary work:

> The Spirit in the life of the believer is so dynamic and transforming that missionaries ought to be able to rest from many of their worries about doctrine, morality, church growth, leadership, finances, standards and a long list of other things that we feel must be carefully managed.[17]

A person is saved when Jesus is Lord and when, by faith, allegiance and worship are directed to the resurrected Christ (Rom 10:9). This is possible only through the Holy Spirit (Rom 8:16). Paul speaks of the Holy Spirit in this spontaneous way because there is no other "law" but that of the Spirit. Our relationship to the Holy Spirit needs to be transparent and spontaneous.[18] It follows that to be a "love prisoner" of the Holy Spirit makes it possible, even joyful, to accept whatever may follow. Paul, says Bruce, "did have serious misgivings about what would happen at Jerusalem. He is ready to surrender his liberty and life itself if need be, which he spoke about frequently (Phil. 1:20; 3:8; Col. 1:24)."[19] It is through the Spirit that he is able to face what lies ahead, not knowing exactly what it will be. Yet, as E. H. Trenchard comments, the threatening situation "could not turn him from his course which must be accomplished irrespective of personal considerations, since his life was not precious to himself but only as a means of serving the Lord."[20]

### Mission Is the Whole Message Reaching the Whole "Field" by Spontaneous Witness

"And now I know that none of you, among whom I have gone about proclaiming the kingdom, will ever see my face again. Therefore I declare to you this day that I am not responsible for the blood of any of you, for I did not shrink from declaring to you the whole purpose of God." (20:25-27)

Paul states these verses in such a way that we need to look at two points already made in verse 20. One is that Paul did not fail to proclaim the complete message, regardless of the consequences this carried for him. A second fact is that he touched every place and all the people he possibly could. These points together give Paul a clear conscience. The result is that Paul chose a radical metaphor to express that he has done all he can humanly do, reaching into all the places available to him: "I am not responsible for the blood of any of you." He takes no blame for those who, having heard, refuse to believe. The reference to "you" speaks in a corporate way about all the people who had been contacted in the entire territory. "[Paul] had sounded the trumpet aloud so that all the province of Asia had heard."[21] This also brings to mind his opening words to the elders when he spoke about the "entire time from the first day that I set foot in Asia" (20:18). His larger context is Asia, while remembering that Ephesus dominates all other places as the greatest of urban centers.

The Asia story is far bigger than what happened in the city of Ephesus. Connected with the months of teaching in the hall of Tyrannus is a statement that has almost incredible implications. Acts 19:10 states flatly that "all the residents in Asia, both Jews and Greeks, heard the word of the Lord." Unless one is to say that Luke is unreliable as a historian and tends to be hyperbolic, we have to agree that a magnificent program of witnessing was opened up among the populated regions around the Lycus River Valley, which included the towns of Hieropolis, Laodicea, and Colossae. Could this be the mission effort that was responsible for planting the churches John addresses (including Ephesus) in Revelation 2—3?[22] With Ephesus as the "mother church," Paul stayed in the city, continuing to teach, while perhaps "gospel teams" evangelized the areas around. This was the exciting, vibrant witnessing that would have been done by recent converts. Paul sent out these messengers of the new life to tell honestly and simply what they had experienced. He knew how important it was for converts to move out in spontaneous, dynamic witnessing.[23] These elders needed no additional reference to the way the good news was spread among the places and people in all of Asia. No wonder Paul could say, "I am not responsible for the blood of any of you, for I did not shrink from declaring to you the whole purpose of God" (20:26-27).

## PAUL'S FINAL EXHORTATION (ACTS 20:25-35)

We have been reviewing the first part of Paul's address to the elders, in which he sets up his own ministry as an example for his friends and colleagues. We turn now to the last section, which is a more direct exhortation. Throughout we have been allowing the text to establish basic lessons or principles for those who aspire to be cross-cultural witnesses. At this point the nature of the address changes somewhat from the personal to a more exhortative style. It shifts also from the witness of Paul as missionary to direct points of admonition for the elders. Paul now repeats in some ways what he has just said, impressing upon these leaders yet again certain points. The tone becomes quite mandatory as he gives additional counsel. In this way the elders know what is most important as Paul, the church planter, transfers the new community of faith into the care of local believers.

### Leaders Must Care about Themselves If They Are Going to Care for the Very Precious Church

> "Keep watch over yourselves and over all the flock, of which the Holy Spirit has made you overseers, to shepherd the church of God that he obtained with the blood of his own Son." (20:28)

These men were referred to as *presbuteros* in verse 18 and here, in verse 28, they are called *episkopos*. However, there is no reason to make a distinction between elders and bishops. These early church leaders are indiscriminately described as, "elders, bishops (superintendents) and shepherds (pastors)."[24] The stereotype we have of elders is that they are seniors in age and experienced as Christians. This would likely not apply in the case of these elders. The point is that even though they are not old in years and may be quite inexperienced as Christians, they do have authority. "These were men on whom the Holy Spirit had bestowed the requisite qualifications for their work."[25]

The likelihood of their relative youth and their recent "turning" from traditional pagan ways gave Paul additional reason to emphasize that, before anything else, they must look out for their own lives. How easy it is to emphasize the need for leaders to "watch the sheep." The phrase "keep watch over yourselves" (*prosekete*, "hold the mind to") is set in the present imperative; that is, at no time can the shepherd of the flock compromise his or her own behavior or neglect mature thinking. "Be taught before you teach" or, as it is now said, "walk the talk." What painful stories we can tell of church leaders (and mission-aries) who, while gifted and zealous, do not watch their own conduct and words. Paul says the elders should first look out for themselves if they are going to teach aright and lead, as they should. Paul advised young Timothy in this same way. "Pay close attention to yourself and to your teaching" (1 Tm 4:16).

The responsibility is great because this is no ordinary or common religious group. This is "the church (congregation) of God." By this reference the infant congregation at Ephesus is linked to the whole of biblical history, through which God works to create a people of God's own possession. The psalmist cried to God,

> Remember your congregation which you acquired
>     long ago,
> which you redeemed to be the tribe of your
>     heritage. (Ps 74:2)

The elders are charged to watch out for these special people whom God says he has "formed for myself so that they might declare my praise" (Is 43:21). Further, they are not to care for some part of the church only (for example, only for those who are well off socially or economically). This charge covers "all the flock"—everyone, including those who cause problems and may not be among the "nice" people. The priceless value of this church cannot be stated in ordi-nary speech, leading Paul to use a more doctrinal phrase. It is the church that God obtained with the "blood of his own Son."[26] No expression can surpass this for describing the exquisite value God puts upon repentance and faith. No price was too high to make in the task of watching over this new living reality, the church of God (Eph 2:11-22).

### Leaders Have to Prepare Themselves for Opposition and Failure

> "I know that after I have gone, savage wolves will come in among you, not sparing the flock. Some even from your own group will come distort-ing the truth in order to entice the disciples to follow them." (20:29-30)

Because certain groups were opposed to the gospel, Paul had enemies from within the Jewish community as well as among non-Jews. Opposition to the gospel is a well-known theme that runs throughout Paul's ministry. The hostility in Ephesus was so intense that he mentioned these dangers twice. In 20:19 he speaks about "enduring the trials that came to me through the plots of the Jews" and warns that "savage wolves" will come in "distorting the truth" (20:29).

The elders are a mixed group, coming from both Jewish and Gentile back-grounds. The picture of the fledgling church in the letter to the Ephesians is one where Jews and Gentiles were brought together in a completely new kind of fellowship. It carries an eloquent description of how the walls between Jews and Gentiles were broken down and how these alienated groups, once so far from each other, were now "brought near by the blood of Christ" (Eph 2:12-13). So

Paul lets the leaders know that vigilance and wisdom are required to meet the fierce opposition from inside and outside, from both Jews and Gentiles.

Leading new churches in locales that are governed by traditional religions is bound to bring conflict. The masses are entrenched in cultural practices. They hold world views that have united the society for generations. When the gospel threatens customs and rituals, a reaction occurs. These elders remember immediately the outbreak that arose in Ephesus over the Artemis cult (see Acts 19:23-41). Both believing and unbelieving Jews pursued Paul relentlessly. Seditious factions would now take advantage of the Christians, especially after Paul's personal influence is withdrawn. Even the leaders themselves would suffer from schisms within their ranks that would undermine the church.

The fact that Christian leaders can be led astray by Satan not only to abandon the church but to work against it is one of the hardest things to understand in Christian work (see Acts 5:3). I can never forget that one of our most eloquent African preachers, whom God used greatly in public evangelism during the 1960s, became disgruntled over a series of personal setbacks. He went back to Islam, from which he had been converted, and actively subverted the church by preaching the Muslim faith. In another case, when the son of a zealous evangelist died, the evangelist took his daughter-in-law, the son's widow, as his second wife. He claimed that as a Christian he was now free from the law, free even from African traditional law.[27] A few of the believers then followed him and his new teaching.

Paul warned that these "wolves" will "entice the disciples to follow them." The Pastoral Epistles and John's message to the church at Ephesus show that Paul's fears were not unfounded.[28] The leaders, then, must stay constantly on the alert. The difficulties that subsequently arose in Ephesus show that they probably failed in this area. They might have been overwhelmed by problems or could have been involved with things other than the church. Whatever the reason, they did not keep watch at all times (see 1 Cor 16:13; 1 Thes 5:6).

To speak about weeping would not be out of character with these men, including Paul. When they really felt deeply about something, they could cry and could do so together. The record says that when they had to depart from Paul there was much emotion, weeping, kissing, grieving, and embracing (20:37-38). This was obviously a culture in which people showed their feelings openly. I am sure that Luke did not stretch what Paul said when he implored them to watch and be alert to the point of tears, so that wolves would not invade the flock.[29]

### *Leaders Will Change, But the Word Remains*

"And now I commend you to God and to the message of his grace, a message that is able to build you up and to give you the inheritance among all who are sanctified." (20:32)

Perhaps the NRSV has somewhat minimized the meaning of the term *logos* by translating it as "message" rather than "word," as in most earlier translations.

The essence of this verse lies in the reference to the message as grace. This may not be understood fully from today's popular usage. There can be nothing superficial about this message. It is not limited to verbal communication. Nor can it have a sectarian, denominational slant. The apostle John will later develop the term *logos* in a unique way, the exegesis of which has become the bedrock of New Testament theology. Throughout the New Testament "word" is used in a variety of ways, often for simple speech (1 Cor 14:9; 2 Cor 1:18) or preaching (Acts 13:15). But here the context calls for deeper meanings, such as "remembering the words of the Lord Jesus" (20:35) or the response Peter gave to Jesus in John 6:68, "To whom can we go? You have the words of eternal life." Paul writes to Timothy about the "word of faith" (1 Tm 4:6) and to the Corinthians about the "word of reconciliation" (2 Cor 5:19), pointing to the deeper level of the term. This is the good news of God's grace that Paul had spoken about in 20:24, where he described his ministry as one "received from the Lord Jesus." Grace flows out from this word for the spiritual work that is now laid upon the elders. This word, all that Paul had taught them, will build up the church, and it is through the word they will receive all the privileges of grace, which he speaks of here as "the inheritance among all who are sanctified."

The use of the phrase "all who are sanctified" is a reference to the church, this "cleansed" community *(hegiosmenois)* that has been separated to God's use, as was God's intention for Israel in the Old Testament.[30] The sure permanence of the word and the church is a gracious and substantial promise. Paul must now separate himself from these leaders, but the church for which Christ gave his life and the Word of Grace is secure. The God to whom Paul commends the church will not abandon it.[31]

I have to confess that during our missionary years we had a deep feeling that if we were to go away the church could not survive. It was something that was difficult to admit even to each other; yet I felt my own presence, my knowledge, and my connection with the American church was indispensable. This conferring of responsibility was the pattern of Paul's whole ministry; that is, plant the church and turn it over to the Holy Spirit and to the leaders the Spirit sets aside for ministry.

Paul's confident transferal of authority was not only because his personal involvement was over, but also because he had no doubt that the word and the church could and would prevail without him. The process of "handing over" from mission to church took our missionaries many months—years, in fact. For a variety of reasons that we thought justified, we did not have enough trust in national leaders or confidence in the Holy Spirit to govern and protect the church without our presence.

### Leaders Must Understand the Self-support Principle
### for Covering the Costs of Church Life

"I coveted no one's silver or gold or clothing. You know for yourselves that I worked with my own hands to support myself and my companions. In all this I have given you an example that by such work we must support the weak, remembering the words of the Lord Jesus, for he himself said, 'It is more blessed to give than to receive.'" (20:33-35)

There were probably other ways for Paul to conclude his exhortation to the elders. Certainly in Luke's account of what Paul said he did not touch on everything that leaders need to know. However, the spontaneous intensity of what Paul says leaves no question that these are matters of first importance. The needs of the church were many, and perhaps this was the most difficult, disappointing feature of the apostle's ministry. Could it be that the young Christians found supporting their own needs difficult or unimportant? Paul had this problem in other places, such as Thessalonica, where Christians were told to "work with your hands . . . and be dependent on no one" (1 Thes 4:11-12).

Paul always asked his church leaders to remember this characteristic of his service among them, even though he admitted to the Corinthians that the "work of our own hands" made him weary (1 Cor 4:12). But he did not fail to lay down this principle of helping others and supporting himself. Lenski asks us to remember his assistants, those evangelists who covered the whole of the province of Asia. He feels Paul is asking the elders to remember that he gave of his own earnings to help them in addition to his own support.[32]

There is no question that Paul ends on a note that has not been solved in mission up to the present. Nothing cuts more quickly to the very nerve of mission than finance. It touches in one way or another almost every aspect of the mission enterprise. It is impossible to plant and nurture churches without facing the question of money. The way Paul supported himself set him apart from professional public preachers and apostles of his day. He was quite sure that his habit of supporting himself and giving the gospel "free of charge" at Corinth was interpreted by some as evidence that he lacked authority as an apostle (2 Cor 11:7-8). Yet this did not deter Paul. The basis of self-support, as Paul taught it, was fundamental to the very life of the new churches. Systematic, sacrificial giving was probably the hardest thing for the new Christians to learn. Yet it was vital to their spiritual lives, vital for their early growth in ministry to one another and to the maintenance of their witness in a hostile world.[33]

Paul does not mention it here, but he also had the conviction that members of the body of Christ should share and have a gracious spirit of receiving from those who offer help. Accordingly, he was at great pains to be sure that churches everywhere, among both Jews and Gentiles, contribute to the offering he was bringing along with him for the poor at Jerusalem. Some have felt that the elders may have come to Miletus with this offering in hand.[34] Paul took this final opportunity to ask them to remember something that Jesus said, even though it is not recorded anywhere in the gospels. Oral recitation was crucial for the first Christians because they had no written record of what Jesus said or what they were taught. This statement of our Lord had become so widely known that Paul made an almost casual reference to it. "For he [Jesus] himself said, 'It is more blessed to give than to receive.'"[35]

This is the note on which Paul ends his address. The matter of self-support was one of the highly visible factors in a much broader conviction—that the church at Ephesus and the churches planted by its mission in the regions around must be independent and able to develop their own life in every way. A church equipped to bear its own burdens will be better able to bear the burdens of others.

It is on this note that the farewell address ends. It remains now for these brothers in Christ to bid goodbye to one another. We close with Luke's description of those touching last moments:

> When he had finished speaking, he knelt down with them all and prayed. There was much weeping among them all; they embraced Paul and kissed him, grieving especially because of what he had said, that they would not see him again. Then they brought him to the ship. (20:36-38)

## EPILOGUE

I would like to add a biographical note to this study. During my lifetime I have had providential situations in my ministry experience. It has been forty-eight years since I graduated from seminary and began my ministry. The first half of those years was spent in Nigeria doing work in church planting and training African leaders. During the second half of those years I have been teaching at Fuller Theological Seminary's School of Intercultural Studies. In working with graduate students who are mid-career missionaries as well as pre-field, I constantly draw upon my own missionary story. Part of that story is how the apostle Paul became a friend, as it were, when, as a young missionary, I became discouraged with what I was doing. I was actually tempted to close my brief African career and look for some other kind of work. It was then that I discovered Paul, the immensely human and honest missionary. Paul, I found, formed his approaches to mission and theology as he learned about people in their cultural environment. The way I had been working in mission was out of touch with the realities of the place where God had put me. I was practically unaware of the power available through intimate relationships with African people. In this period of great personal need I came home for a year's furlough. It was during this time that the apostle Paul came to my rescue. It was through an extended restudy of Paul that the Holy Spirit assured me I could find a way through formidable problems. I returned to the mission field, with Paul at my side, and stayed on for eighteen more years.

As I was working through this narrative and reflecting on my years as a missionary, the principles shared above from the text came to me almost spontaneously. So, this has not been simply an exegetical exercise. It has provided an intensely personal opportunity for me to remember the consequences of my own failure to do the right thing as well as the joys of connecting to African people through the ties of the gospel. While not doing it perfectly, I was able, in time, to make decisions based on remembering events and to trust African leaders to carry out what we had planned together. I am still learning about these blessed secrets.

## REFERENCES

[1] C. Peter Wagner's recent volume on Acts shows how the Holy Spirit directed and empowered the apostolic witness in the beginnings of the New Testament Church. Wagner says of Acts 19: "No chapter in Acts could be more helpful for learning principles of evangelism and more encouraging regarding potential results for those willing to move into enemy territory by the power of the Holy Spirit" (*Acts of the Holy Spirit* [Ventura, Calif.: Regal, 2000], 487).

[2] From the hall of Tyrannus (Acts 19:9) Paul's disciples itinerated throughout the Lycus River Valley over a period of three years, planting churches that are probably those to which John refers in Revelation 2—3. We are told that in this way, "all the residents of Asia, both Jews and Greeks, heard the word of the Lord" (19:10).

[3] *Dielexato,* "revolve in the mind," is translated, "had a discussion," "argued," or, in older versions, "reasoned." This is Luke's favorite term for Paul's way of communicating in the synagogues (as in 17:2, 17; 18:4), reflecting the Socratic method of question and answer (A. T. Robertson, *Word Pictures in the New Testament* [New York: Richard Smith, 1930], 304).

[4] The intimacy between Paul and the elders in this passage is rare for Luke's writing. The words and phrases can only be of Paul himself (W. M. Furneaux, *The Acts of the Apostles* [Oxford: Clarendon Press, 1912], 331).

[5] The only theological/doctrinal reference is made in 20:28 where Paul exhorts the elders to "shepherd the church of God that he obtained with the blood of his own Son."

[6] As professor of contextualized theology I am committed to the analysis of the situational components in each context. Account must be made for the total human experience, that is, cultural and social-psychological as well as religious aspects. This is not only a requirement for an accurate hermeneutic of scripture but without this sensitivity the gospel cannot be communicated in appropriate ways from people to people and place to place. Here I share points 4-6 from the methodological guidelines that I give to students in my course, "Doing Theology in Context": (4) *Cultural agenda:* Give an analysis/description of the issue, providing as much information as possible (history, meanings of rituals, symbols, words) from the various dimensions of the context. (5) *Biblical agenda:* What signs, narratives and insights can you find in the scriptural text(s) that shed light on the issue or theme you are working with and on the intended meanings in the message of the text? In other words, (6) *Integration:* What are the results when (4) and (5) are brought together? that is, how do the realities of the historical situation affect the language, symbolism, and applicational message of the text?

[7] R. C. H. Lenski, *Interpretation of the Acts of the Apostles* (Columbus, Ohio: Wartburg Press, 1944), 838.

[8] I. Howard Marshall, *Acts of the Apostles,* Tyndale New Testament Commentaries (Leicester, England: Inter-Varsity Press, 1996), 333.

[9] F. F. Bruce, *The Book of Acts: New International Commentary on the New Testament* (Grand Rapids, Mich.: Eerdmans, 1956), 413.

[10] John Calvin, *The Acts of the Apostles,* vol. 2 of *Calvin's New Testament Commentaries,* ed. David W. Torrance and Thomas F. Torrance (Grand Rapids, Mich.: Eerdmans, 1965), 172.

[11] Bruce recalls that the Jews' rejection of the gospel had been dealt with very recently in the writing of Romans, just before he came to Ephesus. The doctrinal and deeply emotional treatment of this tragedy—the Jews' rejection of Jesus—is recorded in Romans 9—11 (see Bruce, *The Book of Acts,* 413).

[12] Paul repeats the same phrase in verse 27, where he says, "I did not shrink from declaring to you the whole purpose of God." The fact that it is used twice in this brief speech adds to the importance of the point he is making.

[13] Henry J. Cadbury, and Kirsopp Lake, *The Acts of the Apostles,* vol. 4 of *The Beginnings of Christianity,* ed. F. J. Foakes-Jackson and Kirsopp Lake (Grand Rapids, Mich.: Baker Books, 1972), 260.

[14] Calvin, *The Acts of the Apostles,* 2:175.

[15] The simple act or event of "turning" is conversion. It is enough for Paul that there is a change from the old way and the old gods to the risen Christ (Acts 14:5; 1 Thes 1:9). While this is not a completed act, the change of heart and attitudes constitutes conversion (see Charles H. Kraft, "Christian Conversion as a Dynamic Process," in *Christianity in Culture* [1979], 333).

[16] William Barclay, *Turning to God* (Philadelphia: Westminster Press, 1963), 18-23.

[17] Dean S. Gilliland, *Pauline Theology and Mission Practice* (Eugene, Oreg.: Wipf & Stock, 1998), 124.

[18] Roland Allen writes: "There is a way of thinking and speaking of the Holy Spirit which banishes the vagueness and makes it perfectly clear why the apostles spoke of the gift of the Holy Spirit as being given only to Christians. If we think of this gift as the gift of the Spirit that dwelt in Jesus Christ, in the man Jesus Christ of whom the Gospels speak, instantly the title becomes clear and definite" (A. T. Paton, ed., *The Ministry of the Spirit: Selected Writings of Roland Allen* [London: World Dominion Press, 1960], 56).

[19] Bruce, *The Book of Acts,* 413.

[20] E. H. Trenchard, "The Acts of the Apostles," in *A New Testament Commentary,* ed. G. C. D. Howley (London: Pickering and Inglis; Grand Rapids, Mich.: Zondervan, 1969), 327.

[21] Bruce, *The Book of Acts,* 415.

[22] This assumption is further substantiated by the nature of the letter to the Ephesians. Paul wrote Ephesians from prison (Eph 3:1; 4:1), probably from Rome (Eph 6:20). The letter bears no note of destination; and it is held to be a cyclical letter. Because it was to be shared among the churches in general there is ambiguity about the "you," "your" being addressed (Eph 1:15; 2:1-2; 6:21). In fact, as it was circulated around the churches, local names might have been entered into the salutation. Marcion, who called it a letter to the Laodiceans, may have seen the one sent to Laodicea (see George E. Harpur, "The Letter to the Ephesians," in Howley, *A New Testament Commentary,* 459). Paul would not know these churches personally, certainly not intimately, because his disciples evangelized them while he remained at Ephesus.

[23] The term *spontaneous expansion* (of the church) was popularized by Roland Allen decades ago to describe what he called "unexhorted and unorganized activities of individual members of the church explaining to others the gospel which they have found for themselves" (*The Spontaneous Expansion of the Church and the Causes Which Hinder It* [London: World Dominion Press, 1927], 10).

[24] Bruce, *The Book of Acts,* 414. The term "elder" *(presbuteros)* has mainly Jewish antecedents, while "bishop" *(episkopos)* has mainly Greek antecedents. Even in the Pastoral Epistles the terms still appear to be used interchangeably (see 1 Tm 3:1; Ti 4:1ff.). For other designations by which such men were known in New Testament times, see Rom 12:8; 1 Thes 5:12; 1 Tm 5:17; Heb 13:17 (ibid., 415-416 n. 56).

[25] Ibid., 416.

[26] The Greek is actually *dia tou aimatos tou idiou* ("with the blood of his own"), translated commonly as "his own blood" (e.g., KJV and RSV). The NRSV has "the blood

of his own Son," making obvious what is inferred by the Greek, that is, the sacrifice of Christ as "propitiation through faith in his blood" (Rom 3:25) and Christ as "an offering for sin" (Heb 10:18). The difficulty expressions of this kind might have caused between Paul and the Jews can only be imagined.

[27] A similar situation came up in the Corinthian church, where Paul was led to mete out discipline when one of the church members engaged in a form of immorality "that is not found even among pagans." In this case the man had taken up with his stepmother (1 Cor 5:1-3). Paul suffered the pain of his own disciples forsaking his teaching and following worldly lifestyles; for example, Demas deserted him (2 Tm 4:10), Alexander and Hymanaes suffered shipwreck in their faith (1 Tm 1:10), while the latter, along with Philetus, Paul says, "swerved from the truth claiming that the resurrection has already taken place" (2 Tm 2:17).

[28] The verses referred to above as well as 1 Timothy 4:1ff. and 2 Timothy 3:1ff., were written while Timothy was pastor at Ephesus. Later John the Apostle writes strongly to the Ephesian church that it had been plagued by false teachers, especially the Nicolaitans, causing the church to be weakened in its "first love" (Rv 2:1-7).

[29] It is common to speak of the "sheep" being harassed by "wolves." The wolves in Matthew 7:15 are false prophets, and this is Paul's concern here (see also Ezr 5:18).

[30] Subsequently in Jerusalem Paul will make his defense before Agrippa. He uses this same expression (*the sanctified*) in Acts 26:18, where he refers to the church. In a comprehensive definition of evangelism he testifies that evangelism is (1) *opening their eyes* (i.e., awareness of need), (2) *turn from darkness to light* (repentance), (3) *from the power of Satan to God* (power encounter), (4) *forgiveness of sins* (justification), and (4) *a place among those who are sanctified by faith in me* (identity with the body of Christ, the church).

[31] When Paul writes to the Ephesians, he gives an inside glimpse of serious problems there; for example, he says that people who steal should stop their stealing (Eph 4:28). If this word was not for the church, what reason or right would Paul have for writing it? Cessation from theft is followed by a call to work honestly "with their own hands," and the reason is the same as that given here, "so as to have something to share with the needy."

[32] Lenski, *Interpretation of the Acts of the Apostles,* 855.

[33] Gilliland, *Pauline Theology and Mission Practice,* 248.

[34] The Jerusalem offering is mentioned frequently (see Rom 15:25-27; 1 Cor 16:1-3; 2 Cor 8:7-9; 9:6—12; 16:1-3).

[35] While the exact words accorded to Jesus are not recorded in the gospels, the spirit of these words is shown in other sayings of Jesus such as those recorded in Lk 6:38; 11:9ff.; Jn 13:34.

# 23

## *Do the Right Thing—*
## *But Results Are Not Guaranteed*

### ACTS 21:17—22:36; 24:10–21

### A. Scott Moreau

Life in North American culture is built on the idea that we have certain rights and that these cannot be violated. We have a right to develop freely and express our religious views. We have a right to pursue what life has to offer. We have a right to protection under the law. Parallel to our concept of rights is our understanding of a guarantee. Products are guaranteed for a certain time period. When I buy a new car, I am guaranteed that if something goes wrong the dealer will fix the problem. When I purchase a box of cereal, I am guaranteed a fresh, satisfying product and that the packaging accurately states the nutritional value of the food. We tend to apply those guarantees to life. We want guaranteed liberty, guaranteed happiness, and guaranteed satisfaction with life. We want to be free from pain, from hardships, and from misery.

Real life, however, comes with no guarantees. The same can be said of missionary training and preparation. We can offer no guarantee of smooth sailing in cross-cultural adjustment. We can offer no guarantee in terms of evangelistic results. We can offer no guarantee in terms of ease of life or joy in leadership.

My first term of missionary service in Swaziland with Campus Crusade for Christ was an exciting one in many ways. It was also perhaps the two most difficult years of my life. In addition to culture stress, I faced a relationship in which my romantic hopes were dashed. At the same time my missionary organization was conducting a country-wide evangelistic campaign that was to serve as a pilot project for other countries in Africa. I was responsible for the campaign in the northern section of this land-locked southern African country. In the months leading up to the campaign we had visited numerous churches and set up numerous training sessions. Most of the churches in the northern part of the country were from one denomination. Two weeks prior to the actual campaign, as a result of missionary debates over doctrinal differences that I did not understand at the time, all of the churches of this denomination pulled out of the campaign except the church I attended. In the area for which I was responsible, we went from the excitement and anticipation of more than sixty churches participating in a potentially life-changing country-wide evangelistic event to the grim reality of four churches sponsoring local evangelistic efforts scattered across the region. The scarring issue of doctrinal division interrupted my dreams of evangelistic glory. I was devastated.

My failures in ministry and personal experiences in my first term of service are not unique. In fact, I would say it is more common in missionary circles than we tend to admit. This reality has shaped my missionary thinking and teaching. As a result, the one guarantee I can and do offer my students on a regular basis is that life will occasionally blow up in our faces. The issue is not how to prevent disasters but how to face them and walk through them with perseverance. The Pauline passages explored in this chapter also offer an illustration of the principle that following Christ offers no guarantee, except perhaps the guarantee that life will blow up.

## PAUL REPORTS AND THE JERUSALEM ELDERS RESPOND

At the end of his third missionary journey Paul travels to Jerusalem to report to the elders what has happened throughout his travels (21:17ff.). He comes to the city in spite of being urged in the Spirit by believers in Tyre (21:4), as well as the prophecy of Agabus (21:10-12) that he would be bound, and the subsequent urging of the believers in Caesarea to stay away from Jerusalem (21:12). As Harold Dollar notes, throughout the Book of Acts Paul has a special relationship with the Jerusalem believers:

> Luke very carefully shows Paul's relationship to Jerusalem throughout his narrative. Saul first meets the apostles through the mediation of Barnabas (9:26ff.). After spending some years in Tarsus, Saul is brought into the movement in Antioch through the Jerusalem insider, Barnabas (11:22 with 11:25). Next Barnabas and Saul take a gift from the church in Antioch to the church in Jerusalem (11:27-30; 12:25). Later Paul and Barnabas' mission to the Gentiles receives the approval of Jerusalem (15:1-35). Finally, Paul yields to the request of James and enters into a Jewish vow while attending the Temple in Jerusalem (21:17ff.).[1]

On arriving in Jerusalem, Paul and his company proceeded to meet with James and the elders.[2] He reports to them in detail God's work among the Gentiles through his ministry.[3] Verse 18 ends the "we" section of this narrative. While it may be that the author was no longer present, the change may also indicate that Paul's missionary role was not just the emphasis (as from chapter 13 on) but the sole focus for the rest of the Book of Acts. In addition to reporting to the Jerusalem leadership, he almost undoubtedly presented the offering he was carrying from the Gentile churches. It is not known why Luke relegates this issue to only a side comment in Paul's later defense before Governor

Felix (24:17) without even raising it here. Indeed, this appears to have been the primary motive in Paul's journeying to Jerusalem (1 Cor 16:1-4; Rom 15:25-28), but the subsequent events related in Acts render it somewhat incidental. Thus, Luke's treatment is appropriate.[4]

The very act of accepting such a collection brought forward some of the issues faced by the church in Jerusalem.[5] The inclusion of Gentiles into the church was nonnegotiable but at the same time a stumbling block to the Jews. This would be especially true in Jerusalem, the spiritual capital of Judaism. This is the third time that the Gentile and Jewish relationship plays a role in Acts; it must be important! Robert C. Tannehill explains each scene:

> The issue of the baptism of Gentiles was settled in 11:1-18. The demand that Gentiles be circumcised and obey the Mosaic Law was rejected in 15:1-31. Now the commitment to include both Jews and Gentiles in the mission generates a third problem: overt or covert pressure on Jewish Christians to abandon their Jewish manner of life.[6]

The heart of the problem was the disturbing rumors that the Jerusalem elders heard about Paul's teaching (no source is identified in the text). It was being said that he advocated that Jewish believers forsake their centuries-old traditions, especially circumcision, and thus turn their backs on the Law of Moses. Things were slipping completely out of control for Paul and the Jerusalem elders, an example that we have no guarantees in life.

Today a quick email might dispel such a rumor, but in Paul's day two-way communication between distant cities could take months. Thus the elders in Jerusalem had no means of discussing the issue with him prior to this visit. Further, since Paul was frequently on the move, reaching him with a specific inquiry about the rumors would have been difficult at best. Paul was probably aware of his reputation among the Jewish Christians. The rumors of his denigration of the Law and traditions would likely not surprise him. In fact, he would have been able to give ready answers to them. It appears that the unproved rumors were troubling to the Jerusalem believers. It is not surprising then that they felt it necessary to hear from Paul personally.

One of the obvious points in the passage is that the elders chose to hear Paul before explaining their situation. The strong positive response of the elders to Paul's detailed report showed their acceptance of his ministry and testimony. It may have been a great relief to them that what they heard were only rumors with no factual basis.[7]

The sudden shift in subject (from Paul's report to the accusations against him circulating in Jerusalem) may indicate that Paul did not even know of the accusations, at least in the context of Jerusalem. As noted above, however, there can be little doubt that Paul knew he did not enjoy a good reputation among the Jews (as well as Judaizing Christians) who knew of his ministry but disagreed with him. While perhaps unexpected, it seems unlikely that this accusation would have surprised him.

## THE ELDERS' PLAN

The narrative then takes a turn. Paul's report complete and the context of the rumors circulating about him staged, the elders then asked Paul what they should do. That no pause is indicated in the text between the question and the answer should be seen as an indication of the rhetorical nature of the question.[8] They already had a plan in mind. We still might ask why they were concerned that the Christian Jews would know that Paul was in Jerusalem? Perhaps they were afraid of persecution from the religious leaders. Since Paul would be associated with Jerusalem Christians, accusations against him, if he were discovered in Jerusalem, would reflect on them, resulting in what could be a difficult situation in the spiritual capital of Judaism.

The Christian elders inform Paul of their plans to prove the rumors false. It appears the opposition to Paul's teaching is among some of the Jews who had come to Christ (Acts 21:20). Perhaps this is the same group of Christian Pharisees in Acts 15:5, who wanted Gentile believers to submit to the regulations of the Law before they could be considered Christians.[9]

No negotiation takes place; the elders have already decided what they want Paul to do. This may indicate that they had prepared for his return, keeping close watch on the situation. They apparently thought they had found an opportunity to clear his and their reputations and to provide security for the local believers. Paul's willingness to comply shows that he trusts their leadership and recognizes that they know the local situation better than he does.

Luke records no overt prayer as a part of the discussion. Is he hinting by its absence and the subsequent results that such prayer may have resulted in a better solution? For example, perhaps Paul could have maintained a low profile, not making any public appearances until the rumors had died down. That Luke had a better solution in mind seems unlikely, given Paul's attitude toward what actually happened. Paul does not regret his arrest, trials, and journey to Rome. Instead, we see only a willingness to go where God leads and to do as God commands, no matter what the cost (19:21; 20:24). Paul knew before going to Jerusalem that hardships awaited him (20:22-23; 21:4-12), and this was God's way of working out the details.

Before further exploring the elders' plan, a number of important questions may be asked: What was the foundation of the rumors that were circulating? How far did Paul accommodate himself to Gentile customs in his ministry among Gentiles? Did Paul actually teach Jewish converts that they should not circumcise their sons? While not explicitly seen anywhere in the New Testament, it may be inferred from the culturally sensitive attitude we see in the Pauline epistles that he would not have been uncomfortable with forgoing circumcision.[10] Though relaxed over the necessity of circumcision, it was still true that he circumcised Timothy for the sake of better communication with a Jewish audience (16:3-4). He also apparently took the Nazirite vow (18:18) and participated in the Jewish feasts of Passover and Pentecost (20:5-6, 16).

These Pauline examples help frame the discussion on the missiological concept of accommodation—the "missionary practice of accommodating the rituals, practices, and styles of the missionary's sending church to those of the recipient culture."[11] Accommodation is rooted in the Catholic church in the sixteenth through eighteenth centuries in relation to the so-called Rites Controversy. In China, Jesuits such as Matteo Ricci promoted the idea that ancestral rituals in Chinese culture were social family rituals and could be practiced by Christians. In India, Jesuit Roberto de Nobili sought to become as Indian as possible, even adopting the practices and lifestyle of a Brahmin holy man. The Catholic debates over the extent of accommodation lasted until the mid-eighteenth century, when finally two papal bulls condemned such practices.[12]

Perhaps we could ask, Would Paul have condemned these practices? Based on his maintenance of certain Jewish rituals, it is impossible to answer this definitively from the material presented in Acts. However, it does raise the question that all missionaries must consider: To what extent may we accommodate cultural religious rituals when new churches are planted across cultural boundaries?[13] If we may draw principles from the passage under consideration, it seems that as long as the ritual does not demean Christ or contradict the essentials of the gospel, Paul showed flexibility in what he practiced and allowed. Of course, for a full treatment of the issues, discussion must range far beyond this passage. Other significant passages for consideration include the honoring of specific foods or days (Rom 14:2-6), dealing with meat offered to idols (1 Cor 8), baptism for the dead (1 Cor 15:29), acting like a Jew when Jews are present and like a Gentile when Jews are absent (Gal 2:11-21), and so on.

## SOLUTION TO THE PROBLEM

While the rumors circulating in Jerusalem in Acts 21 were false, it is easy to see how they got started. This serves as a reminder that still rings true today: People read the intent of the missionary in light of their own world view rather than the world view of the missionary. They have to make sense of our attitudes and actions in light of the filters they wear, not in light of our filters. If we are unaware of this or treat it too lightly, we run the risk of being misunderstood and even rejected for what seem to us inappropriate reasons. In this example it does not even matter what the local leaders (the elders) think; the Christians of Jerusalem have heard rumors and the rumors make sense to them—another reminder that life offers no guarantees.

The solution must go beyond teaching; Paul must demonstrate that he is not throwing out the customs that have been given over many generations.[14] In Walter Wink's terminology, Paul's teaching about the customs was a threat to the system and the very identity of Jews as a "called-apart" people, so the system responds to the threat with a counter-attack.[15] In effect, Paul "becomes the lightning rod through which the pent-up energy surrounding this issue is discharged."[16]

The elders propose that Paul sponsor the final purification of four men who had undergone a vow. That the vow was a Nazirite vow seems hardly debatable.[17]

It was an act of special separation unto God on the part of the person undergoing the vow, as described in Numbers 6:1-21. Such an act was allowed under the Law and seen as an act of piety. The Nazirite would pay the expenses for the offerings necessary to complete the vow. Having himself gone through a Nazirite vow (18:18), Paul would hardly object to this as long as it was understood that he was not teaching that Gentile converts must adhere to Judaic practices. Before he could sponsor the Nazirites, however, he himself needed to be purified. Having recently returned from Gentile areas of the world, he was ritually impure and unable to sponsor the men in their ritual.[18] His own purification would take seven days, at the end of which he would be able to pay for their purification.[19] Each day during his purification he would report to the priests,[20] and his very public presence was intended to quell the rumors: "Thus all will know that there is nothing in what they have been told about you, but that you yourself observe and guard the law" (21:24b). At the same time, however, such visibility put him at great risk. Paul undoubtedly remembered the warnings he had personally received from the Holy Spirit that imprisonment and suffering awaited him (20:22-23), the admonition of the Christians in Tyre not to go to Jerusalem (21:4), and Agabus's prophecy of his arrest (21:10-14), but none of these warnings deterred him from trying to fulfill the request of the Jerusalem elders.

Paul had no qualms about participating in both the purification and the Nazirite completion rituals, showing that his willingness to "become all things to all people" (1 Cor 9:19-23) was more than just talk. He certainly did not let the fear of alienating anyone serve as a deterrent, though he did not want to alienate anyone unnecessarily. He saw nothing contradictory to his walk of faith in participating in these rituals, as long as they were not perceived as a means of justification (see Rom 3:21-24; Eph 2:8-10; Gal 1:6-10). His hope, together with the Jerusalem elders, was that his high visibility in participating in the rituals would stop the rumors.

The plan of the elders is followed by a recitation of the policy hammered out several years earlier and described in Acts 15:22-29. Paul, being present at the Jerusalem council and passing the decision on to the church in Antioch before going on his second missionary journey, is aware of the resolution (15:30-31).[21] Perhaps F. F. Bruce best captured the reason for the recitation:

> The elders wish to assure Paul that their misgivings are confined to his teaching reportedly given to Jewish believers. We are glad to know, they say in effect, that you do not teach Jewish believers to abandon the ancestral customs, and we should like you to make this clear to everybody here. As for Gentile believers, of course, we have already agreed that nothing is to be imposed on them apart from the abstentions detailed in the apostolic letter.[22]

## PAUL VICTIMIZED BY THE RUMOR MILL

Unfortunately, no missionary is in charge of the rumor mills found in every culture, and once again we see that we are offered no guarantees. Trophimus, a Gentile from Ephesus in Asia (Acts 20:4; 2 Tm 4:20), was also in the city. Paul is seen with him. When the Jews from Asia, who were aware of this, see Paul in the Temple, they jump to the logical though incorrect conclusion that Paul brought Trophimus beyond the outer court of the Gentiles and into the inner court of the Temple. This was a violation of the worst kind for the traditionalists. In fact, warnings were posted on the barrier to the inner court in Greek and Latin that any non-Jews who entered were themselves responsible for their ensuing death.[23] Luke is clear on the supposition for the rumor and on Paul's innocence in the matter. Even so, Paul is implicated, and mob justice asserts itself.

The charge leveled is greater than that against Paul's teaching. The new charge is that he has actually defiled the Temple. At the time of Pentecost, when Jerusalem's population was swollen with an influx of devout visitors from the Jewish Diaspora, the social tensions naturally would be higher than at other times and the possibility of mob violence greater. This may help explain the quick response of the Roman soldiers, who were probably ready for just such a situation. It did not take much to stir up a crowd of zealous religious patriots with a charge of defilement of their holy place. The "wild card" is that it is the Jews from Asia and not the Jerusalem Jews who stirred up the crowd. Their presence does not seem to be something the elders had taken into account in their prescription for Paul, and he pays the price.

One of the first acts after the accusation of Paul and the stirring of the crowd is that the doors to the Temple were closed (21:30). In a literal sense the intention was to keep the holy place from further defilement. Metaphorically, however, we may also see the closing of the Temple as a closing of Judaism to Paul and the New Testament church. Bruce remarks, "The exclusion of God's message and messenger from the house once called by his name sealed its doom: it was now ripe for the destruction which Jesus had predicted for it many years before (Luke 21:6)."[24] That this is significant is seen in the rest of the narrative of Acts, which focuses on Paul and the defense of his ministry to Judaism.

In addition to the ongoing tension between the Jewish and emerging Christian communities, we also see a shift in Luke's presentation of God's sovereignty. Earlier in Acts, God mainly protected the church through deliverance, but after Acts 21 the church grew in perseverance through trials rather than seeing deliverance from them. Robert C. Tannehill notes the shift:

There are no more wondrous prison releases, as in 5:17-21; 12:1-17; and 16:25-30, although Paul is rescued from danger, he remains a prisoner. Paul's references to his bonds (26:29; 28:20) keep this fact before us. Paul enters this bondage because he is willing to put himself at risk in order to support Jewish Christians who treasure their Jewish heritage. Later he will say to Jews, "For the sake of the hope of Israel I wear this chain" (28:20). This enlarges the point: Paul's whole imprisonment is an act of loyalty to Israel. Paul's lengthy imprisonment and the witness that this prisoner bears to Israel's hope are signs of his loyalty to Israel, although he is being attacked as a renegade. Imprisonment is not just an opportunity for an amazing escape.[25]

That Paul wanted his Jewish brothers and sisters to come to faith in Christ cannot be questioned (Rom 10:1). That he was flexible in the observance of the Jewish law and compliant with the request of the Jerusalem Christian leaders is also undeniable. However, all of these factors together could not prevent his arrest and the subsequent events portrayed in Acts. Even Paul had no guarantees.

## IMPLICATIONS FOR MISSION

In mission circles today we emphasize the need for consultation with the local church when making crucial decisions. We highlight the importance of accountability on the part of the missionary, as well as flexibility in contextualization of both message and method. American pragmatism, however, often overshadows our perspective and demands that good methods bring successful results. Paul's story in Acts 21:17-29 is a case study illustrating that even when we do everything "right," things can go wrong.

What about my experience in Swaziland? Eventually, I recovered from the embarrassment of having the churches pull out of the campaign. I learned how to live through the feelings of failure in the relationships that did not go the way I wanted. In fact, it was because these things blew up in my face that I gained strength to trust more fully in God's oversight of my life. Stripped of my hopes and faced with an almost debilitating sense that I had blown it, I clung to Christ and began to see God walk with me through the failures. As time went by and I continued to persevere in the situation, the Holy Spirit gave me strength that enabled me to live life trusting in his ability to carry me through whatever happened. In fact, if I had not failed, I would not have had the chance to learn the more valuable lesson of trust in spite of the feelings I lived with. In the immediate context, all I saw was failure. Eventually there came the ability to trust God despite circumstances and to know that whatever life brings, walking with the Lord in "ruthless trust" is the only path that makes sense.[26]

## REFERENCES

[1] Harold Dollar, *St. Luke's Missiology: A Cross-Cultural Challenge* (Pasadena, Calif.: William Carey Library, 1996), 134.

[2] In view of what appears to be a description of the large size of the church in Jerusalem (literally, "how many tens of thousands," v. 20), this gathering may have included seventy elders, modeled after the traditional number of Jewish leaders. If so, James must have had a large house to accommodate this group (see F. F. Bruce, *The Book of Acts: The New International Commentary on the New Testament* [Grand Rapids, Mich.: Eerdmans, 1988], 404-405).

[3] This, as well as Paul and Barnabas's reports to the Jerusalem church in 15:4, may be seen as a precursor to contemporary missionaries debriefing in their home churches.

[4] Some feel that this indicates that the Jerusalem elders did not accept the offering or that there was antagonism over it, some even positing that the Jerusalem elders set Paul up for failure. While this is possible in view of the awkwardness of Jewish acceptance of Gentile help, it hardly seems likely (see the discussion in J. G. Dunn, *The Acts of the Apostles* [Valley Forge, Pa.: Trinity Press International], 284-285; and Luke Timothy Johnson, *The Acts of the Apostles* [Collegeville, Minn.: The Liturgical Press, 1992], 377-379).

[5] Richard N. Longenecker, "The Acts of the Apostles," in *The Expositor's Bible Commentary* (Grand Rapids, Mich.: Zondervan, 1992), 9:519.

[6] Robert C. Tannehill, *The Narrative Unity of Luke-Acts: A Literary Interpretation*, vol. 2, *The Acts of the Apostles* (Minneapolis, Minn.: Fortress Press, 1994), 268.

[7] Certainly it should not be overlooked that they were also grateful for the offering Paul brought.

[8] Johnson, *The Acts of the Apostles*, 375.

[9] I. Howard Marshall, *The Acts of the Apostles*, Tyndale New Testament Commentaries (Grand Rapids, Mich.: Eerdmans, 1980), 343.

[10] See the discussion in Bruce, *The Book of Acts*, 405-406; see also Paul's attitude toward circumcision, seen in Gal 5:2-4, 6; 6:15.

[11] George Hunsberger, "Accommodation," in *Evangelical Dictionary of World Missions*, ed. A. Scott Moreau (Grand Rapids, Mich.: Baker Books, 2000), 31.

[12] In 1742 for China and 1744 for India, Hunsberger points out that the term *accommodation* was utilized prior to the now widely accepted Catholic term *inculturation* and Protestant term *contextualization*. With accommodation the missionary remained in charge, focused on external practices rather than the deeper, more meaningful structures, and neglected to question the culture that shaped the Christian faith of the missionary (ibid., 32).

[13] For further discussion, see Mathias Zahniser, *Symbol and Ceremony: Making Disciples Across Cultures* (Monrovia, Calif.: MARC Publications, 1997); Bernard Adeney, *Strange Virtues* (Downers Grove, Ill.: InterVarsity Press, 1995).

[14] Dunn, *The Acts of the Apostles*, 287.

[15] See Walter Wink, *Engaging the Powers* (Minneapolis, Minn.: Fortress Press, 1992).

[16] Tannehill, *The Narrative Unity of Luke-Acts*, 2:270.

[17] Dunn, *The Acts of the Apostles*, 287; Johnson, *The Acts of the Apostles*, 375; Bruce, *The Book of Acts*, 406; Tannehill, *The Narrative Unity of Luke-Acts*, 2:207.

[18] See the helpful discussion in Johnson, *The Acts of the Apostles*, 375-376.

[19] On the possible explanations for this, see Marshall, *The Acts of the Apostles*, 345 n. 1.

[20] Johnson, *The Acts of the Apostles*, 377.

[21] For a more extensive discussion of the missiological significance of the prohibition, see Dollar, *St. Luke's Missiology*, 92-109, 159-162.

[22] Bruce, *The Book of Acts*, 407.

[23] Ibid., 409.

[24] Ibid., 410.

[25] Tannehill, *The Narrative Unity of Luke-Acts*, 2:271.

[26] Brennan Manning, *Ruthless Trust: The Ragamuffin's Path to God* (New York: HarperCollins Publishers, 2000).

# 24

# *The Contextualization and Translation of Christianity*

ACTS 9:1–9; 22:3–33; 26:2–23

## Shawn B. Redford

Like many missionaries, I wish that my own mission practice had greater development, especially in my early years. As a young Christian I had great zeal to proclaim God's message to others and little understanding of God's plan in mission, combined with a terribly awkward way of expressing myself. Often I would bluntly ask absolute strangers, "Do you know Jesus?" resulting in polite responses that were ultimately focused on finding the nearest exit (airplane passengers were an especially captive and annoyed audience). Though the process was similar to extracting impacted wisdom teeth, I came to realize that God was giving me a great deal of grace by allowing for my clumsy steps in mission.

Numerous well-developed perspectives in mission theory have held their place in the history of missionary practice.[1] Some of these include the watchword, ecumenism, the Church Growth movement, cultural anthropology, social action, receptivity theory, signs and wonders, power encounter, contextualization, and recently, the translation model.[2] However, since the introduction of contextualization in 1972, this theory has grown in appreciation to become commonly accepted in evangelical mission theory today with relatively little biblical work done to critique or validate the practice.[3]

The accounts of Paul's conversion in Acts 9, 22, and 26 provide narrative accounts that demonstrate integration between contextualization and the translation model of mission. Moreover, through the repeated accounts of Paul's conversion experience, the theme of Acts 1:8 is illustrated narratively. Beginning in Jerusalem and Judea (Acts 9), moving thematically to Judea and Samaria (Acts 22), and onward to Samaria and the ends of the earth (Acts 26), each presentation of Paul's conversion represents wider socio-cultural circles. Whether or not Luke intends this, these three accounts illustrate evangelism in expanding multicultural contexts, showing the maturation of Paul's witness and the translation of Christian witness through time.

The thesis of this chapter is that Luke's narrative accounts of Paul's conversion demonstrate progressive steps stretching the witness of the church multiculturally, paralleling a progression from (the modern missionary concept of) contextualization to the translation principle in Christian mission. These passages call us to understand the importance of relational integrity in the midst of missionary witness. The encounter of contextual and translation models in Paul's missionary activity provides biblical critique and integration between these two areas.

This progression is a step from the familiar to the unfamiliar, from comfort to discomfort, from small boundaries to greater boundaries, and from one culture to another. In each case the familiar aspects provide solid footing, while the unfamiliar ground is a painful process of understanding God's will. Ultimately the passages demonstrate God's graceful approach to the missionary as the missionary grows in the process of understanding God's mission.

## CONTEXTUALIZATION

Since contextualization and the translation model are often topics in this chapter, some definition will be helpful. I have defined *contextualization* after Arthur Glasser, as follows:

> Contextualization represents the careful and refined use of a people's cultural forms in order that the truth of the gospel can be correctly expressed in their language through a judicious use of their own thought forms.[4]

Contextualization involves communicating well enough so that the communication itself is not a barrier to the presentation of the gospel, that is, presenting the gospel in a timely manner and in appropriate portions. It is communication that is foremost directed and guided by the Holy Spirit for the sake of the salvation of the receptors. Finally, it is a process that transforms and challenges the missionary's understandings of scripture by seeking to remove biases from the missionary's context.

Contextualization is not minimizing the impact of scripture that is to be shared with the receptor for the sake of the receptor's comfort. It is not "watering down" the gospel. It is not reducing the whole of the gospel so that the receptor has no ability to understand the implications of being a disciple of Jesus Christ.

Contextualization might meet the perceived needs of the receptors. It might share a message that the receptors want to hear. It might even be a message that admonishes the receptors and meets their needs at the same time. However, contextualization most often will include loving and graceful elements because the Bible is fundamentally a series of messages about the love and grace of God calling all humanity into redemption.[5]

## THE TRANSLATION MODEL

The translation model focuses on the effect that takes place when indigenous Christians move away from any original missionary influence (often this takes multiple generations) and freely allow their own interests and concerns to bring new questions, shape, meaning, and focus to the Christian message. This results in a translated Christianity (not transplanted) that produces unforeseen and added contributions to the mission of God and the nature of God in their midst. Likening the process to linguistic translation, Andrew F. Walls comments:

> Translation involves the attempt to express the meaning of the source from the resources of, and within the working system of, the receptor language. Something new is brought into the language, but that new element can only be comprehended by means of and in terms of the pre-existing language and its conventions. In the process that language and its system is effectively expanded, put to new use; but the translated element from the source language has also, in a sense, been expanded by translation; the receptor language has a dynamic of its own and takes the new material to realms it never touched in the source language.[6]

This chapter examines the three accounts of Paul's conversion in Acts 9, 22, and 26 in order to show the integration between contextualization and the translation models of mission.

## ACTS 9:1-9

Though given independently Paul's commission was substantially the same as that given to the eleven in Galilee and on Olivet. The fact that the glorified Redeemer felt it expedient to appear in person to this man and to give him his commission from His own lips is most significant.[7]

### *And You Will Be My Witnesses in Jerusalem and throughout Judea*

Geographically, Paul is near Damascus, far from Jerusalem and outside of the Judean region. However, Paul and his companions form the cultural context of this account. Paul is the focus of God's mission in Acts 9, and Paul is deeply rooted in Jewish structures as a Pharisee. Although born in Tarsus, Paul represents Jerusalem in thought and further represents one of the most difficult problems in mission—the problem of those who are convinced that they have everything solved. Paul is representative of Jerusalem and Judea because he is entrenched in the Jewish understandings and structures of his day. Paul's Judaic tenacity is manifest in his headstrong determination to hunt down followers of Jesus Christ to deliver them to imprisonment or death.

### Contextual Issues

Though Paul demonstrates no grace toward God or God's followers, God's grace toward Paul is evident in the highly contextual manner in which God addresses Paul—in Paul's own language of Aramaic (9:4-5; cf. 26:14). While Greek would certainly have been an understandable language for Paul, it is unlikely that Paul could have overcome his ethnocentrism if God had not spoken in the language of the Jews that Paul would have expected. God could certainly have used dreams, visions, or other nonverbal communication, but God chose to use the familiar and expected to reach into Paul's context. It is most likely that the men with Paul "stood speechless" because they heard God speaking in their mother tongue and could not see anyone (9:7). If they could not understand the words of Jesus, confusion would have been the likely response.

Furthermore, God addresses Paul in a culturally familiar and expected Old Testament pattern of intensification ("Saul, Saul"), using the Hebrew form of Paul's name (9:4; cf. Gn 22:11 "Abraham, Abraham"; Gn 46:2 "Jacob, Jacob"; Ex 3:4 "Moses, Moses"; 1 Sm 3:4, 6, 10 "Samuel! Samuel!")[8]

Since we know that this passage is a translation, the Greek phrase translated "I am Jesus" *(egō eimi Iēsous)* is probably based on the underlying Aramaic.[9] Paul, upon hearing the "I AM" phrase from the voice of God, would likely have been reminded of the tetragrammaton YHWH (9:5; cf. Ex 3:14). The impact of God's response would have absolutely overwhelmed Paul as he realized God's authority. Additionally, the "I AM" phrase missionally links Paul with Moses, and Paul would eventually see his calling as having continuity with the Old Testament. Kaiser notes:

> It can hardly be argued that this [Paul's mission] was some sort of late shift in the apostolic plans and that it marked the first time that the message of salvation would now be extended to the non-Jewish world. In fact, Paul cites as his authority the Old Testament.[10]

Paul, like Moses, heard directly from YHWH. More important, Paul was called to break the bondage of Jewish missionary apathy toward the Gentiles in the same way that Moses was called to lead Israel from Egyptian bondage in order that they might become a missionary force for the nations (Ex 7:5-17; 9:16; Rom 9:17).

The entire passage is ultimately one of establishing the proper identity and authority of Paul and Jesus. Just as Jesus' ministry took place in a specific context, Jesus now comes to Paul in a specific context with a specific language demonstrating God's power to halt the self-righteous perceptions and activity of Paul (9:1). Paul is so invested in his own ideas and cultural tradition (9:2) that he must face a greater power for him to stop persecuting Christianity (9:4); Paul could only be stopped by a greater power (cf. Lk 11:21-22). Therefore the use of power is contextual.

Although Jesus could certainly have stopped Paul in numerous ways, he chose to communicate to Paul through power. Paul's self-righteousness on the

Damascus road should be a constant reminder for all modern missionaries repeatedly to seek God's will in mission. Self-righteousness is an extremely powerful and deceptive psychological force that inhibits God's mission because it masks God's real desire in mission and falsely affirms our own misunderstandings.

The interaction between Jesus and Paul is an excellent example of contextual admonishment (9:3-9). It is a mistake to think that contextualization should diminish or soften the message of God. Contextualization is foremost an activity that correctly communicates the message of God, whatever that message may be. However, if someone is called to admonish another person, contextualization is essential for producing an understandable message (2 Sm 12:1-14; Lk 4:16-30; Acts 22:3-22).

### *The Translation of Christianity*

Within this passage we again see the principal example of God reaching into human history and revealing the Christian message for the nations. The first translation of the Christian message is always one of God to humanity. As Andrew Walls states, the "incarnations of Christ are contingent on that first Incarnation with its firm anchorage in time and space, its 'crucified under Pontius Pilate.' Similarly, biblical translation is re-translation, with the original always at hand."[11] We see this translation of the message in God's call to Paul. Just as God called Israel through Abraham for mission, Christ called the Jews for mission, and the Holy Spirit called the church for mission. Archibald McLean sees this translation as so influential that he counts Paul's conversion as a "sixth great commission passage."[12]

God translates the message for Paul, and as Paul understands that message, he begins a process of reshaping Christianity by taking the Christian message in the new direction of Christ for the Gentiles. The blindness of Paul's self-righteousness is replaced with eyes to see God's missional love for all humanity; this results in new questions and directions for Jewish believers, and unforeseen issues spring from the newly developed Judaic Christianity. All this began to reshape the meaning of mission in the first century (Acts 15; 22; 28).

Self-righteousness is hard to address. As a Christian, I was steeped in self-righteousness and legalism with a dangerous passion for evangelism. With a college fraternity as my first mission field, I hoped to share my developing faith with my colleagues. I had taken a communal step by boarding with men that I hoped would find faith in Jesus. Later I realized that the stripping of my own self-righteousness was God's real focus. I learned slowly that God had to do a great work in me before I could genuinely share my faith and cross boundaries "to the nations."

### ACTS 22:3-22

If the church, under the inspiration of its head, Jesus Christ, lives by the conviction that the world is on a course that leads to death, it has no other

choice than to invite men and women to become a part of God's new order, the kingdom of life. The church that is not evangelizing is a church
that does not truly believe the gospel. It is a faithless church.[13]

### And You Will Be My Witnesses throughout Judea and Samaria

The context of Acts 22 is radically different from that of Acts 9. The Jews
are now confounded as they exist in the tension of cultural boundaries. The
prejudice of the Jews toward the Gentiles represents a nearly identical tension
to that which existed between Judea and Samaria, which gave the apostles
missional difficulty (see Jn 4).

Acts 22 represents a mixture of ethnically Jewish and Gentile people (21:27,
29) that includes Jewish Christians (21:20) and Gentile Christians (21:25). The
Jewish Christians are Judaizers. They have blended their newfound Christianity with their own misunderstood forms of Jewish law, resulting in unhealthy
and missionless spirituality. The tension of Acts 15 has not diminished. The
Jewish believers are even more entrenched in their cultural imperialism as their
ethnic values police the spiritual community. Moreover, Paul is the scapegoat
for their wayward spirituality, which eventually erupts in an urban riot.

In addition, it is very likely that Paul is undergoing reverse culture shock
because he has recently returned from his third missionary journey in Gentile
lands. Moreover, Paul has changed radically from his conversion in Acts 9. He
is now an experienced missionary familiar with Jewish and Gentile tendencies
as they relate to God's mission.

### Contextual Issues

The self-righteousness that Paul exhibited in Acts 9 is now being thrust upon
him by self-righteous Jewish believers. Paul's speech is contextual, evangelistic, and reforming in nature. As in Acts 9, contextual admonishment is hard at
work. Paul ultimately admonishes the traditionalism among Jewish believers,
which is not simply their Judaizing tendency. It also includes their lack of understanding that God's missional plan includes the Gentiles as co-believers and
co-workers in sharing Christ's message with the nations.

Paul captures the attention of the crowd by using Aramaic, the street language of Palestine (22:2). He learned from God's grace in Acts 9 to work within
certain expectations of his audience even if those are built on misconceived
perspectives (such as the idea that God is Jewish). Furthermore, Paul uses the
phrase "brothers and fathers" (22:1) and quickly notes his Jewish heritage: "I
am a Jew, born in Tarsus in Cilicia, but brought up in this city at the feet of
Gamaliel, educated strictly according to our ancestral law, being zealous for
God, just as all of you are today" (22:3). Paul even builds upon the common
heritage of both the Jews and Judaizing Christians when using the term "the
God of our ancestors" (22:14). The additional corroboration of Ananias's testimony, noted by Paul as a devout Jew (22:12) and a Christian believer, permits
Paul to declare Jesus' title as "the Righteous One" with understandably little

reaction from the Judaizers (22:14). However, Paul is not merely trying to gain credibility. He is sharing his journey relationally with those who are weak in their own understanding of God's mission.

Paul builds within his speech his conversion and experience with God. The first-time reader might expect that Paul is going to affirm the crowd's existing perception of the Christian faith. However, Paul has a message to deliver with contextual skill that ultimately illustrates the purpose of Israel's privilege: "Go, for I will send you far away to the Gentiles" (22:21). This is not Paul's purpose alone. It has always been the role that God wanted for Israel (see Gn 12:1-3; 17:4-6; 18:18; 22:17-18; 26:4; 27:29; Nm 24:9; Ps 72:17; Is 61:9; Jer 4:2; Zech 8:13).

It is only at this point that the crowd erupts. The news of God's appearance to Paul and his experience with "Jesus of Nazareth" (22:8) is not what causes the eruption, but rather the news that God purposefully seeks out the Gentiles through Jewish agents of mission. This is what causes the crowd to yell "away with such a fellow from the earth! For he should not be allowed to live" (22:22). Robert C. Tannehill has noted that Paul emphasizes "his Jewish roots and the Jewish roots of his mission."[14] Paul is emphatically stating that the Jews and the Judaizing Christians have misunderstood their roles—their relational purpose with God is integrally linked in God's mission.

The apparent discrepancy between the situation in Acts 9:7 and Paul's account of the situation in 22:9 has often been an issue of debate, or ignored altogether, but it has not been addressed from a missiological standpoint. The account of Paul's companions in Acts 9:7 takes place at the beginning of Paul's transformation in mission. "The men who were traveling with him stood speechless because they heard *(akountes;* root, *akouō)* the voice but saw no one." The men with Paul actually did hear the words that God spoke to Paul. We are only told, however, about Paul's response to this message. Paul has no comprehension of the nature of God's mission for the Gentiles nor that this responsibility is being placed upon Paul and his companions.

The context of Acts 22 is critically important as we consider the contrast in Acts 22:9: "Now those who were with me saw the light but did not hear *(ouk ēkousan;* root, *akouō)* the voice of the one who was speaking to me." Paul is using the narrative of his conversion to address this angry audience. Paul is likely saying, "Now those who were with me saw the light but did not listen to the voice."[15] Familiar echoes of Matthew 13:13 come to mind—"and hearing they do not listen."[16] Paul is implying that despite a very similar experience, they never followed God in mission. It is surprising that Luke records nothing of Paul's companions in the years that follow the Damascus road experience. It is highly likely that there is no sign of Paul's companions' involvement in God's mission to the Gentiles.

However, Paul does not make this change simply to tell the Judaizers additional information. He has begun with an indirect style of communication that gives an initial narrative understanding of the situation in order to tell the hardened Judaizers that they have not listened either. This is common in contextualized admonishment, as it helps the listeners manage the difficulty of

the message (2 Sm 12:1-14; Lk 4:16-30). Through Luke's account in Acts 22
we are allowed to see the maturation of Paul's evangelistic skills and missional
comprehension, while the church has remained entrenched in a past that understands very little about God's desire for its involvement in mission. When Paul
finally states this same idea directly in 22:21, the crowd understands what Paul
is saying.

## The Translation of Christianity

This passage represents the birth pains within the translation model of Christianity as the Jewish believers are screaming over their inability to control and
shape the newly maturing Gentile Christianity. Already the Gentile forms of
Christianity have brought uncomfortable and unforeseen questions to Jewish
believers, including the Gentiles' lack of interest in Judaizing (Acts 21:28). Paul
is caught within this stress as a midwife trying to assist in what has become a
recently discovered and unwanted pregnancy. As the Gentile Christians take on
these new forms and understandings in mission, the traditionalistic Jewish
Christians are angry over the freedom that the Gentiles have found in Christ.
Gentile Christianity is about to walk free from the control of Jewish ethno-pa-
ternalism. Andrew Walls states: "Early Christianity was thus already touched
by the translation principle. Not even Jewish Palestine could be culturally and
linguistically sealed off from the Hellenistic world; and the very words of Jesus
come to us in Greek dress."[17]

However, this lesson should not go unnoticed in contemporary mission practice and in missiology as a discipline. The interplay in Acts 22 between a traditionalistic church and Paul's missionary activity has application for today.
The church uninvolved in God's mission can often be a destructive force for
the missionary. Many missionaries (like Paul) have returned from active involvement in God's mission only to be drawn into a missionless church filled
with issues that have nothing to with God's plan for humanity. Like the
Judaizing Christians of Acts 22, the Western church has often been co-opted
by polarized cultural values, such as the fundamentalist-modernist controversy
that has wreaked havoc on missionary practice. Polarization and division in
the church have the capacity to hinder real missionary activity. The good
news, however, is that even this type of church will not ultimately stop God's
missionary plan.

There is a lesson for missionaries in this too. Missionaries can often forget
to build missionally motivated churches. Who was leading the Jerusalem church
to become God's missionary people? Charles Van Engen reminds us:

As the church translates its nature into priorities, . . . it must go one step
further and convert that knowledge and faith into action in the world
through its members. . . . Without such careful and intentional planning,
missionary congregations never emerge and are never built up to become
God's people in mission in the world.[18]

As God began to develop my own missional understanding through talented missionaries working among the Maasai of East Africa, I was also learning first-hand that the church must reflect God's design in being a mission-based community. It was no longer *my* witness but *our* witness, and the missionaries had to avoid the pitfall of being the "mission experts." The entire church had to manifest Christ's presence and witness for there to be a translation of the Christian faith.

## ACTS 26:2-23

Now, in the good providence of God, he [Paul] has the right of way, and with the audience and escort of centurions, chief captains, governors, and kings, leisurely takes up his triumphal procession toward Rome. He had touched the fringes of Rome's domain and now he was closing in on the heart of the empire.[19]

### And You Will Be My Witnesses in . . . Samaria and to the Ends of the Earth!

Stepping into Paul's testimony in Acts 26, we again find a radically different context from Acts 9 and Acts 22. At least two years have passed in Paul's life (24:27), and that time has been spent in prison. Paul is standing before multiple rulers. Agrippa is ethnically Jewish, with knowledge of Jewish customs (26:3), but his cultural makeup is largely Hellenistic.[20] Much like the Samaritans, Agrippa represents a blend of ethnic and cultural values. Little is known about Festus. Caesar is the unexpected and absent participant in this audience. Paul is informed that Festus will be writing to Caesar based on this speech (25:23-27). The context of Acts 26 is then Rome itself, which represented uncharted territory much like "the ends of the earth."

Although Paul is in prison, this discussion is not about securing his freedom because Paul's real trial will take place in Rome (25:12, 21, 25). Paul is primarily concerned about sharing his faith with the rulers that surround him and sending a record of his faith before he arrives in Rome.

### Contextual Issues

The most obvious difference of Jesus' wording in Acts 26 is the added phrase "it hurts you to kick against the goads" (26:14). It is astounding to realize the contextual significance of this phrase. The term *goad,* however, could have two possible cultural meanings.

In Acts 26:14, in Paul's conversion story, Christ tells Paul that it hurts him to kick against the goads. Although the idea of the goad for oxen is common in the Jewish world, Paul (or Luke) seems to be adopting the Greek proverb here; this is most suitable in an address to the Hellenist Agrippa.

... The proverb (also in the plural) is a stock quotation by the first century A.D.[21]

Herod Agrippa II was a ruler who understood the power of the Roman army. In fact, Josephus later attributes a speech to Agrippa in which the main point is "that the Romans were simply too strong to succumb to any uprising which Jewish revolutionaries could mount (*War* 2.345ff.)."[22] The meaning of the phrase "to kick against the goads" for a first-century Hellenistic authority would have been "an expression of futile and detrimental resistance to a stronger power, whether it be that of a god, of destiny, or of man."[23] The use of this phrase helps modern-day readers to see King Agrippa's culture through Paul's eyes. Agrippa is more Hellenistic than Jewish and familiar with authoritarian values. This Greek colloquial phrase would have captured Agrippa's attention in much the same way that Paul captured the crowd's attention in Acts 22 by speaking in its language. More important, the phrase would have conveyed that Paul found himself in the same predicament with God as Agrippa did with the Roman army—one of overwhelming power that can crush at will. To put it in theological rather than missiological terms, in Acts 26:14

> the fact remains that the common Greek and Roman saying *pros kenta laktizein* ["to kick against the goads"] does not occur at all in the Jewish sphere. It thus seems that Christ's warning to Paul not to attempt futile and harmful resistance takes the form of a suitable Greek proverb. To be quite blunt, Paul or Luke puts a Greek proverb on the lips of Jesus. It is, of course, no accident that this proverb should occur in the account of Paul's conversion, which is given to the Hellenist Agrippa. If it comes from Paul himself, this means that he cleverly adapts himself to the situation, as on other occasions. Out of regard for his particular hearers, he works in a suitable proverb, which it is most unlikely that he himself should not have known.[24]

Paul was doing what any good missionary would do. He was translating the message (literally) and adding his own contextual insights in order to share the Christian message in understandable ways for his Greek-speaking audience.

Paul's inclusion of the Greek proverb has merit from the standpoint of linguistic translation as well. Additionally, it should be noted that the likely Aramaic verb for "persecution" in 22:8 had a focus of military attack or revenge, denoting "chasing one's enemies," "pursuing someone," or "hurting someone."[25] However, the Greek verb can communicate religious persecution or positive connotations, such as "following after" or "aspiring after someone."[26] Including the proverb provides consistent meaning with respect to Paul's militant style before his conversion. Paul's choice to include this proverb is as valid from a standpoint of missionary translation as it is contextually. The two are integrated in the process. Noting the reality of what Paul is doing, Andrew Walls states:

> Translation is the art of the impossible. Exact transmission of meaning from one linguistic medium to another is continually hampered not only

by structural and cultural difference; the words of the receptor language are pre-loaded, and the old cargo drags the new into areas uncharted in the source language. In the end the translator has simply to do his best and take risks in a high-risk business.[27]

Paul continues with an expanded version of the former accounts (26:16-18) that combines understandings that Paul developed over time. The message is a merger of various elements in his growth as a Christian that allows this audience to hear God's missionary plan revealed to the Gentiles. Some of these ideas may have been written with Caesar in mind. While God rescued Paul from death, he also rescued Paul from the Jewish and Gentile understanding of God's mission. Some Jews in his audience believed they owned God and may have had little interest in God's mission, while the Gentiles saw the God of the Jews as a foreign deity, insignificant to their own society—"a stumbling block to Jews and foolishness to Gentiles" (1 Cor 1:23).

Ultimately the focus of God's mission is expressed in the crossing of spiritual boundaries (26:18). Paul announces God's plan for the Gentiles to cross from darkness to light, from Satan's power to God, and from sin to forgiveness, giving the Gentiles a "place among those who are sanctified by faith" in God (26:18). For the tri-cultural Herod Agrippa, ethnically a Jew and culturally Greco-Roman, this must have been challenging. Paul's similar cultural background to a Greek-speaking Jew and Roman citizen gave him a very rare opportunity relationally with Agrippa to announce God's plan to break the barriers that divided Jew and Gentile. Paul revealed God's unchanging plan for the very cultures that Agrippa governed in tension. Kaiser notes:

> Paul stood on trial for his life before King Agrippa in Acts 26:22 and affirmed: "I am saying nothing beyond what the prophets and Moses said would happen." He did not see himself as an innovator, or as one who introduced meanings that were not already in the text.[28]

From the Damascus road encounter, the "light from heaven" is the one commonality that has not yet been mentioned, because it can only be fully understood in Acts 26. Paul described the light as a great and brilliant "light from heaven" that left him blind (9:4; 22:6; 26:13).[29] The light that Paul described in this passage is more than an expression of God. The imagery of the light is almost certainly linked to Paul's understanding of "a light to the Gentiles," (22:18, 23; cf. Lk 2:32; Acts 13:47), ringing familiar echoes of the Old Testament theme—a "light to the nations" (Is 42:6; 49:6; 60:3)—and an eschatological hope (Rv 21:24). The light that Paul had seen was the light of God's mission providing a way to Jesus in a world of darkness.

### The Translation of Christianity

For the first time in this comparative study, the human agent of mission has to decide whether or not to translate into another linguistic context. For a second time, we are allowed to see a translation of God's message into a new mother tongue (the first occurring in Acts 9). Although Greek was a secondary language for the Jews, it was most likely the mother tongue for these officials. Paul's comment regarding God's choice to speak in Hebrew or Aramaic in Acts 26:14 indicates that Paul is very likely speaking in Greek at the time (Acts 21:37).

Paul's use of the vernacular may seem like an obvious concept for today's missionaries, but there are many cases where secondary languages are preferred by missionaries, such as Swahili in Maasai-land, rather than the mother tongue, such as Maa (the Maasai language). Contextualization should begin with the heart language of the people because ultimately Christianity will rest in the people's hearts as the translation takes place.

Although Paul may not have envisioned the future of Christianity translated into Gentile thought and practice (this perception would be difficult for any cross-cultural missionary), he was faithfully obedient as a missionary to begin that process and entrust the Gentile world with the Christian message. Even though Festus and Agrippa show little interest in following Christ, they do carry out an uncommon missionary role as they translate Paul's message for Caesar and send it on to realms untouched by Paul; they are the unwitting translators of the Christian message.

## CONCLUSION

Whatever the variety of wording in Luke's three reports . . . the salient fact is clear. Paul has been commissioned to break bounds. And, while taking every opportunity to speak to his fellow-countrymen, he recognizes a particular calling to the world outside the covenant of God's promises, as the Jewish people and he himself had understood them.[30]

The maturing of Paul's ministry provides us with an image of the integration between contextualization and the translation model of mission. God is contextual toward Paul, and Paul contextualized the Christian message for the Gentiles. Missionaries in cross-cultural settings must begin with their best attempt to share the gospel message in the most understandable way possible. However, contextualization alone is not enough.

Like Paul, we must be prepared for an eventual transformation that bursts upon us and expands our own limitations in understanding Christian mission. Eventually this transformation becomes a translated gospel as external paternalism and outside cultural values are replaced with concerns and values that spring from the newly maturing missional community. Just as God entrusted Paul and his Jewishness with God's mission *(missio Dei)* in Acts 9, Paul entrusted the Gentile world with the *missio Dei* and they in turn entrusted mission to others. As this new missional community expresses God's love, grace, and redemption to the world, it too will transform others and be transformed in the process, giving its trust over to another new and unforeseen era of mission.

For instance, returning and remaining missionaries among the Maasai all report fruitful ministries. While many of the missionaries had left frustrated over the lack of evangelistic zeal among Maasai Christians, the Maasai on their own have now begun to take on God's mission with a fervor that is unlike anything the missionaries had witnessed. The very lack of missionary presence for a period was actually a crucial stepping stone in enabling Maasai believers to express their faith in new and creative ways. The missionaries were surprised as Maasai acts of healing and conversion began to take place in their absence.

To experience the translation of the gospel is a rare privilege that we, as missionaries, can rejoice in if we have eyes to see and ears to hear. Andrew Walls noted this privilege for Paul:

> But it looks as though Paul was less impressed by the passing of faith to the Gentiles . . . than by the fact that through Christ one nation had been made out of two. Jew and Gentile, who had not in centuries been able to eat in each other's houses without calling the whole covenant of God into question, now sat down together at the table of the Lord. It was a phase of Christian history that did not last long. Not long after Paul's time, Gentiles so dominated the Christian Church that in most areas Jews were hardly noticeable in it. Christianity became a Gentile matter, just as in its earliest days it had been a Jewish matter. But, for a few brief years, the one-made-out-of-two was visibly demonstrated, the middle wall of partition was down, the irreconcilables were reconciled. This was, surely, not simply a historic episode, but a paradigmatic one, to be repeated, even if briefly, again and again. It is repeated as people separated by language, history and culture recognize each other in Christ.[31]

## REFERENCES

[1] Wilbert Shenk outlines the history of mission theory in *Changing Frontiers in Mission* (Maryknoll, N.Y.: Orbis Books, 1999). He correctly calls for a corrective on the use of the terms *technique, methodology,* and *strategy* in mission theory due to these terms association with modernism, Christendom, and military practice (Wilbert Shenk, *Write the Vision* [Harrisburg, Pa.: Trinity Press International, 1995], 53-64; Shenk, *Changing Frontiers in Mission,* 103-104). Evangelism and mission are ultimately based on relationships. These terms result in a forced persuasion that really has no place in Christian mission.

[2] In personal conversations with Ryan Bolger, Jehu Hanciles, and Wilbert Shenk, there has been a general preference for the translation model over other models of mission. The translation model of mission is discussed in Andrew Walls, *The Missionary Movement in Christian History* (Maryknoll, N.Y.: Orbis Books, 1996), Part 1 and in Lamin Sanneh, *Translating the Message* (Maryknoll, N.Y.: Orbis Books, 1989).

[3] Shenk, *Changing Frontiers in Mission,* 77.

[4] Arthur F. Glasser et al., eds., *Announcing the Kingdom,* pre-publication ed. (Grand Rapids, Mich.: Baker Books, 2002), chap. 7, subheading C.

[5] Ibid., 108-109.

[6] Walls, *The Missionary Movement in Christian History,* 28.

[7] Archibald McLean, *Where the Book Speaks* (New York: Revell, 1907), 33.

[8] Hans Conzelmann, *Acts of the Apostles* (Philadelphia: Fortress Press, 1987), 210.

[9] F. F. Bruce, *The Acts of the Apostles* (Grand Rapids, Mich.: Eerdmans, 1990), 456; cf. Gustaf Dalman, *Jesus-Jeshua* (London: S.P.C.K., 1927), 18.

[10] Walter C. Kaiser, *Mission in the Old Testament* (Grand Rapids, Mich.: Baker Books, 2000), 8, 75-82.

[11] Walls, *The Missionary Movement in Christian History*, 29.

[12] Along with Mt 28:18-20; Mk 16:15-16; Lk 24:46-47; Jn 20:21-23; Acts 1:6-8 (Archibald McLean, *Where the Book Speaks* [New York: Revell, 1907], 31-33).

[13] Shenk, *Write the Vision*, 54.

[14] Robert C. Tannehill, *The Narrative Unity of Luke-Acts* (Philadelphia and Minneapolis: Fortress Press, 1990), 2:276.

[15] The words "they did not listen" would be familiar for Jews who had studied the Old Testament, especially in Isaiah and Jeremiah—Ex 16:20; Jdt 2:17; Ps 81:11; Is 65:12; 66:4; Jer 7:13, 26; 17:23; 25:7; 34:14; 44:5.

[16] For linguistic Greek comparisons, see Lk 10:39; Acts 14:9; Acts 22:22; Mt 18:16; Mk 9:7; Jn 10:8.

[17] Walls, *The Missionary Movement in Christian History*, 32.

[18] Charles E. Van Engen, *God's Missionary People: Rethinking the Purpose of the Local Church* (Grand Rapids, Mich.: Baker Books, 1991), 145.

[19] Charles K. Ober, *Bible Studies in Missions* (New York: The International Committee of Young Men's Christian Associations, 1899), 35-36.

[20] D. N. Freedman, ed., *The Anchor Bible Dictionary* (New York: Doubleday, 1992), 1:99-100.

[21] G. Kittel, *Theological Dictionary of the New Testament: Abridged in One Volume* (Grand Rapids, Mich.: Eerdmans, 1985), 427.

[22] Freedman, *The Anchor Bible Dictionary*, 1:100.

[23] G. Kittel, G. W. Bromiley, and G. Friedrich, eds. *Theological Dictionary of the New Testament* (Grand Rapids, Mich.: Eerdmans, 1976), 3:664.

[24] Ibid., 3:666-667.

[25] Ludwig Koehler and Walter Baumgartner, *The Hebrew and Aramaic Lexicon of the Old Testament* (Leiden: Brill, 1996), 3:1191-1192.

[26] Walter Bauer, William F. Arndt, F. Wilbur Gingrich, and Frederick W. Danker, eds., *A Greek-English Lexicon of the New Testament and Other Early Christian Literature* (Chicago: University of Chicago Press, 2000), 254.

[27] Walls, *The Missionary Movement in Christian History*, 26.

[28] Kaiser, *Mission in the Old Testament*, 61.

[29] Notice that there is no mention of Paul's companions hearing the message in 26:13-14 because the Jewish misunderstandings of God's mission are not relevant to this context.

[30] Max Warren, *I Believe in the Great Commission* (Grand Rapids, Mich.: Eerdmans, 1976), 32.

[31] Walls, *The Missionary Movement in Christian History*, 25.

# 25

## *The Apostle Paul's Acts of Power*

### ACTS 22—28

## Robert C. Linthicum

> The kingdom of God depends not on talk but on power.
> —1 CORINTHIANS 4:20

The apostle Paul, considered among the greatest leaders of the Christian church, tirelessly labored to take the gospel to the Gentile world. He turned Christianity from a Jewish sect into a worldwide religion. His New Testament letters have been formative in the setting of the theology of the church throughout its two-thousand-year history.

How can we understand the impact and influence of Paul of Tarsus? The stunning words Paul wrote in his first letter to the Corinthian church (4:20) give us a profound clue to understanding this man.

### THE KINGDOM OF GOD AND POWER

Both of Paul's letters to the Corinthian church were written to a warring church. In 1 Corinthians 1:10-17 Paul described that struggle for dominance among four factions: those who were loyal to himself, the planter of that church; those who were disciples of its current leader, Apollos; those who belonged to the party of the Judaizers and who named Peter as their patron; and those loyal to none of these leaders but rather looked to Jesus as their leader. Each party sought to be the controlling influence in the church.

Paul masterfully used his position as the founder of the church to exercise influence and power in this situation. He reminded the Corinthian Christians that

---

This chapter was originally written for Robert Linthicum's book *Building a People of Power* (to be released in 2005). It is used here by permission of the author and copyright holder.

he was father to all of them (4:15). Paul stated that, as their parent in Christ, he was going to visit them to confront "these arrogant people" who were tearing apart this church. When he comes, he will test the power of those creators of dissension, and he "will find out not the talk of these arrogant people but their power. For the kingdom of God depends not on talk but on power. What would you prefer? Am I to come to you with a stick, or with love in a spirit of gentleness?" (4:19-21).

Paul was not the least bit bashful about exercising power. His letters, which make up the bulk of the New Testament, are full of his use of power through argument, influence, authority, and logic. The Book of Acts is replete with Paul's use of power to defeat the enemies of Christ, to help shape the course of the church, and to strengthen the spreading of the gospel throughout the Roman Empire.

It is hard for Christians today to resonate with Paul's use of power because power has long had a "bad name" in Christian circles. We are often suspicious of power because we have been victims of its misuse. We have experienced power used to manipulate people, to control and manage situations, to gain the response a leader wants to receive, and to dominate the church.

However, power misused does not somehow disappear when we ignore that misuse. Instead, unacknowledged power "goes underground." Once moved into the corporate unconsciousness of a community and no longer under any countervailing restraint, it becomes highly demonic in its capacity to destroy or injure institutions. Therefore, it is important for Christians to have a biblical theology and practice of power that can be openly acknowledged and understood in order to enhance the relationships among people, the church, and the world.

Power can be good as well as evil. It can be relational instead of unilateral. It can be "power with" rather than "power over," power that sets people free to become what God has created them to be. Rightfully used, power can enable Christians to take action on issues of common importance, work for justice in the world, seek the evangelization of people, and help build a more loving and powerful community of faith.

## THE TRANSFORMATION OF AN URBAN SLUM

As I reached the brow of the hill that rainy day in November 1990, I could see the squatter settlement of Carton City lying below me in the lush Nairobi River Valley of the capital city of Kenya. The stench of burned and charred buildings filled the air.

As the international director of World Vision's Urban Advance, I was in Nairobi to meet with Rev. David Ashiko and other leaders of World Vision Kenya to explore how that national office could join with Nairobi's poor to work for their empowerment. Over several visits I had worked with World Vision Kenya's leadership to develop an urban strategy built around the "Iron Rule" of community organizing: "Never do for others what they can do for themselves!" I had led selected staff through several weeks of intensive training in community-organizing principles and strategies. We were prepared to determine where we could begin our work.

We began down the path leading to Carton City, and soon my eyes could see what my nostrils long since had discerned. Scores of homes lay before me, roofless, with scorched walls, some even burned to the ground. As we arrived in the squatter settlement, angry people, eager to tell their story, immediately surrounded us. Escorted to home after home, we viewed scorched walls, rain-soaked, meager, and roofs open to the sky. A man old enough to remember when the British first came to Kenya (which made him well over one hundred) and who had served in the Kenya forces that finally drove them out, asked, "How could they do this to me after I fought for their freedom?"

Carton City, they told us, was one of the first slums in the city of Nairobi. Dating back generations, it was constructed on government land in the flood-plain of the Nairobi River, close to the military airport. Its inhabitants had simply squatted on that government land after Kenya had won its battle for independence; there they sought to scratch a living from its rich alluvial soil. The name Carton City described giant (now burned-out) cardboard carton homes with thatched roofs.

That night, however, as Nairobi was being lashed by a tropical storm, the police had entered Carton City and rousted the people from their beds. They made the families gather their belongings and stand in the pouring rain. And then, with shouts and waving guns and batons, the police forced the men of each family to set fire to their own homes! One by one they watched their homes burn to the ground. It seemed like the bitter end, because they were unwanted where they were and had no place to go.

"How do you feel about all this?" I asked.

One woman spoke with conviction in only the way Kenyans can accent their words, "I am very, very angry!"

"How about the rest of you," I asked.

"We are angry too," they replied.

"Good," I said. "Stay angry. But don't let them get away with it. Decide what you are going to do with your anger!" And to my surprise, they cheered!

As the little party of World Vision Kenya eventually climbed back out of the valley, leaving the residents of Carton City behind, David Ashiko said to me, "I think we have found our slum!" And we had.

Sixteen months later, on my next trip to Kenya, I returned to Carton City. I could not believe the transformation that greeted me! Solid two- and three-room mud-brick houses filled the slum, and only a few "carton houses" were left. The dirt streets were swept clean with no litter or refuse. Behind each home was a pit latrine rather than a single, polluted community outhouse. Community showers had been installed throughout the complex. There was a demonstration piggery and fowl farm in operation. A large vegetable garden provided food both for residents and for sale.

"What happened?" I incredulously asked. The story was told. Ashiko and other organizing staff had spent innumerable hours sitting in their shacks, drinking tea with them, listening to their stories of government abuse, their difficulty in finding work, and their rejection by the rest of the people of Nairobi due to their poverty. Then the organizers gathered them into small groups to talk about how they could make their community a decent place.

Almost immediately they identified what they had to do. First, they created three income-generating projects. With the production and selling of clothes, baskets, charcoal, and furniture, they began to experience for the first time a steady income stream into their community. Second, the only member of the community who could read and write went into a bank for the first time in her life and opened an interest-bearing account for the monies the community was earning. Third, the people decided to build pit latrines and community showers and created the demonstration farms and vegetable gardens. Carton City began to bounce back.

Eventually, a new government deputy chief visited, saw their improving standard of living, and demanded a "pay off" in return for protection. The people refused. One night the police returned to Carton City. Under the direction of the deputy chief, they began setting fire to selected houses. But this time, instead of cowering in fear, the residents of Carton City rose up. They drove the police out of the community. And at daybreak the next day, they descended en masse upon the appropriate government office. There they met with the immediate superior of the deputy chief, issued a complaint, and demanded action. But the chief refused to cooperate.

This, in itself, had been daring action in a repressive political atmosphere. But when they got stone-walled by the chief, a selected delegation went to the district commissioner and threatened to reveal the whole sordid mess to the newspapers if the deputy chief was not dealt with severely. Intimidated by the resolve of the people, the district commissioner dismissed the deputy chief and disciplined the chief.

The people then began building permanent homes (thus legally staking claim on the land) and monitored every meeting of the District Development Commission in order to hold the government accountable. Such community empowerment led to a significant spiritual transformation of the Carton City residents. They were once "cowed, cringing, broken."[1] But no longer. Carton City is made up of Christians, Muslims, and those following traditional African religions. "God-talk" was a natural part of the organizing of that community. Most meetings open with a reflection. Crops are blessed with prayer, and no action is initiated without public prayer. Faith is freely shared among people, as relationships deepen around shared activities and common risks in dealing with the government. The transformation of Carton City produced spiritual transformation as much as social transformation.

The result has been the building of a substantial permanent community, a communal economy that provides the economic foundation of that community, and a people filled with hope who never have to fear a police raid again. The people of Carton City learned to act powerfully.

## POWER FOR THE SAKE OF THE GOSPEL

No one understood power as clearly as did Paul of Tarsus, as the final chapters of Acts profoundly demonstrate. Much of the Book of Acts is a textbook on Paul's use of power in behalf of Christ's kingdom. For example, Paul confronted a person seeking to undermine his ministry (Acts 13:4-12), called the members of a Jewish synagogue to account (13:13-43), and finally took the gospel to receptive Gentiles (13:44-52). In Acts 15:12 Paul negotiated to allow Gentiles to become Christians without first becoming Jewish. This action would eventually turn Christianity into a worldwide religion. In Acts 16:36-37 Paul utilized tactics of confrontation to gain respect from a Roman magistrate. But the most extensive and thorough use of power by Paul is exhibited in the last seven chapters of Acts.

## PAUL BEFORE THE TEMPLE LEADERSHIP

When we arrived in Jerusalem, the brothers welcomed us warmly. The next day Paul went with us to visit James; and all the elders were present. ... Then Paul took the men, and the next day, having purified himself, he entered the temple with them, making public the completion of the days of purification when the sacrifice would be made for each of them.

When the seven days were almost completed, the Jews from Asia, who had seen him in the temple, stirred up the whole crowd. They seized him, shouting, "Fellow Israelites, help! This is the man who is teaching everyone everywhere against our people, our law, and this place; more than that, he has actually brought Greeks into the temple and has defiled this holy place." (Acts 21:17-18, 26-28)

The story began with Paul's decision to go to Jerusalem (19:21) to report on his missionary work and to worship in the Temple. This was a way of demonstrating his continued commitment to Jewish custom. However, his presence instigated a riot. Paul was arrested by the Roman tribune, Lysias (21:32—22:21) and would now remain under Roman protection and custody.[2] Facing a flogging, Paul told the Roman centurion responsible for his arrest that he was a Roman citizen (22:25). This was in itself a powerful statement.

The tribune directed that he was to be brought into the barracks, and ordered him to be examined by flogging, to find out the reason for this outcry against him. But when they had tied him up with thongs, Paul said to the centurion who was standing by, "Is it legal for you to flog a Roman citizen who is uncondemned?" When the centurion heard that, he went to the tribune and said to him, "What are you about to do? This man is a Roman citizen." (Acts 22:24-26)

This is the *first power action* by Paul in this passage. He informed the arresting Roman officer that he was a Roman citizen. Paul did this to avoid being flogged.

Roman citizens were accorded a different jurisprudence than others. When non-Roman citizens were arrested, the case was disposed of as quickly as possible. On the other hand, Roman citizens were guaranteed due process. They could not be punished without being first found guilty in court. They were accorded rights of safety and decent living conditions under Roman law.[3]

In this case the tribune had assumed that Paul was not a Roman and was therefore about to deny him the rights of citizenship. Paul would have none of it. Through the centurion, Paul informed the tribune of his status. This immediately reversed the treatment of Paul. For the remainder of this scenario, it became Rome's responsibility to protect Paul both from the wrath of the mob and the whims of the Jewish priests and religious leaders who wanted Paul dead.

Having claimed his citizenship and full protection of the Roman state, Paul came before the Sanhedrin for a hearing on his supposed crime. Here he demonstrates his profound knowledge of power.

> When Paul noticed that some were Sadducees and others were Pharisees, he called out in the council, "Brothers, I am a Pharisee, a son of Pharisees. I am on trial concerning the hope of the resurrection of the dead." When he said this, a dissension began between the Pharisees and the Sadducees, and the assembly was divided. (The Sadducees say that there is no resurrection, or angel, or spirit; but the Pharisees acknowledge all three.) Then a great clamor arose, and certain scribes of the Pharisees' group stood up and contended, "We find nothing wrong with this man. What if a spirit or an angel has spoken to him?" When the dissension became violent, the tribune, fearing that they would tear Paul to pieces, ordered the soldiers to go down, take him by force, and bring him into the barracks. (23:6-10)

This is the *second power action* taken by Paul. In order both to manage the situation and to take away from the Sanhedrin control of the trial, Paul used the tactic of "divide and conquer." He perceived that the Sanhedrin was divided between Sadducees (who denied the resurrection of the body) and Pharisees (who believed in the resurrection). So he declared himself a Pharisee (immediately gaining Pharisaical sympathy) and raised the issue of resurrection, knowing the dissent it would cause.

Paul then did something even more extraordinary. He *redefined the issue*. His presence and persuasiveness were powerful enough that, given the political volatility of the situation, he literally tricked the Sanhedrin into changing the crime of which he was accused.

The crime for which Paul was standing trial was his teaching that Jesus was the Messiah and his taking of that gospel to the Gentiles (21:28; 22:14). This was a crime punishable by death in the Jewish court, if not for the Roman protection Paul had demanded. Paul's self-description of the "crime" of which he was accused was "the hope of the resurrection of the dead." Since the issue of resurrection was a combustible issue for the Jewish religious elite, it thoroughly diverted them from the true purpose of the trial. In their righteous indignation they did not realize they had been thoroughly manipulated by Paul. The trial therefore ended in chaos, and Rome had to assert its authority once again, rescuing Paul from the confrontation.

## PAUL BEFORE THE ROMAN TRIBUNE

Conspiring Jews bound themselves by an oath to taste no food until Paul was killed. They manipulated the council to notify the tribune to bring in Paul on the pretext of a more thorough examination of his case. Then they planned to kill him. But the son of Paul's sister heard about the ambush and informed Paul, who told a centurion that a young man had something to report to the tribune (23:12-19).

This is the *third power action* by Paul. The apostle uncovered a plot to assassinate him and reported the same through his nephew to the Roman tribune. The tribune then acted to protect Paul, moving him in secret to be under the Roman governor's protection and giving him a sizeable military escort. This tribune was taking no chances.

At first glance one's reaction to this scripture is to ponder, "How fair the Roman government is and how committed they are to protecting Roman citizens." That may be true, but that is not fairly stating the case. *Paul was protected because Paul demanded protection.* The tribune was already painfully aware of how well Paul knew Roman law. By exposing this plot to the tribune, Paul exercised powerfully his legal rights for protection and a fair trial, and the tribune had no alternative but to provide those rights. This is evidenced in the tribune's effort to give Paul a military escort of two hundred soldiers, seventy horsemen, and two hundred spearmen—to protect one prisoner (23:23). How careful he was to word the letter to the Roman governor of Palestine, Felix, indicating how assiduously he had protected Paul and thus fulfilled Roman law (23:23, 26-30).

"When they came to Caesarea and delivered the letter to the governor, they presented Paul also before him. . . . Then he [Felix] ordered that he be kept under guard in Herod's headquarters" (23:33, 35b). Paul was not placed in prison but under house arrest in the palace Herod the Great had built for his own enjoyment, which was now being used by Rome as the chief residence and administration building of the Roman governor. And Paul was accorded a guard—not necessarily to keep Paul under arrest but to protect Paul from attack! (see Acts 21:32-36; 22:22-29; 23:9-10, 12-22).

## BUILDING RELATIONSHIPS

Acts 24 explains how the high priest of Israel, Ananias, came to Caesarea with "elders and an attorney" to argue the case against Paul. But Paul presented such a strong defense that the governor Felix made no ruling:

Then he [Felix] ordered the centurion to keep him in custody, but to let him have some liberty and not to prevent any of his friends from taking care of his needs.
Some days later when Felix came with his wife Drusilla, who was Jewish, he sent for Paul and heard him speak concerning faith in Christ Jesus.

And as he discussed justice, self-control, and the coming judgment, Felix became frightened and said, "Go away for the present; when I have an opportunity, I will send for you." At the same time he hoped that money would be given him by Paul, and for that reason he used to send for him very often and converse with him.

After two years had passed, Felix was succeeded by Porcius Festus; and since he wanted to grant the Jews a favor, Felix left Paul in prison. (24:23-27)

This is the *fourth power action* by Paul. After presenting a convincing case in his defense, Paul built a relationship with Felix. Thus Felix would not bring a verdict against him. It is also true that Felix was a compromised individual. He accepted bribes, and he hoped to receive money from Paul. Further, he wanted to remain in favor with the Jewish leaders, so he was not going to set Paul free. Paul did not argue for his freedom, probably because he realized that the assassins were still waiting for him (cf. Acts 25:3, which takes place two years later). The safest place for Paul was staying under house arrest in the governor's palace.

Paul made good use of his informal exile. He enjoyed some freedom in the palace, and he met regularly with "his friends," most likely continuing to give direction to the infant Gentile Christian movement (24:23). But a most important power activity was Paul's relationship building with the Roman governor. The text tells us that Felix "used to send for Paul very often and converse with him" (24:26b). Possibly a relationship of trust grew between the two men. Within that relationship Paul was not afraid to share the gospel with Felix "concerning faith in Christ Jesus" and to speak truth to the Roman governor on issues of "justice, self-control, and the coming judgment" (24:24-25).

Thus, what Jesus had predicted some thirty years earlier happened. Through Paul, the church was indeed standing "before governors and kings because of me, as a testimony to them and the Gentiles" (Mt 10:18; cf. Lk 21:12-13). Paul was now able both to argue his case and to present the gospel before this Roman governor, his successor and the king of Galilee, Agrippa, and eventually even Caesar himself. Thus, Paul was able to share "the Way" before some of the most powerful and influential figures in the Roman and Jewish worlds. And they were impressed with his testimony.

## PAUL BEFORE CAESAR

Felix found himself in a dilemma. He knew that he could not find Paul guilty because Paul had broken no Roman law. That was why the Jewish Sanhedrin had brought charges against Paul of disturbing the peace (Acts 24:2-8) rather than the crime of blasphemy, because Rome would not recognize blasphemy as a crime punishable by death. Felix's examination of Paul had exposed the invalidity of that accusation. He knew he could not find Paul guilty.

In addition, Paul was a Roman citizen, and as such, Felix was responsible for his protection and safety. He knew of the plot to assassinate Paul upon his release, so he could not release him. If he released Paul, and then Paul was killed and it was exposed that Felix knew of the plot, his career as a Roman procurator would be over!

What would Felix do in response to this apparently irresolvable dilemma? He did exactly what any government bureaucrat would do. He passed the problem on to his successor, Porcius Festus!

When Festus met with Paul, the Jews who had come down from Jerusalem surrounded him and brought serious charges against him.

Paul said in his defense, "I have in no way committed an offense against the law of the Jews, or against the temple, or against the emperor." But Festus, wishing to do the Jews a favor, asked Paul, "Do you wish to go up to Jerusalem and be tried there before me on these charges?" Paul said, "I am appealing to the emperor's tribunal; this is where I should be tried. I have done no wrong to the Jews, as you very well know. Now if I am in the wrong and have committed something for which I deserve to die, I am not trying to escape death; but if there is nothing to their charges against me, no one can turn me over to them. I appeal to the emperor." Then Festus, after he had conferred with his council, replied, "You have appealed to the emperor; to the emperor you will go." (25:8-12)

This is the *fifth power action* of Paul. With his knowledge of Roman law, Paul likely recognized the dilemma of the new governor. The bind in which Festus now found himself was exactly the same that his predecessor had faced. So Paul realized that Festus would either keep him under permanent house arrest in the governor's palace or send him to Jerusalem and possibly death by ambush. Therefore, Paul acted to break the stalemate. He appealed to Caesar. This was a deliberate power action.

What did it mean to appeal one's case to Caesar? Roman citizens accused of crimes, no matter how poor or how distant from Rome, had the right to have their cases heard directly by Caesar. Each case had to be heard by the emperor, as Caesar would sit as the highest court of Rome, acting as both judge and jury.[4]

From my perspective, there were five clear benefits to Paul deciding to appeal his case to Caesar. First, it would resolve the stalemate in which he might otherwise remain for the rest of his life. Second, it would mean that his case would be heard directly by Caesar, who likely had little patience with Jewish religious arguments. Third, it would be held in Rome, which would physically distance Paul from both his accusers and those who sought his assassination. They were unlikely to travel to Rome to kill him, because if they were caught, they could not be protected by the Sanhedrin and would face possible execution. Fourth, he would be tried exclusively under Roman law, with no concern for sensibility to the Jewish religious establishment; therefore, the case was likely to be dismissed.[5] Finally, appealing to Caesar meant that the emperor himself was going to hear a proclamation of the gospel by Paul.

Paul's decision to appeal his case to Caesar was not a sudden whim on his part. It was a carefully calculated and highly intentional act in which Paul was exercising the power vested in him as a Roman citizen. It was therefore a very deliberate act of power.

"You have appealed to the emperor; to the emperor you will go" (25:12). Of course, going to the emperor did not immediately happen. The governor had to wait until the next Roman sailing vessel, suitable for carrying both Paul and his Roman guards, was available. It could sail only during the safe season, because the safety of Paul was the governor's responsibility until he reached Rome. Therefore, some weeks or possibly months passed before Paul set sail for Rome. During the interim Paul exercised his *sixth power action*.

While under house arrest at the governor's palace, Paul was invited to present his case to King Agrippa, not for Agrippa to adjudicate (the emperor would be responsible for doing that) but for the purpose of enabling Festus to present clearly in writing to the emperor the crime of which Paul was accused and the circumstances surrounding the supposed crime. Festus wanted Agrippa's advice because the governor neither understood nor was sensitive to the nuances of Jewish religious law, and Agrippa was. At the same time, Agrippa was no religious elite, protecting the law at all costs. Because he thoroughly understood both Roman and Jewish law, he was the ideal person to assist Festus in writing the brief for the emperor so that it was both accurate and captured the nuances of the situation (25:13-22).

Marcus Julius Agrippa (c. A.D. 27–100) was the son of Agrippa I and great-grandson of Herod the Great. He was the king of Perea and those portions of Galilee not directly governed by Rome and also had the responsibility of appointing the Jewish high priest. Agrippa II was appointed to this responsibility by Rome and was directly accountable to Rome. Whenever possible, Rome ruled conquered provinces through a local Roman-appointed king, as this tended to make the populace more willing to accept Roman suzerainty. Agrippa II was educated in Rome, was extremely knowledgeable about Roman law, and was deeply committed to the emperor. But he also understood the Jews, being well versed in their law (26:3) and respecting their religious practices (but not their moral requirements since he was likely in an incestuous relationship with his sister) and he was willing to intervene on behalf of the Jews.[6]

Although Agrippa could not adjudicate the case, there was ample reason for Paul to appear before him to present it. The first reason was that, given Agrippa's understanding of Jewish law and scripture, Paul could not only make a defense but could also present clearly the claims of Christ to the king. Second, it would not hurt his case to have Agrippa on his side, especially if the emperor sought the king's counsel. Finally, although Agrippa had no authority to release Paul, there was no one better positioned than he to hear Paul's case, both in helping to form the case for the emperor's ears and to be an advocate for Paul (26:32). So it was in Paul's self-interest to make his case before Agrippa II.

## PAUL BEFORE AGRIPPA AND FESTUS

The defense Paul made before Agrippa and Festus was probably the most powerful apologia Paul made in scripture, brilliant in its simplicity (26:1-29). He began by stating his argument: "And now I stand here on trial on account of my hope in the promise made by God to our ancestors, a promise that our twelve tribes hope to attain, as they earnestly worship day and night. It is for this hope, your Excellency, that I am accused by Jews! Why is it thought incredible by any of you that God raises the dead?" (26:6-8).

Paul then told his story. First, he shared with Agrippa his former status in the Jewish community (26:4-5), making a point of his having been a Pharisee, since King Agrippa was particularly supportive of the Pharisee movement, as over against the priestly and Sadducean movements. He then moved on to tell how he had persecuted the emerging Christian movement (26:9-11). He continued with the story of his conversion and call to minister to the Gentiles. Finally, he concluded with the stirring words, "After that, King Agrippa, I was not disobedient to the heavenly vision, but declared first to those in Damascus, then in Jerusalem and throughout the countryside of Judea, and also to the Gentiles that they should repent and turn to God and do deeds consistent with repentance" (26:19-20). He then noted that the Jewish leaders took offense at his message. "So I stand here, testifying to both small and great, *saying nothing but what the prophets and Moses said would take place:* that the Messiah must suffer, and that, by being the first to rise from the dead, he would proclaim light both to our people and to the Gentiles" (26:22b-23, emphasis added).

Paul argued that both the Hebrew law ("Moses") and the Hebrew prophets predicted the coming of a messiah who would die for the sins of the nation, would be raised again, and that this "gospel" would be proclaimed to Jew and Gentile alike. Paul proclaimed that what was predicted had come true in Jesus of Nazareth. It was for this proclamation that the Jewish aristocracy wanted Paul killed!

At this point Festus interrupted Paul's defense, in essence saying, "This is the craziest story I've ever heard!" But Paul rebutted Festus and challenged Agrippa. "King Agrippa, do you believe the prophets? I know that you believe" (26:27). He was essentially saying to Agrippa, "The perspective of Festus that I am crazy is exactly what we Jews would expect out of an uninformed Gentile. But you know better, don't you, King Agrippa? You know the prophets. You know what they have predicted about the coming and resurrection of the Messiah. And you know in your heart that what I am telling you is true."

## SHARING THE GOSPEL WITH POWER

Agrippa's response to Paul's challenge was significant. He replied, "Are you so quickly persuading me to become a Christian?" (26:28) or, from the New King James Version, "You almost persuade me to become a Christian." Which nuance did King Agrippa mean? Was he courteously evading the challenge by saying, "You will have to present much more evidence than this argument if you are going to win me to your Christ"? Or was he saying, "I am almost persuaded to become a Christian"? We do not know Agrippa's intention in these words. The Greek itself is ambiguous. Literally it says, "In a little, you are persuading me to make a Christian." But whether an evasion or near confession of faith, it was significant. Paul had struck close to home. Agrippa had been moved. This messenger from God had radically disrupted the neat arrangements with which Agrippa had ordered his life.

Paul had the last word. "Whether quickly or not, I pray to God that not only you but also all who are listening to me today might become such as I am–except for these chains!" (26:29). Among those listening were Bernice, Agrippa, and Festus (25:23).

In this sixth power action Paul used his defense as an opportunity to share the gospel with the two highest government officials in Palestine, the king of Galilee/Perea and the Roman governor. In that sharing he shook them at the core of their beings, agitating the governor and provoking the king. Through Paul's use of power, he made an important gain with King Agrippa, because it would be likely that Caesar, uninformed on Jewish law, would turn to his surrogate king in Palestine for enlightenment. The final words of Agrippa capture his commitment to the innocence of Paul: "This man is doing nothing to deserve death or imprisonment. . . . This man could have been set free if he had not appealed to the emperor" (26:31b-32).

Paul's *seventh power action* is unlike the six previous actions because it does not occur in a single place or deal directly with his trial or imprisonment.

> When it was decided that we were to sail for Italy, they transferred Paul and some other prisoners to a centurion of the Augustan Cohort, named Julius. Embarking on a ship of Adramyttium that was about to set sail to the ports along the coast of Asia, we put to sea. (27:1-2a)

Paul's trip to Rome, where Caesar was to hear his case, proved a difficult journey. By the time the Festus administration had completed arrangements for Paul's trip to Rome, the sailing season was nearly over and the inclement weather of winter was fast approaching. The text charts their voyage across the Mediterranean, stopping at several islands to change ships (27:2-8). At one island with a poor harbor Paul could "see" how rapidly the stormy weather was closing in upon them and advised the ship's captain and the centurion to winter there (27:9-12). They chose to put forth to Phoenix, a more secure harbor of Crete, ran into a vicious storm, and the ship was in danger of sinking (27:13-20). Paul stood up and urged them to be courageous, declaring that the ship would run aground on an island (27: 21-26). The ship ran aground as predicted and broke up, but all 276 passengers and crew safely washed ashore (27:27-44).

What gave Paul courage and presence of mind in the midst of such danger and chaos? In reading both the Book of Acts and Paul's epistles, one does not get the impression of a frightened or easily intimidated individual. But Luke reports something far more decisive than that.

> I urge you now to keep up your courage, for there will be no loss of life among you, but only of the ship. For last night there stood by me an angel of the God to whom I belong and whom I worship, and he said, "Do not be afraid, Paul; you must stand before the emperor; and indeed, God has granted safety to all those who are sailing with you." So keep up your courage, men, for I have faith in God that it will be exactly as I have been told. But we will have to run aground on some island." (27:22-26)

An angel of God was the source of Paul's remarkable determination, power, and courage. It was not simply that he was a determined and single-minded man. It was that he was a *called* man. He saw himself as chosen by God, adopted as God's child through Christ, redeemed, forgiven, given the knowledge of God's will for humanity, and marked with the power of the Holy Spirit (Eph 1:1-13). He was called and chosen so that he might "bring to the Gentiles the news of the boundless riches of Christ . . . so that through the church the wisdom of God in its rich variety might now be made known to the rulers and authorities in the heavenly places" (Eph 3:8b, 10)—even to Caesar himself! Thus not even the worst storm at sea discouraged Paul. Assured and buoyed by the angel's visit, Paul took over the leadership of the sinking ship and guided its people to safety.

Acts 28 found the shipwrecked people stranded upon the island of Malta. The former passengers and crew tried to warm themselves around a fire to ward off the bitter cold and rain, as Paul humbly gathered firewood. Suddenly a venomous viper came out of the wood and struck Paul (28:1-4). "They were expecting him to swell up or drop dead, but after they had waited a long time and saw that nothing unusual had happened to him, they changed their minds and began to say he was a god" (28:6).

Those shipwrecked were well received by the residents of the local town, where they wintered for three months. Paul received hospitality at the home of Publius, the "leading man of the island," and Paul healed his ill father. This, in turn, opened a healing ministry for Paul on the island (28:7-9). Finally, when spring returned, Paul and the passengers set sail to Rome. The town residents bestowed "many honors on us, and when we were about to sail, they put on board all the provisions we needed" (28:10).

One must ask of Acts 27:1—28:10, Who was the prisoner and who was in charge? Paul boarded the ship from Palestine as a prisoner of the Roman government. But his powerful leadership on behalf of the passengers and crew is a testimony to his dependence on God. Initially ignored by the Roman officer and the ship's captain, he became the one actually giving the orders as the ship foundered. It was Paul who prepared both crew and passengers for their shipwreck, including instructions as to what they were to do when the ship went down. The prisoner had become the leader of both the passengers and crew, apparently even obeyed by the Roman guard escorting him to Rome. Eventually, Paul was invited into the chief person's house and turned a disaster into a healing ministry.

The *eighth power action* now concludes the Book of Acts. Paul arrived in Rome and settled there, waiting for his trial before Caesar (28:11-31).

> And so we came to Rome. The believers from there, when they heard of us, came as far as the Forum of Appius and Three Taverns to meet us. On seeing them, Paul thanked God and took courage.
> When we came into Rome, Paul was allowed to live by himself, with the soldier who was guarding him. (Acts 28:14c-16)

In spite of his chains, Paul and the gospel staged a triumphant procession into Rome (28:20). Paul strode into the city followed by an entourage of Christians who escorted him. Paul shared the gospel with the Jewish Diaspora in Rome. When some rejected his message, he declared that he would continue to take the gospel to the Gentiles (28:24, 28). The Book of Acts then concludes, "He lived there two whole years at his own expense and welcomed all who came to him, proclaiming the kingdom of God and teaching about the Lord Jesus Christ with all boldness and without hindrance" (28:30-31).

Paul was under house arrest awaiting trial before the emperor. But consider how he powerfully drew upon his Roman citizenship both to protect his life and to advance the cause of Christ. Neither the church nor Paul paid for his travel to Rome; the Roman government did. Under house arrest, the guard would not allow him to leave the house, but anyone he wished to see could have free access to him. There, under Roman protection, Paul provided direction to the church in efforts to reach the Roman Empire with the gospel, composing many of his letters that have now become epistles of the New Testament. He both expanded and strengthened the church that would eventually face Roman persecution.[7] In this sense Paul conducted a Bible school at the emperor's expense (Phil 1:10-15). He even built relationships with those members of the Praetorian Guard (the elite corps responsible for the protection of the emperor), his household, and the prisoners who protected him; apparently several of those soldiers converted to Christ, so that a Christian church was formed and began meeting in their barracks in Caesar's palace.[8] There was a Christian congregation in Caesar's household (Phil 4:22). Thus, Paul took full advantage of his imprisonment to build a powerful church across the Roman Empire while under the protection and unwitting support of Rome!

Paul knew how to utilize power to protect himself, advance the gospel, and position the church to influence profoundly both the present and the future empires.

## REFLECTIONS ON PAUL'S USE OF POWER

We do not know the result of Paul's appeal to Caesar. The scriptures do not inform us directly, but we can get some hints. If the Pastoral Letters (1 and 2

Timothy and Titus) were written by Paul, then they provide clues. These letters list cities where Paul ministered that were not a part of the history of Acts (1 Tm 1:3; 2 Tm 4:13; Ti 1:5; 3:12). Furthermore, 2 Timothy 4:16-17 intriguingly states, *"At my first defense,* no one came to my support, but all deserted me. May it not be counted against them! But the Lord stood by me and gave me strength, so that through me the message might be fully proclaimed and all the Gentiles might hear it. *So I was rescued from the lion's mouth"* (emphasis added).

A possible scenario is that Paul's case was dismissed two years after he arrived in Rome. Roman law stated that if prosecutors did not come to Rome to argue the case within two years, then the accused was to be acquitted.[9] This might explain Luke's otherwise enigmatic words at the end of his history, stating that Paul "lived there two whole years" (28:30). He would have lived under house arrest for "two whole years" only if his accusers had not come forward to press their case. And the Jewish leaders in Rome confessed to Paul, "We have received no letters from Judea about you" (28:21). It is possible that, recognizing it had no case, the Sanhedrin simply chose to drop the matter.

Paul likely made his case, it was dismissed, and he was set free. He then traveled to churches to strengthen them and into new cities to plant the gospel, perhaps even going to Spain, according to tradition. He was later arrested once again perhaps after Rome determined that it was a crime and treason against the state to be a Christian. Finally he made his defense before Caesar in his second trial, and this time was not "rescued from the lion's mouth" but instead was martyred.[10]

The trials and imprisonments of Paul remind the church of its calling to engage in the political, economic, and religious powers. The church is not called by Christ to ignore the systems of the world. When engaging the powers of the world, the church is to understand power and to use it in a wise and sophisticated way for the furtherance of Christ's kingdom. Paul utilized power intentionally and reminded us that "the kingdom of God depends not on talk, but on power" (1 Cor 4:20).

## REFERENCES

[1] Origen, quoted in Robert C. Linthicum, *Empowering the Poor* (Monrovia, Calif.: MARC Publications, 1991), 115.

[2] Harry W. Tajra, *The Trial of St. Paul: A Juridical Exegesis of the Second Half of the Acts of the Apostles* (Tubingen: J.C.B. Mohr, 1989), 68.

[3] For a thorough discussion of the legal rights of a Roman citizen, see Brian Rapske, *The Book of Acts and Paul in Roman Custody* (Grand Rapids, Mich.: Eerdmans, 1994), 139-146; see also, William Barclay, *The Acts of the Apostles* (Philadelphia: Westminster Press, 1976), 163.

[4] Tajra, *The Trial of St. Paul,* 113, 144-147.

[5] Ibid., 171.

[6] Johannes Munck, *The Acts of the Apostles* (Garden City: N.Y.: Doubleday, 1967), 237-238, 240, 245; S. Sandmel, "Herod Agrippa II," in *The Interpreter's Dictionary of the Bible,* vol. E-J, ed. George A. Buttrick (New York: Abingdon, 1962), 592.

[7] Rapske, *The Book of Acts and Paul in Roman Custody*, 177-183.

[8] Barclay, *The Acts of the Apostles*, 193.

[9] Tajra, *The Trial of St. Paul,* 195, quoting Pliny, *Ep.* X, 56.

[10] Rapske, *The Book of Acts and Paul in Roman Custody*, 189-191; G. H. C. MacGregor, "Introduction and Exegesis of the Acts of the Apostles," in *The Interpreter's Bible*, ed. George A. Buttrick (Nashville, Tenn.: Abingdon, 1954), 9:349-350; Tajra, *The Trial of St. Paul,* 187-188, 196.

# 26

## *The Ending Is Prelude: Discontinuities Lead to Continuities*

### ACTS 1:1–11 AND 28:23–31

### Paul Varo Martinson

An authentic entry into the narrative world of Acts inevitably intersects with our personal narratives. Horizons meet and inform. Following are two moments in my horizon.

First, I have recently read an oral history of my paternal aunt Cora. Many of these stories have shaped both my personal and professional life—missionary service in Hong Kong during the 1960s, doctoral work in Chinese studies, teaching of missions and world religions at Luther Seminary since 1972, and contact with China through both my wife's career and my own.

My grandparents, Andrew and Anna Martinson, went to China in 1902 as Lutheran missionaries. They arrived in Henan province, central China, and served in Xinyang, Queshan (Kioshan), and Jigongshan (Kikungshan). Andrew, a twenty-year-old immigrant from a fishing island off the coast of Norway (Varo, now Vaerlandet), and Anna, a first-generation Iowan of Norwegian descent, ventured to a poor region of China; adjustments were not easy. Andrew was mainly in evangelistic work but also tried to help educate young boys. Daughter Cora narrates:

> My father was always running a boys' school. Talk about commitment! I remember very well my mother asking Father (I was about five or six then) if she could get a cabinet for her dishes. Father was silent for a long time. Finally he said, "The boys' school needs desks." He had no fund for this, so naturally would have to pay for the desks out of his own pocket. I remember then my mother cried. I did not know for whom to stick up. My dad was right; my mother was right too.[1]

And so things went for seven years. It was only a year and a half after their return from their first furlough that Andrew came down with dysentery. The

313

antidote forced upon him was strychnine! Cora writes, "Father again gasped for air, jumped two feet in bed, beat the air and carried on. . . . Then Father died,"[2] bellowing out in his big voice the twenty-third psalm.

Poor Anna. How would she handle this loss? What should she do with three small children, Cora, Pearl, and Harold? The salary discontinued, she lived on a pension of three hundred dollars a year. The family in the United States urged, "Bring your children home and give them a chance." My Aunt Cora continues:

> What should she do? I remember many times when we came back from school we would hear her in a trunkroom praying out loud and weeping as she prayed, pleading with God for guidance. . . . Then the thought came that she had felt the call to the mission field when she heard Rev. Skrefsrud speak in Eagle Grove. She had received that call before she ever met my father.

Surely that call was as legitimate as that of her husband! On one occasion my eight-year-old father embraced his mother and promised, "When I grow up, I will take Dad's place." And he did. As for Anna, she knew her calling, even though she was not considered as "a missionary" either by the mission board or other missionaries. She earned what little she could gardening and renting space in her home. Friends, relatives, and congregations provided her with funds. She began a school in a village at the foot of the mountain, traveled to neglected villages, provided salaries for evangelists and teachers. Some six or seven years later the mission board saw what she was doing and offered her a position. But the Lord had provided, and she continued on her own, though the ministries became unofficial outstations of the mission in China.

This memory is one moment in my horizon. Andrew, dead at forty-five, buried in China, and Anna, at over one hundred, reading her Chinese Bible daily to the end, buried in Hong Kong. What about my father, Harold, taking his dad's place? Some years after his death in 1970 my mother jotted on a scrap of paper these words about their early years together in China in the 1930s:

> We always felt that the Chinese are very friendly people! Harold espe-cially got close to them. Many times a year he walked up to fifteen miles into the country villages to spend two weeks to a month teaching and preaching. He lived in their homes, sleeping in a chapel—if there was one—on a camp cot he dragged along, and eating with them out of the common pot. Long evenings were spent listening to their heartaches, their hopes, their superstitions, family lore, home spun stories and many leg-ends, centuries old songs and history they had learned from the traveling minstrels. They shared love and understanding. The Chinese liked his quiet humor, his unrushed manner, his concern. Having learned Chinese from babyhood and up to sixteen years of age, he spoke their language with all the expressive nuances and colloquialisms. Well, they were rich years for him.

A second moment in my horizon follows: During the 1949 Liberation of China there were 700,000 Protestant Christians. In the years leading up to the Cultural Revolution of 1966-1976 the number of active Christians dwindled to a fraction of that number. Suddenly all religious activity was shut down and even the Three-Self Protestant Patriotic Movement, officially sanctioned by the state to represent all Protestantism, was dissolved.[3]

In 1979 government policy changed and religion was again allowed to be practiced on a small scale, though reality overtook governmental caution. Christian home gatherings had already begun and now mushroomed. The officially sanctioned church, under the guidance of the Three-Self Movement and the newly constituted China Christian Council, sought to catch this tiger by the tail and give it some order. Partially successful, some fifteen million Christians are now under its control, although at least that many more form the autonomous Christian communities throughout China, with by far the highest number in Henan. Something remarkable has happened in China. The last two and a half decades span a striking chapter in church history. From the ashes of the past comes a new beginning. Discontinuity leads to a new continuity.

These two moments in my horizon intersect with the Book of Acts. Until recently, much of Acts interpretation by academia has been somewhat sterile theologically. Recent studies are changing that picture and have shaped my approach here.[4] I have chosen the beginning and ending verses in Acts to explore the book as a whole. Luke's presentation is a theologically profound presentation, far exceeding many of his erstwhile interpreters.

## ACTS—A THREEFOLD DYNAMIC

*1. The Spirit's Activity.* Acts, as in the gospel of Luke, presents a parade of unpredictable and often surprising events. Much of this is directly connected with the activity of the Holy Spirit, as well as with the unrehearsed response of humans to the Spirit-inspired activity of evangelism. Pentecost unleashes this series of events, culminating in Paul's preaching from detention in Rome. These surprises involve change and discontinuities.

*2. The Divine Plan.* In spite of discontinuties, beginning and end are held together by the overarching will of God. Whether the surprising narrative concerning Jesus or the seemingly discontinuous events of Acts, all are lodged in God's plan. That plan links past, present and future—the call of Israel, the life of Jesus, the proclamation of the apostles. These in turn are lodged within the time frame that begins in creation and finds consummation in the return of Jesus "in the same way" as he left (Acts 1:11). Everything comes together in God's plan, expressed in continuities and coherence.

*3. Christological Content.* It is Christology that gives content to the narrative, making it go somewhere. That is to say, "the things concerning Jesus" are the substance of God's plan and the focus of the Spirit's work. Following these hints, mission, we might say, is God's way of being God. In Acts, mission is God's plan. Thus, mission, as God's plan, is the life, suffering, and exaltation of Jesus. Christological content in Luke's writings is always connected with the suffering of Jesus. Mission is the empowerment of the Spirit and the proclamation of that message. It is in mission that God's character is both deployed and honored.

Now, if we glance at the beginning and end of Acts we will see this three-fold dynamic—Spirit's activity, divine plan, christological content—at work. Additional dynamics explicitly link beginning and end. A central theme in both is the kingdom of God and the human response to its possibilities. In both the Spirit is the great communicator—"instructions through the Holy Spirit" (Acts 1:2), and "the Holy Spirit was right in saying" (Acts 28:25). Also, we see God's overarching design—"the times or periods that the Father has set by his own authority" (1:7) "the promise of the Father" (1:4), "this salvation of God" (28:28). Explicit in the beginning paragraphs is reference to the passion of Jesus ("suffering), his resurrection ("presented himself alive") and his exaltation ("taken up to heaven") (1:3; 1:2; see 1:11). Implicit in the end is the same agenda through Paul—"trying to convince them about Jesus" (29:23) and "teaching about the Lord Jesus Christ" (28:31). Proclamation of this message is the central activity of God's delegated witnesses, which, anticipated by Acts 1:8, climaxes in Rome (28:30-31).

## A THREE-DIMENSIONAL NARRATIVE

The opening dedication of Acts and Luke raises the question of genre. Is it Hellenistic historiography, biography, fiction, or something else? The arguments keep coming. Perhaps Luke-Acts, infused with proclamation, is a genre unto itself.

Luke makes every effort to sew a tight seam. Luke's gospel ends on four themes: an interpretation of the passion, resurrection, and forgiveness in light of scripture; the appointment of witnesses; promise of the Spirit; departure into heaven. Acts commences on just these four. This threading continues to the end of Acts. There Paul convinces about Jesus "from the law of Moses and from the prophets" (28:23; cf. Lk 24:44).

The ascension that concludes the gospel of Luke is found in the introduction to Acts (Lk 24:50-53; Acts 1:9-11), after which a fresh narrative begins. This ascension story embeds Acts in the gospel of Luke, serving as a hinge that links Luke's two volumes together. Linked to that hinge are key themes of Luke-Acts, in particular, the empowering of the Holy Spirit and the mission mandate to the world (Lk 24:48-51; Acts 1:8).[5]

The sewing together of Luke-Acts is intricate. A jarring note opens Acts: "Lord, is this the time when you will restore the kingdom to Israel?" (Acts 1:6). The reader recalls the disciples' failed insights in Luke. The passion prediction meets only blank stares. Who is the greatest? Snores accompany Jesus' praying. He really wants swords, and we have got them! "Woman, I do not know him." What's with the empty tomb? Who is that stranger on the way to Emmaus? Is the risen Jesus an apparition? (Lk 18:31-34; 22:24, 45-46, 50-51, 54-62; 24:1-4, 13ff.). This failure is woven into the very fabric of Luke-Acts.

Indeed, as the sermons in Acts make plain, especially Stephen's speech, this failure is the habitual response of Israel to Moses and the prophets, a failure that is repeated in Acts to the end. Yet there was a remedy—the coming of the Holy Spirit. Insight dawns. They do not ask such an ignorant array of questions again, misconstruing Jesus' words on God's kingdom and the Messiah's suffering. This is due to the coming of the Holy Spirit. Interlocking, numerous threads characterize Luke-Acts. Following is a detailed discussion of the threefold dynamic described above.

### A Narrative of Surprise (The Spirit's Activity)

Are we surprised at the end of Acts when leaders again gather to hear a Christian preacher only to reject the message? We expect this to happen from Luke's previous narrative. So it was in Paul's first sermon to the Jews in Antioch of Pisidia, then at Iconium, Lystra, Thessalonica, Corinth, Ephesus, and Jerusalem. Peter's and Stephen's sermons elicited similar responses. Taken alone, each disturbance is a surprise, but does not repetition remove the surprise? No, it does not. It is the cumulative nature of rejection that conveys one of the biggest surprises in Acts.

This rejection originates at the beginning of Luke's gospel. In the birth narratives we find eager expectation, joy, and optimism. Elizabeth exclaimed to Mary, "Blessed are you among women, and blessed is the fruit of your womb!" Mary responds by speaking of the exaltation of the lowly, the filling of the hungry, and the remembrance of God's mercy to Israel, "to Abraham and to his descendants forever." Zechariah prophesies, "The Lord God of Israel . . . has looked favorably on his people and redeemed them." The angels announce "to you is born this day in the city of David a Savior." Simeon holds the babe and exclaims, "My eyes have seen your salvation." Anna too gives thanks to God, announcing the anticipated "redemption of Jerusalem" (Lk 1:42, 52-55, 68-79; 2:11, 30-32, 38). Luke begins with great anticipation, only to lead us into the surprising narrative of Christ's rejection and the cross. So, too, Acts begins with great hope only to end with Israel's persistent rejection of the message concerning Jesus.

However, there is a positive surprise as well: the coming of the Spirit, the reception of Samaritans and Gentiles, and the positive examples of many Jews—the courage of Peter, the call of Paul, and the sending out of Barnabas and "Saul" (see Acts 2:2-7; 9:1-31; 10:1-48; 13:2). Every episode and exchange is new and unexpected. Thus the negative surprise of Israel's rejection is matched by the positive surprise of the reception of Jewish-Christian leaders and the Gentiles (Acts 15:2-11, 13-19). In the beginning of Luke's gospel Simeon anticipates "a light for revelation to the Gentiles," and perhaps Mary too in her theme of reversals. Simeon alone sees reversal as a dark moment: "This child is set for the fall and rising of many in Israel, and for a sign that is spoken against" (Lk 1:52-53; 2:32, 34). Paul completes what Simeon anticipates: "Let it be known to you then that this salvation of God has been sent to the Gentiles" (Acts 28:28). The surprises are both negative and positive.

## A Narrative of the Expected (The Divine Plan)

Why should there be surprise? After all, God, is the supreme subject, the guiding hand. What is "the kingdom of God" and the "salvation of God" (Acts 1:3; 28:28) if not God's work? Surely Elizabeth, Mary, Zechariah, the angels, Simeon, and Anna made that clear.

As Acts begins, Jesus deflects the longing for national restoration and points to God's authority, promise, and sending (Acts 1:4, 5, 8; 2:33). There seems little room for surprise—only the expectedness of promises realized, scriptures fulfilled, patterns of resistance repeated, and divine intervention along the way.

The narrative is very sure about divine intervention. Were the believers drunk? Peter replies pointblank that "this is what was spoken through the prophet Joel" (2:16). And Jesus?—"handed over to you according to the definite plan and foreknowledge of God" (2:23). No surprises here. Design, plan, and foreknowledge suggest that each episode has an interior dimension. A surprise to humans may for God simply express the inner significance of an event.

And so the beginning and end of Acts (indeed Luke-Acts) cohere. What is anticipated in the beginning is attained at the end. The movement *into* Jerusalem in the gospel of Luke is continued by a movement *out from* Jerusalem in Acts. Everything serves that mission. They must be in Jerusalem (1:4), since location bespeaks God's faithfulness. Knowledge of salvation to God's people in the forgiveness of their sins has taken place—in Jerusalem! (Lk 1:77; Acts 2:38-39). Yet all must end in Rome, the center of the Gentile world and symbol for "the ends of the earth." Jerusalem and Rome are linked. God's promise to Abraham is that he will be a blessing to all peoples. It must happen by way of Israel; Rome must be reached through Jerusalem. God is faithful. Now, to be sure, it does not happen in the way a human might have predicted, but it does happen. God's will threads events, and there are no surprises.

## A Narrative of Significance (Christological Content)

But what end does this divine will serve? One way to discover this is to explore the meaning of the ascension, which Luke alone records, a hinge that links Luke's two volumes together.

The ascension has to do with dominion and saving efficacy. The rejection of Jesus is its necessary precondition. The post-resurrection appearances and departure to God's right hand are aspects of one thing, the exaltation of the crucified Lord and Messiah. The Pentecost sermon announces this meaning from the beginning: "Therefore let the entire house of Israel know with certainty that God has made him both Lord and Messiah, this Jesus whom you crucified" (Acts 2:36).

In assessing significance, we see that the ascension points in three directions. First, it points to the lordship of Jesus, "Lord" being the preferred designation for Jesus in Acts up to the end of the book (Acts 28:31). Second, it refers to the saving consequences of that lordship, expressed in forgiveness of sins and the giving of the Spirit. Third, it points to the passion of Jesus as the necessary condition of both lordship and saving implications. Lordship, efficacy, and passion—here is the heart of Acts, the basis of God's design and the presupposition of the Spirit's work.

Perhaps the most stunning title for Jesus in the New Testament is *Lord.* It dramatically re-envisions the inherited biblical message. This is clear already in Peter's Pentecost sermon. Among the several texts cited from the Septuagint, one is from Joel 2:28-32a and another from Psalm 110:1. In both passages the key term is "Lord."

Peter uses the Joel passage to link salvation "in the name of the Lord" with forgiveness "in the name of Jesus Christ," and the signs of Joel with the "gift of the Spirit." Later, Acts 4:12 states that salvation is in Jesus alone. An affirmation that in Joel applies only to God (Yahweh) now refers to Jesus. In Acts "the name of Jesus" is now equivalent to "the name of the Lord."[6] It is interesting that this use also characterizes Paul's thought.[7]

So also, in Acts 2:39 the word "Lord" of Acts 2:21 is applied to God just after the name has been used to refer to Jesus in Acts 2:38. To intensify the complexity, it is God in Acts 2:36 who establishes Jesus as both Lord and Christ. Thus in this complex weaving of texts we find a hint of identity with continued distinction.[8]

Moreover, the use of Psalm 110:1 retains a distinction between two "lords": divine and messianic. However exalted the name of Jesus might be, even appropriating divine status, it is not as simple as "Jesus is Yahweh" or "Yahweh is Jesus." Yahweh is not collapsed into Jesus. There is identity in difference, a principle underlying the trinitarian doctrine formulated later. This principle, which led to the church to talk about God in a threefold way, is already present here in Luke.

The ascension in Acts exalts Jesus to divine status as a basis for his role as divine mediator. Yet however far into the regions of the divine it places Jesus as Lord, God's being God is never compromised but enhanced. The exaltation of Jesus enhances God's being God, just as God's plan and design enhances the role of Jesus. Nevertheless, that divine will requires suffering for the Jesus who is to be exalted. How does this link to the other two aspects of lordship and efficacy?

Many interpretations of Acts at this point have been less than adequate. For some, the suffering took place because that is the way God willed it.[9] For others, the pattern of suffering/exaltation is some kind of sacred pattern that is felt to be important even if not understood.[10] Or perhaps it is simply a law of life. God allows a bad world the freedom to act and so exposes God's agents to suffering.[11] All these fail to see Jesus' suffering as constitutive of God's gift of forgiveness.

Surely the suffering of Jesus dictates the result—forgiveness. But how so? Let us note four elements. First, the human and divine patterns are consistent. Humans kill. God raises. God reverses human wrong. Second, the necessity of Jesus' suffering lies partly in the realm of human sin. Humans will violate God's good gift—Jesus, the Righteous One (Acts 3:14). Third, in Luke-Acts the context of the language about the divine plan for Jesus' suffering is always in connection with God's relation to Israel, not to the Gentiles.[12] So what? Surely God's faithfulness to Israel is at stake. Fourth, God's purpose from the beginning was to reach the nations through Israel.

These four elements in the narrative of Luke-Acts yield the following: God will endure human wrong, reverse its consequences, and persist in offering forgiveness and the gift of the Spirit. Also, God will do so in a way that honors God's commitment to and through Israel, God's promise to the nations. Had God acted through Jesus in any way other than through suffering, such as through power and judgment, it would have been the end of Israel, with no divine faithfulness and no gospel for the nations. Suffering becomes the way of salvation. Death brings life. Take any one of these above four elements (God's power of reversal, human penchant for wrong, the requirements of faithfulness, Israel's mission to the nations) out of the equation and nothing is left. Necessity and design reveal the hidden dimension of God's work threading through all of these. Yet, in the end, many of God's people refuse the promised gift.

## ENDING AS PRELUDE

We have argued that three characteristics of the Acts narrative—Spirit's activity (discontinuities), divine plan (design), and christological content (passion)—assure an integral theological connection between beginning and end. Moreover, Jesus gives substance to the ascension Christology of Acts in which the lordship and efficacy of exaltation depend upon the mandate of suffering implicit in God's relation to Israel.

The Spirit-induced surprises of the narrative, the unity given through God's will and the significance of the ascension Christology, are motionless without the witness of the believing community. Pentecost leads to preaching, preaching to community, and community to further mission. The call of the church in Acts is first of all a call to witness. Acts 1:8 outlines the threads of that movement.

The ascension, which separates and joins Luke-Acts, is absence. But it is not a mystical leap, transcending space and time. Only what happens in the mundane concerns the believers. "Why do you stand looking up toward heaven?" (Acts 1:11). Go back to Jerusalem and wait. Absence becomes presence, a presence in mind and heart that impels them to engage the world. Ending, as the absence characteristic of ascension, is prelude to a new presence.

Acts ends in one final confrontation. Once again, to Paul's dismay, his compatriots dismiss his arguments concerning Jesus. As before, their rejection becomes the opportunity for the Gentiles. Here again the ending is a prelude to a new and wider mission. This rhythm is typical of Acts.

The meaning of this rhythm is not hard to discern. It is the rhythm of mission through all of time. Witness passes on to witnesses, and passes on yet again to witnesses. Jesus' absence became the occasion to draw the Christian community into full participation in God's mission. If humans do not bear witness to all that Jesus said and did, who else will?

Since suffering is integral to mission, mission does not take place through a triumphal mindset. Just as in God's overarching plan for Jesus, suffering is taken up into the substance of Jesus' lordship itself. "I am among you as one who serves" (Lk 22:27). So is it for the disciples. "I myself will show him how much he must suffer for the sake of my name" (Acts 9:16).

## INTERSECTING HORIZONS

Horizons intersect. Paul's horizon intersected with the horizon of the Jesus narratives. In turn, the early church's horizon intersects with that of Peter, Paul, and others in Acts. The open ending of Acts opens the door for us to take stock of these connections. The last account of Paul's mission opens to the future account of our mission. Likewise, the ending of the so-called missionary era, and the ending of public worship in China, is a prelude to a resurrected church, the beginning of a new wave for the church.

One final vignette. Recently I was in a major city in China and visited with the leaders of a house church, an autonomous Christian community. Much was shared about their history and their experience. Ways for mutual strengthening were discussed.

Many of their experiences reminded me of Acts—small beginnings, imprisonment, healings. For instance, a woman had long suffered a football-size growth on her neck. In coming to faith in Jesus, her growth disappeared. Subsequently, in a leaflet, a communist official denounced the excessive growth of Christianity based on false claims. The leader of this Christian community objected and demanded that an official investigation be made. Inquiry from the locals elicited an "Oh, yes, we know her." When the investigators asked how it happened, they replied, "We don't know." So they asked her how the growth disappeared. "I don't know," she replied. Asked if she had seen a doctor, she replied, "Of course! Who wouldn't see a doctor with a big thing like that? They couldn't do anything." Then how did it happen, they inquired. "I believed in Jesus and soon I felt an itching in my neck and it began to shrink until it disappeared." After this investigation the matter was never brought up again.

Meanwhile, having heard of some of these things, a communist cadre came to the Christian community leader. He complained of a persistent headache that hindered his speech. The leader curtly dismissed him, saying that healing was not a matter of simply getting some desired benefit but was a matter of faith in Jesus Christ and the gospel. How could healing be dispensed to an atheist who did not care about these things? But the next day he returned. "If you want healing," he was told, "the first thing you have to learn is to pray to God, confess that you are a sinner, and ask God's mercy for Jesus' sake." The next day he came back again, having done just that, and his headache had disappeared. Spiritual healing brought psychological healing. He and his family became Christians.

These examples of God's surprising work in China remind us that the Acts of the Holy Spirit do not end in Acts 28:31 but are a prelude to a growing Christian movement. The book concludes not with Paul's death but with Paul "teaching about the Lord Jesus Christ with all boldness and without hindrance." However much Paul's journey to Jerusalem was patterned after the final journey of Jesus, including the passion predictions (Acts 20:23; 21:4; 21:11), passion was not its point. Paul was no Jesus. Rome was Paul's destination. To conclude with Jerusalem, or with another passion, would have violated Acts' own rhetoric. And so it has no ending.

Mission is finally God's way of being God—faithful to an eternal design, bound to suffering, turning contingencies into opportunities, granting forgiveness and healing, and pouring out the Spirit. As a community of witnesses sent to the ends of the earth, this is what being church is all about. Perhaps if we allow our contemporary horizons to intersect with that of Acts, we will discover our opportunities and deal rightly with our complexities.

Recently, a relative from Vaerlandet visited the United States. She told of the final visit of grandfather Andrew on his furlough. As he left, soon to die himself, he stood on the bow of the boat, arms raised, and fingers pointing to heaven. Thus he remained till withdrawn from sight. Was this a pointing to the lordship of the ascended Jesus, to the God of eternal design spoken of in Acts, to the source of forgiveness, to the empowerment of the Spirit, to the way of the cross as the way of service? It was all of these. China's horizon and our horizons intersect with the mission horizon of Acts.

The ending is the prelude. A continuous thread holds the discontinuities in the Luke-Acts narrative together. Yet, this thread of continuity derives its meaning from discontinuous events of the story itself. This takes place within an open, not closed, temporal frame in which new discontinuities will give ever-new meaning to the ongoing continuity. Thus, each end, each discontinuity, harbors a fresh beginning. "Why do you stand looking into heaven? This Jesus . . . will come in the same way" (Acts 1:11). That distant or near ending is yet another prelude, a prelude to God's eternal dominion. Toward this we move.

## REFERENCES

[1] Jane Koons, interviewer and editor, *Cora Martinson* (St. Paul, Minn.: Midwest China Oral History and Archives Collection, 1980), 9.

[2] Ibid., 15. The strychnine was forced upon him by a missionary, an untrained "practical nurse." The nearest medical facilities were at least a day's travel away.

[3] "Three-self" refers to self-support, self-government, and self-propagation. For a short analysis, see Paul Varo Martinson, "Giving Account of a Vision: China and the Christian Community in Relation to North America," in *Mission at the Dawn of the Twenty-first Century*, ed. Paul Varo Martinson (Minneapolis, Minn.: Kirk House Publishers, 1999), 78-101.

[4] Some of the studies that I have found helpful as my background reading include Robert L. Brawley, *Text to Text Pours Forth Speech: Voices of Scripture in Luke-Acts* (Bloomington, Ind.: Indiana University Press, 1995); F. F. Bruce, *The Acts of the Apostles: The Greek Text with Introduction and Commentary* (Grand Rapids, Mich.: Eerdmans; 1990); Joseph A. Fitzmyer, *The Acts of the Apostles*, The Anchor Bible (New York: Doubleday; 1998); David J. Lull, *Society of Biblical Literature 1990 Seminar*

*Papers,* Series 29 (Atlanta, Ga.: Scholars Press, 1990); Charles H. Talbert, *Literary Patterns, Theological Themes, and the Genre of Luke-Acts* (Missoula, Mont.: Scholars Press; 1974); Robert C. Tannehill, *The Narrative Unity of Luke-Acts,* 2 vols. (Minneapolis, Minn.: Fortress Press, 1986, 1990); Ben Witherington III, *The Acts of the Apostles: A Socio-Rhetorical Commentary* (Grand Rapids, Mich.: Eerdmans, 1998). Recent studies are of increasing interest.

[5] This hinge metaphor is found in Michael Prior, *Jesus the Liberator: Nazareth Liberation Theology (Luke 4:16-20)* (Sheffield, UK: Sheffield Academic Press, 1995), 24.

[6] Referring to "the name of Jesus," see 4:10, 12, 30; 10:43; cf. 13:38-39. Referring to Jesus as "lord," see 2:36; 9:5, 17; 15:11; 16:31-32; 28:31, and numerous uses of "lord" by narrator. On exegesis, see also Brawley, *Text to Text Pours Forth Speech,* 75-90.

[7] Romans 10:13 and 1 Corinthians 1:2 both use Joel 2:32a in the same way. Furthermore, the Christ hymn in Philippians 2:5-11 presents a Christology almost identical with that of Acts.

[8] Interestingly, a similar use of the title of the Lord of lords, which belongs properly to God (Dt 10:17; Ps 136:3), is applied to Jesus in Revelation 17:14.

[9] See comments on this in David P. Moessner, "The Script of the Scripture in Acts: Suffering as God's 'Plan' (Boule) for the World for the 'Release of Sins,'" in *History, Literature, and Society in the Book of Acts,* ed. Ben Witherington III, 218-250 (Cambridge: Cambridge University Press, 1996), 218.

[10] Tannehill, *The Narrative Unity of Luke-Acts,* 1:288.

[11] Ibid.

[12] To my knowledge this has not been clearly pointed out in the literature.

# Index

Abraham, 76-77

accommodation, 278

Acts: appearance of Jesus, 3; characterization in, 205-6; dating of, 5; divided into speeches and stories, 89-90; incorrect reading, 2; interested in Gentile mission, 6; intertwined with Paul's letters, 4; missionary strategy of, 192; settings for narrative, 198-200; six-part structure, 9-10; speeches in, 88-100; three-dimensional narrative, 316-20; threefold dynamic, 315-16; three-part structure, 8-9; two-part structure, 10; unique genre of, 2-3; watershed of narrative, 197

Agabus, 279

Agrippa, Marcus Julius, 291, 292, 293, 294, 306, 308

Agrippa II, 306-7

Allen, Roland, 244-45

almsgiving, 39-40

alternate spirituality, 177-78

American Religious Identification Survey, 182 n. 53

Ananias, 119, 126-27, 128-29, 303

Antioch: center of mission to the world, 158; model for urban ministry, 146-53

Apollos, 150, 250

apostles, role in conflict mediation, 64, 67

apostolic decrees, 203-5

apostolic strategy, 189-93

Aquila, 243-44, 250, 251

Aratus, 231

Aristobulus, 231

ascension, 12, 318-19, 320

Ashiko, David, 298, 299-300

Asia, Paul's larger context, 264-65

Asian culture, table fellowship, 34, 35 n. 7

Athens marketplace, significance, 223

Attard, Mark V., 245

Augustine of Hippo, 209

Augustus, 170

Azariah, V. S., 148

Bakke, Ray, 145

baptism: commissioning for grassroots lay evangelism, 148; inseparability with repentance, 106; in person and body of Christ, 26

Barclay, William, 262

Bar-Jesus, 168, 174-76

Barnabas, 119; addressing Jerusalem council, 202; giving according to need, 151; mentoring and recruiting Saul (Paul), 129, 149, 225; missionary work in synagogues, 185, 187; passive protagonist, 206; sent to Antioch, 147, 148; speech to Gentiles at Lystra, 95-97, 99

Barr, James, 222-23, 233

Barrett, C. K., 160

barriers, eliminating, 151-52

Barth, Karl, 222

*bat kol,* 217

Bauckham, Richard, 202

Bavnick, J. H., 191

Betz, Hans Dieter, 173

biblical agenda, 271 n. 6

biblical interpretation, 14

Biblical Theology Movement, 222

birds, role in divination, 212

birth narratives, 317

Bolman, Lee G., 65

boundaries: among religion, witchcraft, and magic, 169; removing, 120. *See also* cultural boundaries

breaking of bread, 31, 33. *See also* table fellowship

The American Society of Missiology Series, published in collaboration with Orbis Books, seeks to publish scholarly work of high merit and wide interest on numerous aspects of missiology—the study of Christian mission in its historical, social, and theological dimensions. Able proposals on new and creative approaches to the practice and understanding of mission will receive close attention from the ASM Series Committee.

## Previously Published in
## The American Society of Missiology Series

*Changing Frontiers of Mission*, Wilbert Shenk

*In the Light of the Word: Divine Word Missionaries of North America*, Ernest Brandewie

*Gospel Bearers, Gender Barriers: Missionary Women in the Twentieth Century*, edited by Dana L. Robert

*Changing Tides: Latin America and Mission Today*, Samuel Escobar

*Church: Community for the Kingdom*, John Fuellenbach

Made in the USA
San Bernardino, CA
11 January 2018